TRAVEL GUIDE

SERBIA

in your hands

Gwa
De

Second Edition

Author and Editor:
Vladimir Dulović

Publisher:
KOMSHE d.o.o. Beograd

For Publisher:
Nikola Milivojević, director
Igor Stamenković, director

Photos:
Dragan Bosnić
National Tourism Organisation
of Serbia
National Museum Belgrade
Alessandro Gori

Maps:
Aleksandar Stanojlović

Translation:
Nadja Leuba
Hazel Slinn
Jadranka Mašić
Zrnka Mišković

Additonal texts:
Uroš Milivojević
Stefan Stojanović

Promotional and Marketing team:
Ana Jovanović
Dimitrije Stamenković

For information and distribution
address: KOMSHE d.o.o.
www.komshe.com
+381 65 5667431
+381 65 KOMSHE1

In association with:

NATIONAL TOURISM ORGANISATION OF SERBIA

NATIONAL MUSEUM
Caffe&Bar

Morning mist on Kamena Gora, near Priboj

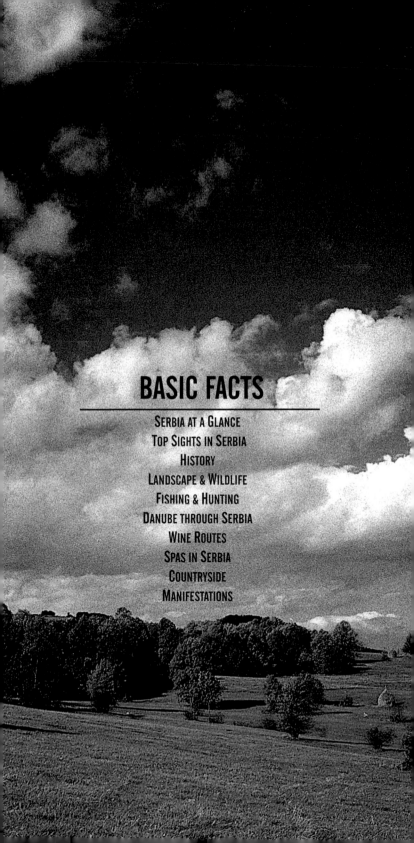

BASIC FACTS

SERBIA AT A GLANCE

In terms of tourism, Serbia is still an undiscovered, "unknown" country in the heart of Europe. Although it is not a usual tourist destination and is probably not likely to become one, countless attractions of this land are unjustly neglected. Rarely in Europe is such a small piece of land home to so many wild animal species. There are few countries with such rugged and beautiful mountains. Several cultural monuments are protected by UNESCO, and a visit to a monastery in this part of the world is a unique experience. Many of Serbian towns have more to offer than meets the eye. And in the end, it is almost needless to mention the proverbial hospitality of a Serbian peasant who gives the impression that the less he has the more he offers.

Welcoming smile

If for no other reason, tourists should visit Serbia to overcome their prejudices. Recent events have given Serbia a bad name, but any visitor will tell you that after only a couple of days spent here, his opinion about Serbia was changed. In many aspects, Serbia is an under-developed and even archaic-looking country, yet today it is, for the most part a modern European country, open to various influences from all over the world. However, the essence of Serbia is all about mixed influences. There were so many of them, that even Serbs themselves are not sure about them all, except that their identity is made of many different cultural layers that have created a distinctive racial, linguistic, and cultural mixture rarely found amyhere else. As noticed eight centuries ago by St. Sava, the most celebrated Serbian saint, Serbia will always be viewed as the East in the West, and as the West in the East. This can be applied even today, for both neighbouring and more remote nations.

Location & Regions of Serbia

One of the keys to understanding the Serbian temperament is its location and the geographical features that have produced several distinguishable regions.

Serbia occupies territory in central Balkans and lies on the crossroads of several important European routes. The Pannonian plain, open on all sides, presented the final destination for all the peoples comming from the Asian steppes. The Danube, the second longest and most important European river, begins in southern Germany and flows eastwards into the Black Sea, to the very borders of Europe; starting from the times of ancient Greek explorers to German colonists in 18th c., this river brought here many diverse influences. The valley of Morava, the Danube's tributary, is the most accessible way through the Balkan Peninsula. Along this route, following the valley of Nišava River, and further on through Bulgaria led the roman

Winding stream of Uvac River near Priboj

road *Via militaris*, connecting the Middle East and Constantinople with central Europe. Contrary to these areas, susceptible to various influences, some parts of Serbia were covered in thick woods and hidden in mountain massifs were isolated from most of the historical events as well as from the blessings and curses of the civilised world.

Walls of Smederevo Fortress on Danube

Belgrade, the capital of Serbia, lies at the confluence of the Sava and the Danube rivers, overlooking the Pannonian plain. Its position on such an important spot provided a tumultuous history – Belgrade was repeatedly destroyed only to rise again on the same site. Today, it is a metropolis bursting with life, be it traffic jams, vibrant night life or cultural events.

The north of Serbia is the autonomous province of Vojvodina. It is a fertile plain with only two mountains, but on the other hand, with several sandpits only recently domesticated.

Serbia in a nutshell

Full name: Republic of Serbia
(Republika Srbija)

Population: 9,979,752 (2002)

Area: 88,361 sq km (34,116 sq mi)

Capital: Belgrade / Beograd,
1,594,483 (1998)

Ethnic groups: Serb, Albanian, Magyar (Hungarian), Bosniak, Roma, others

Language: Serbian, Albanian in Kosovo

Religion: Orthodox Christian, Muslim, Roman-Catholic, Protestant

President: Boris Tadić

Prime minister: Vojislav Koštunica

GDP: US$ 28.37 Billion (2005)

GDP per capita: US$ 3200 (2005)

Inflation: 16.5% (2005)

Unemployment rate: 18,50% (2005)

Vojvodina built its identity during the time of Habsburg rule (1699 – 1918) when different people came and lived here together. The most numerous, and the oldest of its inhabitants are the Serbs, but Hungarians left here a deep impact, especially in terms of toponyms; in Banat, there are many Romanians, who moved there from the Carpathian mountains as stock-breeders; the hard-working Slovaks also live here, and people of many other nationalities, such as Ukrainians, Bunjevci, Croats, Czechs, Germans, etc. The capital of the province is Novi Sad, an enchanting town which gives a new meaning to the phrase "chilling out".

South of Belgrade lies Central Serbia. Its north is still a large plain, but the altitude rises as one moves south. In quiet corners of Serbian mountains lies the country's greatest cultural heritage: ancient monasteries with their unique architecture and exceptional frescoes. Fresh air and unpolluted water are the best guarantee that local traditional products are still competitive. Flocks of sheep and herds of cows graze on pastures next to rich orchards that yield the basic ingredients for high quality products like cheese, milk, *kajmak* cream, fruit and *rakija* brandy. The Turkish legacy is best preserved in the Raška region inhabited by a large number of Muslims, and of course in Kosovo where Albanians outnumber people with other nationalities.

Geography and Climate

Two thirds of Serbia are mountainous and the rest of the territory is composed of plains. All of the Balkan mountain ranges meet south of the Sava and Danube rivers. The Dinaric mountains and the Šara-Pind

Curves of River Drina forming the border between Serbia and Bosnia

mountain range end in the western part of the country, whereas parts of the Carpathian, Balkan and Rodopi mountain ranges spread eastwards. Fifteen mountains in Serbia are higher than 2000m, and the highest peak is Djeravica in the Prokletije Mountains (2656 m). On the other hand, northern Serbia is almost all flat. The whole of Vojvodina is actually a part of the Pannonian plain and at its edges lie the plains of Mačva, the Morava valley, Stig and Negotinska Krajina. In the south, the largest plains are Metohija and Kosovo; other plains are actually broader river valleys, like that of the Western Morava, Niš, Toplica, Pirot etc.

With the exceptions of the Beli Drim River basin, that belongs to the Adriatic watershed, and the Lepenac and Pčinja rivers that belong to the Aegean, all the other rivers in Serbia belong to the Black Sea watershed. Only the Danube, the Sava and the Tisa are navigable along their entire courses within Serbia. The longest river is the Danube, whose course through Serbia is 588 km long.

There are three climate zones in Serbia. The Pannonian plain and northern parts of central Serbia have a continental climate that is characterised by warm summers (up to +40°C) and cold winters (down to -20°C). Central and southern parts have a moderate continental climate without such extremes. Regions surrounded by high mountain peaks (large parts of the Raška region, the Šara Mountain, and Stara Planina) have a mountain climate, with pleasant summers, but very cold and snowy winters.

Due to these climactic characteristics, the best time of the year for visiting Serbia are the spring months of April and May, as well as early autumn, from the beginning of September to mid-October.

Politics and Economy

The Republic of Serbia is a parliamentary democracy. It has two autonomous provinces – Vojvodina in the north, and Kosovo-Metohija in the south. Vojvodina has its own government and assembly that deal with local issues. Kosovo-Metohija is under UN administration, and has an undefined status - Albanians believe that it is an independent area, and Serbs that it is still part of Serbia. Serbia and Montenegro constitute the State Union of Serbia and Montenegro. It is a confederate state that may be dissolved if citizens of any of its member states decide so by referendum. The referendum in Montenegro will be held on May 21st this year. Forced by the civil wars of the 1990s, a great number of people from Croatia, Bosnia-Herzegovina, and Kosovo-Metohija fled to Serbia that still has the largest number of refugees in Europe. This complicated situation is, for the great part,

Ships and barges on Sava in Belgrade

Kneza Mihaila Street, central Belgrade shopping area

the economy is doing good, the political system doesn't follow even this slow pace of progression.

Everyday Life

Despite the fact that life was not easy for the majority, or maybe just because of it, Serbs like to talk about it in jokes and without any bitterness. It's not surprising that the basis of a good joke is often expressed through black humour and self-criticism, and sarcasm knows no bounds. In general terms, people here are open and relaxed, and friendships are easily made. Serbs are also cheerful and loud, often careless of consequences and ready to live for the moment. Other important characteristics of thir character are complaisance and hospitality, especially in the more remote parts of the country, where one must be really persistent in saying no to another glass of brandy, juice or coffee. Don't be surprised if your host won't let you pay for your drinks or invites you to a family dinner.

As there have never been big social differences between Serbs, social etiquette has never been fully developed. Although few pay much attention to formalities, long introductions and manners, one should show interest in the local culture, general opinions and politics.

At the end of the 18th century, a German traveller on his way through Novi Sad, noticed that members of all social groups are dressed far better than one could think they could afford. The situation has not changed

the result of the criminal regime (1989 – 2000) of Slobodan Milošević which also left the legacy of the quite unstable political situation. Every new parliamentary election (regular ones are held every four years) is of uncertain outcome. The three main political parties are DSS (centre right), DS (centre) and SRS (far right). In order to form a government these three have to bargain between themselves and to cooperate with other smaller parties. Presidential elections are direct, but the post has limited prerogatives. The public turnout is sometimes below fifty percent. The reason for this is a general disillusionment with the pace of political changes and due of the still tough economic situation. Painful and unpopular transitional decisions are hard to make and so necessary economic reforms are still far from being accomplished. Although largely inefficient, the system works much better than it did few years ago. Crime and corruption rates have been lowered, but the citizens' distrust of institutions is still very high. A big boost for the economy has occurred through loans from European and international institutions. The introduction of the regulated procedures create more opportunities for banking and foreign investments. Although it cannot be said that

Monk with **klepetalo** *in front of the Sopoćani Monastery*

Kolo - *the Serbian national dance*

much today. Although nobody likes overdressing, sloppiness and carelessness are even less appreciated. At almost every occasion one should be decently dressed, and for a casual night out the majority will prepare as if it were their wedding day!

Religion and Customs

About two thirds of population of Serbia are Orthodox Christians. Apart from the Serbs this is also the religion of Romanians and Bulgarians. Each of these three nations has its own national orthodox church. The ethnic and religious composition of Vojvodina is very complex, as there seem to be more churches of different denominations than there are ethnic groups. After the Orthodox Christians the second largest religious group are the Roman Catholics made up of Hungarians, Bunjevci and Croats, along with the Greek Catholic Ukrainians, Lutheran Slovaks, and Calvinist Hungarians. A number of other small religious communities, with followers in almost every part of Vojvodina, are not to be omitted. Muslims live in the southwest of Serbia, in the region of Novi Pazar and Kosovo-Metohija, as well as in the area of Preševo and Bujanovac. In no part of Serbia religious laws and practices are too strictly observed, however the occasional outbursts of extreme religious behaviour are all the more turbulent due to this. Despite the fact that alcohol is available everywhere, even in the most Muslim of the Serbian cities, its consummation in the streets is not appreciated. The Orthodox Church observes many fasts, but only a small percentage of Orthodox Christians really live by those rules

and, those who do, do not impose them on others.

The Serbian Orthodox Church still uses the old Julian calendar that now runs thirteen days late behind the Gregorian one. This is why the Serbs celebrate Christmas on the 7th of January. In addition – puerly as another excuse to celebrate – Serbs organize the so-called "Serbian New Year" on the 13th of January. These two weeks are often turned (unofficially!) into a small winter holiday. The greatest day in every family is the patron saint's day, called *slava*. This is a unique Serbian custom dedicated to the celebration of each family's patron saint. On that day the family's friends and relatives come to the feast; the celebration sometimes lasts two or even three days.

Language and Culture

Serbian belongs to the South-Slavic subdivision of Slavic languages. The same language is spoken in Montenegro and, only under different names, also in Bosnia-Herzegovina and in Croatia. It's closely related to the Macedonian and Bulgarian languages. Along with christianity, Serbs received the so-called "Old church Slavonic" as their written language from SS Cyril and Methodius who translated

Miroslav Gospel (12th c), included in UNESCO's World Heritage list

religious books into Slavonic and created the first Slavonic alphabets – Glagolic and Cyrillic – according to Slavonic phonetics. The first literary works in Serbian originate from the Middle Ages such as: "Maria's Gospel" (10th century), Temnić Inscription (11th century) and "Miroslav's Gospel" (12th century), famous for its splendid beauty. At the time it was written in the Serbian redaction of Old Church Slavonic, used only by educated men, rarely found in those times. In time, spoken language of common people diverged further and further from the written langauge. The language of common people gained the upper hand only in the first half of the 19th century, largely thanks to efforts of Vuk Karadžić. By collecting and publishing the Serbian oral tradition of tales, songs and poetry, Karadžić showed to the world and to Serbs themselves that popular language possessed a unique beauty, means of expression, as well as also being functional. Vuk also created the first Serbian grammar and reformed the Cyrillic alphabet reducing it to only thirty letters holding to the principle: "one letter for one sound". Until 1918 the Latin alphabet was unknown in Serbia, but from then on it was used alongside Cyrillic. Today, both alphabets are used equally and there are no laws regulating when one or the other should be used.

Serbian culture has always been divided between the East and the West. It is visible from very early on, for example in the architecture of the Raška School (12th – 14th c.) with its Romanic exterior decorations but Byzantine structure and frescoes. After the loss of the independent state in the 15th century, Serbs found themselves divided between three different states: the Islamic Ottoman Empire, the Roman-Catholic Habsburg Empire and the Venetians. The Serbian Orthodox Church preserved not only the religion but also the state traditions from the times of independence. Aditionaly, epic poems glorified the lost Serbian empire. Turkish influences were the most predominant, so that even today they can be sensed in the language, cuisine, music etc. From the end of

the 17th century the centre of Serbian erudition and culture shifted northwards to the lands under Habsburg rule. Despite their reluctant adoption

Nadežda Petrović's impressionist painting "Peonies of Kosovo" (1913, National Museum Belgrade)

of novelties for fear of conversion to Catholicism, influences of the baroque and rococo slowly but firmly gained ground. Connections with Russia had been already established by the end of the Middle Ages, and Russian tsars often donated to the Serbian Church and monasteries thereby spreading Russian influence. This reached its peak during the 18th century when the written language itself was shaped according to Russian.

Independent Serbia of the 19th century was for a long time under the cultural influence of the educated Serb elite from Austria. However, towards the end of the century Serbia found its own independent path looking towards the modern ideals of France and Great Britain. From the beginning of the 20th century, Serbia followed European models in culture and art, with its cultural elite adopting contemporary art movements such as impressionism, expressionism, surrealism, post-modernism etc. After a short period of time (1944 – 1948) during which the Soviet cultural model was entirely imitated, Yugoslav communists opted for "their own path to socialism". Supervision of cultural life was still rigid, but everything that wasn't directed against the state and the Communist party was tolerated, so cultural circles were followed up to date trends in jazz and rock, pop-art and artistic performance unlike in other surrounding countries.

TOP SIGHTS IN SERBIA

Fruška Gora
Rising from a vast plain, this low mountain is covered in woods and vineyards and adorned with sixteen baroque orthodox monasteries

Belgrade
The capital of Serbia is a bustling metropolis full of life, best known for its impressive fortress, fascinating nightlife and its unique situation at the point of confluence of the Sava and the Danube.

Topola
The town is inseparable from the fight for Serbian independence, housing the stunning mausoleum of the Karadjordjević royal dynasty

Studenica Monastery
Listed by UNESCO as a World Heritage site, this 12th-13th c. monastery complex has for centuries been regarded as the birthplace of Serbian art and architecture

Mount Kopaonik
This beautiful mountain is transformed every winter into an attractive tourist resort, the centre of Serbian winter sports

Vrnjačka B
The undisputed capital
spas for over

Subotica
Due to its geographic location, inter-ethnic mix and beautiful Art Nouveau architecture, this town is regarded as Serbia's gate to Europe

Location of Serbia

Novi Sad
The elegant capital of Serbia's northern province will enchant you with its buildings, museums, festivals and, above all, its uniquely relaxed atmosphere and friendliness

Iron Gates Gorge
The magnificent Danube is squeezed to the width of only hundred metres into a gorge, running between magnificent mountains that have for millennia concealed spectacular archeological findings

Manasija Monastery
Mighty battlements protect this imposing masterpiece of monastic architecture and its frescoes (15th c.) that opened the way to a new era in the development of art

Djavolja Varoš
One of Nature's magnificent works of art, with hundreds of earthy columns subject to constant change

apeutic

HISTORY

The Slav tribes overran the Danube basin from their homeland north of the Carpathians in the 4th and 5th centuries. Their advance was checked briefly at the borders of the Byzantine Empire but continued the moment that Constantinople was caught off guard. Together with the Asiatic Avars, the Slavs pushed inwards down the Balkan Peninsula around the year 600 AD. The local Romanised population fled to the coastlands or to the mountains but was eventually Slavicised over the next centuries.

The Serbs, one of the Slavic tribes, came in the second wave from somewhere in the region of the present day Czech Republic and eastern Germany. Together with the Croats, these warrior tribes took the upper hand over the unorganized Balkan Slavs. The first Serb states took root in the mountainous Adriatic hinterlands in present-day Bosnia-Herzegovina and Montenegro, far from major roads and midway between Rome and Constantinople.

In the second part of the 9th c. the Serbs adopted Christianity on the basis of a Slavic liturgy created by Greek Brothers, Cyril and Methodius, often dubbed the "Apostles of the Slavs". However, over the next centuries the increasing differences between the Western and Eastern Churches left the Serbs open to both influences, caught between the Byzantine wish to subdue them and the unpopularity of Rome's Latin liturgy. Finally, the Orthodox rite prevailed but the connections with the west remained strong in affairs of state and art.

The 9th and 10th centuries saw the struggle of the Serb states to remain free from their mightier neighbours, the Byzantines and the Bulgarians. In **1077** Duke Mihailo of Duklja received the crown and title of King from the Pope, securing for the first time international recognition of the sovereignty of a Serb state. But his state did not last long since it was lost in a new war with the Byzantine Empire.

Taking advantage of the weakness of the Byzantine state, grand župan **Stefan Nemanja** (1168-1199) united all the Serb lands except Bosnia, expanded the borders to the Morava valley and Skopje, and forged the foundations of a more lasting political structure. His eldest son Stefan, married to a Byzantine Princess, was crowned in **1217** by the Pope and became known as the "First Crowned", while his youngest became a monk, Brother Sava, (future Saint Sava) and secured the independence of the Serb Church from Constantinople in **1219**. These political ties, the newly established institutions and ideology, the founding of an independent Church, together with the building of many monasteries, secured the power of the Nemanjić dynasty for 200 years (1168-1371). This is regarded as the true cornerstone of Serb history.

Saint Sava, fresco in the Mileševa Monastery

The three sons of Stefan the First Crowned, Radoslav, Vladislav and Uroš, took no great part in Balkan politics but maintained the independence of Serbia, enhancing its wealth by bringing in foreign traders and miners as well as promoting internal colonization. Uroš's sons, Dragutin and Milutin, continued the territorial expansion of Serbia. Milutin (1286-1321) conquered large parts of Byzantium, in present day Macedonia and Albania, and secured them through marriage to a Byzantine princess. His son, Stefan "Dečanski" (1321-1331), defeated Bulgaria and pressed Byzantium to even more grants, securing the status of Serbia as the most powerful state in the Balkans. Serbia reached its heyday under the rule of King **Dušan**, who used the civil war in Byzantium to push southwards in several vanquishing waves. In **1345** he was crowned Emperor and the Serb Archbishopric was raised to the status of Patriarchate, thereby ruining relations with the Byzantine Church. Serbia stretched from the Adriatic to the Mesta River in Bulgaria, and from Belgrade in the north to the Gulf of Corinth in the south.

Meanwhile, **Bosnia** was developing its own identity. Pressed between Serbia and Hungary, it had its own version of Orthodox Christianity that was under constant persecution by Catholic Hungarian kings. It was a small territory under the Ottoman rule of the Bans and lay along the river Bosna. A more independent foreign policy and expansion came only with Stjepan II (1314-53) who was succeeded by his nephew Tvrtko.

After Dušan's sudden death in 1355, his son Emperor Uroš (dubbed "The Weak") was unable to maintain the same tight grasp over the nobles, who had grown stronger during the rapid period of conquest. Their greed and disunity soon turned the mighty state into a feudal anarchy in which the emperor was a mere figurehead. The most powerful of the nobles, Vukašin Mrnjavčević, from the region of Macedonia, tried to promote himself as successor to the childless Uroš but he had only a few allies and the other lords blocked his aspirations. The disputes and dilemmas of the nobles were cut short by the growing Turkish threat. In **1371** Vukašin and his brother died in battle on the river Maritsa and their lands became vassal to the Turks. Shortly after, Uroš died without an heir.

In the north, Vukašin and Uroš's deaths brought about a redistribution of power. The Bosnian Ban, **Tvrtko** conquered the western tracts of Serbia and, in **1377**, crowned himself King of

Nemanjić Family Tree, from the Dečani Monastery (National Museum Belgrade)

Serbs on the grave of St Sava in the Mileševa Monastery. The other noble to profit from the changes was **Prince Lazar**, who conquered the valleys of the three Moravas and the town of Novo Brdo, which encompassed the largest mine in the Balkans. He tried to reassemble the Serb state by marrying his daughters to other prominent nobles. He re-established good relationships with the Byzantine Church, and thus won for himself the status of the "first among equals". In **1389** he joined forces with King Tvrtko and Vuk Branković (a noble who controlled the territory of

Paja Jovanović, "The Crowning of Emperor Dušan" (National Museum Belgrade)

Kosovo) in an effort to stop the Turkish advance. The bloody battle of Kosovo Polje ("Field of Blackbirds"), near present-day Priština, resulted in the deaths of both the Ottoman Sultan Murad I, and Lazar. With a decimated army and an underage son, Lazar's widow, Milica, accepted vassal status with the Turks. In Bosnia, after the death of King Tvrtko in 1391, the state deteriorated under weak kings.

Lazar's son, **Stefan**, served Sultan Bajezid faithfully and, with his help, unified again most of Serbia. After Bajezid's demise in **1402**, the Ottoman Empire fell into disarray and Stefan continued on an independent course, receiving the title of "Despot" ("Lord") from the Byzantine Emperor, who was cornered in Constantinople. His good relations with Hungary, which more closely resembled true vassal status, prospered when, in 1403, he was granted Belgrade which he made into his magnificent capital. The relief from the Ottoman grip and the relative peace that lasted for two decades made possible the rise of urban centres, a renaissance of trade and mining, combined with a new splendid style in architecture and fresco painting, as well as literary activity led by the poems of Despot Stefan himself. Stefan (died 1427) was succeeded by Djuradj Branković, an older cousin. Djuradj's rule was troubled – the Ottomans rose once again and attacked in full force. In 1455 Novo Brdo fell, together with the southern half of Serbia. The last stronghold of Djuradj's sons, Smederevo on the Danube held on to **1459**, the year that marks the end of Serb statehood

Despotes Stefan Lazarević, painting in the Manasija Monastery

in the Middle Ages. Bosnia, torn apart by its nobles, fell in **1463**; Herzegovina, under the Kosača family, followed in **1482** and finally, Montenegro of the Crnojevićs succumbed in **1499**.

By the beginning of the 16th c. the great migrations that were to reshape the ethnic map of the Balkans were well underway and masses of Serbs were fleeing to the north and west. The Hungarian kings used Serbs as soldiers to guard their depopulated southern borders and continued to nominate the Despots. The fall of Belgrade to Suleyman the Magnificent in 1521 and the destruction of the Hungarian state in the Battle of Mohacz in 1526 brought an end to all hope that the Turks would be defeated and Serbia regained. In the shadow of these events Pavle Bakić, the last Serb Despot in Hungary, was killed in 1537. With the Ottoman conquest of central Hungary almost all Serbs were living under the Sultan's suzerainty. However, some local autonomy was preserved and many Serbs joined the auxiliary Turkish forces.

In **1557** the good relations between Serbs and Ottomans reached their zenith when the Grand-Vizier, who was of Serb origin, Mehmed-Pasha Sokolović (known in Turkish as Soccoly), re-established the Serb Patriarchate with its seat in Peć. The Patriarchy embraced all Serbs in the Empire, from Buda to Skopje, and from Zadar to Sofia. The Serb Church emerged as the keeper of state traditions. With its newly found power, the Church made discreet moves to rebuild its monasteries and a modest artistic revival followed.

Aleksandar Dobrić, "Miloš Obilić at the Battle of Kosovo" (National Museum Belgrade)

The custodian of tradition under Turkish rule - "Blind guslar" by Rista Vukanović (National Museum Belgrade)

The good relationship did not last long. In **1594** the Serbs rebelled in Banat and later also in Herzegovina, responding to the calls of the Habsburgs during their war with the Ottomans. The Turkish response was to burn the relics of St Sava, the greatest Serb saint. Due to the rise of mutual suspicion, an aftermath to these rebellions, Serbs were no longer granted the status of spahi (nobles).

In the meantime the Habsburg Empire was fighting for its life and, short of funds to finance regular army in its devastated and depopulated territory of the Croatia, welcomed anyone who would come to fight the Turks, giving them privileged rights as freemen, with the obligation of guarding the frontier. Soon a chain of settlements, populated mostly by Orthodox Serbs, was formed on the Austrian side of the Empire that was to be organized as a Military Frontier (*Vojna krajina*). The free settlements threatened the landed nobility and Eastern Orthodoxy infuriated the Catholic prelates. In the centuries to follow Serbs in Croatia and Slavonia had to fight off repeated attempts to strip them of their rights and religion. The only way to protest was to be loyal to the Habsburg Emperor and hope for his protection, both in law and in practice.

The first Serb land to win back its freedom was **Montenegro**. With its rear protected by the Venetian Republic, the local clans united under the leadership of the Metropolitans of the Petrović-Njegoš family and decided at the end of the 17th c. that they would no longer pay taxes to the Ottoman

Porte. This defiance by a small and barren mountainous region led to several Turkish raids but none of them managed to bring it back to full submission and stop the Montenegrin raids into the neighbouring districts.

In 1683 the Ottomans received a devastating blow before Vienna. The tide turned and by **1689** the Habsburg army, with the help of the local Christian population that rose to arms, had liberated Serbia, reaching Niš, Prizren and Skopje. The Ottomans regrouped, pushed back the Habsburg forces and with them also the mass of refugees fleeing their retribution. The flood of people, led by Patriarch Arsenije III, asked the Austrian Emperor to grant them religious and personal freedoms as well as autonomy under the church prelates. In grave need of soldiers, Leopold agreed and the refugees settled in Hungary. The Privilegium that the Emperor issued, but had no intention of acting upon, led to a long-running struggle against being reduced to peasantry and being forced to give up Orthodoxy. Still, the Serbs of the Habsburg Empire managed to develop an elite, drawn from church dignitaries, officers, new nobles and men of commerce, that was to lead the way in art, culture and education.

During the course of the 18th c. Austria took and lost Serbia twice (1717-39 and 1789-91). These failures brought the Serb trust in the Habsburgs to an end. As a frontier region of the Ottoman Empire, Serbia was already governed with a broad autonomy that was intended to

Petar Ranosović, "Jova Kursula Among the Turks" (National Museum Belgrade)

keep the population calm. The province soon developed as a trading area. However, the Sultan's control over his representatives was deteriorating fast. When rebellious Janissaries killed the local Ottoman administrator in Belgrade and took control of the town, bringing in

Uroš Knežević, "Prince Miloš" (National Museum Belgrade)

irregular taxations and appropriating land, the Serbs rose to arms.

The mutiny, which started in **1804**, soon turned into a general Serb rebellion and after talks with the Sultan failed in 1805, it became an insurrection against all Ottoman authorities. Led by the legendary Djordje Petrović – Karadjordje ("Black George"), the Serb peasants organized and fought off numerous Turkish offensives, liberating the area from Drina and Novi Pazar to Leskovac and Vidin. It was not only a national but also a social movement; in the words of respected historian Leopold Ranke, the "Serb Revolution". Caught in diplomatic manoeuvres between Napoleon, Austria, Russia and the Ottomans, the Serbs could find neither recognition nor protection and, after almost a decade of resistance, gave way in **1813**.

The brutal Turkish repression could not wipe out the sweet smell of a decade of self-rule and freedom from feudal lords. Another insurrection followed in 1814 and yet another in **1815**. The leader of this last, Miloš Obrenović, a cautious and cunning man, used his early victories to start talks with the Sultan and settled for moderate autonomy. In the course of the following years he begged and threatened, bribed and blackmailed, all in the best oriental fashion. He secured a *de facto* autonomy in 1817, murdered Karadjordje, who tried to re-start the rebellion, and in **1830** and 1833, as a final point, won charters from Istanbul which secured the status of Serbia as a self-governing principality with the Obrenovićs as hereditary princes, paying tribute to the Sultan, but with the Turks occupying only six fortresses in Serbia.

Miloš's autocratic rule led to a resistance that in **1835** produced the first Serb constitution, which did not last long in the reactionary atmosphere of Europe. In the same year, land was granted to the peasants. Miloš finally abdicated in 1840, but his son Mihailo, suffering from the bad name of his father, was overthrown and replaced by Aleksandar, Karadjordje's son. However, the real power was in the hands of the so-called "Constitutionalists" (Ustavobranitelji), the learned elite notable for its modernizing zeal. In 1858 Miloš returned to power briefly, to be succeeded once again by Mihailo. The second reign (1860-68) of this European-educated ruler was marked by his enlightened absolutism but is best remembered for his great success in forcing the Turks out of their six remaining fortresses on Serb territory (**1867**).

The Austro-Hungarian revolution of 1848 brought bloody clashes in southern Hungary between Serbs and Croats on one side and Hungarians on the other. Serb loyalty to the Emperor was rewarded with the long-sought-after territory called *Srpska Vojvodina* (Serb Dukedom). However, it was soon clear that absolutism and Germanic bureaucracy held sway in this purely administrative district that survived up to 1860.

Meanwhile, from the late 18th c. Montenegro was all but internationally recognized as an independent state. Through its frequent wars with Turkey it was gaining a reputation as a fearsome opponent and earning respect from

Uroš Predić, "Herzegovinian refugees" (National Museum Belgrade)

neighbouring Serb clans. Herzegovina recurrently rose to arms. A crisis provoked by the rebellion of 1875 pushed Serbia and Montenegro into a war against the Ottomans in 1876, bringing Russian intervention in 1877 and finally the Congress of Berlin in **1878**. Both Serb states achieved territorial gains but more

Strategist of Serbian victories - "Živojin Mišić" by Uroš Predić (Narional Museum Belgrade)

importantly they finally received international recognition as sovereign states.

In Serbia, Prince Milan's reckless rule (1868-1892) saw the promotion of Serbia to the rank of Kingdom in 1882. After a long struggle, in 1888, Milan agreed to submit himself to parliamentary control, under the terms of a new liberal constitution, but he could not bear it for long. His son Aleksandar produced constant parliamentary crises that, combined with personal scandals (he married a widow that could not bear him children), left him friendless and vulnerable, and in 1903 a group of plotting officers assassinated him.

Petar Karadjordjević, grandson of Karadjordje, was brought to the throne. Willing to submit to the vote of the parliamentary majority, he opened an era of true democracy in Serbia. However, he could not fully control the officers that had brought him to power. The change of dynasties also meant the final break with the unpopular tutelage of Austria-Hungary. The first clash was in the field of economics: for several years a tax war was waged and Serbia emerged victorious, managing to free itself from economic dependence on its northern neighbour. Austria-Hungary, insecure in its own power and position, started to view Serbia as its most dangerous foe. The two Serb states presented a powerful attraction to the Serbs and other South Slavs in the Empire; moreover, they blocked the only possible route to territorial advance. In 1908 Austria-Hungary annexed Bosnia & Herzegovina and started a series of politrulless trials against prominent Serbs in Croatia and Bosnia that gave its statehood and justice a bad name.

Meanwhile, Serbia and Montenegro joined forces with Bulgaria and Greece in a Balkan Alliance and surprised the European Great Powers by acting on their own in a joint venture against the Ottomans (1912, First Balkan War). The Serb army established a mutual border with Montenegro and liberated Kosovo, Macedonia, Albania and northern Greece. When Austria-Hungary promoted an independent Albania, Serbia wanted to hold the territories it had liberated in Macedonia as compensation for what she did not get in Albania. The idea was opposed by Bulgaria who recklessly declared war on its former ally but was defeated in 1913 (Second Balkan War).

After these two bloody wars both Serbia and Montenegro were hoping for respite. However, in 1914 the heir to the Habsburg throne visited Sarajevo on Vidovdan, the greatest Serb holiday. This was viewed as a challenge by a group of Bosnian students and on the 29th of June a young Serb named Gavrilo Princip shot dead Archduke Franz Ferdinand and his wife Sophie. Austria-Hungary chose to use the occasion and act against Serbia, making impossible demands; it did not anticipate that Serbia's allies, Russia, France and Great

Belgrade 1914, first line of defence

Britain would act on obligations created in earlier treaties. This miscalculation by Austria-Hungary turned what was expected to be a local war into the first global conflict.

In 1914 and 1915, Serbia, together with Montenegro, managed to win three battles against the superior Habsburg forces but in 1915 it fell back before the joint attack of Austro-Hungarian, German and Bulgarian forces. Sheltered by its Montenegrin ally, the Serb army together with King Peter and the government managed to withdraw through the snow-covered mountains of Albania and join the French and British forces, forming the Saloniki front in northern Greece. Montenegro was also occupied but King Nikola conducted negotiations with Austria-Hungary and then fled to Italy, an event that would later be held against him.

In 1918 the Allied offensive started; well motivated, the Serbian troops led the way. In three weeks they were in front of Sofia and Bulgaria was eliminated from the war. They soon reached Belgrade and advanced into Austria-Hungary. The defeated empire

Aleksandar Karadjordjević, King of Yugoslavia (1921-34)

crumbled and after Montenegro and Vojvodina had declared unification with Serbia, representatives of the Serbs, Croats and Slovenes opted for unification under the Karadjordjević dynasty on the **1st of December 1918**. Serbian troops secured the borders of the newly established state and remained under arms until 1920. Eight years of warfare had left Serbia crippled: 1/3 of the population died including 50% of men able to bear arms.

The many differences within the Kingdom of Serbs, Croats and Slovenes derived from four state systems (Austro-Hungarian, Serbian, Montenegrin, Turkish), plus geographical and ethnic diversity. They were all considered manageable with a presumption of good will. But this crucial ingredient soon disappeared as internal disagreements arose. The first problem was that of was Croatia: a Serb majority in the new state and an army that was still Serb-domi-

nated, rather then being Yugoslav left little space for a Croatia that was economically more developed. The new state hoped to achieve shared power within a loose federal system but the constitution of 1921 defined the Kingdom as an almost unitary state - seen as the only guarantee that a country of so many differences could survive. A decade of tense parliamentary life reached a climax in 1928, when, in parliament a Serb Deputy shot Stjepan Radić, leader of the strongest Croatian party. In **1929** King Aleksandar, son of King Petar, in an attempt to prevent the state from disintegrating, and not being particularly inclined to democracy, abolished the Parliament. He took to active promotion of the Yugoslav concept, recognizing no nations within the kingdom, as a ruling ideology. His dictatorship, coinciding with the hard times of the world economic crisis, was ended in 1934, when he was assassinated by separatists. However, a return to parliamentary rule could do little to prevent the internal struggles. When, in 1939, Croatia finally achieved autonomy within the state it was too late - national tensions were too high and faith in Yugoslavia too low.

For some time it seemed that Yugoslavia would manage to stay outside the new World War: a favourable treaty was signed with Nazi Germany in **1941**. But only two days later, on March the 27th, the goodwill was broken by a military coup spurred on by the British intelligence services and followed by anti-Axis demonstrations in major Serb towns. Enraged, Hitler ordered an immediate attack as a reprisal for this insulting act and on the 6th of April 1941 Belgrade was bombed without a declaration of war. In no position to wage a war, a multinational Yugoslav army put up resistance in only a few places and the war was over in two weeks. Young King Petar II and his government fled to England. Parts of Serbia were annexed by Hungary, Germany, Bulgaria and Albania (controlled by Italy) while Bosnia-Herzegovina along with Srem were turned over to Croatia, which was led by the fascist Ustašas, who fanatically hated the Serbs.

The army was defeated but the spirit of armed resistance lived on. In May, Colonel Dragoljub Mihailović, encouraged by the London-based government, proclaimed the continuation of the war and started attacking the Germans. Following the German attack on the USSR, the communist Partizani also took up arms in July. A brief coopera-

Hanged patriots in Belgrade, 1941.

tion between the two groups resulted in a large liberated territory in western Serbia with its centre in Užice. The German reaction was reprisals against civilians using a notorious rule: 100 civilians for each German soldier killed. Seeing that the toll was too high for the Serb people, Mihailović and his Četnici settled for maintaining a low-profile resistance and waiting for an allied landing. In contrast, the Communists, led by Josip Broz "Tito", were fighting not only for freedom but also for power and thus decided to continue. Defeated in Serbia, in 1942 they moved their main forces to Bosnia and Croatia. Here, the horrifying slaughters of tens of thousands of Serbs forced many people to the mountains. The Partizans offered them the opportunity to fight the executioners and so the core of their army was made up of Serbs, either from Serbia proper or from western parts of the country. The other nations of Yugoslavia did not join the resistance in great numbers until mid-1943. Tito's forces kept on fighting a bitter and uneven guerrilla war against the Germans and their axis partners and in this way caught the attention of the Allies who shifted their support from Miha-ilović's royalists to the more efficient Partizans. In **1944**, with the help of the Red Army, Tito took control over the eastern part of the Yugoslavia including Belgrade. The class struggle, masked with

charges of collaboration, led to mass executions of the Serb elite. The war, still raging as the Partizans liberated Croatia and Slovenia unaided, was to claim over a million Serb lives and inflict colossal material damage. The year 1945 saw a transitional period in which the Communists gradually marginalised all the other political forces and eventually proclaimed Yugoslavia a Federal Republic that followed closely the example of Stalin's USSR.

Yugoslavia was envisioned as a Communist spearhead towards the west but it soon became clear that Tito was not willing to turn over all his successes to Stalin and reduce his country to the status of Soviet satellite. In **1948** Stalin decided that he had had enough of Tito and started a propaganda campaign against him. However, Stalin underestimated the strength of Tito's grasp on power. The majority of the Yugoslav Communists opted for Tito and the Stalinists were eliminated. The shadow of war loomed over the breakaway Yugoslavia but the lost sheep was embraced and saved by the West. Thus the major principle of Tito's politics was born: Yugoslavia remained Communist in its own independent way while Western help kept it afloat, making it an example for other countries behind the Iron Curtain. In the two decades to follow, the country was rebuilt and the standard of living rose far beyond that of the rest of eastern Europe. Political freedoms were also greater but the Communist Party kept its exclusive hold on power and defeated all attempts to share it.

The new way of Yugoslav Communists was named "self-government" (samoupravljanje), which meant that workers had all the control over their factories and production. In fact, as all life was controlled by the almighty Party, self-government was symbolic and the economy was managed in a centralized manner that was to fail over and over again. The national question was deemed solved by federalism and all disputes were hushed up. Another

Banknote, post WWII

Josip Broz "Tito", the lifelong president of socialist Yugoslavia

experiment was the independent foreign policy based on collaboration with Third World countries and criticism of both Cold War blocs.

By the mid-sixties the golden age had passed and the residual economic problems were stirring up the social and ethnic unrest. In 1968 Belgrade students revolted against the growing inequalities in a socialist society, while in Kosovo the ethnic Albanians rioted demanding a separate republic. In 1971 Croatia tried to take an independent course but was stopped when Tito threatened to bring in the army. Tito proved that he was still in control but the multitude of challenges was proving too much for an already old man. The new constitution of 1974 tried to solve the problems in a recognizably bureaucratic way and created one of the most complicated state systems ever. The six republics were turned into almost independent states and the unity of the country depended on the Communist Party, the Army and above all on Tito's guidance. The only republic that exercised limited power was Serbia: only Serbia had two autonomous provinces, Vojvodina and Kosovo, which the new constitution raised in all but name to the rank of republics. Furthermore, the provinces could veto the government of Serbia as a whole, while the reverse was not possible. Voices raised against such an injustice were labelled nationalistic and reactionary.

In **1980** Tito died and his place was taken by a rotating presidency, with an incumbent appointed annually and taken from a different republic in turn. The 1980s brought further economic perils but also unimagined freedoms. With no one in full control, more and more dissatisfied voices could be heard. Finally, with the disappearance of the bi-

polar world in 1989, Yugoslavia with its independent communism was needed no more. Powerless to reorganize and deal with its own problems, it was doomed to perish.

Several problems appeared simultaneously. As early as 1981 an armed rebellion in Kosovo sought to achieve republic status or full independence. The underprivileged Serbs of the province were in desperate need of someone to help them and this came in the person of Slobodan Milošević. A younger generation communist on the rise, he quickly realised that Serbia's problem with its provinces was his opportunity for advancement. Cutting through the red tape and speaking directly to people in a manner they could understand, he seemed like a leader able to reassert the dignity of Serbia. Soon he had many notable followers and in 1987 he took full control of the Communist Party of Serbia. In the next two years he used populism and Serb nationalistic rhetoric together with the cry for legalism and power invested by the Communist state system to bring down the leaderships of the autonomous provinces. While the whole thing was done with little trouble in Vojvodina where the Serbs constituted a majority, in Kosovo the ethnic Albanian majority protested and finally resorted to a boycott of all state institutions. In 1989 Milošević was joined by the new leadership of Montenegro and achieved 4 out of 8 voices in the collective presidency. The possibility of a new authoritarian leader ruling the whole of Yugoslavia scared Slovenia and Croatia and awakened their old ideas about independence. The Communist Party of Yugoslavia disintegrated along national lines in **1989** and a boycott of the Yugoslav National Army by Croats, Slovenes and Albanians turned it into a Serb-dominated communist relic of the past. While Slovenian nationalism took on an economic face, in Croatia voices appeared that sounded much like those of the fascist Ustašas in WWII. Milošević now acted as a protector of Serbs in Croatia and Bosnia-Herzegovina, encouraging them to rebel against unconstitutional proclamations of independence. None of the sides wanted to back off or lower their voices and clashes were inevitable. Moreover, attempts by the "international community" to ameliorate the situation were confused, uncoordinated and insincere and did little more than exacerbate the conflict.

After an attempt to prevent Slovenia from leaving that led to a ten-day war in July **1991**, the Yugoslav Army retreated.

*Church of St Sava, a symbol of the religious revival
prevailent throughout Serbia from the end of 1980s*

decided to submit to talks and in late 1995 the Dayton peace agreement was signed. This provoked the Kosovo Albanians to act and in 1998 the Kosovo Liberation Army emerged, attacking police and army forces together with Serbs, and Albanians loyal to the Federation. Milošević responded in his harsh manner once again and the fighting escalated, leading the way to another NATO intervention, this time against Serbia and Montenegro. The spring bombardment and war in Kosovo in **1999** ended with the retreat of the Serbian army and police from the province; together with them some 200,000 Serbs and other non-Albanians also left. The defeated nation saw this as a sell-out and when, in the year **2000**, the Serb opposition finally managed to join forces, the regime was overthrown in massive demonstrations that hit their highest point on the 5th of October.

However, this relatively peaceful hand over of power to democratic forces was accomplished with the help of Milošević's long-time helpers from special operations units. This and other painful compromises meant that the system was never completely cleansed of Milošević's supporters and that all reforms met with silent opposition in some high circles. The final shock came in 2003 when the leading reformist, Prime Minister Zoran Djindjić was assassinated by a group that combined high-ranking state security officials, special units and suspected criminal elements.

On the 4th of February 2004 the Federal Republic of Yugoslavia transformed itself, becoming the State Union of Serbia and Montenegro, a loose confederation of the two states.

In Croatia the fighting between Croats and Serbs had already started. The Army tried to separate the two sides but it was clear that it preferred the Serbs to hostile Croats. By late autumn the crisis had turned into a bloody civil war, with atrocities on both sides. In 1992 the fighting spread to Bosnia; the Army left the newly recognized independent state but left its arms to local Serbs who, with these means soon controlled two thirds of the Bosnia's territory. In the meantime, Macedonia left the Federation peacefully and Serbia and Montenegro formed a new, third incarnation of Yugoslavia in 1992. Due to its direct and indirect help to Serbs in former republics, international sanctions were imposed on the new Yugoslavia. International isolation and the total collapse of the social and administrative systems left space for Milošević's Socialist Party to join with all kinds of criminals that could help him maintain power. The pyramidal bank system and galloping inflation of 1993 robbed ordinary citizens of their incomes and reduced many to poverty, while a small minority close to the centre of power amassed wealth. Although Milošević lost the popular support he once enjoyed, he managed to cling to power by controlling state-owned factories, the police and the media, combined with selective violence and election fraud. In addition, the boycott by Kosovo Albanians gave him the opportunity to gather all their seats in parliament, leaving him with a clear majority there. After the NATO intervention against the Serbs of Bosnia and the collapse of the Serb state in Croatia that generated a flood of 300,000 Serbs to Serbia, Milošević

*Rocketed in NATO bombing campaign of 1999, the
Liberty Bridge is now again in use*

LANDSCAPE AND WILDLIFE

Serbia has a very rich and diverse natural environment. Mountain ranges stretch south of the rivers Sava and Danube, which divide Serbia into two major areas – the mountainous area and the Pannonian plain.

famous winter tourist resorts. The eastern Serbian mountains are much warmer, sunnier and drier with a more Mediterranean type of climate and vegetation. Here, the vegetation is generally marked by xeric oak forests in lower altitudes and mesic

Jerma River Canyon, near Pirot

Mountains

Lush natural forests, pure mountain lakes (called "mountain eyes") and rivers, mountain bogs, natural and semi-natural mountain meadows are typical of the rocky landscapes of much of Serbia. Livestock farming, mostly sheep, goats and cattle, is the main activity for most of the population in the mountains, especially at higher altitudes. Lower altitudes are suitable for growing potato, corn, cabbage, rye and fruit, especially plums and grapes. The Morava valley divides Serbia's mountains into two different mountain areas – the Western and the Eastern. Western Serbian mountains are generally higher and have a damper and colder climate. Some of these mountains stay covered with snow for more than 8 months a year. Coniferous forests of spruce and pine, and broadleaved beech forests are the most common type of vegetation. The most significant of these mountains are: Tara, Kopaonik, Šar-planina, Zlatar, Zlatibor, Golija and Prokletije. These mountains are

beech forests in higher altitudes. The most significant mountains in eastern Serbia are: Stara Planina, Suva Planina and Homoljske Planine. Many of the Serbian mountains have been declared national parks and areas of special protection.

Plains

Agricultural land, steppe and steppe-like grassland, floodplains, swamps, canals, dead river arms and

The endless Vojvodinian plain

Mountains in autumn

traditional way of living with nature. A visitor can choose between a hotel and traditional home accommodation in many of the picturesque villages within a national park.

Forests

Until the end of the 17th century, Serbia was a land of unspoiled nature. More than 90 percent of Serbia was covered in lush natural forests of oak and beech. The population was very scarce until the 17th century, especially in the lowlands, which where almost completely deserted after the Turkish invasion and left to Mother Nature (hence the name of the central hilly province Šumadija – "Foresty"). Most of the forests have been turned into rich agricultural land over the past three centuries. Nowadays, forests cover only about 27 percent of Serbia's territory, land mostly

lakes surrounded by reed and willows, isolated low mountains covered with thick forest and vineyards, are all typical of plains. The largest plain in Serbia is the Pannonian plain, which lies almost entirely in Vojvodina, north of the Sava and Danube rivers. This area has been almost completely turned into agricultural land. The main crops are: cereals, corn, sugar beet and soya bean. The main crop on the higher ground is vine, out of which are produced excellent wines. There are two isolated mountains, long time ago the islands in the Panonnian see – Fruška Gora and Vršačke Planine Mountains. Climate in the plain is continental – very hot, dry summers and cold, windy winters are typical for the area. Originally, the vegetation here was wooded steppe, but very little of this type of land is left in the area. The Deliblatska Peščara sand plain, a protected area, is one of such places. It is a complex mosaic of forest and steppe patches, constantly resisting the shifting sand dunes.

National Parks

There are 5 national parks in Serbia: Fruška Gora Mountain, Iron Gates Gorge, Tara Mountain, Šar-Planina Mountain and Kopaonik Mountain. 31 areas of special protection exist, while another 32 are to become areas of special protection in the years to come. All of Serbia's national parks are readily accessible. They have a relatively free organizational regime which allows people to live within a national park and continue with their

Serbian Spruce, an endemic species found in the Drina Gorge

restricted to the mountains. The most common tree species are beech, 10 species of oak (the most widespread are Hungarian and Turkish oaks), poplars, spruce, Scots and Austrian pine. Oak forests are typical of lowlands and hills all over Serbia, while beach is typical of mountains. Coniferous forests are common at high mountain altitudes, mostly in west Serbia. Many of Serbia's national parks hold rare or endemic tree species, such as: southern nettle tree (Iron Gate national park), wild walnut population (Iron Gate), Serbian spruce (Tara), Bosnian and Macedonian pines (Šar-Planina), Macedonian oak (Šar-planina) and Turkish hazel (Iron Gate).

Hoopoe

Wildlife

The Serbian forests make a good habitat for wildlife. Some of the wild animals common in Serbia have become rare, endangered or even extinct in the rest of Europe. The wolf thrives in great numbers in Serbia, while it is extinct in most other European countries. Brown bear can be found in almost all of Serbia's national parks, and the biggest population lives in the Tara mountain national park. The lynx population is restricted to only several areas of special protection (the biggest population lives in the Iron Gate national park). Wild horses can be found on the Suva Planina Mountain. Jackals are very common, especially in eastern Serbia. Wild boar, roe deer and rabbit are common in all parts of Serbia. Red deer is typical of old lowland English oak forests in Vojvodina.

Lakes and Wetlands

Serbia is not very rich in lakes since it has a dry and hot climate. The largest lakes are artificial, created by erecting dams to provide hydroelectric power. The largest of all is the Iron Gate Lake. One of the most interesting accumulative lakes is Vlasinsko Lake by the town of Surdulica, which was created by sinking a small mountain stream which used to flood the former Vlasinsko Blato Bog. It is famous for its floating peat islands with its unique flora. Most of Serbia's natural lakes are situated in the Pannonian plain, especially in Vojvodina. The most significant of these lakes are the Obedska Bara Bog by the Sava River, and Carska Bara Swamp between the rivers Begej and Tamiš. The Zasavica Swamp near Šabac is in fact

White-headed vulture over the Uvac River

a very slow river that most people consider an elongated swamp. It has a rich bird and fish population and it is one of the few habitats in Europe where endangered European mud minnow still can be found. The Ludaško Jezero Lake near the town of Subotica is also a very important nesting place. More than 200 bird species thrive and nest by each of these bodies of water and all have the status of areas of special protection. Bird watching, boat excursions and sport fishing is offered to tourists by the management services of these areas.

Daičko Lake in the woods of Mt Golija, a wildlife reserve under UNESCO protection

Rivers

The longest river entirely within Serbia is Morava. The Morava valley is the most heavily populated area in Serbia with very rich soil excellent for farming. Other major rivers that flow through Serbia are Danube, Sava, Tisa, Tami{, Drina, West and South Morava and Ibar. Danube, the second largest river in Europe, is a very important waterway, connecting Serbia with other European countries and the Black See. There are 94 fish species in the Serbian waters, with 79 indigenous species living only in Danube and its watershed, which makes it the richest area in Europe in terms of fish species. Most of Serbia's fish species are rare in the rest of Europe, endemic or endangered. High degrees of river pollution are common in Serbia, but most of Serbia's mountain streams are still impeccably clean. These include Drina, Uvac, Mile{evka, Pek and some of the lowland streams, such as Tisa, Bosut and Studva. Tisa, a unique habitat among Serbia's big rivers, was heavily polluted by a Romanian mining company in 2002, but the river soon regained its large population of otters, water birds and many endangered fish species. The canyons of Drina, Uvac and Mileševka are protected as habitats of Serbian spruce, bald eagles and other endangered species. Forests in the flood plains around Bosut are protected for their richness of wildlife.

Caves and Gorges

Rocky limestone landscape of Serbia is very rich karst elements, especially caves and gorges. Some of these caves, such as Resavska, Rajkova, Ceremošnja and Zlotska have become tourist attractions. Gorges and canyons are typical of all mountain rivers: Drina, Danube (Iron Gates), Ibar, Uvac and Mileševka, West Morava (Ovčarsko-Kablarska Gorge)… During the Ice Age they have become refugiums for many thermophilic plant species nowadays typical of canyons: butternut, sweet chestnut, downy oak...

Potpećka Cave near Užice

FISHING AND HUNTING

There are 94 fish species in Serbia, which makes it one of the richest areas in fish species in Europe. 79 fish species are said to be indigenous to the river Danube and its watershed. Some of the fish species living in Serbia's waters are restricted only

Good catch of carp

to this area or became rare in the rest of Europe: 4 species of sturgeon, sterlet, Danubian salmon, marble trout, European mudminnow, Tracian barbel, whiteeye bream, Danubian roach, moranec, checon, vimba, stripped ruffe, Balon's ruffe, Volga zander, streber, zingel.
The largest freshwater fish in the world – **wells** – is abundant in Serbia's rivers and lakes. There are historical records that the wells used to grow up to 400 kg, but nowadays specimens over 80 kg have become rare and the average weight is usually about 1 kg. The most attractive fishing grounds in Serbia for wells fishing is the Danube (especially in the Iron Gates Gorge), Morava, Tisa and a number of lakes. The best baits for wells are leeches and earth worms, but the biggest specimens are caught on live minnows and pieces of dead fish. The best spots for catching **zander** are on the Danube around the town of Novi Sad and in the Iron Gates

Gorge. They are usually caught on wobblers and silicon minnows. **Pike** is abundant all over Serbia, especially in canals and ponds in Vojvodina. The best baits are all sorts of streamers and spoons, but the biggest fish is caught on live minnows. **Danubian salmon** has become rare in the past years, but the Drina still holds a fairly good population of this fish. **Carp** can be found all over the country, usually in larger rivers, such as: Morava, Tamiš, Danube, Tisa; but it is the most numerous in shallow lakes and canals. Some of the best lakes for fishing trophy carps are: Srebrno Jezero, Ada Safari and all the lakes in the Fruška Gora Mountain. The best bait for catching carp in Srebia is corn. **Bighead** has become very common in Serbia's big rivers and catching a 10 kg fish is not unusual. They usually weight about 2-3 kg, but specimens over 30 kg have been recorded. The best places for catching them are: the Sava River (especially around Belgrade), the Danube and Tisa.
Hunting

Serbia is a very attractive country for hunting and has a great variety of available game: red, roe and fallow deer, mouflon, fox, jackal, wild boar, hare, pheasant, partridge, chamois and wild duck. Linx, bear, wolf, wild horse and all species of falcon and eagle are permanently protected in Serbia.

Fishing in the shallow waters of Visočica

Hunting activities are well organized: all the hunting grounds are
easily accessible and have organized
hunting service that can provide
guidance and accommodation both
in hunting loges and hotels.

The most famous hunting
grounds in Serbia are: Deli Jovan,
Južni Kučaj, Apatin, Karadjordjevo,
Kozara and Morović.

The **Deli Jovan** hunting ground
lies within the Iron Gates national
park and is accessible from the
towns Negotin and Gornji Milanovac. Available game: deer, wild boar,
hare, pheasant and partridge. **Južni
Kučaj** lies 250 km from Belgrade and

Winter hunting on Stara planina

the closest town is Juprija, where accommodation is available in a local
hotel. Available game: deer, fallow
deer, doe, wild boar and pheasant.
The **Apatin** hunting ground lies in
Vojvodina by the river Danube, 160
km north of Belgrade. The closest
town is Apatin, and accommodation
available in Makarske Livade hunting lodge. Available game: deer, roe
deer, wild duck and wild goose.
Karadjordjevo spreads along the
left bank of Danube in Vojvodina
some 160 km from Belgrade. For
centuries it has served as a representative hunting ground for roy-
alty and high statesmen and only
recently has become open for the
public. Accommodation facilities:
luxury class "Dijana" country house
and "Vranjak" bungalows. Available

*Heard of wild boars in the Deli Jovan
hunting grounds*

game: red deer, fallow deer (210
points), white tailed deer, wild boar
(137 points), roe deer, badger (24
points - world champion), hare,
mouflon (242 points - world champion), pheasant, wild goose, wild
duck. The **Kozara** hunting ground
lies some 180 km north of Belgrade
near the town of Sombor in Vojvodina. Accommodation is available
in the hunting ground itself, in the
"Štrbac" hunting loge. Available
game: deer and wild boar. **Morović**
hunting ground is a well forested
area lying some 100 km west of
Belgrade in Vojvodina. Accommodation is available in hunting
loges and bungalows in the hunting
ground itself. Most of the game that
lives in Serbia can be found in this
hunting ground, but it is most famous for its abundance of deer. For
those who prefer to observe rather
than hunt wild animals the Carska
Bara Swamp and the Obedska Bara
Bog are just the places to be.

*Red deer in Gornje Podunavlje
hunting grounds near Apatin*

Serbian Fishing Association:
011/361-3379, 361-3590
011/361-3590

Serbian Hunting Association:
011/344-2653,
lovacs@technicom.net

Vojvodina Hunting Association:
021/456-529
Karadjordjevo hunting ground:
021/767-660, 765-254
021/765-222

THE DANUBE THROUGH SERBIA

The Danube, Europe's second largest river, has always fascinated men. It is not surprising that many of the first European cultures such as those at Vinča or Starčevo, were formed on its banks. The Danube's course presses on from the Black Sea directly into the heart of the Old Continent and has therefore been the communication line between civilizations for centuries. Describing the known world in the 5th century B.C., the Greek historian Herodotus concluded that Istros (i.e. the Danube) is the largest river of all and that it is evenly abundant in water both in summer and in winter. At the beginning of the 1st c. AD the Romans conquered its

Pliny the Younger made the most impressive quote when he praised this powerful river by saying: "Magnum est stare in Danubii ripa" ("It is magnificent to stand

Cruise on the Danube through Serbia

on the banks of the Danube"), an experience shared by many to this day.

Today we know that the Danube is not the largest river in the world, but it certainly is the most important river in Europe as it connects the southeast with the centre and, after the opening of Rhine-Main Canal, it is now also connected with the North Sea. For any lover of river cruising, especially for the owners of boats and yachts, the Danube represents the ultimate pleasure as it runs through different states and

right shore and saw it as a protective border between the civilized and the barbaric world. One century later Emperor Trajan led his army to the conquest of Dacia (present day Romania) along the first road built through the Iron Gates Gorge and then across the bridge, a magnificent structure designed by the ingenious Apollodorus of Damascus. This bridge has been highly praised and noted as one of the world's wonders.

landscapes with dazzling contrasts.

The part of the Danube which runs through Serbia is 588 km long and it is exactly in this part that the river becomes wildly potent. The calm passage of the flow through the Pannonian Plain rapidly turns into the rough wilderness of the Iron Gates Gorge.

Through the Plain of Vojvodina

The Danube River enters Serbia at its 1488 kilometer, at the point where the state borders of Hungary, Croatia and Serbia meet. In this part, the Danube has all the features of a lowland river. In many places it still floods when the water level is high and meanders making numerous sandbars, armlets and oxbows. These places present unique natural oases with

Veliki Kazan, the narowest part of the Danube

various plant and animal species. Along the course of the Danube through Vojvodina there are several large hunting and fishing grounds offering an insight into a world different from the tamed and bountiful countryside that surrounds it. Most people come here to observe rare bird species or to hunt prime specimens of red deer and wild boar. The most significant natural resources are: the National Park "Fruška Gora", Apatin Fenland, Karadjordjevo, Petrovaradin–Kovilj Fenland and the Deliblato Sands. Most of them can also be reached by boat by winding through a maze of armlets. Vojvodinian towns are a mixture of cultures and religions that can be best observed by noting all the churches of various religious denominations. Novi Sad is the charming capital of Serbia's northern province with an immense Petrovaradin fortress, the largest on the Danube.

Trajan's Tablet in the Iron Gates Gorge

From Belgrade to the Iron Gates

Belgrade, the capital of Serbia, is situated at 1170 km of the Danube's trajectory. It is one of the oldest European cities and certainly one with a most tempestuous past. A striking feature is its extraordinary geographic location at the mouth of the Sava River into the Danube, on the main roads connecting Central Europe with the Middle East. On the shores of Belgrade there are numerous natural, and several man-made beaches, pleasant picnic areas and an uncountable number of private barges and boat-restaurants. Above the confluence of the two rivers rises the Belgrade fortress around which many nations and armies fought bloody battles. It dates back to the days when the Celts lived here and its history reflects   the

rope. By definition, it stretches from the village of Vinci in front of Golubac (1048 km) to the village of Kostol, across the river from Turnu-Severin (931 km). In front of Golubac and its captivating fortress, the Danube reaches its maximum width of an incredible seven kilometres. The Gorge is composed of several spectacular ravines, the first being the Golubac Ravine followed by Gospodjin Vir, Kazan (at the river's narrowest point of just 150 m) and, in the end, the Sip Ravine. Due to its specific geological, hydrological and archeological features, as well as the rich flora and fauna to be found here, the Iron Gates Gorge has been proclaimed a national park. The once wild waters roaring across the dangerous crags sticking out of the water that filled all but the most experienced captains with fear are today quite calm. This was achieved through the construction of the "Djerdap I" dam 35 years ago. The dam created a considerable rise in the level of the river especially at the narrowest and once most dangerous points. On the other hand this led to the submerging of many coastal villages as well as several towns. The most famous archeological sites thankfully escaped this destiny as they were raised on higher positions inland.   In this way the traveller can   still admire the

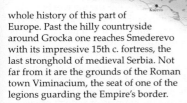

whole history of this part of Europe. Past the hilly countryside around Grocka one reaches Smederevo with its impressive 15th c. fortress, the last stronghold of medieval Serbia. Not far from it are the grounds of the Roman town Viminacium, the seat of one of the legions guarding the Empire's border.

Through the Iron Gates Gorge

The Iron Gates Gorge (in Serbian Djerdap) is the largest river gorge in Eu-

Trajan's Tablet commemorating the termination of the construction of the road through the Gorge and the Lepenski Vir settlement where Europeans created their first sculptures some 6000 years ago.

WINE ROUTES

The history of wine making in Serbia stretches back over two millennia. The wines made by the indigenous tribes were enhanced by the better Mediterranean grape varieties brought over by the Romans at the beginning of our era. Emperor Probus (276-282 AD), born in Sirmium (today Sremska Mitrovica), abolished the monopoly of the Roman viticulturists and initiated the planting of the first vineyards with prime varieties of grape on the slopes of Mt Fruška Gora. One of the reasons why his troops rebelled and killed him was that they had been made to work hard on the clearing of land for the new vineyards.

With the arrival of the mead-drinking barbarians from the North and general insecurity in the region, the laborious task of producing wine was abandoned throughout the inner Balkan region. The Byzantines restored viticulture and wine production in the whole region but most of Serbia remained poor in vineyards until the 12th century, except along the Adriatic coastline. Better times for wine growing came with the rise of the Nemanjić dynasty. The legend says that the wise St. Sava Nemanjić, the greatest Serbian saint, actually taught the people how to make wine. Large numbers of newly built monasteries required wine for liturgical services and as a result new planting took place everywhere. Especially well known was the region of Metohija where many monasteries owned villages where wine production became the sole activity. Soon, wine was drunk by all classes

A toast not to be missed

of society and was made on vast royal plantations as well as in the modest wineries of ordinary peasants. Laws regulated the whole process of wine making from the planting to the sale. With the arrival of the Turks and the displacement of the center of the Serbian state northwards, new wine growing areas grew along the rivers Morava and Danube. The counties around the capital cities of Prince Lazar (Kruševac) and the despot Djuradj (Smederevo) are still famous wine growing regions. Even Bertrandon de la Broquière, a Burgundian knight travelling to Constantinople in the 15th century, was impressed with the multitude of Serbia's vineyards. Since Islam prohibits wine consumption, the Turkish conquest and rule brought wine production to a standstill. However, many regions still lived from wine making, like the town of Sremski Karlovci on Fruška Gora and the neighboring monasteries that paid their rents to the Sultan in wine.

Habsburg rule revitalized the ancient craft once again. The wines of Sremski Karlovci, above all the aromatic vermouth-like bermet, were now used to secure the granting of Serbian privileges by the Viennese court. Consequently, the wines of Fruška Gora became highly regarded all over Europe and, already in the 18th century, were being exported

Roman wine jug from the Museum of wine, Ravna near Knjaževac

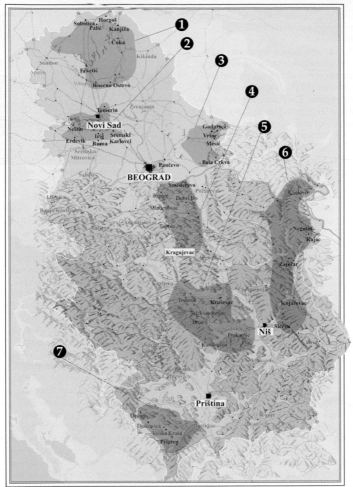

1 Subotica-Horgoš wine region

2 Srem wine region

3 Banat wine region

4 Šumadijsko-Velikomoravski wine region

5 Zapadnomoravski wine region

6 Timok wine region

7 Metohija wine region

to London and other major European cities. The knowledgeable winegrowers from the Moselle region who were colonized in Vršac became renowned in the 19th century for their production. The sandy grounds of northern Vojvodina, around Subotica and Čoka, owned by the wealthy noble families, were turned into great plantations that produced some celebrated masterpieces of wine-making.

When Serbia became independent, the re-establishment of vineyards attracted much attention from the new rulers. Particularly well known in this context was King Petar who, at the very beginning of the 20th century,

planted huge vineyards at his property on Oplenac Hill that still give top quality wines.

The different regions, each with their specific climates, yield a variety of distinct wines. The main wine growing areas all lie along rivers: the Danube, all three Moravas, the Timok or the Nišava. There are several indigenous wines like the pale Smederevka or Slankamenka and ruby Prokupac and Župljanka, that each bear the names of the towns or regions where they originated.

If you're eager to learn more about Serbian wines you can follow the suggested wine routes and visit the places where you can try them and perhaps buy some from the manufacturers themselves.

Sandy grounds, a temperate continental climate with much sun during the summers and fine grape varieties are features of the **Subotica-Horgoš wine region**. The main producers here are two large wineries in Čoka and in Palić. Čoka produces wines such as Merlot, Muscat Ottonel or "Ždrebčeva krv" ("Stallion's Blood"). The winery "Sololac" from Novi Bečej makes Muscat Crocant, a very rare variety, which is produced solely on Biserno Island in Tisa River. The wine named "Francuski poljubac" ("French Kiss") is prepared from the local grape variety – *Kevedinka*.

For several centuries the **Srem wine region**, whose focal point is the famous Sremski Karlovci, center of the Serbian Orthodox Church, was one of the leading wine producing areas in Europe. Distinctive local specialities and techniques go into specially prepared wines like *Ausbruh* (*Samotok*) and the aromatized *Bermet* that accord perfectly with deserts. The winery in Čerević produces a recently created but equally attractive wine, Neoplanta. Basking in the sun's rays and their reflection in the broad waters of the Danube - varieties including Italian-, Rhein- or the local Fruškogorski Riesling, and also others such as Traminer, Bouvies, *Župljanka*, Portugieser or Blaufränkisch - each have their own distinctive taste and qualities.

Already famous in the days of the medieval Hungarian kings, the **Banat wine region** centered around the Vršac Mountains, continued wine production throughout the days of Turkish rule up until the wine growing renaissance in the 19th and 20th centuries. Small villages east of Vršac, such as Gudurica or Veliko Središte, still base their living on wine growing. In Gudurica, the wine growers come from 16 different ethnic origins, all tending their vineyards in harmony. The biggest maker here is "Vršačko vinogorje" with its 1,7 thousand acres of vineyards and equally huge cellars,

View through the vineyards to Vršac Hill

most famous of which is the 1880 "Helvecija" in Vršac. The most widely produced wines are Muscat Ottonel, Chardonnay, Pinot Bianco, Rhein and Italian Riesling, as well as the local *Kreacer* and the sparkling "Kabinet".

The **Šumadijsko-velikomoravski wine region** borders on the rivers Danube and Great Morava, with local centers in Topola and Smederevo. The traditions of the royal vineyards of the Karadjordjević dynasty, on the hill of Oplenac above Topola, is maintained by the "Aleksandrović" winery. Their most famous wine, prepared according to the old recipe, is Trijumf ("Triumph"). The villa of the rival Obrenović dynasty, on Zlatni Breg above the Danube, is surrounded by plantations founded at the beginning of the 19th century. Apart from the local *Smederevka*, with a fruity, fresh taste in two varieties (dry or demi-sec), the other white wines – Chardonnay, Rhein Riesling, Cabernet - are equally worth trying here. Further up the Morava River is the village of Krnjevo and in it the "Small Cellar 'Radovanović'" whose wines have won several awards.

With its mild climate, the valley of the **Timok wine region** stretches along the river of the same name from Knjaževac to Negotin, both with big wineries. At the turn of 19th and 20th centuries this region became famous as one that was not affected by Phylloxera, such that French winegrowers came to buy wine here. Austro-Hungary even maintained a consulate here with the sole purpose of importing the local wine!

Wine pressing tool

Nevertheless, one of the biggest attractions here is the *pimnice* in villages such as Rajac, Rogljevo or Smedovac. Pivnice are groups of houses separated from the villages themselves and specially designed for wine making and wine storage. The old stone houses formed streets and small squares so that a pivnice today constitutes a sort of wine hamlet. Apart from the local *Bagrina*, the Gamay and Semillon produced here are also exquisite.

The **Zapadnomoravski wine region** is famous for the producers in Kruševac ("Rubin"), Prokuplje and above all in Aleksandrovac, center of the Župa district. Župa is a term for a valley with a mild climate, and župa along the river Rasina is perfect for wine growing. All of the wealthy medieval monasteries had their vineyards here and that tradition was never abandoned in this quiet and beautiful corner of Serbia. Akin to *pimnice*, here we find *poljane* made by villagers to live in during the long periods of work in the vineyards required in springtime and summer every year. During the wine harvest season in Aleksandrovac, one of the fountains flows with wine instead of water. Most widely grown here are the indigenous *Prokupac*, named after the town of Prokuplje, and *Tamjanika*, a Muscat variety that originated in France but has been very popular in Serbia since the Middle Ages.

The **Metohija wine region** encompasses the south-western angle of Kosovo province, with local centers in Suva Reka, Orahovac, Velika Hoča (with its twelve medieval churches) and especially in Mala Kruša village, whose "Kosovovino" was among the largest wine producers in the country

Grape harvest in Župa

before the war. The tradition was established at the end of the 12th century by Stefan Nemanja, the founder of the Nemanjić dynasty, who himself planted the first vineyards here.

The winegrowers of Serbia celebrate St. Tryphon as their patron saint (14th of February). In the same way as St. Tryphon remained persistent and steadfast under persecution, so they believe, their patron will grant that long months of labor will pay off with a rich grape harvest and quality vintages.

During the grape harvest all of the wine regions organise festivities to honor the event. These are wonderful occasions for savouring wine, music, singing and dancing and, most important of all, for enjoying the assorted specialties of Serbian cuisine that accord so perfectly with their local wines.

Pivnica *interior in Rajac near Negotin*

SPAS IN SERBIA

Serbia is considered one of the richiest country in mineral springs - there are three hundred enumerated so far. Twenty among them are evaluated as mineral springs with the highest healing caracteristics. Mineral waters in Serbia are very versatile and can be divided after their physical (cold, worm and hot) and chemical characteristics (acid, base, neutral, mineralised from a lesser to a greater degree etc.).There are alkaline spas such as Bukovička, Vrnjačka, Mataruška or Ribarska, radioactive – Niška, Sokobanjska, the ones with healing mud bath from their pools as Palić and Rusanda, salt water spa in Slankamen and iodine spa in Novi Sad. The number and abundance of their water sources mostly depend on geological composition of the ground. Some of these springs are appearing on the hights over five hundred meters witch is very rare to find worldwide. Thermo-mineral water from Vranjska banja with its 92°C is the hotest in Europe. In Sijarinska banja there are two geysers , and one of them is jeting water to 45 meters of hight!

Most of these mineral springs were used already by the Romans who built around them thermae and villas, the remains of which were found in Niška, Vrnjačka and Sokobanja Spa. In Medieval times springs were used sporadicly by common people creating miths about their megical healing powers. The Turks rediscoverd and made a great use of them. Turkish baths are still in use today in Novi

Pazar, Sokobanja and Brestovačka banja. Soon after the country was liberated from the Turks, educated experts aknowledged natural resources of mineral and thermel waters in Serbia and became interested in their healing characteristics so that during the first half

Pool at Vrnjačka Banja Spa

of the19th century several mineral spas emerged as health resorts. It didn't take long for these spas to become places of leasure and recuperation for urban people who found their retreat there during summers and who started building houses and villas there. Just before the World World I, spas In Serbia were very fashionable places, with beautifuly designed parks and lakes which attracted visitors from Serbia as well as from abroad. At that time, the special law on spas and health resorts was passed which regulated their organization. Further delopment took place within resorts between two wars, when

19th c. "Staro zdanje" Hotel at the Bukovička Banja Spa

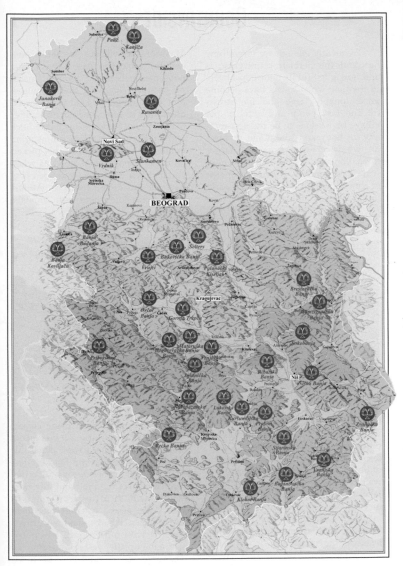

modern hotels and boardinghouses were built. That was the heyday of health resosrts who were leading the way within the Serbian tourism. During the following decades large hotels were erected to accomodate thousands of visitors eager to find the cure for their diseases but also tourists who were just enjoying in their charm.

Today , spas in Serbia can offer modern accomodation, well maintained parks, sport grounds, beauty salons, saunas, fittness centers, indoor and outdoor swimming pools and conference halls. Within all health resorts, there are specialise medical institutions with modern equipment for diagnostic pourposes and treatments. Wooded hills and mountains are suitable for walks, picnic, picking medicinal herbs and forest fruits, rivers for fishing and rafting, a very active holiday in general. There are a lot of monuments from passed times as monasteries, fortresses or archeological excavation sites. The most famouse among health resorts in Serbia are also very lively cultural centres during the season, with lots of manifestations – theatrical and cinematic events, folk performances, concerts...

COUNTRYSIDE

Frequently enough we forget how beautiful the Serbian countryside is and how plentiful its nature has been. In the time when towns have become uncomfortably large and life stressful and fast, peace and quiet of the village idyll seems to be the best remedy for body and soul. Only an hour or two-drive away from any larger town, you will be able to find scenery with a completely different concept of time: although people get up early in the morning and work all day, here

Most of the villages in Serbia are, genuine ecological oases. Every true housemaster is proud about his natural products, knowing that his ancestors left him healthy land to be passed on as such to new generations. Apples that were not sprayed, raspberry juice without any preservatives, plums dried in old-fashioned way or freshly picked tomatoes often taste as good as when you had first tried them and open new flavours and aroma horizons. Almost every household keeps farm animals,

The rolling countryside of the Zlatibor region

the hurry will lead you nowhere. And when you visit a village as a guest, the time passes quickly, for the joys of old-fashioned life never end. In villages of Serbia, you can take relaxing slow walks, sleep to your heart's content, take a breathe of fresh air, but also meet the life of a peasant, and if willing, learn something as well.

Someone unobservant often misses the beauty of the countryside. To unveil its disguise takes patience and time, takes turning from the main road, exchanging a few words with a peasant, climbing on a hilltop, tasting wild strawberries and sitting by a cauldron over a slow crackling fire. In Serbia, every village has its stream or its river, its wood or its mount, and every household - its field or its hill, orchard or raspberry patch Hidden valleys between mountains, or solitary farm in never-ending plains, leave you with an opportunity to face yourself and your loved ones and for a few days devote yourself entirely to them. Do not forget the sunsets behind the faraway hills, nights with thousands of stars and crystal clear mornings.

offers fresh milk, home made cream, eggs from this morning… If you take a walk, you may come across hedges full of wild strawberries and blackberries, branches full of cherries or mulberries that band over the path and lure passengers with their ripe fruit. You will also come across fragrant meadows full of remedial herbs, shadowy groves covered with mushrooms, which are springing up after yesterday's rain.

The large hotels could be a bit more comfortable compared to simply decorated rooms, but the familiarity and kindness that is offered to you as the guest from a village host is something

Playful moments in nature

you will not find anywhere else. For the guest is the sanctity here and is welcomed as the first who ever came and seen off as the dearest.

Apart from visiting natural and cultural sights of the countryside, many households offer you the opportunity to learn how to milk a cow, how to stock hay, how to prepare winter stocks. And if you roll your sleeves up and try your newly acquired skills, the master of the house will be more than happy. With little attentiveness, you may also learn how to make excellent rakija (brandy), how to make buckwheat pie and what the most important in a quince preserves preparation. The

Interior of "Ruža Gruže" in Bare village

best souvenir you can take home from a village is something that you yourself helped to be made and offer to your friends, knowing the love and effort you invested in it.

MANIFESTATIONS

JANUARY

THE STREET OF OPEN HEART,
Belgrade
011/3248-404
office@tob.co.yu
www.tob.co.yu

FEBRUARY

SLANINIJADA, The Bacon Festival,
Kačarevo (near Pančevo)
013/711 094, 711 223

FEST - INTERNATIONAL FILM
FESTIVAL , Belgrade
011/3346 946
info@fest.org.yu
www.fest.org.yu
  During ten days there will be screening of
films of the latest world and local production.
Organised in several programmes' categories-
Currents, Facts and puzzels, Europe out of Europe, Certain view at French movie, Lighthouse
and Filmeur.

Sauseges in "Kobasicijada" of Turija

KOBASICIJADA, Sausage Festival,
Turija (near Srbobran)
021/731 279

MARCH

IN VINO,
INTERNATIONAL WINE FESTIVAL
011/455 986
invino@yubc.net
www.invino.co.yu
  This is the largest wine festival in the Central
and Southeast Europe. The festival runs parallel
with wine instrument exhibition, and a promotion of tourist offerings of Serbia's wine growing
regions.

APRIL

The Belgrade Marathon

BELGRADE MARATHON
011/3309 425
  Belgrade's largest sportingrecreational event
gathering marathon runners from more than 30
countries and over 20,000 participants in other
running disciplines.

MAY

LILAC DAYS, Kraljevo
036/333 585

STERIJA THEATER FESTIVAL,
Novi Sad - „Sterijino pozorje"
021/451 273
sterija@eunet.yu
www.pozorje.org.yu
  The Sterija Theater Festival, a national drama
festival and theater contest, was established in
1956, the 150th and 100th anniversaries of play-
wright Jovan "Sterija" Popović's birth and death,
respectively. The theater festival gathers local
and international professional theaters, which
stage plays written by local playwrights. The
permanent national drama festivity promotes
theatrical art and encourages the development
of drama.

*Ethno-music concert in the Belgrade
Fortress*

MOLJE MOTIFS & GOLDEN
ANDS OF KUČEVO, Kučevo
)12/850 666
tokucevo@ptt.yu

This event focuses on the old way of panning for gold in the Pek River. It also features contests in the preparation of Wallachian dishes, spindle making, sheep milking and wool spinning, as well as all-round shepherd sports competitions. Traditional folk music players, dancers and singers from all parts of Serbia perform at the event, which also showcases folk arts and crafts and stages a selling exhibition of Homolje cheese.

Folklore performance in Kučevo

JUNE

INTERNATIONAL SWIMMING MARATHON, Šabac
015/347 383
tossabac@verat.net
www.swimmarathonsabac.com
The best-known swimming marathon in Southeast Europe has been held for the past 36 years. The route is 18.8 km-long. The contest is accompanied by a cultural and entertainment program, fish soup contests, etc.

TOUR DE SERBIE INTERNATIONAL CYCLING RACE
011/3292 128
tds@eunet.yu
www.tds.co.yu
Tour de Serbie is an event with the longest tradition in our country. It dates back to 1939. For the third time the race will take place under a slogan "Cycling and tourism together". The goal of the race, besides its recreational character, is also the affirmation of Serbian tourism, its natural beauty, cultural heritage, and hospitality of our people.

DANUBE DAY, Danube
011/2013 357, 2134 903
ruzica.jacimovic@minpolj.sr.gov.yu
www.minpolj.sr.gov.yu
www.danubeday.org
www.icpdr.org
Danube Day manifestation started on June 29, 2004 to mark the tenth anniversary of the signing of the Danube Convention. Each year on that day, a day of festivities take place across the whole Danube River Basin. The water games, exhibitions, excursions, seminars, workshops and other activities.

JULY

BELEF - SUMMER FESTIVAL, Belgrade
011/3238 341
office@belef.org
www.belef.org
A summer time multimedia festival, BELEF is staged in open air or in alternative city spaces. It unifies three great arts – that of theater, music and painting. The festival explores various city spaces and facilities, contents and innovative forms of artistic expression. BELEF strives to reflect the sensibility of Belgrade citizens and artists in all segments of its program.

MERRY DOWN THE IBAR RIVER, Kraljevo
036/312 682, 316 000
webmaster@veselispust4t.com,
www.veselispust4t.com,
www.jutok.org.yu
Rafting on the Ibar River; outdoor lunch features national dishes.

EXIT - MUSIC FESTIVAL, Novi Sad
021/420 735
info@exitfest.org
www.exitfest.org
The largest music festival in Southeast Europe, EXIT has been staged in Novi Sad's enchanting Petrovaradin Fortress every year since 2001. The number of EXIT visitors is growing with each year, with young people flocking from all over the country, but also from all over Europe. The festival attracts such an overwhelming turnout not only thanks to its attractive music program, but also thanks to great fun, the good atmosphere inside the Fortress, and positive energy of Novi Sad.

REAPING ON MT RAJAC
014/85 242
info@ljig.org.yu
www.kosidba.com
www.ljig.org.yu
An event dedicated to reaping and harvesting carried out by husking bees. Local and foreign participants compete in the reaping of mountain grass. Reapers wear national costumes, straw hats, and colorful shoulder bags. The best among them is pronounced the winner, or "didija". Folk ensembles from surrounding villages wear colorful national costumes and perform traditional songs and dances, while traditional dishes are served on embroidered white tablecloths.

Reapers of Rajac

SHEPHERD DAYS, Kosjerić
031/782 155
tokos@verat.net
www.kosjeric.org.yu
A festivity showcasing shepherd lives and customs, songs and dances; girls' beauty contests, and costume, traditional cooking, and handicraft competitions; exhibitions of paintings, field tools, artisan objects, fruit and vegetable preserves and honey products; shepherd story-telling.

SERBIAN FRULA-PLAYER FESTIVAL, Prislonica (near Čačak)
032/342 360
toc@ptt.yu
www.turizamcacak.org.yu
Indigenous music performed on the frula – a Serbian national instrument – and on other instruments derived from the frula. This is a competitive event, which includes choosing the best frula-player, and is accompanied by traditional activities such as the participation of dance and song troupes, poetry readings, etc.

A young contestant

AUGUST

GITARIJADA, Zaječar
019/422 086
A guitar-playing event.

HACKNEY COACH FESTIVAL, Ravno Selo
021/722 092
Hackney coach-driving state championship evaluating the appearance, beauty and grace of horses, horse-drawn carriages, and drivers.

ATFISH FISHING COMPETITION, ja
01 690
n@kladovocity.net
adovo-turizam.org.yu
e tourist and fishing event of interna-
rtions, with a variety of accom-
ral, entertainment, and sporting

The art of driving a hackney-coach

DUŽIJANCA, Subotica
024/554 589
info@duzijanca.co.yu
www.duzijanca.co.yu
A traditional harvest-time custom consisting of the weaving of wreaths from the last sheaf of wheat, which is then taken to church to be blessed. The entire event takes approximately four months. It ends with a reaping contest, followed by a ceremonious procession of the participants dressed in national costume, and riding in elaborately decorated, horse-drawn carriages.

BEER FEST, Belgrade
011/3240 784
office@belgradebeerfest.com
www.belgradebeerfest.com

DRAGAČEVO TRUMPET FESTIVAL, Guča
032/854 110, 854 765
domtrube@eunet.yu
Competition of brass bands and vocal and instrumental groups from all parts of Serbia and abroad. It is accompanied by all-around folk sports, exhibitions of folk handicrafts, traditional dishes and self-taught artists – painters, sculptors and poets.

BEER DAYS, Zrejnanin
023/523 160, 581 890
office@zrenjanintourism.org.yu
www.danipiva.co.yu
www.zrenjanintourism.org.yu
Zrenjanin beer days, Banat's busy hands, Ino-coop international fair of enterprise, Innovation, Sunflower international pop music festival, Lala international folklore festival.

Revellry at the Guča Festival

BOAT CARNIVAL, Belgrade
011/3248 404
office@tob.co.yu
www.tob.co.yu
www.publicart-publicspace.org
　Belgrade Boat Carnival is a one-day event organized on the Belgrade rivers and their banks. It involves various activities, such as exhibitions, competitions on water and banks, Belgrade boat tours, festive boat carnival, fireworks and similar.

TEŠNJAR EVENINGS, Valjevo
014/221 138
tovaljevo@ptt.yu
vaturist@verat.yu
www.valjevo-turist.co.yu
　Literary evenings and concerts showcasing traditional song and dance, theater productions, fashion shows, and exhibitions of agricultural products from the Valjevo region.

SEPTEMBER

LJUBIČEVO EQUESTRIAN GAMES
012/221 941, 555 323
to_pozarevac@ms012.net
www.turizampozarevac.com
www.kdknezmihailo.org.yu
　An international equestrian sporting event. The traditional all-round competition includes: show-jumping, relay riding, and arrow, lance, and mace-hurling, as well as sword-cutting in full gallop. Cultural and entertainment activities accompany this event.

ROŠTILJIJADA, Leskovac
016/233 260
toleskovac@sezampro.yu
www.toc.co.yu
　A competition involving local and foreign ćevapčići-makers, along with professionals and hotel management students. The event is accompanied by cultural and entertainment activities.

Wine-making in Vršac

GRAPE-PICKING, Vršac
013/822 554, 822 909
tovrsac@ptt.yu
kultcentar@hemo.net
www.to.vrsac.com
　A traditional event of wealthy winegrowers, including wine balls and festivities, celebrations of the first racking, and diverse cultural and entertainment programs.

On stage at the Natonal Theatre

BELGRADE INTERNATIONAL THEATRE FESTIVAL, Belgrade
011/3243 108
vesna@bitef.co.yu
www.bitef.co.yu
　Since the 1960s, BITEF has been a festival of theatrical tendencies, reflecting most directly the tumultuous evolution of the theatrical art.

GRAPE-PICKING, Sremski Karlovci
021/881 250
srem.karl@eunet.yu
www.sremskikarlovci.org.yu
　Held in the unique environment of this town- museum, its purpose is the affirmation of cultural and touristic values of Sremski Karlovci and its neighbourhood, promotion of viniculture and wine production, as well as preservation of grape-picking customs.

BEMUS - MUSIC FESTIVAL, Belgrade
011/3239 916
bemus@jugokoncert.co.yu
www.bemus.co.yu
　An international music event presenting the best musical achievements from international and domestic competitions. Besides renowned artists, every year BEMUS also opens up its stages for young musicians.

AUTUMN IN SMEDEREVO, Smederevo
026/222 952
toosd@sezampro.yu
　An event devoted to grape-picking and wine-making. A procession of costumed and mounted medieval knights, accompanied by ladies of the court dressed in highly ornate garments, is followed by grape-pickers and cultural and entertainment activities taking place in the famous Smederevo Fortress, and in the city of Smederevo itself.

OCTOBER

LUDAJA DAYS, Kikinda
0230/26 300
dragisa.ugarcina@kik

NO

NISVILLE
FESTIV
018/5

SERBIA BY REGIONS

BELGRADE

1.753.800

Dečanska 1
11000 Beograd
011/3248-404, 3248-310
www.tob.co.yu
www.belgradetourism.org.yu

The Serbian capital, a city of over two million people, lies on the confluence of the Sava River into the Danube, dominating the Panonnian plain to its north. Thanks to its position it has, since ancient times, been a vital crossroads between the Orient and the Occident, the North and the South. Today it is also the hub of road and rail networks in the country. The city has a continental climate marked by harsh winters and very hot summers, with barely discernible springs and falls. The best times to visit are April and May when the whole city seems to celebrate the end of winter, or September - which here looks more like a summer than an autumn one.

Belgrade has many interesting sights including a magnificent fortress that rises above the confluence of the two rivers, Serbia's major museums, royal palaces and many other historical monuments, however, the city's greatest attraction is its spirit: lively crowds, street bars always filled with the both young and old alike and a sparkling nightlife.

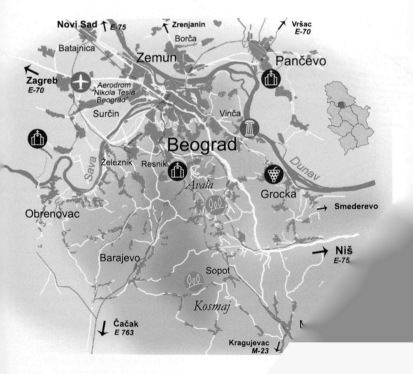

...zije Square in downtown Belgrade, with a view of "Albar...
...ube behind it

HISTORY OF BELGRADE

A steep hill above the confluence of two mighty rivers that rams itself into the Pannonian plain, was a good strategic position from the earliest of times. Data of a settlement in Belgrade goes back as far as 4000 years BC. The first people known by name to have lived here were the Thracian Singi tribe. Around 270 BC they were replaced by the Celtic Scordisci who settled here returning from their unsuccessful raid on Greece. The Celts gave the settlement its first name – *Singidun*, "the town of Singi".

"The Belgrade Cameo" representing Constantine the Great in battle against the Danubian barbarians (National Museum Belgrade)

Around the date of Christ's birth, the Romans took possession of the area and Romanised the name to *Singidunum*. However, it was not until **91 AD**, when the Legion IV forming of a civil settlement next to the military castrum that occupied the site of the present-day Upper Town of the Belgrade Fortress. The city flourished in the 2nd and 3rd c. but remained in the shadow of neighbouring Viminacium (today Kostolac, in Eastern Serbia) and famous Sirmium (Sremska Mitrovica).

Singidunum endured troublesome times during the barbaric invasions until finaly in **441** Attila and his Huns ruthlessly sacked the settlement.

A revival came with the great Emperor Justinian, yet instead of the reconstruction of the city Justinian only built a small fortress on the spot where the "Victor" monument stands today. Soon afterwards, the fortress was taken over and destroyed by the joint forces of the Avars and the Slavs in 582 and than again in 602. This was the last of the ancient Singidunum (or *Singedon* as the Byzantines called it) - along with the Byzantine Empire, the name of the city disappeared amidst a sea of Slavic newcomers. In 878 the city is mentioned again, and here for the first time as Belgrade in a letter from Pope John VIII to the Bulgarian Khan Boris I Michail concerning the conduct of a local bishop (*episcopatum belgradensem*). The 8th and 9th centuries saw Bulgarian predominance in the city, as it was

...ic position of Belgrade as ... many old engravings

...t here to fight the ...n the other side ...e city's strategic ...l. The station- ...and all the ...l to the

a border fort on the western edge of their empire. Then, as soon as the Byzantines crushed the Bulgarians, another adversary emerged, the Hungarians, and in the 11th c. Belgrade changed hands several times. Most of the First, Second and Third Crusades passed through Belgrade bringing with them insecurity and occasional looting. After the death of Emperor Manuel I in 1180 the Byzantines lost possession of Belgrade for good and the Hungarians turned it into an important fort on the southern border of their Pannonian realm.

In **1284** King Istvan V of Hungary ceded the town to his son-in-law the Serbian King Dragutin and thus Belgrade came into Serbian hands for the first time. After Dragutin's death his brother Milutin tried to keep hold of it, contrary to agreement with the Hungarians. The town then became a regular target of Serbian rulers who encountered fierce resistance.

The rivalry between the Serbs and Hungarians ended in **1403** in face of the grave threat from the Turks. In that year the Hungarian King Sigismund handed the town to the Serbian Despotes Stefan Lazarević who became his vassal and principal ally against Turkish onslaughts. Stefan Lazarevic transformed it into his capital and, after years of hard work, also into one of the strongest fortresses in Europe. After Stefan's death in 1427 Belgrade passed back into the hands of the Hungarian king but retained its Serbian population. In **1440** the town experienced its first Turkish siege; it had been set back after 7 months of desperate defense. But this was just a splash in the pan for the ordeal that was to come in **1456**: a 150,000 strong army led by Sultan Mahomet the Conqueror laid siege to the town which was saved only by the united efforts of the defenders inside the city walls and the Crusaders' army that came to rescue. The wounded Sultan had to flee leaving behind 24 thousand of his best soldiers dead and, all of his cannons. Belgrade was celebrated as the bastion of Christianity and the Pope ordered for all the churches to ring their bells at noon every day as a reminder of

The first visual representation of Belgrade (14th c)

this glorious victory. For the Turks it became known as *Dar-ul-Jihad*, "The Home of Holy War". However, the Turkish power was on the rise while the Hungarian kingdom was falling into disarray. When, in **1521** Suleiman the Magnificent marched on Belgrade, the town could not expect any outside help. Cut off from all sides by the precautious Sultan, Belgrade waited for two months but after hearing that the Hungarian king was still mustering his army in Buda, all hope was shattered and it surrendered. The whole of the Serbian population was taken into slavery and settled in Istanbul. With the fall of Belgrade, Hungary was soon lost as well and, as early as 1529, Vienna lived its first Turkish siege.

Finally away from the frontlines, Turkish Belgrade made the best of its position and grew into a huge trade and administrative centre. 170 years

View of Belgrade in Turkish times

Eugene of Savoy's 1717 victory in front of Belgrade

could not be subdued after they had tasted the fruits of liberty and rose up again in 1815. This time the solution was reached by an agreement which was finally ratified by the Sultan in 1830: the Turks would leave the countryside and reside in only six forts in an autonomous Serbia ruled by Prince Miloš Obrenović. Belgrade developed slowly under this dual government and the European looks and manners substituted oriental neglect painfully. Nevertheless, in this period Belgrade obtained its first theatre, library, museum and university. After the 1862 Čukur-česma incident and the subsequent bombardment of Belgrade from the fortress, the problem of the Turkish provinces was brought to international attention that led to, in **1867**, the Turkish garrison being forced to leave the fortress. New perspectives were created with the Turkish departure: a railway connection through Europe came in 1884, electric lighting in 1893…

of peace brought the town unrecorded benefits and its populace rose to some 100.000 inhabitants.

In 1683 Kara Mustafa-Pasha was defeated at the gates of Vienna, making the tidal wave of Ottoman victories stop and he and his armies were forced back. The Habsburg armies reached Belgrade in **1688** taking the unprepared city whose fortification was neglected and out-of-date. Austrian rule was brief – the Turks returned victorious two years later. Once again Belgrade became a frontier fortress town. In **1717** the military genius of Prince Eugene of Savoy ensured Christian victory over the far more numerous enemy in front of the Belgrade gates and the town again fell into Habsburg hands. The new rulers transformed it into a baroque city with a fascinating new fortress in the Vauban style.

The Turks returned in **1739**, destroyed all the European-looking edifices and rebuilt the fortress that had to be pulled down due to the peace agreement. Once again the Austrians took possession of the city in 1789 and lost it in 1791. By this time the population had been reduced to just a few thousand living in the ominous shadow of the fortress.

The terror of the janissary troops, in an empire unable to control them, provoked the Serb rebellion of 1804. In **1806** Belgrade was taken by the insurrectionists and became again the capital of Serbia. Although the Turks managed to crush the insurrection in ˃813 and take over the town, the Serbs

The town's progress was halted by the First World War, whose initial shots were fired on the **29th of July 1914** from the Austro-Hungarian ships onto the first lines of Serbian defense

Street scene from the middle of the 19th century

by the Sava riverfront. The years 1914 and 1915 saw heavy shelling and street fighting in three of the Central Powers offensives against Serbia. After that, occupation followed, a painful time in which all that was Serbian was prohibited. In 1918

Belgrade emerged stripped of most of its industry, devastated by economic standstill and economic exploitation and with population just half of its pre-war size.

Old Belgrade Fairgrounds, 1939.

Things soon got better as the city became the capital of the new, far bigger state, the Kingdom of Serbs, Croats and Slovenes (from 1929 called Yugoslavia). The need for larger buildings meant that construction flourished, new boulevards and parks were created, and the first plan-built suburbs emerged as well as the first bridges across the Sava and the Danube. Along with the material renewal, Belgrade eagerly tried to follow all of the world's trends: from fashion shows and jazz to skyscrapers and a commercial airport.

All of this came to a halt, when in demonstrations on the 27th March **1941**, the Serbs repulsed the possibility of joining Nazi Axis powers. Hitler took this as a personal and national insult and turned on Yugoslavia. On the morning of the 6th April the Reich attacked without the proclamation of war and its planes viciously bombed Belgrade. The city fell into the hands of the Nazi's and suffered greatly: in the vicinity of Belgrade there existed two concentration camps and a mass execution site. To add insult to injury, the city was bombed several times in 1943-44 by the Allied forces. In the end, the Nazis were forced out of the town through the joint efforts of the Soviet Red Army and Yugoslav communist partisans taking it back, street by street. On the **20th of October 1944** the city was free of Germans, but it was then to be ideologically cleansed by the new authorities.

The post-war period was marked by rapid industrialization fed by the influx of people from the countryside into the new suburbs and the new town across the river – New Belgrade, founded in 1948. Luckily, disputes between the Soviet and Yugoslav way into communism brought a break with Stalin and Yugoslavia managed to escape being part of the Soviet block and ended up balancing between the East and the West. The 1960's saw a definite break with austere communist reality as Belgrade embraced western influences such as rock'n'roll and hosted some of the biggest film and music stars of the day. This cosmopolitan atmosphere, that reached its climax during 1980's, was abruptly stopped when the country fell apart in 1991.

Milošević's Belgrade of the 1990s lived through streams of refugees, the second highest inflation rate in the world ever (in 1993/94), mafia shootings, anti-regime demonstrations, police beatings and in the end, the **1999** NATO bombing that left many scars on the city still visible today.

After the bloodless revolution of October 2000, the city returned back to its prior course but the wounds inflicted by a decade under an isolated and corrupt regime are still the cause of most of its current problems.

Belgrade's "Western Gate" seen from the motorway

OLD TOWN

Up until the end of the 17th c. the nucleus of the town used to lie where the Fortress and Kalemegdan Park are situated today. The splendid views in all directions, mighty medieval and baroque fortifications and a pleasantly modeled park with many old monuments are a sight not to be missed. The Old Town is the core of the city, the onetime "Town within a Moat", from where Belgrade again began to develop in the 19th c. After the Turkish departure in 1867, most of this area was remodeled, influenced by the modern rectangular street plan that can be best observed in the Dorćol quarter sloping towards the Danube which is nowadays packed with trendy cafés. Many important institutions located in fine palaces can be found here, such as the National Bank, the Serbian Academy of Arts & Sciences, University buildings and the National Museum. The main shopping avenue, Kneza Mihaila Street runs through the middle of the Old Town presenting the shortest route between Kalemegdan and the Republic and Terazije squares.

1 Trg Republike	**11** French Embassy	**21** The ZOO
2 Kneza Mihaila Street	**12** Kalemegdan Park	**22** Eastern Outwork
3 Obilićev venac	**13** The Roman Well	**23** Ružica Church and St. Petka Chapel
4 Topličin venac	**14** The Victor	**24** Pedagogical Museum
5 Museum of Applied Arts	**15** Upper Town	**25** Frescoes Gallery
6 Kosančićev venac	**16** Lower Town	**26** Bajrakli Mosque
7 Palace of Princess Ljubica	**17** Gallery of the Natural History Museum	**27** The Vuk & Dositej Museum
8 Orthodox Cathedral	**18** Military Museum	**28** Studentski trg
9 Patriarchal Palace & Museum of the Serb Orthodox Church	**19** Clock Gate and Tower	**29** Ethnographical Museum
10 Kralja Petra Street	**20** Art Pavilion „Cvijeta Zuzorić"	**30** Church of St Alexander Nevsky
		31 Skadarlija

w of Orthodox Cathedral and New Belgrade in background

❶ Trg Republike

Belgrade's central square emerged in the empty space in front of the now non-existent Istanbul-gate, which formed the principal entry to the walled city. The colossal gate, symbol of the Turkish occupation, was demolished immediately after their expulsion in 1867. Today, the square is a favourite meeting spot and a place where all kinds of events, celebrations or protests are held. The "republic" referred to in the name of the square, commemorates the communist abolishion of the monarchy and the proclamation of the Federal Republic of Yugoslavia in 1945.

The **Monument to Prince Mihailo Obrenović** is the central feature of the square. This excellent neo-renaissance work by Florentine sculptor Enrico Pazzi was unveiled in 1882. Mihailo Obrenović (1839-42 and again 1860-68) was the first Serbian ruler to experience European education and to adopt western manners in the 19th c. During his reign the Turks were finally made to leave their last six fortresses in Serbia. The names of these can be seen on the sides of the monument's plinth while in the front is the coat-of-arms of Serbia, from the time it was a principality.

Behind the monument is the **National Museum**. The edifice was constructed in 1903 by the renowned Stevanović-Nestorović architectural team to house the Administration of Funds

Prince Mihailo Monument in Trg Republike

of the National Bank. The Museum (founded in 1844) moved into the premises after WWII. Currently, the neglected building is awaiting major reconstruction work and therefore the museum organizes only temporary exhibitions. The collection comprises master works of Serb and European art. The black marble caryatides by sculptor Ivan Meštrović adorn the main entrance to the museum from Vasina St. *Tel. 011/330-6000, www.narodnimuzej.org.yu; open Mon, Tue, Fri & Sat 10 a.m. – 5 p.m., Thu 12 a.m. – 8 p.m., Sun 10 a.m. – 2 p.m.*

To the right of the monument stands the **National Theatre**. Its construction started in 1867, upon the departure of the Turks, under the patronage of Prince Mihailo who was a keen theatre lover. The stone from the demolished Istanbul-gate was used for the foundation of the building designed by Aleksandar Bugarski. Unfortunately, the brutal assassination that claimed Prince Mihailo's life prevented him from seeing its completion in 1869. After the destruction caused by shelling in WWI the theatre's façade was renovated in 1922, creating its present appearance.

❷ Kneza Mihaila Street

Following the Ottoman departure from the town in 1867, the Serb government purchased their estates and soon, instead of small winding streets, there emerged a straight and broad European-looking street. The street was named after the ruler whose diplomatic action had led to the expulsion of the Turks. It is one of the rare streets in Belgrade that did not change its name later. The main commercial street ever since, in 1987 Kneza Mihaila was turned into a pedestrian zone and is the favourite promenade of Belgrad-

National Theatre by night

ers, leading from Terazije and Republic Sq to the Kalemegdan Park.

At the corner with Obilićev Venac is the elegant and richly ornamented building of the **"Ruski Car"** ("Russian Tsar") café, dating from 1926. No. 18 is the **Mesarović Building**, a fashionable house of a rich merchant built in 1884 by the court architect, Aleksandar Bugarski. Facing it stands a building erected by Vladislav Vladisavljević in 1940/41 that successfully combines modern with traditional details. On the right hand corner of Zmaj-Jovina St is the building of **Prometna Bank**, the work of Danilo Vladisavljević built in 1912 with Art Nouveau decoration.

No. 33 belonged to Serbia's richest merchant of the day, Nikola Spasić. As he left no heir, Spasić used his huge wealth to create a charitable trust for helping poor students. Viennese architect Konstantin Jovanović designed the house in 1889 in his favourite neo-renaissance style, one he cherished throughout his life. . It is considered one of his most successful works and the best of this style in Belgrade.

As the street widens, the dominant feature is the **Palace of SANU**

Pedestrian street, Knez-Mihailova

(standing for Serbian Academy of Arts & Sciences) with its impressive frontage and numerous statues on top. It was started in 1912 but finished only in 1924 due to the three exhausting wars that swept across Serbia. It houses two galleries: the large one at the corner of Vuka Karadžića St organizes temporary exhibitions in the fields of art and history; the small gallery in Djure Jakšića St belongs to the Museum of Science & Technology. The fountain in front of the SANU Palace is a 1987 reconstruction of the old **Delije Well** (*Delijska česma*).

Three houses in a row, **numbers 46, 48 & 50**, were all constructed between 1869 and 1870, immediately after the street was laid out, and they contribute to a harmonious whole. Across the street stands the massive grey building commissioned by the **Nikola Spasić Foundation**. It was designed in 1930, by a Parisian student Kosta Najman in the French neo-renaissance style,

which was very popular at the time.

After the intersection with Kralja Petra St, on the left is the building of the **"Grčka kraljica"** ("Queen of Greece") café, the successor to the older Despot's Han Inn. The building dates from 1835 and is the oldest in the street. It owes its unusual arrangement to the fact that it was built before the existence of planning regulations. Opposite is the entrance to the "Akademija" nightclub, famous in the 1980's as one of best underground clubs in Europe.

The last building in the street before the Kalemegdan Park, is used today by the **City Library**. It was built in 1869 to house the "Srbska kruna" ("Serb Crown") hotel when it was the most modern and best equipped in the town. In its cellar are the remains of the south gate of a Roman *castrum* (camp), which, together with some other Roman artefacts, forms a "Roman hall" (*Rimska sala*).

Palace of Serbian Academy of Arts and Sciences

"Palace" Hotel in Topličin venac

❸ Obilićev Venac

This street, actually a Venac ("wreath" i.e. crescent) together with Topličin Venac and Kosančićev Venac follows the line of the 18th c. town fortifications. It starts from Kneza Mihaila St, takes a right angled turn (the former bastion of St Charles) and continues north in a gentle curve. Since a good part of Obilićev Venac has been closed to traffic in recent years the "City Passage" and "Millennium" shopping malls have developed here, as well as a dozen or more cafés making it a popular venue both day and night.

❹ Topličin Venac

The park in Topličin Venac emerged on the site of the St Francis Bastion constructed under Austrian rule from 1717 to 1739. Later, it was used by the Turks, and then in WWI it became an ad hoc Austro-Hungarian cemetery for the soldiers that died in street-fighting.

The **monument** in the centre commemorates Lieutenant Colonel Vojin Popović, better know by his guerrilla nickname Vojvoda Vuk. He was a fearless fighter in a multitude of battles that are listed on the sides of the monument. Initially he fought with a group of volunteers for the Serb cause in the then Turkish province of Macedonia. He later fought in both of Balkan wars and in World War One. He died in 1916 fighting to take Mt Kajmakčalan on the Allied Saloniki front. His monument, the work of sculptor Djordje Jovanović, dates from 1936 and was erected thanks to money donated by his fellow combatants.

The grand building with its richly decorated eclectic façade, lying to the west of the park is the **"Palace" Hotel** dating from 1923. It is still one of Belgrade's finest.

❺ Museum of Applied Arts
Muzej primenjene umetnosti

Vuka Karadžića 18; tel. 26-26-841;

Behind the monument to Vojvoda Vuk lies the Čelebonović Palace (1927) today housing the Museum of Applied Arts. The sons of lawyer Jakov Čelebonović, Marko and Aleksa, became world renowned painters.

The museum has a large gallery in which it organizes temporary exhibitions, while on the first floor a new exhibition is prepared annually by one of the 11 departments of the Museum. *Open Tue, Wed, Fri & Sat 10 a.m.-5 p.m., Thu 12 a.m.-8 p.m., Sun 10 a.m.-2 p.m.*

❻ Kosančićev Venac

This tranquil neighbourhood is a rare reminder of what Belgrade looked like in the 19th c. The winding cobbled street follows the line of the baroque era city walls. On the bend where once was the point of the bastion stands a small dilapidated house with a **Bust of Ivan Kosančić**, a hero of epic songs and a brother-in-arms of Miloš Obilić, the knight that killed the Turkish Sultan Murad in the battle of Kosovo (1389) - the focal point of Serb epic poetry.

The gaping space opposite was the site of the National Library, hit by German firebombs on April 6th 1941 in an air raid that marked the beginning of the Nazi onslaught on the Kingdom of Yugoslavia. In this cultural catastrophe innumerable printed books together with thousands of medieval manuscripts in Serbian perished.

Down the street at

Detail from the exterior of Mika Alas' House

No. 22 stands the house of famous mathematician and university professor Mihailo Petrović who preferred, due to his passion for

Princess Ljubica's Palace

St Michael and dating from the 18th c. was about to crumble when prince Miloš decided to finance a new grandiose edifice as a symbol of the newly acquired religious freedom. Modelled on churches built by Serbs in the Habsburg Empire the new cathedral church was finished in 1841 in a classicist style with a baroque tower.

To the left and right of the entrance lie the graves of Vuk Stefanović Karadžić (1789 – 1864), reformer of the Serbian alphabet and collector of folk songs and stories, and Dositej Obradović (1739 – 1811), propagator of the Enlightenment and rationalist philosophy.

fishing, to be known as "Mika Alas" ("Mike the Fisherman"). Among other things he was also a violin virtuoso, writer and the first Serb to reach the North Pole. His modest house (1910) with a grand view over the Sava River exhibits a mixture of Art Noveau and Serb medieval style. The water lilies on the façade and a fish carved on the door are reminders of the original owner.

❼ Palace of Princess Ljubica
Konak kneginje Ljubice

Kneza Sime Markovića 8;
tel. 638-264

This small palace was built in 1831 by Prince Miloš as his new home in the town. However, he soon changed his mind, being fearful of the nearby Turkish fortress and guardsmen and decided to reside and rule from his estate in Topčider, some miles to the south of Belgrade, leaving this palace to his wife Ljubica and their children. The building is the work of Hajji Nikola Živković, the first architect of free Serbia. Though basically still an edifice in the oriental style, its decorative elements show that the final step to European architecture had been taken. Later palaces were constructed fully in the European manner. Partic-

ularly noteworthy is the small lookout on the roof used by the guards. The layout of the rooms holds to the old style, with the osmanluk, a large central room for welcoming guests. The palace also includes a private hammam (Turkish bath), to the rear. Miloš's firstborn son Milan, who ruled for only three weeks, died here in 1839. He was succeeded by his underage brother Mihailo who set up his court in this building.

Today the palace is used by the Museum of Belgrade. The rooms are furnished to resemble the look of houses of the period using furniture, paintings and memorabilia from the time. The cellar, which Miloš used as a treasury, is now used for temporary exhibitions organized by the Museum. *Open Tue-Fri 10 a.m.-5 p.m., weekends 10 a.m.-4 p.m*

❽ Orthodox Cathedral
Saborna crkva

The crossroads of Kralja Petra and Kneza Sime Markovića streets was in Turkish times the centre of the Serbian part of the city, facing the river Sava. The old wooden church, dedicated to

Interior of the the Cathedral Church

The highlight of the unpretentious interior is the impressive iconostasis whose icons were created by Dimitrije Avramović and represent one of the earliest examples of romanticism painting in Serbia. The wall paintings are the work of the same artist. In front of the iconostasis lie the relics of the great martyr Saint

Uroš V, Serbian Emperor (1355-1371), and Saint Stevan Štiljanović (who died ca. 1540). They were brought here in 1941 from the monasteries of Fruška Gora, which faced the threat of destruction by Croatian fascists.

To the right of the entrance stand the graves of Prince Miloš and his son Mihailo (with a statue of St Michael looking over it) and to the right, facing them is the grave of Patriarch Gavrilo Dožić, the only church leader to be imprisoned in a Nazi concentration camp (died 1950).

❾ Patriarchal Palace & Museum of the Serb Orthodox Church

Patrijaršija i Muzej Srpske pravoslavne crkve

Standing on the site of the old Metropolitan court, the Patriarchal Palace (better known just as Patrijaršija – "Patriarchy") was built in 1934/5 to the designs of Viktor Lukomski, one of many Russian refugees that had fled from the Bolshevik terror. He combined the elements of Serb-Byzantine with academic and modernistic features that spoil the whole effect. The main entrance from Kneza Sime Markovića St is decorated with the coat of arms of the Belgrade-Karlovci Metropolitan Diocese. By the apse of the chapel, dedicated to St Simeon Mirotočivi and St John the Baptist, the latter is depicted in a mosaic. The edifice is, among other things, the residence of the Serb Patriarch.

The entrance to the **Museum** is round the corner (*Kralja Petra 5; tel. 638-875; open Mon-Fri 8 a.m. -3 p.m.., Sat 9-12 a.m., Sun 11 a.m.-1 p.m., closed on all Orthodox church holidays; admission 50 din, students and children 20 din*). After purchasing a ticket climb to the first floor and continue turning to the left as far as the museum. Despite being housed in only five rooms, it has an extensive collection of documents and religious artefacts. Especially attractive among them are: the vestment of Prince Lazar (late 14th c.), the "Praise to Prince Lazar" embroidered by Sister Jefimija (1402), the ciborium from the Ravanica Monastery (1705), the Gospels (16th c.), the sceptres (18th c.), charters of the Habsburg Emperors regarding Serb privileges, the shroud of King Milutin (late 13th c.), and the unusual votive gifts dating from the 19th c. The information accompanying the exhibits is displayed only in Serbian.

❿ Kralja Petra Street

King Petar Street is one of the oldest thoroughfares in the town. It was the shortest connection between the Sava and Danube rivers, climbing up and descending down the ridge upon which the city centre lies today. Up to the 1870's when Kneza Mihaila Street was laid out, it was the foremost trading street in Belgrade.

Café "?" (*Znak pitanja*), across the street from the Orthodox Cathedral, is situated in a house typical for Belgrade, or any other Balkan city from the beginning of the 19th c. It was constructed in 1823 by Greek builders for Naum Ičko, a merchant and trade representative of the Principality of Serbia in Istanbul. The house was later obtained by Ećim Toma, the personal physician of Prince Miloš, who opened a café here to make the best use of the building's prominent position. The house and café changed hands several times and in 1892 the new owner decided to rename the café as "At the Cathedral". The church authorities took this as an insult and threatened to close him down if he did not change it. This task proved more difficult than it might have appeared since all the good names had been apparently taken and so, while reflecting on it, the owner hung out a sign with a "?" which people mistook for a new name. And so it remains to now, strange but appealing. Inside, low wooden chairs and tables give it a picturesque appearance.

At the corner with Gračanička Street stands the **"King Petar I"**

The old "?" cafe in Kralja Petra Street

from the beginning of the 18th c. The present building was erected in 1906 by Jelisaveta Načić, the first woman architect in Serbia. The first basketball game in Belgrade was played in its courtyard in 1923.

On the other corner of this intersection stands

KALEMEGDAN

Elementary School, the oldest school in town. It traces its origin to the old Serbian school that stood next to the church

the neo-renaissance building of the **National Bank** (*Narodna banka*) erected in 1889 and extended in 1922 following the plans of Konstantin Jovanović.

In it there is a permanent **Numismatic Exhibition** (*entrance from Kralja Petra No. 12, open on workdays 10 a.m. – 4 p.m.*) which presents the development of metal and paper money from antiquity till modern day. The display is hosted in the attractively decorated teller-hall of the bank.

Not far from the bank, at **No.16**, stands one of the finest examples of Art Nouveau architecture in Belgrade. It was constructed in 1907 to house a modern department store that followed the construction innovations of the time: large windows, concrete walls, the use of steel to decorate the façade and the arrangement of unbroken inner space across all three floors around the central staircase.

Beyond the intersection with Kneza Mihaila Street, **Nos. 39 & 41** are excellent Art Nouveau buildings constructed in 1907. The first one is the only remaining work of a prominent Belgrade architect, Stojan Titelbah whose other works have all been destroyed or altered; the other, commonly known as the "Building with the Green Tiles" (*Kuća sa*

The French Embassy in the Art Deco style

zelenim pločicama) is the finest achievement of the Stevanović - Nestorović architectural team.

Facing them stands the pride of modern Belgrade architecture - the **"Zepter" Palace**. This work of Branislav Mitrović and Vasilije Milunović from 1997 stands out with its daring composition of both the façade and the interior.

⓫ French Embassy
Francuska ambasada

At the height of the Franco-Yugoslav alliance and friendship in the 1930s, parallel with the unveiling of the monument of Gratitude to France, the new edifice for the French Embassy was finished at this prestigious location in Pariska ("Paris") Street. The stunning white structure with a large courtyard was executed to the plans of French architect Espere and Serb architect Najman and is regarded as the finest example of Art Deco in Belgrade. The three woman statues holding hands at the top represent liberté, fraternité and egalité.

Above the first floor windows of the side wings are the high reliefs of Jeane d'Arc and Louis the XIV.

⓬ Kalemegdan Park

In front of the Belgrade fortress stands the Kalemegdan Park. The name of this pleasant park comes from two Turkish words: *kale* – "fortress" and *meydan* – "field". Therefore it could be translated as "the field in front of the fortress", which is precisely what it was: a barren field separating the fortress from the town, preventing a concealed approach by potential attackers. After the Turks left Belgrade in 1867, it was gradually turned into a public park. Along its pathways a number of busts from the turn of the 20th c. are displayed, commemorating writers, composers and other

public figures.

The most prominent is **"The Monument of the Gratitude to France"** (*Spomenik zahvalnosti Francuskoj*) facing the approach from Knez-Mihailova St. Unveiled in 1930, the monument commemorates the strength of the Yugoslav-French alliance between the two world wars. It was paid for by Serb Francophiles, in particular students who had finished their education in France while Serbia was occupied during WWI. The monument was created by the most prominent Yugoslav sculptor of the time, Ivan Meštrović. France is allegorically portrayed as coming to the rescue with a drawn sword, while the two side reliefs represent the military and educational assistance given to Serbia during the war.

To the left of this monument is a fountain and statue called **"The Struggle"**, the work of Simeon Roksandić from 1906. Behind it is the main park **Promenade** stretching parallel with the Sava River and, commanding superb panoramic view of the New Belgrade and the Sava districts. This extraordinary position was much praised through-

Promenade in Kalemegdan Park

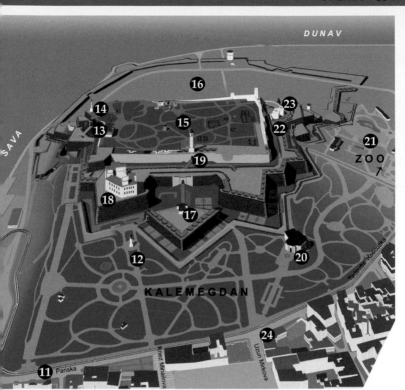

out history, not least by Turks who called it *Fikir-bayir*, "The Hill of Contemplation".

From here there are three possible routes to follow. The first passes the King's Gate and Roman well /13/ leading directly to the Victor monument and the Upper Town; the second heads to the right of the "Gratitude to France" monument through Karadjordje Gate past the Gallery of the Natural History Museum /17/ and Inner Istanbul Gate to the Upper Town. The third leads past the "Cvijeta Zuzorić" Gallery /20/ and the ZOO, taking a roundabout way to the Eastern Outworks.

13 The Roman Well

Having passed alongside the promenade and the Tomb of "National Heroes", one arrives at the King's Gate. Its exterior originates from 1725, the time of the second Habsburg rule over Belgrade. It was built in a modest baroque style, while ogee arches, common for oriental buildings, decorate the interior. Just behind the gate is the entry to the so-called Roman Well. Although it may have existed in Roman times, there are no records of it until 1721-31, when the Austrians constructed it in its present shape. It is actually a cistern imbedded in the rock on which the fortress lies, that provided water supply during sieges. The Well is 62 metres deep, 10 metres below the level of the Sava and Danube rivers! It was made in brick, and the water (35 metres under the ground level) was accessed by two curved stairways, one for going down and another for going up. *Opening hours (during the season): 9 a.m.–7 p.m.*

14 The Victor
Pobednik

This wide plateau offers a remarkable view of the confluence of the river Sava as it flows into the Danube. It is the very nucleus of Belgrade. This strategic spot was occupied by the first settlements and later fortresses. The core of the mighty fortress, built at the beginning of the 14th c. by Despotes Stefan Lazarević (see a model of it on the east side of plateau), stood here until 1683 when, during the Austrian siege of the town, a gunpowder depot in one of the towers was hit, blowing up a good part of the medieval fortress.

Sunset over the Belgrade Fortress

"The Victor" monument was designed by Ivan Meštrović to commemorate Serbian victories in the Balkan wars (1912-13) but it could not be erected because of the outbreak of WWI. When finally set in this place at the end of the war, it also signified the victory over the Austro-Hungarian Empire that once stretched to the other side of the two rivers. Originally, the monument was intended for Terazije Sq. but it was exiled to this place in 1928 because of its problematic nudity that scandalized the more puritan citizens. Sited in an excellently chosen position, it blended well with the walls and soon became a well-known emblem of Belgrade.

15 Upper Town
Gornji grad

This is a wide plateau situated on the top of the hill, enclosed by rectangular, double walls (since this was the most exposed part of town) built by Despotes Stefan at the beginning of the 15th century. In the Middle Ages, a hospital and noblemen's palaces were located here, and later, in the 18th and 19th c, here stood the buildings belonging to the commanders of the fortress.

In the middle of this plateau lies the **Tomb of Damad Ali-Pasha**, a typical 18th century tomb of an Ottoman dignitary. Ali-Pasha, the Grand Vizier of the Ottoman Empire, was fatally wounded in 1716 during the Battle of Petrovaradin, when his army was defeated at the hands of Prince Eugene of Savoy.

There are four gates from which to exit the Upper Town, one on each side. Towards the north-west, the Defterdar's Gate leads to the Lower City. Next to it one can find **Mehmed-Pasha's Drinking Fountain** built in 1575, a fine relic from Ottoman times.

16 Lower Town
Donji grad

The Lower Town is also a result of Despotes Stefan's building activity that transformed Belgrade into both his capital and the strongest fortress on the Danube. During the Middle Ages, houses in the Lower Town were owned by merchants, crafts-

men, and other common folk, making it the commercial centre of town. Episcopal and several other Serbian Orthodox churches were also situated here. However, all of this disappeared during the baroque reconstruction of the city, when the inhabitants were relocated and their houses demolished. The area created was used for barracks and as military training grounds. However, this too vanished in 1914-15, under the Austro-Hungarian artillery fire, when the Lower City became the frontline of the city's defense. Today it is an open field on which sport competitions, concerts and other events frequently take place.

Directly beneath the "Pobednik" monument lies the **Large Gunpowder Depository**, better known as "Barutana" to those who attend concerts in its courtyard. Inside, in three always chilly halls made of stone (so that the gunpowder could stay dry), are exibited Roman gravestones found in Belgrade.

"Victor" statue, a symbol of Belgrade

Charles VI Gate. Lower Town

On the east side of the medieval Lower Town stands Belgrade's most beautiful baroque monument, a work of a renown German architect, Balthasar Neumann - **Gate of Charles VI** (*Kapija Karla VI*), built in 1736, during the reign of the Austrian Emperor Charles VI. The Gate was designed as a triumphal arch and had no military significance. Further to the east, stands the **Inner Vidin Gate**, which leads to Cara Dušana Street.

On the left-hand side of Gate of Charles VI stands the tall **Nebojša Tower** (*Kula Nebojša*), the only remaining tower in the Lower City. It was built in the 15th century to protect the port that once lay in front of it. In Ottoman times it was used as a dungeon. The most famous prisoners to have been incarcerated here were Rigas Feraios, a Greek patriot who was executed here in 1798, and Jevrem, Prince Miloš Obrenović's brother. *Open for visits on weekends from 10 a.m. to 9 p.m. (during the season)*

17 Gallery of the Natural History Museum

Galerija Prirodnjačkog muzeja

Tel. 011/328-4317

The Natural History Museum has a rich collection of minerals, fossils, flora and preserved animals but it has no permanent exhibition since its building is not large enough. Nevertheless, its gallery makes the best of its position and organizes many attractive exhibitions on nature which are popular both with children and their parents. The gallery is situated in the house once used by the Turkish guardsmen who were in charge of the two gates on either side of it. Interestingly, though built by Turks in 1835, the

Nebojša Tower in the Lower Town of the Belgrade Fortress

house bears the hallmarks of the classicist style.

Facing the Gallery is the **Inner Istanbul Gate** that attained its present appearance from 1740-60. As the most striking gate of the fortress it symbolically represents Belgrade in its coat-of-arms. *Open (summer) every day from 10 a.m. till 9 p.m.; (winter) from 10 a.m. to 5 p.m. except Mondays*

18 Military Museum

Vojni muzej

Tel. 011/33-43-441

This imposing building was constructed in 1929, yet, with it's resemblance to the medieval fortress, it suits its surroundings very well. Around the edifice are cannons, tanks and other machinery from various 19th and 20th c. wars. The museum still has the old exhibition representing the military development of all Yugoslav peoples and emphasises the Communist Partisan Movement in the Second World War. In the last section there is a small collection of artefacts from the conflicts in ex-Yugoslavia including parts of the F-117, shot down during the NATO bombing in 1999. *Open from 10 a.m. to 5 p.m. except on Mondays*

In the trench between the two walls is an interesting assortment of tanks, guns and similar artillery from the First and Second World Wars.

During the tourist season one may also visit the **Casemates**, extensive vaults below the bastion on which the Military Museum stands (*open from 9 a.m. to 9 p.m.*).

Military Museum in the Fortress walls

the development and different incarnations of the fortress over the many centuries of its existence. Also exhibited are Roman gravestones and medieval building tools, all excavated here.

⓳ Clock Gate and Tower
Sahat-kapija i kula

The only entrance to the walled area of the Upper Town from the side of the city is through the **Clock Gate** (*Sahat kapija*), which dates from the end of the 17th c. when the Turks started restructuring the fortress for defence against the fire arms. The decoration of these new walls with cannonballs is noteworthy. Standing above the gate is the high **Clock Tower** (*Sahat kula*), an 18th c. construction by the Austrian masons. During the tourist season one may climb to the top to view its mechanism and take in the views of fortress (*open 9 a.m.-9 p.m., admission charged*).

On the other side of the gate, next to the enormous cannon, is the entrance to the **Exhibition "Belgrade Fortress"** (*Izložba "Beogradska tvrđava", open during the tourist season from 9 a.m. to 9 p.m.*). From the drawings and models one may follow in detail

⓴ Art Pavilion „Cvijeta Zuzorić"

The Art Pavilion was opened in 1928 on the initiative of dramatist Branislav Nušić with donations collected by ladies belonging to Belgrade elite of the period. This was the first permanent gallery in the town and has since played an important role in presenting various authors and exhibitions to the public. It is named after a 16th c. Dubrovnik lady whose beauty was praised by poets on both sides of the Adriatic. In front of the pavilion is the sculpture **"Awakening"** (Dragoslav Arambašić, 1920).

㉑ The ZOO
Zoološki vrt
Tel. 011/2624-526

When walking down the side of Mali Kalemegdan Park one comes to the entrance to the Belgrade ZOO that was founded in 1936. The zoo is still situated in the same place as when it was founded, underneath the fortress walls, even though it has expanded considerably. It was severely damaged in the 1941 bombing; animals that survived were to be seen roaming freely through the streets of Belgrade. During the international sanctions, in 1993/4, animals were badly malnourished due to food shortages. After these many desperate times, the ZOO has made every effort to enlarge the number of animals and to house a variety of animal species. Although it is located in a relatively small area of only 6 acres, it is home to more than 2000 animals of 200 different species. The zoo's gardens are well maintained and include a gallery of wooden sculptures, a fountain, and even monuments of the most famous animal residents. *Opening hours 8 a.m.–8.30 p.m. in summertime and 8 a.m. – 5 p.m. in wintertime*

㉒ Eastern Outwork

This is the most recent part of the Belgrade medieval fortification and

Clock Gate and Tower

also the best preserved one. It was built in the late 15th century and consists of several well preserved towers and gates. Outworks are walls usually raised either on a vulnerable spot of a fortification or to give an additional protection to a fortress entrance from a sudden attack. Later, in 18th century, the new walls were just leaned on the outwork.

If you approach the outwork from the direction of the ZOO garden, you will first come across the small baroque **Leopold's Gate**, named after the Emperor Leopold I (1657 – 1705), during whose short reign over the city (1688-90) the gate was constructed. Right behind it stands the medieval **Zindan Gate** flanked by two protecting towers. The name means "prison" in Turkish, which was exactly what it was used for, once it had lost its primary defensive purpose. Flat tops of its towers offer a nice panoramic view of the Danube. Behind the Zindan Gate is the **Despot's Gate** built in the beginning of the 15th century. Just next to it is the high **Dizdar's Tower**, today the home of one department of the Belgrade Observatory.

On the right-hand side from the Zindan Gate is the hexagonal **Jakšić Tower**. This very well preserved, four storey tall construction is situated right on the corner of the outwork. It was named after the Jakšić brothers, Serb feudal lords in medieval Hungary and well-known heroes of Serb epic poetry.

Zindan Gate, Eastern Outworks

㉓ Ružica Church & St Petka Chapel

On a fascinating site, shadowed by the fortress walls, two picturesque churches are located. The one with the steeple is **Crkva Ružica**, named after a Belgrade medieval church that no longer exists. The present-day building had originally served as a Turkish gunpowder depository. After the departure of the Turks in 1867, it was adapted for the needs of the Serbian garrison. It suffered substantial damage during World War I and was reconstructed in 1924 in order to fit better its medieval surroundings. Just next to the entrance are figures of Serbian soldiers from both the Middle Ages and World War I. Being a military church, its candelabra

was made of sabres and gun shells. The frescoes executed by Andrej Bicenko portray both biblical characters and portraits of contemporaries, for example those of Russian Tsar Nikolas II and the King of Serbia, Peter I. The iconostasis was designed by Saint Rafailo Momčilović, a painter and a monk who was killed by Croatian fascists in 1941.

A little bit further downhill is the **Chapel of St Petka** (in Serbian, *Sveta Petka* is a popular name for Holy Mother Paraskeva). It was built in 1938 over a spring that is believed to be miraculous, especially in healing the women who gather here in large numbers on St Petka's feast day (27th October). The relics of this saint were brought to Belgrade in 1403 when the city was proclaimed

The Ružica Church and the Dizdar Tower

Pedagogical Museum

a new capital of Serbia. When the Turks took all inhabitants of Belgrade into slavery in 1521, the people took the relics to Constantinople with them. They are now in Jassy, Romania.

24 Pedagogical Museum
Pedagoški muzej
Uzun Mirkova 14;
011/2625-621

The Museum is sited in a small classicist style house with strong Doric pilasters. It was built for Cvetko Rajović, the Mayor of Belgrade, in 1838. When finished, it was one of the first buildings to fully follow the current European style, without any oriental features. Some time later it became the home of the British Consul J. L. Hodges, who organized first diplomatic balls and banquets here.

The Pedagogical Museum presents the development of schooling and education from the 9th c. and the first monastic schools up to present day, though most of the items on display are from the 19th c. Of special interest are the old schoolbooks and the schoolroom, furnished as it would have been used in the mid-19th c. *Open Tue-Fri 10 a.m.-5 p.m., weekends 10 a.m. – 3 p.m.*

25 Frescoes Gallery
Galerija fresaka

20 Cara Uroša St;
tel. 011/621-491

From 1904 until the Nazi destruction in 1944 this was the site of the New Sephardim Synagogue. The present-day building was erected after the war in a so-called "voluntary youth action" as a community cultural centre. In 1953 it was altered to house the fresco paintings from Serb medieval monasteries, copied a few years earlier for an exhibition in Paris that met with great success. Since then the Frescoes Gallery has been dedicated to copying and preserving the medieval frescoes.

On display are copies of some of the world-famous frescoes, many of them from UNESCO World Heritage sites. They offer an insight into religious life, medieval ideological conceptions reflected in interesting iconographical programs, as well

Christ the Almighty, Fresco Gallery

as the master skills of the anonymous painters. Although a visit to the Gallery cannot replace the feel of a real

monastery, it has its advantages since many of the paintings are from far-flung churches or are sited in obscure corners. The Frescoes Gallery is a perfect starting point for learning more about the Orthodox religion and its art. *Open 10 a.m.-5 p.m. except Thu 12 a.m.-8 p.m. and Sun 10 a.m. – 2 p.m.*

26 Bajrakli Mosque
Bajrakli džamija

Today the only surviving mosque in Belgrade is the Bajrakli mosque which was constructed between 1660 and 1688. This makes it the oldest surviving religious edifice in the town. It is a modest but classical temple of Ottoman provincial architecture. The name of the mosque comes from its unique purpose: because the mosque stood in a prominent location in the center of the Turkish part of the town, it was thus visible from all other mosques and became the one that determined the exact time to initiate the daily calls to prayer. When the muvekit, a specialist who calculated the right moment to start the call, estimated that the time was right, the flag (in Turkish *bayrak*) at the top of its minaret would be hoisted. Bajrakli mosque has had a troublesome history: during the period of the second Austrian reign of Belgrade its minaret was torn down and it was transformed into a Jesuit church. When the Turks left Belgrade the mosque was closed down, along with all the others as there were no Muslims in the town. However, Bajrakli mosque is the only one that was reopened in 1893 and thus survived. Since the outburst of civil war in Yugoslavia it was attacked several times by extremists but, luckily, it has escaped serious damage.

27 The Vuk & Dositej Museum

Muzej Vuka i Dositeja

Gospodar Jevremova 21; tel. 011/2625-161

Although Vuk Stefanović-Karadžić and Dositej Obradović belonged to different generations, both had the same goal: to bring Serbia closer to Europe by means of education and enlightenment. Dositej started this by fighting against the Church's monopoly over education and by promoting the philosophy of rationalism. Vuk devoted his life to reveal to the world, and more specifically to the Serbian elite, the beauty of the language of ordinary peasants, which, thanks to his efforts, was adopted as the literary standard of the Serbian language.

The museum building dates from the mid 18th c. It was built for a rich Belgrade Turk, in the style of the so-called "Turkish baroque" which evolved as more and more contemporary European influences penetrated the weakening Empire. During the First Serbian Insurrection (1804-1813), the building housed the Grand School, the highest educational institution in Serbia. Its founder and principal teacher was Dositej Obradović and one of its pupils, Vuk Karadžić. The ground floor is dedicated to the life and work of Dositej

Vuk Stefanović Karadžić

(Tršić, West Serbia, 1787-Vienna, 1864) was one of the most illustrious figures in modern Serbian history and culture. He was born in a simple peasents' family. However, with the help of his wealthy uncle, young Vuk learned how to read and write, which was very uncommon in the age of Ottoman domination. During the First Serbian Rebelion, Vuk served as a clerk in Serbian administration, but after Turkish reconquest of Serbia in 1813 he escaped to Austria. Eager for further learning, he moved to Wiena, which was also a cultural center of Southern Slavs. There he started his capital work as a reformer of the Serbian lanquage and Cyrillical alphabet and collector of oral forms of folk tradition such as epic poems, fairy tailes and proverbs. Karadžić wanted to introduce popular language instead of highly artificial Church Slavonic and base it on a simple rule – „Write as you speak, read as it's written". As a restless linguist, Vuk Karadžić traveled all around Europe, as well as through Serbian-speaking areas of the Balkans. Collections of Serb epic poems astonished with their beuty personalities such as Walter Scott, Johann Wolfgang Goethe and Jacob Grimm. He published first Grammar book of modern Serbian (1814), first Dictionary (1818) and in 1847 he translated New Testament in contemporary Serbian. He was also praised as a historian since he recorded memories of the participants and contempories of the Serbian Rebelions. Finally, his reformist work was also accepted by Croatian cultural elite in 1850, basing Croatian language on the same principles. Vuk's reform of Serbian language and alphabet were oficially accepted in Serbia in 1868. Today Vuk Stefanović-Karadžić is recognised as the father of modern Serbian national and cultural identity.

and the first-floor to Vuk. Amongst the exhibits are the first editions of their books, correspondence as well as some personal items. *Open Tue, Wed, Fri & Sat 10 a.m.-5 p.m., Thu 12 a.m-8 p.m., Sun 10 a.m.- 2 p.m.*

28 Studentski trg

This large open area in the centre of the town remained empty for a long time as the Turks had used it as their central burial ground. Later, as the cemetery fell into disrepair the grounds were gradually taken over for use as a marketplace. Following the

Turks departure from Serbia, the northern half of the square was turned into a park that finally ousted the market from this prestigious location in 1927. In the park there are **monuments** to (from N to S): botanist Josif Pančić (1814 – 1888) dating from 1897, geographer, ethnographer and anthropologist Jovan Cvijić (1865 - 1927), erected in 1995, and the enlightened educator Dositej Obradović (1739

Interior of the Vuk & Dositej Museum

Captain-Miša's Edifice

- 1811), erected in 1914.

At the lower side of the square, on the corner of Višnjićeva St stands the **Tomb of Sheikh Mustafa** (*Šejh-Mustafino turbe*). This hexagonal structure dating from 1783, once stood in the grounds of a dervish lodge, the leader of which was Sheikh Mustafa.

The dominant structure of the upper side is the red and white **Captain Miša's Edifice** (*Kapetan-Mišino zdanje*). Miša Anastasijević was a merchant who obtained his enormous wealth by trading on the Danube (hence "captain"). In 1857 it became obvious that the reign of Prince Aleksandar would not last much longer, so Miša broke with the Prince and decided to build a palace for the Prince's nephew and his own son-in-law, Djordje Karadjordjević, whom he intended to make the new ruler of Serbia. However, his plan failed and the palace (finished in 1863), at the time the biggest building in Serbia, was left without a purpose. Since his daughter refused to live in it he endowed it to the state. Over the next half a century it housed almost all of the main institutions of culture and education, such as the University, the National Museum, the National Library, the High School, the Ministry of Education, many of them at the same time. Gradually, they were all moved out to new premises leaving the palace to the sole use of Belgrade University that has its Rector's Office here. The architectural style of the palace is a romanticist blend of influences, notably renaissance and Venetian gothic. On the top of the building is a glass lookout, once used by the firemen. The colonnaded entrance hall bears four plaques with the names of students of Belgrade University killed in WWI. In 1968 this building was the centre of student protests against the corruption of the communist society, when the university was renamed "Red University 'Karl Marx'" and the building was adorned with pictures of Marx, Che Guevara and Tito.

The second building to the right is that of **Kolarac's Endowment** (*Kolarčeva zadužbina*), usually referred to only as "Kolarac". It has a gallery, lecture hall and an excellent concert hall. The latter thanks its remarkable acoustics to the musically educated architect Petar Bajalović, who constructed the building in 1932.

Linked to the Captain Miša's Building on the left is the new building of the **Faculty of Philosophy** (1974). The quadrangle between the two buildings (known locally as the "Plateau") has a **Monument to Petar II Petrović Njegoš** (1813 - 1851), Prince-Bishop of Montenegro and one of the greatest Serb poets. The Plateau is the starting point of many students' protests. The most famous were those that lasted for four months during the winter 1996/7 against the electoral fraud by the Milošević regime committed to 'win' the local elections.

29 Ethnographical Museum
Etnografski muzej

Studentski trg 13;
tel. 011/32-81-888

The Museum is situated in a noteworthy modernist style building completed in 1934 to house the Stock Exchange. In the planned economy of the communist regime a Stock Exchange wasn't needed anymore so that, in its stead, as of 1951, the Museum took over.

The permanent exhibition (partly on the ground floor, as well as on the first and second floors) is attractive and well displayed, presenting the life and folk traditions of Serbs through many photos, models and artifacts. The ground floor also features interesting temporary exhibitions. *Open Tue, Wed and Fri 10 a.m. – 5 p.m., Thu 10 a.m. - 7 p.m., Sat 9 a.m. – 5 p.m., Sun*

St Alexander Nevsky Church

9 a.m. – 1 p.m., closed on Mondays; admission 100 din.

㉚ Church of St Alexander Nevsky
Crkva Svetog Aleksandra Nevskog

The cult of this Russian saint was brought to Serbia by the Pan-Slavic voluntary corps of General Černjajev that came to fight alongside Serbs against the Ottoman Empire in 1876/77. When the Russians headed home they left behind their field church dedicated to their saint. The work on the present day church lasted from 1912 to 1929 resulting in a striking edifice inspired by the Serbian medieval Morava-style (note the massive belfry and rose windows). The iconostasis, originally intended for the Karadjordjević dynasty mausoleum at Oplenac, is the donation of king Aleksandar. There is also an altar dedicated to the soldiers who fell in 1912-18 wars.

㉛ Skadarlija

"Skadarlija" is a popular name for Skadarska and several other smaller streets around it that form the old bohemian quarter. The street was initially a gipsy settlement just outside the city walls, already well known for its cheap cafés. In the second part of the 19th c. it took on a more dignified appearance when the poorer inhabitants were joined by actors who found its proximity to the National Theatre and low rents convenient. With the arrival of the actors the cafés of Skadarlija became centres of literary and artistic life, an era which had its heyday at the very beginning of the 20th c. After WWII it was gradually becoming an ordinary street but this was reversed in 1966, when the old, so-called "Turkish" cobblestone, lanterns and fountains were reinstated bringing much of its former charm. Today almost every house is a café starting from the illustrious **"Three hats"** (Tri šešira) in a small house from the mid 19th c. and **"Two stags"** (Dva jelena), founded in 1865, to the new and trendy nightlife locations and popular beer gardens.

At **No. 36** stands the house in which, up to his death, lived the famed

Gypsy musicians in Skadarlija

romantic poet, painter and no less notorious bohemian, Djura Jakšić. His tormented-looking statue is in front of the house. The lower right hand side of the street is occupied by one of bear brewing facilities of the **"Belgrade brewing industry"** (*BIP*), that originally belonged to the Bajloni family. Its façade is covered with a colossal mural that took some years to finish.

At the bottom of Skadarlija stands the **sebilj** fountain a gift of the city of Sarajevo to Belgrade during the first conference of the Non-aligned Nations in 1961. It is a copy of a fountain that stands in Sarajevo's Baščaršija Street.

THE CENTRE

The central part of Belgrade stretches from the onetime city walls to Savinac Hill which is crowned by a vast temple dedicated to St Sava, one of the largest domed churches in the world. This part of the town is a product of the progress Belgrade made in the 19th and the first half of the 20th c. Most of the sights are located at a short distance from Kralja Milana Street, running along the ridge between the two rivers. At the top of this ridge is the Beogradjanka Tower, the highest point in the town. The Republic and State Union Parliament, the Main Post Office and St Mark's church are all positioned near each other. Also from here, Kneza Miloša Street runs down the hill, lined with grand government edifices and old villas turned into embassies, but also some of the most impressive ruins left in the aftermath of the 1999 bombing campaign. This is the part of the city where most of the theatres and businesses are; however, there are also many street cafés, restaurants and traditional old kafanas.

1. Terazije
2. Trg Nikole Pašića
3. Union Parliament
4. Postal Museum
5. Church of St Mark
6. Bulevar kralja Aleksandra
7. Krunska Street
8. Nikola Tesla Museum
9. The Old and New Royal Courts
10. Beogradjanka
11. Cvetni trg
12. Vračar Plateau
13. Karadjordjev Park
14. Ulica kneza Miloša
15. Main Railway Station
16. Mali pijac
17. "Atelje 212" Theatre
18. The Automobile Museum
19. "BITEF" Theatre
20. Botanical Gardens

...verbeds in front of the Old Court, today the Belgrade City Hall

❶ Terazije

This long oval space stands midway between a square and a street. It owes its form to the ponds that stood in the middle when the Serb blacksmiths from the town were relo-

Terazije Fountain and Hotel "Balkan"

cated here in the early 1830's by Prince Miloš. The name is short for *terazije za vodu*, ("water scales"), a structure that stood in the centre and distributed water from the Turkish aqueduct to the various drinking fountains in the walled town.

The focal point of Terazije is the **"Albania" Palace** (*Palata "Albanija"*) standing at its northern end. This first skyscraper in Belgrade was finished in 1939 and in contrast to its modern look it took the name of the small crooked café that it replaced.

Hotel "Moskva" ("Moscow") was built in 1907 as the hotel of a St. Petersburg insurance company. Thanks to its prominent position it became a distinct feature of the town silhouette and, with its high green roof, tiled walls and ceramic decorations, one of the finest buildings in Belgrade. In front of the hotel stands the **Terazije**

Fountain (*Terazijska česma*), constructed in 1860 to commemorate the return of Prince Miloš to the throne.

Further down Terazije stands the small **Krsmanović House** dating from 1885 and decorated in a rich neo-baroque style.

Following the liberation of the city in 1918, the Prince Regent Aleksandar moved in, using it as his temporary residence since both royal courts were damaged and looted during the Austro-Hungarian occupation in WWI. On the 1st of December 1918 representatives of the South Slavic nations and provinces gathered here and proclaimed their unification in the Kingdom of Serbs, Croats and Slovenes, which in 1929, became the Kingdom of Yugoslavia.

Down the street, No. 39, built for **Smederevo Credit Bank** in 1910, has a vivacious façade and charming Art Nouveau decoration. Next to it stands the well-proportioned and calm neo-renaissance structure of the former Min-

istry of Justice, designed by Svetozar Ivačković in 1893. Terazije continues south changing its name to Kralja Milana Street and following the route of the old Kragujevac Road. Across the road from where Dragoslava Jovanovića meets Kralja Milana St stands the edifice of **Vuk's Endowment** (*Vukova zadužbina*). Its façade was changed in 1912 using plans drawn up by Branko Tanezević in his recognizable mixture of medieval Serb and decorative Art Nouveau styles, resulting in one of the smartest frontages in the city. The interior was designed by Dragutin Inkiostri – Medenjak in a mixed style leaning strongly towards Art Nouveau.

❷ Trg Nikole Pašića

Quite new in origin, the square emerged after WWII on the grounds of bombed out houses. Its shape was determined when the **Trade Unions Palace** (*Dom Sindikata*) was completed in 1957.

The tiled exterior of Hotel "Moskva"

Trade Union Palace in Nikole Pašića Square

The palace is the last offspring of socialist-realism architecture in Belgrade and its most important example. When finished, the square was named Marx & Engels, after the founding fathers of Communism, what was changed in the early 1990's signifying among the first the change of attitude towards the long-undisputed Communist ideology. Today it bears the name of Nikola Pašić, the most important figure in Serb politics for almost half a century up to his death in 1926. His statue, the work of Zoran Ivanović, dating from 1998, stands tall in the middle of his square.

To the right stands the building of the **"Borba"** **("Struggle") newspapers**, an accomplishment of inter-war modernism architecture from 1939. It was built to suit the needs of "Vreme" ("Time") newspapers, the second most popular daily between the two world wars. In 1944 it was changed into "Borba", an official herald of the Communist party for a long period of time.

The corner with Vlajkovićeva St is occupied by a massive building erected in 1934 following the plans of the brothers Krstić to house the **"Agrarna banka"**. Later, from 1948 to 1965, it was the seat of the Central committee of the Communist party of Yugoslavia, the highest authority in the State. The first floor was reserved for the ideologically equally important Museum of the Revolution of the Peoples of Yugoslavia. Today this building hosts the Museum of Yugoslav History (currently under reconstruction).

❸ Union Parliament

Skupština Državne zajednice

Started in 1907 to house the Serbian Parliament, the building was almost completed when, in 1929, King Aleksandar of Yugoslavia abandoned the unstable parliamentary form of government and commenced his rule of a dictator, making the parliament redundant. After Aleksandar's death in 1934 the parliamentary system was gradually reintroduced and work on the Parliament building continued until it was finally opened in 1936. After WWII it became the seat of the Federal Parliament of Yugoslavia, which dwindled from six to only two member states as the Federation collapsed in 1991/92. The name "Yugoslavia" was finally abandoned in 2003 and now the building houses the Parliament of the new State Union of Serbia & Montenegro. The richly decorated interior was heavily damaged in the bloodless revolution of October the 5th 2000 when the angry crowd of several hundred thousand people stormed the building from which State Security Forces were throwing tear-gas. The event marked the beginning of the end of Slobodan Milošević's regime.

To the right of this edifice stands the bulky building of the **Main Post Office** built in 1935. Its short Doric columns and dark rustic front reflect the influences of the contemporary fascist architecture.

State Union Parliament

④ Postal Museum
Muzej PTT-a

Just behind Serbia-Montenegrin Parliament, on the corner of Palmoticeva and Kosovska streets lies the former **Main Telephone Exchange** building from 1908. It is considered to be the best work of Branko Tenezević, an architect who was interpreting the architectural legacy of medieval Serbia in a new, imaginative way. He

The old post-box in front of the Main Post Office

combined geometrical shapes and rosettes of the Serbian medieval Morava School with some elements of the secession style.

Just behind this building lies the edifice housing the **Postal Museum** (*Majke Jevrosime 13; Tel. 011/321-325; open Mon-Fri from 9 a.m. to 3 p.m.*) Ministry of post and telecommunications founded this small but a very interesting museum in 1923 and assigned it to collect and exhibit all the evidence about the development of the postal service in Yugoslavia. The museum possesses a variety of displays, from an old postal coach and uniform to telecommunication devices and a post stamps collection. It is located in a formidable building designed for the needs of the abovementioned Ministry. Built

in 1926 according to the plan of Momir Korunovicj, it shows us his views on national style in architecture. Two statues above the entrance from Palmoticeva Street represent architect Korunović as a constructor.

⑤ Church of St Mark
Crkva Svetog Marka

This church lies on the north side of **Tašmajdan Park**. The name of the park means "stone quarry" in Turkish, relating to the fact that most of the stone needed to build in old Belgrade was found underneath the park leaving the hill on which it lies hollow. The caves of the quarry were made into air-raid shelters for the Gestapo during WWII.

The **Church of St Mark** was erected between 1935 and 1939 by the Krstić brothers, who modeled it on the much-praised 14th c. Gračanica monastery (near Priština, Kosovo). It lies next to the site of a small, old church dedicated to the same patron, which was destroyed in the 1941 bombing. In 1830 the Sultan's orders were read out to the public in front of the old church granting self-government to the principality of Serbia and the title of hereditary prince to Miloš Obrenović. These grounds were also the Belgrade's principal burial grounds until the opening of the New Cemetery in 1886. Contrasting with the

richly ornamented outer decoration, the interior of St Mark's is unimpressive owing to the fact that it was left unpainted with the outbreak of war and again untouched during communist rule. The disproportionately small iconostasis, the work of the outstanding Vasa Pomorišac, was brought here after the Second World War from a Belgrade high school. To the right of the entrance one finds the tomb of Stefan Dušan (1331-1355), the first and greatest Serbian emperor. In the crypt lie the bodies of the unfortunate King Aleksandar, the last of the Obrenović dynasty, and his wife Draga; both were killed in an officer's coup in 1903.

To the back of St Mark's stands the tiny **Russian Church** built in 1924 by the refugees from the October revolution.

Slightly further along stand the horrific **ruins of the State TV**. 16 people met their end here when it was hit by a rocket on April 23rd, 1999 during the NATO bombing.

St Mark's Church in Tašmajdan Park

"Why?" - title of the Monument beside the ruins of State TV building

➏ Bulevar kralja Aleksandra

Commonly referred just as "The Boulevard" this street is one of the longest in Belgrade and follows the line of the ancient Via militaris that led to Constantinople. Since its beginnings in the 19th c. it has been a lively trading street; during the 1990's it became notorious for its outdoor retailers selling cheap daily commodities, a practice that can be seen on a much lower scale even today.

On the corner of Starine Novaka St stands the **Law Faculty** (*Pravni fakultet*), in a 1939 building inspired by Italian modernism. Behind it is the imposing **"Metropol" Hotel** built in 1957. Opened to host the delegates of the first summit of the Non-aligned nations, it was the best hotel in town for a long period. Just beyond the hotel a small street branches off to the left leading to the massive **Archive of Serbia** (*Arhiv Srbije*), designed by Nikolaj Krasnov in 1928. Statues of lions guard the entrance and on the top stand the figures of Plato and Aristotle.

Back on the Boulevard stands the **University**

Library (*Univerzitetska biblioteka*), a small academic masterpiece by N. Nestorović and D. Djordjević. Dating from 1926, it was paid for by donations of the Carnegie foundation to the war-stricken Belgrade. Next to it stands a grandiose edifice which houses the **Technical Faculties** (civil & electrical engineering, architecture) of Belgrade University. The work of N. Nestorović and B. Tanezević, this was built from 1925 to 1931 in a style that was even then considered inappropriate for the faculties of such exact sciences. To the right of the entrance stands the **Monument to Nikola Tesla** (Fran Kršinić, 1961), one of the greatest inventors in the field of electricity. The Technical Faculties and

Vuk Karadžić Monument

the University Library stand on the grounds where many sporting events took place: firstly, this was the site of the old horse racing track; later it was occupied by the football fields and stadiums of the first Serbian clubs.

Just beyond the faculties building, the descending stairway leads to the elegant **"Vukov spomenik" underground train station**, opened in

1995 as the nucleus of the Belgrade underground system-to-be. On the other side of the street stands the **Monument to Vuk Stefanović Karadžić**, the work of Djordje Jovanović, erected in 1937 for the celebration of the 150th anniversary of his birth. Behind the park lies the building of the **"King Aleksandar I" Students' Dormitory**, the work of yet another Russian émigré, Viktor Lukomski, from 1926.

➐ Krunska Street

Starting from Kneza Miloša St. and running south to the Kalenić green market, Krunska ("Crown") St. is a pleasant place to stroll, especially in its latter part where it becomes a tree-shaded avenue lined with many old villas.

House No. 8 is the **Schoolgirls Hostel**, dating from 1911 and decorated with elements of Serbian medieval style. Part of it still serves the original purpose under the name "Jelica Mitrović" and during the summer, when the school children go home, it is open as a commercial hostel.

At No. 23 stands the modest church dedicated to Christ the Saviour, the oldest Catholic church in town, which serves as the **Catholic Cathedral** of Belgrade. It was originally built as a chapel for the **Austro-Hungarian Consulate**, whose building can be seen around the corner. The Consulate became the focus of worldwide attention in July of 1914 as the unacceptable Austro-Hungarian ultimatum was rejected by Serbia, the event that led inevitably to the Great War.

8 Nikola Tesla Museum

Krunska Street 51,
tel. 011/2433-886,
www.tesla-museum.org

The Museum is located in a luxurious mansion that belonged to Djordje Genčić and was built in 1929 by architect Dragiša Brašovan who skilfully enriched an academically designed building by modern elements.

The museum researches and presents the life and inventions of Nikola Tesla, a famous American scientist of Serb origin. The museum was founded after Tesla's lawful heir, Sava Kosanović, transferred all of the belongings left behind the eccentric scientist. Among these are many of his drafted and never fully developed projects, his diary, personal writings, and even the urn with his ashes. The museum rooms present different periods of his life. The most interesting part of the museum are certainly models that explain principles of functioning of his inventions. *Open Tuesday – Friday 10 a.m. – 6 p.m., weekends 10 a.m. – 1 p.m.*

The Man Who Invented 20th Century

Nikola Tesla (1856-1943) was one of the greatest innovators and scientists whose work pioneered modern electrical engineering. He was born in the village of Smiljan in rural Croatia as the son of an Orthodox priest. Already as a boy Tesla was fascinated by physics and mathematics, and although not among the best students, he graduated at the Polytechnic Institute in Graz and the University of Prague. In 1881, he joined Edison's Continental Company in Paris. Three years later he accepted Edison's invitation and moved to New York, but soon the two great minds clashed. Edison tried to protect his investments in the direct current, while Tesla wanted to promote the more powerful polyphase alternating current. After he left Edison, Tesla founded his own company and though he never had great financial success, he registered over 700 patents worldwide – examples of his best known discoveries being the fluorescent light, the laser beam, wireless communication (radio) and robotics. During his life Tesla was recognized as a striking but sometimes eccentric genius (in 1915 he refused to receive the Nobel Prize for physics!). Today he is praised for his great achievements: in 1895 he designed the first hydroelectric power plant at the Niagara Falls and his alternating current (AC) induction motor is considered one of the greatest discoveries of all time. Nikola Tesla's name has been honoured with the International Unit of Magnetic Flux Density called „Tesla" (T).

9 The Old & New Royal Courts
Stari i Novi dvor

Standing opposite each other are the so called Old and the New Royal Courts. The first court that used to stand here, in the middle of the two existing ones, was a stately home built in 1835, bought by Prince Aleksandar in 1842, and fitted out as his residence. This modest court was demolished after the 1903 assassination of the last Obrenović ruler King Aleksandar and his unpopular Queen Draga.

The so called **Old Court** occupies the northern side of the collection of buildings. It was constructed in 1883 for Milan Obrenović, whose new title of King needed an appropriate residential setting. Architect Aleksandar Bugarski, chosen for his excellent work on the National Theatre, created lavish façades, particularly the one facing south. Despite the damage inflicted in both World Wars, and missing its cupolas, the Italianate neo-renaissance front is still striking. The main entrance on east side, facing the

Nikola Tesla Museum in Krunska Street

View of the Old Court

at no 8, where he lived. His apartment has been transformed into the **Ivo Andrić Memorial Museum** (*tel. 32-38-397, open Tue, Thu & Fri 10 a.m.-5 p.m., weekends 8 a.m. – 2 p.m.*) in which his study, his manuscripts, awards and other documents connected with his life and work can be seen.

⑩ Beogradjanka

The "Belgrade lady" is a 23-floor black skyscraper that measures exactly 100 metres in height.

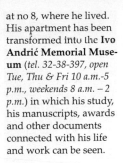

State Union Parliament, was reconstructed after the war in a well-chosen style that harmonized with the rest of the building. The **New Court** was constructed between 1912 and 1920 following plans by Stojan Titelbah, but its present appearance comes from the 1948 reconstruction by Milan Minić after it was severely damaged in WWII. From 1935 through to 1941 it was used as the Prince Pavle Museum, displaying the rich collections gathered by the art-loving Prince Regent. Today the reconstructed Old Court and the New Courts are used as the Town Hall and the seat of the Serbian President, respectively.

The geometrically simple edifice facing the New Court houses the **Parliament of Serbia**, the hub of political life of the Republic.

Behind the New Court lies Andrićev venac, a quiet pedestrian alley named after Ivo Andrić, Nobel prizewinner in 1961 for his novel "The Bridge over Drina". The statue of the only Serb to have won this prestigious award stands at the top of the stairway in front of the building

Young girl looking up to the "Belgrade Lady"

As it stands on top of a ridge it is some metres higher than the "Western Gate" which lies in the flat land of New Belgrade. Finished in 1974 according to the plans of Branko Pešić and his associates for the "Beograd" chain of department stores, it soon became one of the symbols of the city and stands out as part of the Belgrade skyline. It is used mainly as offices including the municipal Radio and TV station "Studio B" that opened in 1990 as the first independent station in the country. Unfortunately, the excellent viewpoint on the top floor is closed for visits.

Ivo Andrić (Dolac 1892 – Belgrade 1975), the only Serb Nobel prize winner, was born into a family of catholic father and an orthodox mother near Travnik in Bosnia. He graduated from the university in Zagreb in philosophy, Slavic literature and history. After graduating he took to writing poetry. Being a member of the "Young Bosnia" organization that was behind the Sarajevo assassination, he spent most of WWI behind bars. After the war he obtained a doctorate in letters from Graz university and then got job at the Belgrade Ministry of Foreign Affairs; in very little time he became a diplomat whilst continuing to write, mostly short stories. When Germany invaded Yugoslavia in 1941, Andrić returned to Belgrade and lived there in seclusion throughout the Second World War writing his three major works "The Bridge on the Drina" (*Na Drini ćuprija*), "Bosnian Story" (*Travnička hronika*), and "The Woman from Sarajevo" (*Gospodjica*). Already a well known figure in literary world, he became the president of the Writers Association of Yugoslavia and received a number of awards, the most prestigious being the Nobel Prize for literature in 1961. He is best known for his novels dealing with the history of Bosnia, describing it through the legends and the eyes of ordinary people and their tragic existence through troubled times, bringing forth universal human problems.

Decoration of SKC, once the Officers' Club

The **Students' Cultural Centre** (*SKC*) is situated in front of Beogradjanka. Since its opening in 1971 it has become one of the city's centres for artistic life. The yellow-painted neo-renaissance edifice (Jovan Ilkić, 1895) was built for the Officer's Club, as the coats-of-arms and armors on the façade indicate.

Facing it stands the **Officers Cooperative**, a sort of a warehouse reserved for the army, still used for the same purpose today. With its long glass panels, dominating verticals, floral decoration and mascarons it is an excellent example of Belgrade Art Nouveau architecture from 1908.

⑪ Cvetni trg

The block bounded by Kralja Milana, Njegoševa and Svetozara Markovića Streets was, 150 years ago, an open air green market where peasants from the vicinity of Belgrade would bring fresh milk and other dairy products to sell. The name Cvetni trg ("Flower Square") came about in 1884 when the site was rearranged on the initiative of the Society for the Beautification of Vračar, with the aim of making

this quarter a better place to live. The new building of this Society stands just by the corner of Kralja Milana and Njegoševa streets. It is the work of M. Antonović from 1902 with a preponderance of Art Nouveau elements.

Across the busy Kralja Milana St. stands the brand new building of the **Yugoslav Drama Theatre** (*Jugoslovensko dramsko pozorište*), with the old façade covered by a glass screen. The building served as a riding school and National Assembly before it was thoroughly reconstructed for theatrical use in 1947. The new company was composed of the best actors from the whole of Yugoslavia in order to present the biggest and the most representative theatre troupe in the country. The building caught fire in 1997 and was afterwards renovated to its present appearance.

Further up the Njegoševa St. at **No. 11** stands another building created by Branko Tanezević in an unusual combination of Serbian medieval and Art Nouveau styles. It was built in 1913 at the height of the Serbian successes in the Balkan Wars and thus was painted in red, blue and white - the flamboyant colours of the Serbian flag.

Across the Svetozara Markovića St. stands the **3rd Belgrade High School**. Constructed in 1906, it is widely considered to be the most beautiful of Belgrade school buildings. On the first floor windows above the entrance stand the busts of Josif Pančić, Vuk Karadžić and Dositej Obradović created by renowned sculptor Petar Ubavkić who taught in the school for some years.

⑫ Vračar Plateau
Vračarski plato

Following the Serbian rebellion in Banat in 1594, the Turkish Grand-vizier Sinan-Pasha decided to break the morale of the rebels and punish the Serb people by burning the relics of their greatest saint, Sava, in the fields of Vračar. Although the original location of this infamous event was probably closer to the church of St Mark and the Tašmajdan Park, on the 300th anniversary (1894) this raised site was chosen for the location of the grand church that would commemorate it. However, the smaller of two temples standing today, built to the plans of Vladimir Lukomski, was finished only in 1935. The huge church next to it was started the same year after much controversy over its design, but by the beginning of the war in 1939 the construction had progressed by only a

New building of the Yugoslav Drama Theatre

The imposing view of Saint Sava Church

few meters. The war and Communism halted the works until 1985 when they were resumed under the direction of architect Branko Pešić. Once again the design, based on the church of St Sofia in Istanbul and having nothing to do with the Serbian ecclesiastical architecture of St Sava's time, created disputes. The overall structure was finished in 1989 and a 12-meter golden cross was erected atop the building. In 2003 the church was finally covered with white marble and 2004 saw the landscaping of the park in front of it. The interior still awaits completion.

To the right of the church stands the **National Library of Serbia**, the work of Ivo Kurtović from 1973, inspired by traditional rural forms. In front of the whole complex stands the **Monument to Karadjordje**, created in 1979 by Sreten Stojanović on the site where it is believed that the leader of the first Serbian insurrection overlooked the attack on the town in 1806.

⑬ Karadjordjev Park

On the site where Karadjordje's insurrectionist army set up camp before the1806 assault on the then Turkish Belgrade, today stands a park of unusually elongated shape. In it are three interesting monuments. In the upper part stands the **Monument to the Men of the Third Call-Up**, the work of S. Djurdjević, finished in 1915 but only erected after the First World War. It stands in memory of the mostly elderly men that held the less important positions

Early morning walk in Karadjordjev Park

of the front in a war in which Serbia lost half of its male population. Slightly further along stands the **Bust of the French poet Alphonse de Lamartine** created in 1933 on the centenary of his stay in Belgrade that he described very positively in his work "Journey Eastwards". The third monument is the oldest one in Belgrade: it was unveiled in 1848 by Karadjordje's son Prince Aleksandar Karadjordjević (who ruled from 1842 to 1858). The monument commemorates the fallen liberators of the town from the year 1806, whose original, modest gravestones can be seen surrounding it.

⑭ Ulica Kneza Miloša

When in 1835 Prince Miloš Obrenović realized that the Turks were not going to evacuate Belgrade he decided to found a new, Serbian Belgrade that was to encircle the old walled town and thereby seal its fate. The streets in this new Belgrade were straight and wide, placed in a grid system and lined with European

The now overgrown ruins of the 1999 bombing campaign

style houses. The main street was Prince Milos Street, created in 1842 to connect the town with Miloš's residence in Topčider.

The busy intersection with Kralja Milana St is known as "London" after a hotel that had stood here in previous times. The upper part of the street is occupied by two fine structures: to the left stands the edifice of the **Vračar Savings Bank** (1906), in an attractive northern neo-renaissance style, and to the right is the seat of "Jubanka", constructed in 1924 for the **"Danube-Adriatic Bank"** which is extraordinarily rich in imaginative sculptures depicting gods and creatures of the waters.

Down the street is the **Ascension Church** (*Voznesenjska crkva*) with its leafy courtyard (entrance is from Admirala Geprata St.). The church was built in 1864 by Prince Mihailo to suit the needs of soldiers from the nearby barracks. It is remarkable only for the fact that it is the first church built in 19th c. Serbia to be erected imitating the medieval style. From then onwards Eu-

ropean styles were abandoned and research began into the heritage of the Serbia's heyday. The exterior is severe and monotonous while the inside gives a more pleasing impression with the frescoes of Andrej Bicenko and an iconostasis by Steva Todorović. To the right of the entrance stands a plain granite cross, that marks the death of 180 people in the destruction of an improvised shelter hit by a Nazi bomb on the 6th of April 1941. On Ascension Day, it is from this church that a colourful procession departs from commemorating the *slava* (patron day) of the city.

Across Kneza Miloša St stands the old **Ministry Of War**. This imposing building is the work of the Russian architect, V. Baumgarten from 1928. At the summit,

this destroyed building became one of the most impressive sights in the city. This excellent modernistic building with its playful cascading forms is the work of the architect Nikola Dobrović finished in 1963. It symbolizes the canyon of the Sutjeska River (in Bosnia) where, in 1943, a bloody battle was waged by the Partizan communist forces against the occupying forces.

The other two corners of this busy crossroad are dominated by the large buildings of **various Ministries**, designed in the 1920's by the Russian Nikolaj Krasnov, the favourite architect of King Aleksandar at the time. The academism style observed here is typical of Krasnov and can also be noted in his earlier works within the service of the Russian emperor. Both buildings were heavily damaged both in WWII and in the NATO bombing of 1999 but were soon repaired. The building standing

Seat of the Serbian Goverment

groups of figures representing ancient warriors saving their wounded comrades can be seen.

Adjoining it on both sides of Nemanjina St. stands the edifice of the **Ministry of Defense and the General Staff**. After it was bombed in 1999,

on the upper part of the street is used by the government of Serbia. It was in its courtyard that the reformist Prime Minister Zoran Djindjić was shot by sniper bullets on the 12th March 2003.

Two more interesting Ministries can be

und down Nemanjina St. To the right are the ruins (again from 1999) of the **Ministry of Construction**. Finished just before the start of the Second World War it bears clear influences of Third Reich architecture as represented by the tall Corinthian columns and the rows of bare window openings. On the other side of the street is the former **Ministry of Transport**, dating from 1931, with soberly composed pseudo-classical elements. In the same building a small **Railway Museum** is situated (*Nemanjina 6; open Mon-Fri 9 a.m. – 2 p.m., Sat & Sun only for scheduled group visits; admission free*) which traces the development of railways in Serbia and the former Yugoslavia.

The rest of Kneza Miloša St is also worth checking out for several of the old villas, many of which have today been turned into embassies. The most interesting one, in terms of its architecture is **No. 54.** Imaginatively and skillfully used elements of the Serbian medieval style (chess-fields and half-cupolas) distinguish it as the best work of Jovan Novaković, done in 1910.

The end of the street is marked with another wreck from 1999: the **Federal Ministry of the Interior**, now with an airy hole in its middle. Above its main entrance still stands the coat-of-arms of Socialist Yugoslavia.

The steam-engine of Marshal Tito's "Blue Train"

15 Main Railway Station
Glavna Železnička stanica

Savski trg ("Sava Square") lies on the once marshy grounds of Crni Lug ("Black Grove"), later humorously called the "Venice Pool" (*Bara Venecija*). The square was finally finished at the beginning of 1880's during the construction of the Railway Station. Finished in 1884, the station was the first upon entering Serbia and lay on the busy railroad connecting Vienna and Istanbul. Heavy damage in both World Wars caused much destruction, however the original exterior has been retained. To the left of the main entrance stands the old steam locomotive that, between the years 1947 and 1957, towed the renowned "Blue train" (*Plavi voz*), used by Marshal Tito to travel across Yugoslavia.

16 Mali pijac

Parallel with the Sava River is Karadjordjeva Street, the most important street in this part of the city known as Savamala. Mali pijac ("Small Square") is the old name for the broadest part of Karadjordjeva, at its intersection with several other streets. This area was always associated with trade, primarily the river trade with Bosnia and Croatia. At the beginning of the 20th c. it developed rapidly thanks to the efforts of a prominent merchant, Luka Ćelović-Trebinjac. After heavy destruction in both World Wars and along with the fall of river trade, the neighborhood became one of the most dismal spots in downtown Belgrade. The area is in much need of renovation and is eagerly expecting the execution of politicians' words, namely - the return of Belgrade to its rivers.

The most impressive edifice here is the new palace of the **Belgrade Cooperative**. This association was founded in 1882 as the

Belgrade Cooperative Palace in Mali trg

Manak House, a rare survivor of the oriental style in Belgrade

first Serbian insurance company and it soon grew to become the largest financial institution in the country after the National bank. Ćelović-Trebinjac, the president of the Cooperative, commissioned the renowned Stevanović – Nestorović architectural duo to build the new palace. Finished in 1907, it is an eclectic structure influenced mostly by contemporary French architecture and neo-baroque. The interior is equally striking due to its statues and lavish use of marble.

To the left lies the **Hotel "Bristol"**, once owned by the Cooperative. It was constructed in 1912, according to the plans of Nikola Nestorović, as one of the largest buildings in the town. The exterior is decorated in lavish Art Nouveau style.

Across the street stand several buildings of other rich Savamala merchants. The yellow **Vučo House** with its attractive balconies and bay windows was carried out by D. T. Leko in 1908. Number 1 Kraljevića Marka St. is the **Home of ...ka Ćelović-Trebinjac ...m 1903)** in which he ...d in a modest manner ...his death. Adjoin-...o the left stands ...he houses of the ...manović family.

This house is the work of M. Savčić and G. Becker from 1894 and is modeled after the Kinsky palace in Vienna.

A small way uphill, at the corner of Kraljevića Marka and Gavrila Principa streets is **Manak House** (*Manakova kuća*) from 1830, a rare survivor of Balkan oriental architecture in Belgrade. Inside there is a permanent exhibition displaying folk costumes and jewelry (*tel. 30-36-114; open Tue-Sun 10 a.m. – 5 p.m., closed on Mondays; admission free*).

with reference to the number of chairs that could fit into the small atelier of the "Borba" newspaper where the first performances were held. The same year "Atelje 212" was founded it was the first theatre in Eastern Europe to stage Beckett's "Waiting for Godot". The theatre carried on in same manner putting on plays by the likes of Ionesco, Camus and Sartre, whilst also discovering talented new Serbian writers such as Aleksandar Popović or Dušan Kovačević who later became famous after the performances of several successful comedies at "Atelje". The building of the theatre was completely reconstructed in 1992 when it obtained the innovative appearance it has at present.

Today "Atelje 212" seats 385 in front of the main stage and 141 in the "Theatre in the Cellar". By the main entrance stands the statue of the actor Zoran Radmilović (1933-85), shown in

A successful performance

🕗 "Atelje 212" Theatre
Pozorište "Atelje 212"

The theatre was opened in 1956 with the aim of promoting new and avant-garde drama. It got its name

"King Ubu" costume, a part he played. Radmilović captured the hearts of audiences with his masterful performances, making his interpretations proverbial and the shows legendary.

An example from the Automobile Museum

18 The Automobile Museum
Muzej automobila

Majke Jevrosime 30,
tel. 303-4625

The most recent museum to open in Belgrade derives its collection from that of Bratislav Petković. It is located on the premises of the first public garage in town that was erected in 1929 - itself a technical monument. It housed the automobiles of the participants of the first international car and motorcycle race ever held in Belgrade, on September 3, 1939.

The museum's collection includes 50 historically valuable old-timers, the oldest being an 1897 *Marot Gardon*. Other exhibits include various other devices connected with driving - driving-licenses, the first traffic regulations and laws, number-plates, tools as well as works of art and objects of applied art. Along with film and photographic records, technical and scientific literature, the museum offers an enhanced understanding of the history of motoring. *Open Mon-Sat 10 a.m.-6 p.m., Sundays 10 a.m.-2 p.m.*

19 "BITEF" Theatre

The theatre is situated in the German Evangelical Church designed in 1931 in a manner reminiscent of the North German Gothic style. The theatre evolved around the festival of the same name (Belgrade International Theatre Festival) started in 1967 and devoted to experimental theatre and the exploration of new tendencies. Currently most of the festival's interests lie in modern dance and physical theatre. The theatre itself has a somewhat calmer repertoire. The small square in front of the theatre bears the name of the festival's founder Mira Trailović.

20 Botanical Gardens
Botanička bašta

Takovska 43

The "Jevremovac" Botanical Gardens were founded in 1874 by the Ministry of Education of the Kingdom of Serbia upon the suggestion of the biologist Josif Pančić, who became its first manager. It originally lay by the Danube but was moved due to the constant threat of flooding.

In 1889, King Milan Obrenović donated the estate he had inherited from his grandfather Jevrem to the Grand School in Belgrade as a site for the Gardens. His sole condition was that the gardens be called Jevremovac. Today, the name remains and the Gardens are still a part of the Biology faculty. Though they have stood neglected for a long time, the Botanical Gardens are currently being redeveloped. They cover an area of about five acres, with over 250 kinds of trees including rare domestic, European and exotic plant species (with a total of 500 individual trees, bushes and herbaceous plants). Part of them has been developed as an attractive "Japanese garden". It also includes a 500 sqm greenhouse from 1892, which contains tropical and subtropical plant species. The offices of the Belgrade Institute of Botany are also situated on the premises. *Open workdays from 9 a.m. to 7 p.m., weekends 11 a.m.-6 p.m.*

Japanese garden found in the Botanical Gardens

ZEMUN

Although Zemun existed as a separate city until 1934, its history was always closely connected with the one of its larger neighbour, Belgrade. It was often the case that one of the cities prospered due to the misfortunes of the other - an example being when in the 18th century Belgrade merchants fled to the Austrian-controlled Zemun and consequently boosted trade there. On the other hand, in the 19th c. Zemun became the window looking to Europe and the world for the still oriental Belgrade. Living off the Danube River, this small town developed around Gardoš

Hill from where there is a fascinating view over the town and its churches below as well as Belgrade proper further down river. The general atmosphere found in the charming, small, Zemun streets still reflect its past spent under the rule of the Habsburg Empire. As a part of Belgrade, Zemun lost much of its unique quality becoming just another old quarter in the metropolis; still, its local municipal pride is alive and well and the locals retain much love and pride for their small houses and streets as much as they do for the vast waterway on their doorstep.

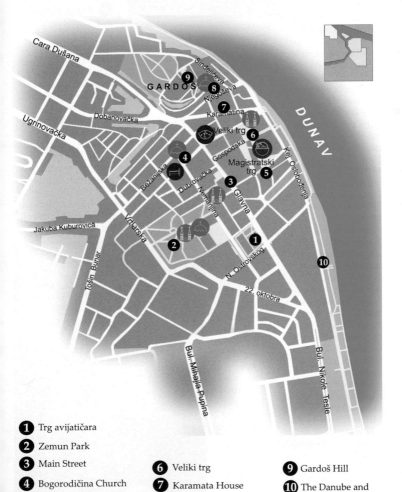

1 Trg avijatičara

2 Zemun Park

3 Main Street

4 Bogorodičina Church

5 Magistratski trg

6 Veliki trg

7 Karamata House

8 Nikolajevska Church

9 Gardoš Hill

10 The Danube and Sava Embankments

e steeple and the tower, Gardoš Hill

❶ Trg avijatičara

The Aviators' Square, up until recently called the Square of Yugoslav National Army, is on the way to the baroque centre of Zemun. The squre is dominated by the **Air Force Command** building, a masterpiece of the modernist architecture, constructed by Dragiša Brašovan and built in 1935. The building was located here because Belgrade Airport had been based along the southern outskirts of Zemun until 1962. The Air Force Command was bombed during the Bombing Campaign in 1999 and although the parts of it have been rebuilt, it is still not used in its full potential. Here is also a plaque in the memory of the members of the Air Force and Antiaircraft Defence who died in 1999.

In the middle of the square and the park is the **monument** in the memory of citizens of Zemun who died in during the „National Liberation War" (World War II). This work of Jovan Kratohvil was unveiled on the 24th October 1954, at the 10th anniversary of liberation.

Behind the monument stands the **Primary School „Svetozar Miletić"**. Built in 1913, it is attractive in its simplicity and neo-classicist details.

The **Faculty of Agriculture**, built in 1933, is on the other side of the school, in Nemanjina street. This Faculty is still the only part of

Relaxing on an autumn afternoon in Zemun Park

Belgrade University that is located in Zemun, owing to its fertile surroundings.

❷ Zemun Park

Zemun Park (also known as *Gradski* or Municipal Park) opened in 1880 on the site of *Kontumac*, the largest of the quarantines on the border between Austria and Turkey. As there existed no sanitary regulations to restrain the infectious diseases in Turkey, deadly epidemics occured regularly and the quarantine functioned constantly throughout the 18th and first part

of the 19th c. The only remains of the complex are **two chapels**. The Orthodox one (1786) is dedicated to St Archangel Michael and the Catholic (1836) to St Roch. The orthodox chapel now serves as a nunnery for the sisterhood that escaped from Croatia during the civil war. Behind the chapels is **Zemun High School** (*Zemunska gimnazija*) modeled in 1879 in the strict academic neo-renaissance style.

❸ Main Street
Glavna ulica

The main street of Zemun is also its oldest one: the main street of Roman *Taurunum* was also situated here. Later, it was part of a much longer road connecting the two major Austrian forts in the region – Belgrade and Petrovaradin (today part of Novi Sad). However, besides its importance in communication, it was also the main merchant street. Though it has lost a lot of its old

Zemun Highstreet

time charm, the street still boasts a number of interesting edifices.

Just behind the ever-busy bus station on the right side of the street (at No. 6) is the **Birth House of Dimitrije Davidović** (1789-1838), a journalist, diplomat and the main creator of the first Serbian constitution of 1835. Across the small street named after him stands the **Main Zemun Post Office** designed in 1896 by the municipal architect Dragutin Kapus in a mixture of neo-renaissance and northern baroque styles.

Across the street is the **neo-gothic house** (1840) of the rich Spirta family. In it is located the Zemun Municipal Museum which is currently closed for renovation.

At the corner joining to Dubrovačka St. is the so-called **Sundial House**, built in 1823 in the empire style. It gets its name from the sundial at its side. The famous Serb politician and writer Jovan Subotić (1817-1886) lived here for some time.

Further along the street one reaches the edifice of the **"Madlenianum" Chamber Opera**. This edifice was built for the Zemun Theatre in 1969 to replace the row of tradesman houses destroyed in the 1944 Allied bombing that crippled the core of the city. In 1998 and then in 2004 its main façade was successfully remodeled to suit the stylish reputation of this institution.

Madlenianum Chamber Opera

④ Bogorodičina Church

This orthodox place of worship dedicated to the Nativity was constructed between 1775 and 1783, replacing an older church. It had a baroque façade but stood without a bell tower and with only a small dome until the end of 18th c. It still is, as it was at the time when it was finished, the largest church in Zemun. The high iconostasis was carved, and plated in gold, by Aksentije Marković, while the icons are the work of Arsa Teodorović. Executed in 1815, they are regarded by many as this classicist painter's finest work. Enclosing the churchyard on two sides is the **Serb House** building (*Srpski dom*). This monumental neo-romanticist edifice was used as a Serbian

school, a congregation centre, as well as flats and shops.

Around the corner at No. 18 Bežanijska Street lies the attractive **Ičko House** (*Ičkova kuća*) built in 1793 in the classicist style with a high gable. It is named after the tradesman Petar Ičko who spent here the winter of 1802 running away from the Turkish violence in Belgrade. Later on, Ičko became one of the most important diplomats of insurrectionist Serbia and in 1807 concluded a peace agreement that

Bogorodičina Church with a view towards New Belgrade

Oath Cross and Catholic Parish Church

would become the basis for Serbian autonomy.

⑤ Magistratski trg

This elongated square has always been the seat of the town administration as it still is today. The brightly coloured blue edifice was designed in 1832 by Josef Felber in a simple but consistent classicist style to house the **Town Magistracy**. The building is painted in the tones of the Serbian Radical Party who ruled Zemun from 1997-2000. In a odd turn of events, they bought this building back from themselves at the auction they organised.

To the left of it is the **Zemun Local Council**, once the seat of the municipal authorities. After the destruction resulting from the 1944 bombing the building was remodeled by D. Tadić to look as it does today keeping the general stylistic elements.

On the other side of the square stands the so-called **"Oath Cross"** (*Zavetni krst*) erected in 1863 by the merchant Lazar Urošević to repent for his sinful gambler's life. Facing it lies the picturesque house of the **Treščik Pharmacy**. Built in 1828, it has a simple classicist façade and a high roof, used as a herbarium, which gives the house a special air of antiquity.

⑥ Veliki trg

The "Large square" was always the centre of the town's trade while today there is only a lesser greenmarket selling fresh goods and the characteristic cheap bits and bobs of transitional economies. The catholic **Church of the Blessed Virgin Mary** lies on the site where in Turkish times stood the only mosque in Zemun. The present day edifice dates

back to 1794 and has features from the empire and baroque styles. On the façade are the sculptures of Saint Florian and Saint John of Nepomuk. From the courtyard can be observed the column capital of the catholic church of the Zemun suburb Francenstal, inhabited by Germans until 1944. Directly after the liberation of the town, the church was torn down while the suburb was populated with homeless families from Bosnia and Croatia. Symbolically, the name of the suburb was changed to Sutjeska, a Partizan battle against the Nazis.

On the other side of the square, at the corner of Zmaj Jovina St, stands the 1911 building of the **"At Snail's"** (*Kod puža*) café. It is adorned with a large dome and four statues representing personages from Greek mythology.

⑦ Karamata House
Karamatina kuća

The house is located at No. 17 of the street of the same name. Its oldest part (with a mansard roof) was built in 1762 while its present appearance, with three distinctive tracts, dates

The previous site of the Treščik Pharamcy

Zemun rooftops by the Danube

from 1824. The house was bought in 1772 by Dimitrije Karamata, a merchant freshly arrived from Macedonia; it has since been in the possession of this family from which come many important personalities in Serbian history. During the war with the Turks in 1788 it was the seat of the Austrian commander-in-chief, Marshal Laudon. At the time of the siege of Belgrade of that same war, Emperor Joseph II stayed here while visiting the frontline.

8 Nikolajevska Church

At the corner of Njegoševa St and Sindjelićeva St is located the Orthodox Church dedicated to the Transfer of the remains of St. Nicolas. This saint is the protector of fishermen and boatmen who constituted a major part of the church's local congregation. The small wooden temple on this spot was recorded as early as 1573. The present church was constructed between 1721 and 1731 and is therefore the oldest in Zemun as well as the whole of Belgrade. Dimi-

trije Bačević, who mixed the Byzantine with the renaissance and baroque elements in a distinctive combination, painted the 18th c. high iconostasis. The church preserves the remains of St. Andrew the First-called (the brother of St. Peter) and the colourful flags of the Zemun guilds.

Stained-glass window in Svetonikolajevska Church

9 Gardoš Hill

This stumpy little hill is the heart of Zemun. With a castle at its peak, this is where the first settlements grew up with most of the houses dug into the hillside. The

castle was also made out of earth (serb. *zemlja*), this being where the name of the town came from. The hill itself is known as Gardoš, a Hungarian pronunciation of the Slavic word grad meaning "castle". This scenic neighbourhood rising above the Danube was inhabited by fisherman living in tiny mud huts thatched with reeds, in rows one above the other. Shamefully neglected, today it has lost much of its charm but is still a favourite destination within Belgrade. The waterfront clenched between Gardoš and the Danube is lined with cafés and restaurants: from the illustrious "Šaran" and trendy "Reka" to more inexpensive venues such as "Radecki".

The simplest way to climb to the top of Gardoš is up Sindjelićeva Street, however, one can take any of the small alleys and stairways that lead up the hill. Crowning the top, stands the Millennium Tower, better known as the **"Tower of Sibinjanin Janko"** (*Kula Sibinjanin Janka*). Sibnijanin Janko is the name of a medieval Hungarian Duke John Hunyadi in Serbian epic

The Millenium Tower also known as Kula Sibinjanin Janka, crowning Gardoš Hill

Svetozar Ivačković in his recognizable neo-Byzantine style. The wall paintings and those on the iconostasis are work of Pavle Simić.

⑩ The Danube and Sava Embankments

This pleasant promenade starts at Gardoš Hill and follows the Danube to its confluence with the Sava continuing on further pass the Brankov Bridge up to Gazela Bridge. A considerably long stroll in the fresh air will give one a feel of the river and will also take one pass some interesting monuments from modern times. Starting from the Zemun side the first noticeable edifice is the **Hotel "Jugoslavija"**. Completed for the first conference of the non-aligned movement countries in 1961, with its one thousand beds it was the biggest hotel in Southeast Europe. In 1999 it was bombed because the notorious criminal and warlord Arkan had his car-retailing business here. Between the hotel and the river stands the Monument to the Pilots who died defending Belgrade in 1941.

Several hundred metres further to the right there is a view of the new **Chinese Embassy** (*Kineska ambasada*) an attractive combination of the modern style alongside traditional details of pagodas. It was bombed on the same night as the neighboring hotel - three Chinese citizens were

folk poetry. It was here in 1456 that Hunyadi died of the plague just after he won his greatest victory over the Turks who had besieged Belgrade. The tower was erected for the 1896 celebration of 1000 years since the Hungarian arrival to the Pannonian Basin. This remarkable structure in a mix of historic styles, served as a vantage point yet is unfortunately almost always closed today. Nevertheless, the hilltop itself offers grand views of Zemun, over the confluence of the Danube and the Sava and a magnificent panorama of Belgrade spreading across a ridge. The tower stands in the middle of the pitiable ruins of the castle. One can still faintly see the remains of four round towers on its corners,

shattered by time and negligence.

Behind the tower lies the old graveyard divided into Orthodox, Catholic and Jewish sections. The most noticeable structure in it is the yellow **Hariš Chapel** constructed in 1875 by the architect

Hariš Chapel in Zemun Graveyard

killed and Beijing broke diplomatic relations with Washington. The official Pentagon explanation was that it was a mistake that occurred due of the outdated maps! Recently an unexploded rocket has been removed from the building and now it is expecting renovation though it will not host the embassy any more.

Relaxed conversation on Zemun Embankment

From the walk one can only observe the

Monument to the Pilots who died in 1941

backside of the grandiose **SIV** building. It was started in 1947 as the first major project in New Belgrade, the area supposedly intended to encompass all the major state institutions contrasting with the old "reactionary" edifices in the town centre. It was finished only in 1960 and has since housed a number of socialist institutions with complicated names that presented the complexity of socialist Yugoslavia's constitutional system. It retains its name after the last one, the Federal Executive Council (*Savezno izvršno veće*). Today, with the reduction in size of the state, it is fairly empty and out of use.

Again to the right one will notice a tall column. Pathetically named **"The Eternal Flame"** this unimaginative monument commemorates soldiers and civilians killed in the NATO bombing of 1999. Opened in the following year by Slobodan Milošević and his wife Mira, it became a target for anti-regime minded people that soon brought it to the poor state its in at the present. The real flames of on the top of it disappeared after the fall of Milošević"s when the gas supply was cut off. The monument lies in the so-called **Friendship Park** (*Park prijateljstva*) in which, during the socialist times, visiting heads of states would plant a tree.

On the other side of the park rises the **"Ušće" Tower**. It was designed in 1968 by Mihailo Janković in architecture of glass and steel for the needs of the Central Committee of the Communist Party and is therefore still known to many simply as "CK". The building was also rocketed in 1999 with the justification that it housed the of Milošević's daughter's radio station. It was re-opened in 2005 having been refurbished and with a viewpoint from the top floor.

The glass-fronted Ušće Tower

AROUND THE CENTRE

There are numerous sights worth visiting further away from the historic centres of Belgrade and Zemun. In their rapid development during the 20th c, the outskirts of Belgrade soon embraced the surrounding hills like Topčidersko brdo where Marshal Tito's mausoleum is situated or Dedinje with its complex of Royal Courts. At the foot of the latter lies Topčider Park where one can find the old manor house that belonged to Prince Miloš, a favorite picnic place during the 19th c. Nearby, the island of Ada Ciganlija has been transformed into a recreational area with a four kilometre long artificial lake, open-air cafés and countless homes on barges. The wooded Mount Avala, with its monument to the Unknown Soldier, and the Rakovica monastery beneath it, guard the southern approach into Belgrade.

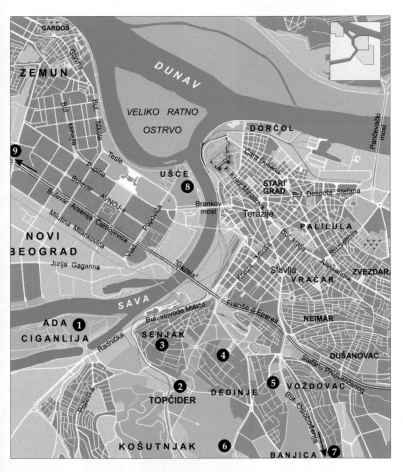

1 Ada Ciganlija

2 Topčider Park

3 Museum of African Art

4 The House of Flowers

5 Museum of FC Red Star

6 The Royal Courts in Dedinje

7 Mount Avala

8 Museum Of Contemporary Art

9 Air Museum

arica marina next to Ada Ciganlija

❶ Ada Ciganlija

This is a river-island between Belgrade and New Belgrade. In 1967 it was linked to Belgrade on two spots thus creating an artificial lake

"Geyser" at Ada Ciganlija

4,2km long, approximately 200 metres wide, and 6 metres deep. In that way Belgrade got not only an exceptional lake, but also a park spreading on more than 700 hectares (mostly covered by deciduous trees), and all that only 4km from the city centre.

Being well connected with all parts of Belgrade, Ada is a Belgrade's favourite sporting resort, especially during the summer, often with a daily visit of up to 300,000 swimmers. There are all necessary infrastructures on the beach, together with slides, water-skiing, and pedal boat and boat rentals. There are also football, basketball and volleyball fields and the only Belgrade golf course. Close to the north extreme of the island is the "Ada Safari" with a small artificial lake turned into a rich fish pond. Near this is a "weekend" resort of

small cottages sunken in the greenness. Numerous bars and restaurants ashore and on rafts are also not to be omitted. There is a tourist train that goes around the lake and a lot of other attractions.

Various water sports competitions often take place on the Ada Island, distinctively those in rowing. A quay harbouring boats and small ships is situated on the north side of the small Čukarički Bay.

Ada Ciganlija is reachable from New Belgrade side as well. Boats are operating during the day from Blok 70.

❷ Topčider Park

The Sultan's charter of 1830 granted Serbia autonomy but did not surrender Belgrade and the five other fortresses. Since Prince Miloš Obrenović could not have total control over the town, he decided to rule Serbia and Belgrade at a safe distance from the Turkish cannons and soldiers. For his residence he chose an estate in the valley of the Topčider River that he had obtained some

years earlier after a dispute with the pasha of Belgrade. At the end of the 19th c. Topčider became the best-loved excursion site for Belgraders who came here in their numbers especially after the introduction of the electric tramline in 1894.

The **Mansion of Prince Miloš** (*Konak kneza Miloša*) was built between 1831-34 in a mixture of the Balkan-oriental and classicist style resulting in an original and memorable edifice. Miloš preferred it to all his other palaces due to its tranquil character and relative isolation. This is where he held the sessions of the Serbian parliament, where he signed his abdication in 1839 and where he later died in 1860. His son Mihailo favoured the more European-looking courts in the town, however Topčider still retained its importance as the Prince's summerhouse. Today the mansion hosts a permanent **exhibition "Serbian Revolution 1804"** dealing with the history of the First (1804-13) and the Second (1815) Serbian Uprisings (*tel. 660-442,*

Swimming for the ice cross on the feast of Theophany

open every day except Mondays from 10 a.m. to 5 p.m.). It is home to documents, paintings, flags and arms as well as some personal items of Karadjordje and Prince Miloš. The most interesting features of the interior are the carvings and paintings on the ceilings as well as the friezes depicting various flora and fauna. The gigantic plane tree in front of the mansion was planted at the time of the building's construction and now has a 7.40 m circumference.

Prince Miloš Mansion with a gigantic plane tree

In the pleasant though slightly forgotten **park**, stretching at the front of the palace, one can see three monuments. The **Obelisk** commemorates Miloš's return from exile in 1859 and shows his coat-of-arms. The **Statue of the Reaping Goddess Ceres** dating from 1852 is the first park sculpture in Belgrade. A small way further stands the **Bust of Dr Rudolf Archibald Reiss** (1876-1929), a professor of criminology from Lausanne, Switzerland who came to Serbia in 1914 to witness the atrocities against the civilian population

perpetrated by the Austro-Hungarian and Bulgarian troops and, so shocked at what he saw, joined the Serbian army, remaining with it until 1918. His professional testimonies revealed the suffering of Serbian people during World War I to the world.

Behind the mansion is the small **Church of SS Peter & Paul** (*Crkva svetih Petra i Pavla*), better known simply as Topčider Church. Dating from the same time as the mansion, it was erected by Prince Miloš in gratitude to God for saving his life at this very place. During the siege of Belgrade in 1806, Miloš left his position; when Karadjordje, the

supreme leader of the Serbian forces, learned about this he decided to make an example of this and kill him on the spot. Luckily, Karadjordje's hand was pushed aside as he was shooting and the bullet missed Miloš. The decoration of the western and southern portals was executed in the naïve fashion of the rural churches, and is a prime example of the local stonecutters' craftsmanship. The present day iconostasis is the work of S. Todorović and N. Marković from 1874.

③ Museum of African Art

Muzej afričke umetnosti

Andre Nikolića 14;
Tel. 011/2651-654

The museum is located in the quiet residential suburb of Senjak in a neighbourhood consisting chiefly of the residences of ambassadors and large villas. It opened in 1977 after a donation by Veda and Dr Zdravko Pečar, diplomats who spent most of their careers in various African coun-

Carriage ride in Topčider Park

tries. Their valuable collection presents the core of the museum that consists of cult, magical and decorative objects mostly from West Africa. *Open Tue-Sat 10 a.m.-6 p.m., Sundays to 2 p.m., closed on Mondays*

❹ The House of Flowers
Kuća cveća
Botićeva 6; Tel. 3671-296

Behind this poetic name is hidden the grave of the long-lived president of the Socialist Federal Republic of Yugoslavia – Josip Broz, known by everyone as "Tito". The "House of Flowers" was a part of the far bigger memorial complex that included the "25th of May" Museum (Tito's birth date) and access into his residence. However, during the 1990's the museum was closed, many of the valuables disappeared, while a part of this luxurious residence was taken over by Slobodan Milošević for his personal use. The first view of the complex is the superb **new building of the museum** (M. Janković, 1962). This edifice is used today for art

Josip Broz "Tito" (Kumrovec 1892 – Ljubljana 1980) was born into the family of a peasant blacksmith in a village on the border of Croatia-Slavonia and Carniola with ancestry on both sides. He was not a good student at school and became a locksmith apprentice in Sisak. This is where he first became aware of the leftist movement. Three years later (in 1910) he joined the Social Democrat party and, after completing his training, became an itinerant metalworker across Austro-Hungary and Germany. He was conscripted into the army in 1913 and, in 1914 served on the Serbian front where he was wounded and won a medal for bravery. He was imprisoned for some time in the Petrovaradin fortress on the grounds of communist agitation. In 1915 he was sent to the Russian front where he was seriously wounded and captured. On leaving the hospital Broz was sent to the work camp in Ural where he came into contact with the October Revolution. He escaped and joined the Red Army. After the war he returned to his home country where he worked as an illegal Communist Party organiser. For this he was prosecuted and jailed from 1928-34. Broz, now adopting the pseudonym Tito, carried out additional training in Moscow. On his return he purged the Yugoslav Communist Party of the defying elements and became Secretary General in 1937. Here he strongly promoted the Comintern view that Yugoslavia, as the supposed Serbian hegemony, should be disintegrated. When this actually happened, in 1941, the Communists regrouped and acted only after the German attack on the USSR. Tito became the leader of the communist partisans who started the anti-fascist insurrection (*see* "History"). In 1943 he became a Marshal, the head of the newly proclaimed Federal People's Yugoslavia. He and his movement enjoyed support from Stalin and from 1944 also from Western Allies. In 1945 he set up a one party dictatorship and loyally followed Soviet model. After the break with Stalin in 1948 he embarked on an independent course and the promotion of his own personality cult. Until his death, in 1980, he held a number of state positions including that of life-long president, firmly holding the reigns of power.

exhibitions and there are only a few of the earlier memorabilia displayed there (like two of Tito's limousines). To the left of the principle entrance is a smaller entrance, still guarded by the army, which leads the way to a quiet garden. The main path splits in two; to the right is the hall containing **Tito's grave**. This was once filled with voluptuous flowers that gave the compound its name, today it stands sadly barren with a white marble tomb in its midst. In the adjoining halls are some of the items connected with Tito's life including the batons that were passed

through the entire country and in the end presented to Tito himself on his birthday. On the other side of the garden is the so-called **Old Museum** that safeguards a selection of the presents Tito received during his life. *Open every day except Mon from 11 a.m. to 7 p.m.*

❺ Museum of FC Red Star
Muzej FK "Crvena Zvezda"
Ljutice Bogdana 1a; Tel. 011/367-4664

The Museum of this most popular Serbian football club was opened in 1985 to mark the 40th anniversary of the Sport Society "Crvena zvezda", which contin-

Tito's Grave in the "House of Flowers"

Red Star Stadium

ues the tradition of the "Jugoslavija" (earlier "Velika Srbija") football club, founded at the turn of the 20th c. Here, one can find the cups and trophies won by the club's sportsmen, as well as acknowledgments, posters and other memorabilia. Red Star Belgrade was the Champions Cup winner in the season of 1990/91 and the Intercontinental Cup winner in 1991. It has been the Yugoslav Champion 23 times and the Yugoslav Cup winner 20 times. *Open Mon-Sat from 10 a.m. to 2 p.m. Closed on Sundays*

❻ The Royal Courts in Dedinje

Wishing to build himself a summerhouse not far from his capital city, King Aleksandar Karadjordjević of Yugoslavia bought an estate on the top of Dedinje Hill in 1924. This new royal court (today usually referred to as the Old Court – *Stari dvor*) soon became the King's favorite residence, far from the bustle of the city. Already

during its construction, he decided to build another court nearby, intended for his three sons when they grow up. As Aleksandar was assassinated in Marseille in 1934 he never lived to see the second palace, the White Court (*Beli dvor*), which was finished by his brother, Prince Regent Pavle. Interestingly, both courts were built from the private incomes of the dynasty and the Karadjodjevićs regularly paid their taxes on them. In 1945, the new communist rulers of Yugoslavia dethroned the dynasty, and the royal complex was taken away from its owners becoming the property of "the state and its people". In fact, it became one of the many residences

of Marshal Tito, the totalitarian ruler of communist Yugoslavia. The White Court was also used by Milošević as his official residence during his time at the head of Federal Republic of Yugoslavia. The complex was returned to the royal family in 2002 and today the grandson of King Aleksandar, Crown Prince Aleksandar II resides there with his family.

The **Old Court** was built between 1924 and 1929 according to the projects of Živojin Nikolić, while the interiors were created by the Russian émigré and favourite architect of the King, Nikolaj Krasnov. The Court's architecture is calm and harmonious with reminiscences of the so-called Serbian-Byzantine style, visible especially in details, such as the capitals of the columns. The whole of its exterior is covered in white marble that came from the island of Brač in today's Croatia. Inside the building, among the many rooms decorated in different styles and filled with antiquities and works of art, the most beautiful are the Entrance hall, the baroque Blue

The Old Court in Dedinje Royal Complex

Salon, Gold Salon in the renaissance style, as well as the large dining hall. The ground floor was used for receptions, offical and large gatherings while the first floor apartments were the living quarters of the King and his family. The basement, with a wine cellar and a cinema, was used for more intimate receptions and dining with private guests. It is painted in the style of the Kremlin Imperial Terem Palace with representations of scenes

from folk mythology on the walls. Among the many worthy works of art, the works of Palma the Elder, Andreas of Assisi, Biaggo d'Aantoni and the inevitable Ivan Meštrović stand out. Behind the Court, connected by a colonnade, lies the **Court Chapel** dedicated to St Andrew and modeled on the King's Church at the Studenica monastery. The frescoes in it are copies of the ones found in Serbian medieval monasteries. At the back of the Old Court is a beautiful park with a view looking towards the southeast.

The **White Court** was built between 1934 and 1937 by Aleksandar Djodjević in the academic style reminiscent of French and English manors. After the King was murdered and his sons moved into the Old Court, this edifice was used by Prince Regent Pavle. Apart from the main entrance hall and the central hall with a staircase, there are several rooms furnished in the style of Louis the XV. The most valuable works of art to be

Billiards Room in the Old Court

seen here are those by Nicolas Poussin, Rembrandt, Albert Altdorfer, Canaletto and other domestic and foreign artists.

The whole of the royal complex in Dedinje covers an area of some 100 acres, out of which about a third has been turned into a park while the rest is covered with dense woods.

Open to visitors from 1st of April to 31st of October in prearranged groups (twice daily). Tickets booking: Tourism Organization of Belgrade office beneath Albanija Tower or 011/635-622, 064/81-81-016, dvor@belgradetourism. org.yu

❼ Mount Avala

Being just 11 metres above the qualification for a mountain, Avala (511 m) is the lowest of the mountains descending from central Serbia towards Belgrade. This forested blunt mass is a pleasant oasis with the somewhat untouched feel of nature set amidst overgrown suburban villages.

On the way to the top there is a small clearing where the **Monument to the Soviet Veterans** lies. On October the 19th 1964, as they were heading to the 20th anniversary celebration of the liberation of Belgrade, their airplane crashed on this precise spot. Amongst the 33 dead were several high-ranking officers including Marshal Biriuzov, who commanded the liberating Soviet troops in 1944.

The parking lot is situated in front of **Hotel "Avala"**, built in 1938 in an unusual combination of modern and national styles, with a touch of the exotic (note the sphinxes).

The top of the mountain is crowned by a black marble **Monument to the Unknown Soldier** (*Spomenik Neznanom Junaku*), the work of sculptor Ivan Meštrović from 1934-38. The gigantic caryatids standing by both entrances are dressed in traditional Yugoslav folk costume. Until the start of the monument's construction, the ruins of the 15th c. Turkish castle of Žrnov stood here, Žrnov being the name of the mountain in Turkish times. Its present day name was taken from the castle's function: in Turkish havale means a dominating high spot apt considering that the castle overlooked the main road from Christian

Monument to the Unknown Soldier at the top of Mt Avala

Belgrade to central Serbia that was already under Turkish rule. In the field on the other side of the parking lot stands the **"Mitrovićev dom"** (1924), the first mountain hut in Serbia. Next to it are the **ruins of the Avala TV tower**. The 195m high structure (from 1966) with a viewpoint and a restaurant on the top floor was turned into a pile of rubble in 1999 by the NATO bombing campaign. As the tower was an important symbol of Belgrade, a scheme to rebuild it is being developed.

8 Museum Of Contemporary Art
Muzej savremene umetnosti

Ušće bb; Tel. 3115-713,
www.msub.org.yu

The museum is located in a wonderful position near the confluence of the Sava into the Danube. Its building (I. Antić & I. Raspopović, 1961-65) has a peculiar form: there are six crystal shaped structures resembling a diamond all with large glass surfaces.

The museum's exhibition covers the best works of art from 20th c. Yugoslav artists. Scores of avant-garde and provocative paintings, collages, sculptures and installations are arranged in several thematicaly separated spaces, each one exploring a leading idea of their creators. *Open every day except Tuesdays from 10 a.m. to 5 p.m. Free admission on Wednesdays.*

9 Air Museum
Muzej vazduhoplovstva

Belgrade Airport,
tel. 011/2670-992,
airmuseum@yubc.net

In this museum, located in an exceptional building (Ivan Štraus, 1989), over 50 original planes, hydro-planes, helicopters and gliders are exhibited. They were constructed in various European countries, in the United States, and in Serbia or Yugoslavia. Among them, we can draw your attention to those from World War II such as Meserschmitt Me-109, Spitfire Mk.Vc, Jak 3 or Thunderbolt P-47. All types of Yugoslav planes, including the one of the aviation pioneer Ivan Sarić from 1910, are exhibited. Two permanent exhibitions are: "Serbian Aviation 1912-18" and "Aviation in the April War 1941". There is a section of the museum dedicated to the bombing campaign of 1999. *Winter opening hours: all days (except Mondays) 9 a.m.–2 p.m. Summer opening hours: Tue – Sun 8.30 a.m. –6.30 p.m.; Mondays 8.30 a.m. –3.30 p.m. Entrance fee: 400 dinars*

Cubic structure of the Contemporary Arts Museum

Mama, Čumićevo sokače (hidden passage by the fountain), alternative, rock
F 6, Francuska 6, r'n'b, domestic pop
Republika, Simina 22, rock, pop
Plato, Akademski plato 1, jazz, latino
Havana, Nikole Spasića 1, latino, jazz
Voodoo, Nikole Spasića 3, rock
Akademija, Rajićeva 10, www.akademija.net, alternative, hip-hop
Bassment (aka Zvezda), opposite "Akademija", house
Cvijeta Zuzorić, basement of the art pavilion in Kalemegdan Park, disco

Sava embankment

Anderground, Pariska 1a, house, disco, rock
Sargon, Pariska 1a, rock, house
Baltazar, Karadjordjeva 9, house, electro
Ana 4 Pištolja (aka Lagum), Svetozara Radića 5, alternative

Dorćol

Sinatra, Braće Jugovića 3, evergreen, jazz
Scandal, Višnjićeva 6, pop
Radionica, Rige od Fere 4 (basement), rock
ŠKD, Gospodar Jevremova, house
Atom, Cara Dušana 13, rock, pop
Bitef Art Café, Skver Mire Trailović 1 (same entrance as the theatre), rock, jazz
Ptica, Šantićeva 8, jazz

Palilula

Optimist, Bulevar despota Stefana 22a, evergreen
Bollywood, Šafarikova 11, house
Dali, Hilandarska 20, house, r'n'b
Idiott, Dalmatinska 13, alternative, rock
Plastic, Takovska 43, rock, alternative, techno
Flash (aka Bus), Aberdareva 1a, disco
Taš, Ilije Garašanina 20, r'n'b

Around "Beogradjanka" Tower

Beggars Banquet (aka Resava), Resavska 24, rock
Gutenberg (aka Štamparija), Resavska 28, house, dance
Fili, Resavska 32, www.fili.co.yu, alternative, rock, electro
Irish Pub "The Three Carrots", Kneza Miloša 16, rock
Lava Bar, Kneza Miloša 77, evergreen
Ghetto (aka Incognito), Hajduk Veljkov venac 2-4 (by the corner of Sarajevska and Nemanjina), house, r'n'b

Barge-restaurant on the Sava River

Drama (aka XL), Sarajevska 26, house, pop
Mr Stefan Braun, Nemanjina 4, 9th floor, disco house

Around Vukov Spomenik

Tramvaj (aka Žagubica), Ruzveltova 2, jazz, evergreen
Mamolo, Ruzveltova 13, house
KST, Bulevar kralja Aleksandra 73, www.kst.org.yu, rock, metal, domestic rock
Kuća Piva, Mileševska 42, pop, rock

Floating clubs

Exile, Savski nasip, drum'n'bass
Sound, Savski nasip, house
Posejdon, Staro sajmište, dance, house

Cafe culture on Obilićev venac

Blaywatch, by Hotel "Jugoslavija", dance
Amfora, by Hotel "Jugoslavija", pop, dance
Prestige, by Hotel "Jugoslavija", dance

Further around

Gaučosi, Vojvode Bojovića 17a (below Belgrade Fortress on Sava), pop-rock, gypsy
Fest, "Pinki" Sports Hall, Gradski Park in Zemun, rock, latino, gypsy
Burence, Strma 2 (Gardoš Hill, Zemun), gypsy, pop
Ellingtons, "Hyatt Regency" Hotel, Milentija Popovića 5 (New Belgrade), evergreen, latino
KPGT, Radnička 3 (near Ada Ciganlija), house, dance
Nana, Koste Glavinića 7 (Senjak), dance

Vox, Lješka 26 (Banovo brdo), blues, rock

Cafés

There is a plentitude of cafés of all sizes and arrangements around Belgrade but there are some streets around which a great many of them are clustered, these being **Strahinjića Bana St.** in Dorćol, **Obilićev Venac** parallel to Knez-Mihailova, **Nušićeva St.** by Terazije, and **Njegoševa St.** between Beograđanka and the Third Grammar School.

Casinos

Fair Play, Terazije 25, tel. 323-36-13
Film, Kneza Miloša 9, tel. 324-1290
Aleksandar, Čumićevo sokače 55, tel. 324-3114
Fun, Uskočka 4, tel. 627-605
London, Kralja Milana 28, tel. 688-530

SHOPPING

If one prefers good folk-art souvenirs visit the shop of the **Ethnographical Museum** at Studentski trg 13, "**Artefakt**" – the showroom of the Women's Textile Workshop Network at Trg Nikole Pašića 8, or the "**Zdravo Živo**" shop situated in Terazije's underground pedestrian passage (in front of the "Moskva" Hotel).

Most locations visited by tourists will sell postcards as well as various items of artistic value or those for

"City Passage" Shopping-mall in Obilićev venac

everyday use – mugs, plates, T-shirts, organizers etc. The most interesting selection of these is to be found at "Beogradski izlog" (on the corner of Kneza Mihaila St. and Republic Sq.) or on the line of street stalls at the top end of Kneza Mihaila St. that sell various handmade items many of which have a Belgrade theme.

For art lovers there are many **Art galleries** in Belgrade selling paintings, sculptures, or even icons made in the traditional Orthodox manner.

Singidunum, Knez Mihailova 40
Kolarac, Studentski trg 11
Dada, Čumićevo sokače mall, local 54
Beograd, Kosančićev venac 19
Grafički kolektiv, Obilićev venac 27

Almost all of the **bookshops** in the centre of the city have a wide selection of English-language books including works about Belgrade and Serbia and even some of the novels of distin-

guished Serbian writers.

Stubovi kulture, Trg Republike 5
IPS, Kneza Mihaila 6 (down the stairs in the basement)
Dereta, Kneza Mihaila 46
Plato, Kneza Mihaila 48
Mamut, corner of Kneza Mihaila and Sremska streets

For a good choice of foreign and Serbian **music** try **IPS** (same as the bookshop), **Round Records** (Makedonska 22), or for jazz and classical music, **Ptica** (Gospodar Jovanova 42).

PUBLIC TRANSPORT

Buses, trolleys and trams. There is a wide network of buses reaching to all the corners of the city. The buses may be privately owned or run by the "Lasta" company and therefore lack uniformity (even in colour!) yet they all have the same paying system. There is only one type of ticket – those valid for one uninterrupted bus ride. They can be obtained from kiosks and small supermarkets for 25 dinars or from the driver for 35 dinars. If you're getting one from the driver have the exact change ready. *Jednu kartu / Dve karte, molim Vas.* – "One ticket / Two tickets, please." After buying a ticket, cancel it: put it upside down in the machine and pull the upper part towards yourself. Keep the card for control.

The first bus starts running usually at 4.30 a.m. and the service runs to midnight. There are nightlines with buses departing at 12.10, 1.10 and 2.10 while some may even operate the 3.10 bus. The price of the night ticket bought from the driver is 50 dinars.

If one intends to use the service for going to some of the far-flung suburbs note that the rate is different for zone 2. Buses that travel there can be identified through their three-digit number. The

PANORAMIC PLANS
APPLIED CARTOGRAPHY

Tel:013/346-129
ravno@panet.co.yu
www.komshe.com/ziza

ticket for these journeys purchased from the driver is 45 dinars.

At almost all of the bigger stations there are notice boards with the public transport system timetable and with information about the first and last departures written in both Serbian and English.

Shuttles

These operate only on main lines but can be a very good solution when there is a traffic jam. They are more comfortable and faster, largely as they do not stop at every station. They are listed as E1 to E4. The tickets (70 dinars) are purchased from the driver and are valid for one ride only.

Taxis

These are always available and relatively cheap. Registered taxis are recognisable through the blue plastic sign with a serial number on the roof, a functioning meter and a sticker portraying the rates. During the night and on Sundays the rate is slightly higher and is indicated by the number 2 on the meter. The ride from downtown Belgrade to Zemun should not cost more than 300 dinars. Most of the taxi companies give a discount of 20% on call. It is customary to round the sum up instead of tipping.

central Belgrade. Beovoz is by far the best way to reach Pančevo. The service consists of both the regular intercity trains and local trains. The trains run at intervals of about half an hour to an hour. Tickets are bought as for the trains and cost 50 dinars. Centrally located stations are "Vukov spomenik" (on the Bulevar Kralja Aleksandra underneath the monument of the same name), "Karadjordjev Park" (on the intersection of Bulevar Oslobodjenja and the Highway) and "Pančevački most" (on the Belgrade side of the bridge across the Danube).

Parking

The centre of town is divided into three parking zones: red, yellow and green (listed by the priority) in which parking is restricted from 7 a.m. to 9 p.m. In the red one, parking is limited to one hour, in the yellow – 2 and in the green – three hours. Follow the instructions seen in the box.

There are several garages in the centre of town that charge by the hour. "Obilićev venac" is next to Knez-Mihailova Street, "Masarikova" is just by the Beogradjanka tower and "Narodnog fronta" is close to the Zeleni venac greenmarket and the bus terminal.

Do hotela "…", molim. – To the hotel "…", please.

Do Trga Republike, molim. – To the Republic Square, please.

Beovoz trains

This is a train service that connects Zemun in the west, Pančevo in the east and Rakovica in the south, passing underground through

Busy Slavija roundabout: buses, trams, taxis and vans

Hotel

Motel

Villa/Private Pension

Agrotourism accommodation

PRICE RANGE - for one person in a two-bed room (including breakfast, service and tax). Small icons present facilities in each Hotel.

number of rooms   number of beds

308/373

> 50 EUR
35 - 50 EUR
25 - 35 EUR
12 - 25 EUR
< 12 EUR

★★★★★ HYATT Regency

✉ Milentija Popovića 5
11070 Beograd
☎ 011/301-1234

308/373

VISA MasterCard

The Hotel is placed in New Belgrade, across the Business Centre Usce. It offers an excellent service and international cuisine restaurant, fitness centre, business centre and several conference halls.

★★★★★ Aleksandar Palas

✉ Kralja Petra 13-15
11000 Beograd
☎ 011/330-5300

9/18

VISA MasterCard Maestro

Fantastic business hotel situated in the very epicentre of the city. All rooms have internet access, gym and efficient service. There is also a nice summer terrace.

ALEKSANDAR PALAS HOTEL
BELGRADE, SERBIA AND MONTENEGRO

★★★★★
One of the
GREAT HOTELS
OF THE WORLD

HOTEL ALEKSANDAR PALAS

Highly intimate. Highly peaceful.
In the very heart of Belgrade.

Kralja Petra 13-15
11000 Belgrade
Serbia and Montenegro
Phone: +381-11-33-05-300
Fax: +381-11-33-05-334
www.aleksandarpalas.com
aleksandar@legis.co.yu

★★★★★ Intercontinental

✉ Vladimira Popovića 10
11070 Beograd
☎ 011/311-3333

415/534

VISA MasterCard Maestro
DinersClub

The Hotel is in New Belgrade, right behind the Sava Centre. Within the Hotel, there are international cuisine restaurant, fitness centre, business centre, several conference halls and tennis courts.

★★★★ M-Best Western

✉ Bulevar Oslobodjenja 56a
11000 Beograd
☎ 011/309-0401

167/288

VISA MasterCard Maestro

One of the hotels of the Best Western group situated 5km from the very centre of Belgrade, offering distinguished quality of services.

LOCATION
• 20-min ride from the Belgrade Intl. Airport
• 10-min ride from downtown Belgrade

ACCOMMODATION
• non-smoker rooms • air conditioning
• mini bar • balconies with park view
• direct-dial telephone lines • satellite TV
• internet access

FACILITIES
• Restaurant "Exclusive" • Open-air restaurant
• Conference hall • Travel agency • Mini Market
• Currency exchange office • Safe deposit box
• Room service • Laundry service
• Parking with security

Best Western

BEST WESTERN
★★★★ HOTEL M

Serbia and Montenegro
11000 Belgrade
Bulevar Oslobođenja 56a
Tel: +381 11 39 72 5
          +381 11 30 90 4
Fax: +381 11 30 95 5
E-mail: office@hotel-m.c
Web: www.hotel-m.co

r·u·ž

Accommodation:

308 of the city's largest and most elegant guest rooms, including King, Twin, Premium, Regency Club rooms, Junior, Executive, Diplomatic and Presidential suites. Handicapped and non-smoking rooms available.

Restaurants and Bars:

All-day dining is available at the stylish **Metropolitan Grill**, serving wide selection of Serbian and international cuisine. In its warm, homely setting, the **Focaccia Restaurant** combines the authentic Italian cuisine and modern details. The **Tea House** is Belgrade's favorite meeting spot, known for its air of calm sophistication, its wonderful cakes, fine coffees and teas, while **Ellington's Club** offers the best local entertainment available and a wide combination of hand picked trendy cocktails, creating a absolute vibrant atmosphere.

Recreational facilities:

Club Olympus Fitness Centre & Spa offers indoor pool, Jacuzzi, fitness, steam room and sauna, affusion showers, as well as Spa massages, facial and body therapies.

Hyatt Regency Belgrade
Milentija Popovica 5   11070 Belgrade   Serbia and Montenegro
Tel: +381 11 301 1234   Fax: +381 11 311 2234
E-mail: belgrade.regency@hyattintl.com   Web: www.belgrade.regency.hyatt.com

★★★★★ Zlatnik
Slavonska 26
Zemun, 11080 Beograd
011/316-7511

31/43

A new bussiness hotel in a quiet part of Zemun with well-known national cuisine restaurant and remarkable service.

★★★★ Balkan
Prizrenska 2
11000 Beograd
011/363-6000

80/171

A classic amongst Belgrade hotels, in its "new" building from 1936. Centraly located, with classic interior, contemporary furnishigs and all the comfort one can ask for.

★★★★ President
Kovilovo, Zrenjaninski put 170
11211 Beograd
011/207-5200

27/50

Hotel is situated on the left Danube riverbank, 12km from the Belgrade centre. Among various facilities, there are excellent shooting galleries and fields.

★★★★ Šumadija-Best Western
Šumadijski trg 8
Banovo Brdo, 11030 Beograd
011/355-4255

76/98

Newly opened hotel situated near Kosutnjak surrounded by nature just few kilometres from the very centre of Belgrade.

★★★★ Slavija LUX
Svetog Save 2
11000 Beograd
011/242-1120

167/288

This modern style hotel with casino and piano bar is situated in the centre of Belgrade.

★★★★ Moskva
Balkanska 1
11000 Beograd
011/268-6255

133/263

Hotel is situated in the centre of Terazije in monumental building with Terazije fountain just in front of it.

★★★★ Palace
Topličin Venac 23
11000 Beograd
011/218-5585

85/140

It the very centre with several business halls and casino is this excellent hotel.

★★★ Rex
Sarajevska 37
11000 Beograd
011/361-1862

92/142

This recently renovated hotel in the centre of the city is remarkable for business tourism. There is also and excellent national cuisine restaurant.

BALKAN HOTEL

since 1936

Prizrenska 2, 11000 Belgrade, Serbia & Montenegro
tel: +381 11 36-36-000 fax: +381 11 2687-581
for more information & reservations please visit
www.balkanhotel.com

Welcome to the very elegant botique Balkan hotel. This beautiful historical building has been completely restored to reflect the traditions of the past with all the modern conveniences that international travelers have come to expect.

All our guest rooms are equipped with all the amenities that you will find in an international 4 star hotel: cable TV, DVD player, mini bar, coffe maker, telephone and wireless internet connection for your business needs.

Enjoy the classical interior, dating from the last century, and contemporary furnishings and equipment. Blended together they give comfort and efficiency. Those are the Balkan hotels' amenities at first glance.
But it's true uniquness lies in the warm welcoming atmosphere...

★ ★ ★ ★ Majestic

✉ Obilićev venac 28
11000 Beograd
☎ 011/328-5777

🛏 78/110

Just next to Knez Mihailo Street is this Hotel with beautiful outdoors café offering well-known quality.

★ ★ ★ Country club - Babe

✉ Milovana Milinkovića 3
11233 Babe
☎ 011/826-0077

🛏 69/194

Because of the excellent climate and 350m height above sea level, hotel complex is an ideal environment for all who wish for peace and fresh air.

COUNTRY CLUB hotel BAB
Milovana Milinkovića 3, 11233 Babe, SC
tel/fax: +381 (11) 826 00 7
e-mail: info@cch-babe.co
www.country-club-hotel-babe.co

COUNTRY CLUB HOTEL

A genuine sanctuary for body, mind and soul... For all your business ventures

★ ★ ★ Le Petit Piaf

✉ Skadarska 34
11000 Beograd
☎ 011/303-5252

🛏 12/24

This very nicely decorated business hotel is places in the very heart of Belgrade, in Skadarska Street. Due to its excellent service and offer, a reservation in advance is required.

★ ★ ★ Metropol

✉ Bul. Kralja Aleksandra 69
11000 Beograd
☎ 011/323-0910

🛏 85/126

For years one of the most prestigeous hotels in the town with exclusive clientele.

★ ★ ★ Jugoslavija

✉ Bulevar Nikole Tesle 3
11000 Beograd
☎ 011/260-0222

🛏 235/326

The Hotel is a symbol of Belgrade, on a Danube riverbank, at the Zemun Quay. The rooms overlook Danube and the Great War Island.

★ ★ ★ Kasina

✉ Terazije 25
11000 Beograd
☎ 011/323-5574

🛏 84/111

At Terazije, just across the Terazije Fountain, there is this Hotel with own brewery and casino.

★ ★ ★ Union

✉ Kosovska 11
11000 Beograd
☎ 011/324-8022

🛏 66/107

Behind the Parliament building this familiar hotel offers very good service.

★ ★ ★ Park
✉ Njegoševa 4
11000 Beograd
☎ 011/323-4723

131/227

The Hotel is suitable for congress tourism, situated at the Flower Square in the centre of Belgrade.

★ ★ ★ Prag
✉ Kraljice Natalije 27
11000 Beograd
☎ 011/361-0422

118/209

The Hotel is placed in the old trade zone at the corner of the Balkanska Street, in the very centre of the city.

★ ★ ★ Royal
✉ Kralja Petra 56
11000 Beograd
☎ 011/26-26-426

105/187

Good weekend hotel in the centre of the city is situated near Kalemegdan.

★ ★ ★ Skala
✉ Bežanijska 3
Zemun, 11080 Beograd
☎ 011/307-5032

16/25

This family Hotel is situated in Zemun, very near to the Glavna Street.

★ ★ ★ Splendid
✉ Dragoslava Jovanovića 5
11000 Beograd
☎ 011/323-5444

49/83

In the very centre of the city there is this excellent garni hotel with very good service.

★ ★ ★ Lav
✉ Cara Dušana 240
Zemun, 11080 Beograd
☎ 011/316-3289

10/18

Very interesting garni hotel in Zemun, suitable for business travellers.

★ ★ Excelsior
✉ Kneza Miloša 5
11000 Beograd
☎ 011/323-1381

58/101

The Hotel with excellent offer is situated just across the Pioneer Park in the very centre of Belgrade.

Fish Restaurant    National Restaurant   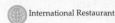 International Restaurant

Kraljevina
✉ Kralja Petra 13-15
11000 Beograd
☎ 011/330-5388

    12-12

Situated next to the Orthodox Cathedral stands this prestigious national restaurant with a touch of the modern to the traditional cooking.

Byblos
✉ Kneginje Zorke 30
11000 Beograd
☎ 011/244-1938

    12-01

Lebanese restaurant with minimalist decor in the oriental spirit, offers traditional arabic cuisine with a good selection of wines. Belly dancing on Thursdays and Saturdays from 9 p.m.

Dačo
✉ Patrisa Lumumbe 49
11000 Beograd
☎ 011/278-1009

    12-24

Interesting design of this restaurant is inspired by country inns and houses of rural Serbia, with the pretty terrace where chickens roam freely. Restaurant has 20 tables in garden.

Daka
✉ Djure Daničića 4
11000 Beograd ·
☎ 011/322-2068

    11-01

Businessmen just love this place, because of the long list of national and international dishes: various meats, sea or fresh water fish, game, escargot... The atmosphere is very pleasant, the staff efficient and kind.

Djordje
✉ Šekspirova 29
11000 Beograd
☎ 011/266-0648

    12-24

Restaurant is located in close proximity to the stadium of FC "Red Star" and combines traditional Serebian cuisine and international specialities.

Franš
✉ Bulevar Oslobodjenja 18a
11000 Beograd
☎ 011/264-1944

    09-24

The interior of the restaurant Franši s very pleasing to the eye, especially in spring and summer when the garden is in use.

Greenet
✉ Masarikova 5
11000 Beograd
☎ 011/361-8533

    08-24

Greenet is a nice place to have a breakfast, but it is even better to enjoy lunch or a light dinner. Prices are very affordable, so booking is advisable.

Gušti mora
✉ Radnička 27
11000 Beograd
☎ 011/355-1268

    12-24

This restaurants seafood is among the best in the city, and all the dishes are prepared in the well-known Adriatic style.

Langouste
✉ Kosančićev venac 29
11000 Beograd
☎ 011/328-3680

    12-24

An expensive, but exclusive restaurant with a stylish interior. A stunning view over the confluence will take your breath away.

The **LANGOUSTE** has been opened with the aim to foster, maintain and promote the idea of Mediterranean hedonism, the original and relaxed lifestyle that requires a love and knowledgeable enjoyment of good company ever better meals, and the best possible wines.

Kosančićev venac 29, Belgrade
Call us to make a reservation: (011) 3283-680. Parking is available.
www.langouste.net

Kod Radeta
✉ Baja Sekulića 29a
11000 Beograd
☎ 011/340-6715

  14-02

Located in a privately owned house rather far from Belgrade's center, the restaurant is decorated in the classic city style of the 19th century.

Madera
✉ Bul. Kralja Aleksandra 43
11000 Beograd
☎ 011/323-1332

 10-01

Known as the gathering place for numerous famost persons, the Madera restaurant has luxurious garden, which spills over into Tašmajdan park, and is one of the prettiest in the city.

Pane e vino
✉ Dobračina 6
11000 Beograd
☎ 011/303-6011

 10-23

The restaurant has imaginative cuisine with a prevailing Italian touch. Its simple and modern interior extends even to the menu.

Peking
✉ Vuka Karadžića 2
11000 Beograd
☎ 011/181-931

 13-24h

"Peking" still remains the best Chinese restaurant in the city, although it was at the height of its fame during the 70's and 80's. The decor is classical Chinese with lanterns and huge fans adorning the walls.

Reka
✉ Kej Oslobodenja 73b
11080 Zemun
☎ 011/611-625

 12-24

It is a perfect restaurant for those who like a relaxed and joyful setting, a happy crowd and a live music.

Santiago
✉ Majke Jevrosime 20
11000 Beograd
☎ 011/323-7953

 10-24

This is the only representative of Latin American cuisine in the city. The decor is quaintly Mediterranean and the food on offer very diverse.

Sport Cafe
✉ Makedonska 4
11000 Beograd
☎ 011/324-3177

 09-02

This centraly located cafe is dedicated to sports: large screens, sporting memorabila and the acompanying crowds are sure to turn every match into a unique event.

Sport Café International
Makedonska 4
11000 Beograd
011/3243-177
www.sportcafe.co.yu

Sport Cafe is located in the very center of Belgrade, just 50 meters from the central Trg Republike Square. It is the favorite meeting place of celebrities, sportsmen, musicians, actors... The restaurant is packed with large TV screens in which you can at all times enjoy sporting, musical and fashion events from all over the world. Numerous original items of local and foreign sportsmen adore its walls.
Sport Cafe runns the official catering service for large-scale events of Football Association of Serbia-Montenegro as well as for the Volleyball Association.

Ikki Sushi Bar
✉ Gospodar Jovanova 46
11000 Beograd
☎ 011/218-4183

 12-24

The restaurants kitchen was set-up by authentic Japanese cook. One of the specialties is Teriyaki salmon. One more hting that shouldn't be missed is green tea ice-cream.

Indian palace
✉ Ljubićka 1b
11000 Beograd
☎ 011/344-6235

 12-24

A pleasant setting with dominant orange coloring and tastefully matched Indian detailes are what give this place its identity.

Sindjelić
✉ Vojislava Ilića 86
11000 Beograd
☎ 011/241-2297

  12-24

Sindjelić is a spacious tavern, often crowded, but the prices are very afordable. Booking is essential.

Šaran
✉ Kej Oslobodjenja 53
11080 Zemun
☎ 011/618-235

 10-01

One of the most famost and elegant Zemun restaurants is thematically divided into two entities, both with prevalent terracotta coloring with a great garden and beautiful terrace.

Suri
✉ Nebojšina 41
11000 Beograd
☎ 011/344-3725

 10-24

A famous restaurant previously located in Kopaonik National Park offers delicious traditional dishes with inspired names.

Located in a house built at the beginning of the 20th century in one of the most beautiful streets in the Vračar municipality. The house has been renovated in the original old style. "Violeta, old chap – hedonists club" is a pleasant place, at the same time a cafe and Italian tavern.

Topolska 4
Tel: 011/ 243 14 58

Violeta, kuća stara
✉ Topolska 4
11000 Beograd
☎ 011/243-1458

Tribeca
✉ Knez Miuhailova 50
11000 Beograd
☎ 011/328-5656

Balkan Ekspres
✉ Despota Djurdja 22
Zemun, 11080 Beograd
☎ 011/615-906

Ipanema
✉ Strahinjića Bana 68
11000 Beograd
☎ 011/328-3069

Kalemegdanska terasa
✉ Mali Kalemegdan bb
11000 Beograd
☎ 011/328-3011

Kapric
✉ Kralja Petra I 44
11000 Beograd
☎ 011/262-5930

Klub književnika
✉ Francuska 7
11000 Beograd
☎ 011/627-931

Srpska kafana
✉ Svetogorska
11000 Beograd
☎ 011/635-160

Stara koliba
✉ Ušće bb
11070 Novi Beograd
☎ 011/311-7666

 09-01

Boosting with the hedonist spirit of the old days this classic restaurant has also a cafe part, cigar and wine bar. Especially nice are its classic furnishings.

 09-02

Tribeca is situated in in an elite location. Restaurant is divided into several different theme sections, but it's equally pleasant whether sitting in the partnerre or upstairs.

 12-24

An interesting restaurant situated in a train coach on top of the Gardoš Hill in Zemun with a magnificent view over the Danube and a large summer garden.

 12-24

Of very simple and urban design, with one huge dinning area in the basement and an equally large terrace on the street pavement, the restaurant is an ideal spot for a short lunch or longafternoon chats.

 12-01

There is no better located restaurant in Belgrade, with spectacular view of Belhgrade's two rivers. The wine list is one of the best in the city.

 12-01

A small but very prominent Italian restaurant at the heart of city, pleasantly decorated and extremely clean and orderly, where you can choose from a large variety of pasta and risotto.

 07-01

Restaurant is located in the building previously occupied by the Turkish and American missions and also was a "gray zone" during the Communist era, a place where dissidents and party leaders met on an informal basis.

 10-24

The famous kafana, always closely connected with "Atelje 212" Theatre and its actors. Recently renovated it keeps the old spirit.

 10-24

Pleasant restaurant, with a comfortable setting, esspecially by the fireplace during winter is more popular for lunch than for dinner.

Luda kuća

✉ Vlajkovićeva 23
11000 Beograd
☎ 011/334-1591

10-24

Traditional chinese cooking of excelent quality at reasonable prices in a leisure modern style atmosphere.

Stara Hercegovina

✉ Carigradska 36
11000 Beograd
☎ 011/324-5856

09-23

Old style *kafana* decorated with the portraits of famous personages from Herzegovina. The national cuisine menu is enriched with the specialties from this region.

Verdi

✉ Terazije 5
11000 Beograd
☎ 011/303-2360

12-24

Very exclusive restaurant with a long tradition. The interior is pleasant, elegant and very neat. Menu is based on Italian cuisine, but of very high class.

Vuk

✉ Vuka Karadžića 12
11000 Beograd
☎ 011/629-671

10-24

For those who like Serbian national dishes, Vuk is the right place to come. Ideally located at the heart of the city, but in the quiet neighborhood, with a beautiful garden.

Žabar

✉ Kej Oslobodjenja bb
11070 Novi Beograd
☎ 011/319-1226

12-24

With a very pleasant and woodsy ambiance, unobtrusive music, excellent service and good selection of wines, "Žabar" is a right place for those who love to light a Cuban cigar with their cognac.

Zaplet

✉ Kajmakčalanska 2
11000 Beograd
☎ 011/404-142

08-23

A favorite restaurant of Belgrade's intellectual elite. The ambience is discreet and minimalist with pleasant lighting while the service is quick and efficient.

Zorba

✉ Kraljice Marije (27. marta) 71
11000 Beograd
☎ 011/337-6547

07-01

The city's only representative of phenomenal Greek-Cyprian cuisine, with very pleasant interior similar to an ikea funiture store. The atmosphere is equally pleasant, crowded with guests from all over the world.

Tabor

✉ Bulevar kralja Aleksandra 348
11000 Beograd
☎ 011/412-466

10-01

Although well out of the city centre, this restaurant manages to maintain its prestigious position for decades with high-class athmossphere and cuisine. Live music.

Kafana "?"

✉ Kralja Petra 6
11000 Beograd
☎ 011/635-421

07-23

The oldest *kafana* of Belgrade is situated in a Turkish-style house from 1823. The interior follows the pattern: wood, small chairs and honest Serbian dishes in a unique atmosphere.

Zlatar

✉ Preradovićeva 9a
Zemun, 11080 Beograd
☎ 011/754-651

08-01

The restaurant is famous for its domestic cuisine and regional specialities. Its uniqueness lies in the fact that it is daily supplied with cheese, kajmak, smoked ham, buckwheat, all kinds of meat, brandies made of wild pears and plums grown in the valley of Lim, near Zlatar.

VOJVODINA

Geographically, Vojvodina is the opposite of Serbia – Serbia is as mountainous as Vojvodina is flat and Serbia is as flat as Vojvodina is mountainous. Apart from the hills of Fruška Gora and Vršačke Planine, there is nothing to disturb the view over the endless plain, once upon a time the bottom of the Pannonian Sea. Today, only tractors and combines sail across this "sea", fighting the waves of wheat or sunflowers. Standing out like islands are the bell towers of Orthodox, Catholic, Uniate, Evangelist or Calvinist baroque churches or silos that are never empty.

Three great rivers flow through this region – the Danube, the Sava and the Tisa – and divide it into three parts

with its own parliament and unobtrusively protects its individuality.

"Hurry at leisure" is a motto in these parts. The people, as if somewhat sleepy, do their work slowly but with certainty, knowing that the rich plain brings deserved rewards. This breadbasket of Serbia gives more than enough for all those who live here, and hence, all do live here: Serbs, Hungarians, Romanians, Slovaks, Ukrainians, Croats, Czechs and many more, all of who have come here in search of a better life and all of who have learned to appreciate it. Vojvodina's beautiful cities are spattered with buildings dating back from the days of the Habsburg Monarchy. Though the Germans are

Pictures made out of straw are characteristic of the north Bačka region

– Srem, Banat and Bačka. For a long time these were different provinces until, in 1848, they united for the first time, as demanded by the Serbs living in all three of them. On this occasion the newly established land of the Habsburg Empire was given another name – "Srpska Vojvodina", that is "Serb Dukedom". Today, Vojvodina is an autonomous province within the Republic of Serbia

gone, quite a bit of their efficiency and order has remained, achieved without tension or force.

Situated on the wide banks of the Danube and shadowed by the mighty Petrovaradin Fortress, lies the city Novi Sad, the administrative and cultural centre of the province. Even though this is a relatively large city, the atmosphere here is relaxed, calming and inspiring at the

...rmen on an armlet of the Danube near Pančevo

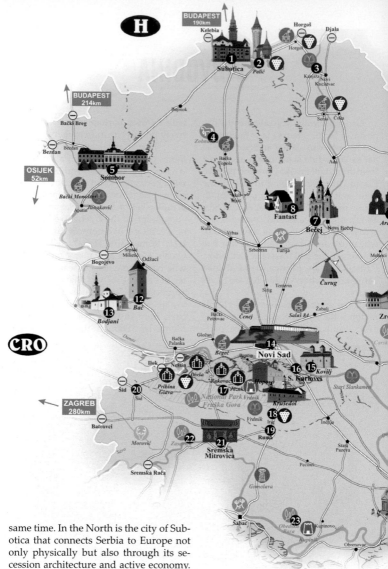

same time. In the North is the city of Subotica that connects Serbia to Europe not only physically but also through its secession architecture and active economy. Sombor, a town that, though it seems to have been left by the way side, is steeped in history and enjoys much greenery and a leisurely pace of life. The town of Sremska Mitrovica, called *Sirmium* in Classical Antiquity, was one of the four capitals of the Roman Empire and gave the name to the entire province of Srem. Tucked in between the Danube and the hills of Fruška Gora, lies the town of Sremski Karlovci, the spiritual centre of the Serbs for many centuries, but also one of the centres of European viticulture. From these vineyards the wine was made that bought privelidges for the Serbs from the Habsburg monarchs. Another town which grew up beside the vineyards is

Vršac with its low, yet wild mountains. Today, only bogs and swamps remain of the Vojvodina landscape before the land drainages. However this scenery from a time gone by, with its richness in flora and fauna can be enjoyed in places like Carska Bara or Obedska Bara bog.

There are many events that celebrate the ethnic and cultural diversity of the nations of Vojvodina. Competitions take place, which honor the abundance of nature and the enthusiasm of the inhabitants who, after all, love most of all to enjoy the fruits of their work with food, drink and song.

1. Subotica
2. Palić
3. Kanjiža
4. Zobnatica
5. Sombor
6. Kikinda
7. Bečej
8. Fantast
9. Arača
10. Zrenjanin
11. Carska Bara
12. Bač
13. Bođani
14. Novi Sad
15. Kovilj
16. Sremski Karlovci
17. National Park Fruška Gora
18. Irig
19. Ruma
20. Šid
21. Sremska Mitrovica
22. Zasavica
23. Obedska Bara
24. Pančevo
25. Kovačica
26. Vršac
27. Mesić
28. Bela Crkva

A typical Vojvodinian salaš, Cvetni salaš

Subotica

148.400
024/554-809
024/555-344
024/555-606
112 km - Novi Sad

Subotica, or *Szabadka* as it is called in Hungarian, was first mentioned in 1391 as a free (*szabad*) trading center under the protection of the Hungarian King himself. Soon after, the place lost its independence and fell under the authority of the famed John Hunyadi, the most powerful lord of the Hungarian kingdom. One of the inheritors of Hunyadi's large estate built a little castle here in 1470 to protect his estate from Turkish attacks. In the turmoil after the battle of Mohacs in 1526, where the Turks had devastatingly defeated the Hungarian army, Subotica briefly became the capital of the self-appointed emperor, the mysterious Jovan Nenad, also known as "Black Man". He gathered the Serb peasants who recently inhabited the region and who now refused to go back under feudal lords. In the end, Subotica was taken over by the Turks who ruled the town from 1542 to 1686. In Habsburg Monarchy, the town changed its name to *Maria Theresiopolis* in the honor of the Empress who, in 1779, accredited it the status of a free royal town. This significant privilege enabled a more rapid development of the town, but its real flourishing started only after 1869 when the railway reached Subotica. The railway facilitated not only a convenient disposal of agricultural products from the surrounding and a rapid industrialization, but it also led to the increase of the number of inhabitants to 100,000 at the beginning of the 20th century. After the territorial changes caused by the end of the First World War, the town suddenly became a part of the Kingdom of the Serbs, Croats and Slovenes, located at the very borderline with Hungary. Although it was the third largest town in the new country (right after Belgrade and Zagreb), the border location and bad relations with the neighboring Hungary that lasted both in interwar and in the post-war period led to the general stagnation of Subotica. In the last few years, the town has gained more of its significance as the main gate of Serbia towards Europe.

❶ Town Hall
Gradska kuća

It took only two years (1908-1910) to build the magnificent new Town Hall in the place of an old one. This structure that with its high tower noticeably rises over the town center soon became the pride and symbol of the booming town. Town Hall was then, as it is today, the largest edifice of Subotica and its main sight. It was built according to designs of architects from Budapest, Marcel Komor and Deže Jakab. Their construction plans were based on Hungarian version of Art Nouveau, which became extremely popular among the residents of Subotica by the beginning of the 20th century. The building is characterized by unusually imaginative variations of naïve folk motives, which are stylized and combined with Art Nouveau elements. The rich decorations are even more distinctive inside. On the floor above the main entrance is a ceremonial council roo

Fountain by the side of the Town Hall in Subotica

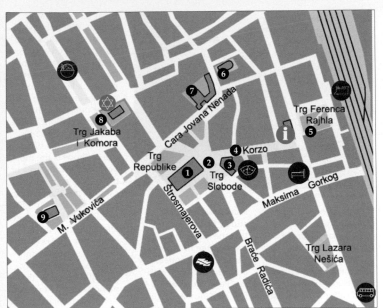

1 Town hall
2 Trg Slobode
3 The National Theatre
4 Korzo
5 Trg Ferenca Rajhla
6 Church of the Holy Assumption
7 Franciscan Church
8 Trg Jakaba i Komora
9 The Cathedral

decorated with stained glass with pictures of significant Hungarian rulers, from the medieval kings all the way to Franz Josef, who was the Austrian Emperor and the Hungarian king at the time of the construction.

In the Town Hall building is located the **Town Museum** (entrance from Štrosmajerova Street, to the right from the main entrance; *tel. 024/555-128; open on Tue,*

Detail from the Town Hall

Wed and Fri 10 a.m.-4 p.m., Thu to 6 p.m. and Sat until 2 p.m.), with a permanent collection housing archeological findings from Subotica and the surrounding area, historical documents that illustrate development of the town, as well as the items describing the everyday life of its residents. You can also see items done by ancient craftsmen, folk dresses or household furniture from peasants' homes of this multinational region.

"Dr Vinko Perčić" Gallery houses mostly the works of the local artists, but there are also a number of paintings by famous Yugoslav and Hungarian authors.

On the 45 meter high **tower** there is a viewpoint, which offers a magnificent view of this lowland town. The admittance is allowed only at noon and at 1 p.m. every day. There is no lift!

2 Trg Slobode

A **monument to the Emperor Jovan Nenad** dominates this central town square that is located on the side of the Town Hall. It is the work of the sculptor Petar Palavičini, put up in 1927 on the 400th anniversary of the Emperor's death. Together with Jovan Nenad, there are also the figures of his associates Subota Vrlić and Fabijan Literata. During the World War II and the Hungarian occupation, the monument was removed, but almost intact awaited to be erected again at its old place in 1991.

The spacious **fountain** built entirely of the

Town Library

famous *Zsolnai* ceramics from Pecs was designed by Svetislav Ličina in 1985.

Behind the fountain stands the **Town Library**, with its neo-baroque façade abundantly decorated with sculptures among which the most distinctive are the two atlases supporting the balcony. It was built in 1897 for the needs of the National Club, by the projects of the famous native of Subotica, architect Ferenc Rajhl.

❸ The National Theatre
Narodno pozorište

At the beginning of the 19th century Subotica lacked both a purpose-built theatre building and a modern hotel. The work on an edifice that would unite both of these functions began in 1848 by the construction plans of Janoš Skulteti, who studied thoroughly the designs of many European theatres. Unfortunately, the construction works had to be stopped almost immediately owing to revolutionary events. Continued soon afterwards the works were soon finished so that this striking neo-classicist edifice could be opened for public in 1854. The main entrance,

emphasized with six sturdy Corinthian pillars became the favorite motif of the first post-cards from Subotica. The building together with its "Pest" Hotel and a few elegantly arranged taverns facing the Korzo became the center of social life. After the big fire in 1915 devoured a larger part of the building, the theatre and the hotel were rebuilt between the two wars, but in a more moderate style that did not repeat old neo-classicist elements. In time, the theatre hall was more and more used for cinema projections, while the hotel lost its prestige. As there was almost no money invested in the maintenance of this building in the last few decades, it has become utterly ruined, so that today its greatest part is closed for public and waiting its renovation.

❹ Korzo

At first, this street was only a starting point of the road to Szeged that winded through the swampy lands of Rogina Bara Pond, at a place of

today's Ferenc Rajhl Square. When the pond was drained, the street was prolonged and made wider, and it soon became the prestigious promenade and a commercial area where some of the most beautiful houses of Subotica were built during the 1880s. Even today, this street full of shops is the most popular walking area of the residents in Subotica, same as it is the main artery of social and nightlife. For all these reasons, after changing its numerous names during its short existence, the street is, as of recently, officially called by the name known to everyone – short and clear – Korzo ("Promenade").

Starting from the Liberty Square, the first edifice that attracts one's attention is **Vojnić Palace** (J. Jedlička, 1893) with its red front, the finest example of neo-Gothic style in Subotica.

Rural ambiance in the centre of Subotica during the "Dužijanca" harvest festivities

The main motif on the facade is a triangular bay window with sculpture of a knight who holds the shield with a Vojnić family coat-of-arms.

Children in traditional Hungarian dress, Subotica

On the first corner to the right, there is a former **bank building**, today an office of the travel agency "Putnik". It was built by the designs of the celebrated Jakab and Komor in Hungarian Art Nouveau style that made them famous. Among the versatile decorations inspired by folk culture, the most dominant are the beehives that symbolically represent the saving. Right next to it is the **House of Jovan Dimitrijević**, in rich neo-renaissance style, built in 1881. It is the work of the architect Titus Mačković, who in his half-a-century-long career designed several of the most beautiful edifices of this town.

Across the little street decorated with a small but interesting fountain, there is the **Palace of Stanko Manojlović**, another work of the architect Mačković, in a generous mixture of renaissance and baroque elements. Two houses further, at number 4, you can find the **House of Djura Manojlović**, Stanko's father, built as a detached villa in 1881 at the outskirts of town. Opposite to it is the **Prokeš Palace** (G. Kocka, 1887) in the strict neo-renaissance style. At one time, it was the largest building for rent in Subotica.

❺ Trg Ferenca Rajhla

In place of this square once stood the Rogina Bara Pond that circled the town form its eastern side and blocked the expansion of Subotica this way for a long time. Even when in 1864 the Railway Station was built, an embankment facilitated the connection to town across the pond. The notorious pond was drained in 1888 and, because of its vicinity to the town centre, this area immediately became attractive to the well-off residents of Subotica, who encircled the newly formed square with their exquisite villas.

On the corner in front of the Railway Station stands the imposing neo-Gothic **Šimegi Palace** from 1893. **Leović Palace** is next door to it (Eden Lehner & Djula Partoš, 1893). On it you can catch a sight of the first signs of Art Nouveau architecture that would soon triumph in Subotica.

Opposite the Station is the **Rajhl Palace**, a wonderful masterpiece of Art Nouveau architecture. This striking edifice of vivid mass and decorated with colorful ceramics was built in 1904 as home of the architect Ferenc Rajhl, after whom the square was

The eye-catching Art Nouveau facade of the Rajhl Palace

❸ Kanjiža

🏠 8.400

🚌 37 km - Subotica

Kanjiža developed next to the best possible crossing of the river

Famous red peppers of Horgoš village near Kanjiža

Tisa. Tradition has it that Hungarian tribes crossed the river here in 896, entering Pannonia and subsequently conquering it. In 1751, after the Serb frontier guards had left for Russia, the town and its vicinity were colonised by Hungarians who, to this day, are a majority here. For a long time constricted between the Tisa and the adjacent bogs, Kanjiža began developing only towards the end of the 19th c. In 1908 it obtained the title of 'town' and a spa was opened just a stone's throw away in 1913. The territorial changes after WWI, that made it Vojvodina's northernmost town, were harmful to its further development. Only recently has it regained its former fame, mainly due to the spa in its vicinity which is the largest and best maintained in Vojvodina.

The focal point of the town is Glavni trg (the Main Square). The **Town Hall** was built in 1911, at the height of Kanjiža's glory. Just behind the Town Hall is the pleasant Narodni Park separating the town from the spa. The **Spa** (*banja*) is centred around three thermo-mineral springs with hydro-carbonated waters that were found by shepherds drilling for water. The three large spa hotels offer full programs for wellness. They are especially well known for their mud baths. Mineral water and mud are used for the treatment of rheumatism and joint injuries, as well as for recreational activities.

❹ Zobnatica

4 km - Bačka Topola

Zobnatica estate is located in the middle of Bačka region, some 30 km south from Subotica, on a heath that once belonged to this city. It owes its fame to its horses: since 1750, thoroughbred English steeds have been bred here, making it the oldest horse farm in Serbia. Today its tradition still exists through well-kept stables, a covered manege, museum of horse breeding and horsemanship, and above all a racetrack that hosts the "Horse Games of Zobnatica", with the well-known horse races on the first week of September. Apart from this aspect, Zobnatica also covers vast hunting grounds (2500 ha) and numerous rather small lakes intended mostly for fishing carp, pikeperch and catfish. Zobnatica also has capacities for congress tourism with its hotel complex and sports centre.

❺ Sombor

🏠 74.300

ℹ️ Trg Cara Lazara 1 25000 Sombor 025/434-350, 434-330

🚌 025/441-751

▯ 025/28-922

58 km - Subotica

The first settlements here grew amidst the branches of the river Mostonga that, in the past, divided the land of the present-day town into 14 islands. The name of the city was first mentioned in 1360 as *Cobor Sent Mihalj* when it became the property of the noble Cobor family. In 1478 the Cobors built a castle to defend what became their most important possession yet nevertheless it fell to the Turks in 1541. Under Turkish rule Sombor became the seat of the regional administration and an

Hackney-coach ride in the vicinity of Sombor

important centre for artisans, best known for its silversmiths. The name changed from Cobor to the more Serbian sounding *Sombor*, clearly testifying to the change of populace. The town suffered greatly in the Long War (1593-1606) with Austria when Tartars who were stationed here plundered the vicinity. The Serbs fled north and their place was taken in 1622 by the Bunjevci (Catholic Serbs), settlers from Dalmatia and Bosnia. The town recovered in the 17th century: with 14 mosques and over 200 shops it was again the most important town in the Bačka region. Sombor was taken by the Habsburgs in 1687. For some time it was a šanac, a settlement of Serbian soldiers, as a part of the military frontier. When, in the mid-18th century, the military frontier was no longer in use as such, the Serbs managed to organize themselves and gather enough money to buy the privileged status of a free royal city (1747) for the town allowing it to develop faster. Sombor became especially important when, in 1786, it became the seat of the Bač-Bodrog County, the administrative and legislative body in which only nobles were allowed membership. In

Diploma granting Sombor the status of the "Free Royal Town"

the 20th century Sombor grew steadily but much more slowly. Spared from the fast development, it retained much of its former charm such as the old family houses nestled under the shade of well-maintained rows of trees. Called *Ravangrad* ("Flat Town") by its most famous writer Veljko Petrović, Sombor is also known today as the "Green City" for the multitude of trees (17.000) and parks (150.000 square meters) within it. It is the town with the most greenery per capita in Serbia. Sombor is also famous for the horse carriages (*fijaker*) in use there and much praised in old songs. In 1975 there were still 19 of them operating; unfortunately, today there is only one.

The town centre, enclosed by four streets bearing the names of the four commanders of the liberating Serbian army in 1918, is where most of the monuments are. The principal square, **Trg Svetog Trojstva**, is also called "Bald Square" (*Ćelavi trg*) due to the small number of trees around by Sombor standards. The most distinguished building found in this square is the **Town Hall** with its high tower. To begin with, in 1718, it was the palace of Graf Jovan, the prodigal nephew of the famous Graf Djordje Branković, the self-proclaimed "despotes of Illyricum". Jovan quickly squandered the family's wealth so that he had to sell the palace to the town magistrate who, in 1749, transformed it into the Town Hall. Its present-day classicist appearance was obtained through its reconstruction in 1842 and a tower was added in 1892. Nowadays it is the seat of the local newspapers and radio.

Facing it stands the Gale house named after the pharmacist Emil Gale who built it in 1838 on the site of the town's first pharmacy, "At the golden lion". Today this Biedermeier edifice houses the **Milan Konjović Gallery** (*tel. 025/22-563, www.konjovic. co.yu, open Mon-Fri 8 a.m.-7 p.m., weekends 9 a.m.-1 p.m.*), that keeps

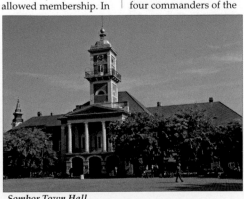

Sombor Town Hall

the legacy of the famous expressionist painter, who memorialised his native Sombor in many of his works.

To the right of the Gallery is the **edifice of Graf Grašalković**, the notorious Catholic and a great enemy of Orthodox Serbs. It was erected in 1763 and served as the immigration centre for the German's colonisation of Bačka. Two buildings along lies the **Historical archive**. It is located in two edifices that are today joined together. The older one is the two-storied **"Turkish Tower"**, the only remaining part of the medieval fortification. Next to it, in 1771, the modest **Krušper palace** was built. Beside this complex stands the 1751 **Chapel of St John of Nepomuk**, who was – among other things – known as the protecter against flooding, which was a frequent worry to Sombor's citizens.

Facing the chapel is the **Catholic Church of the Holy Trinity** (1763) and, adjoining it, the monastery building (1749). Until the suppression of Franciscan monasteries, both were in the possession of the

Order, the only one highly revered by local Catholics. Just after the completion of these buildings, privileges were bestowed on the town in 1749. County meetings were held here until the construction of the Županija building (see below). On the wall of the monastery is a sundial with the inscribed *memento mori*, "One of these (hours) is your last". Where once stood the monastery garden, now lies the central town marketplace called the "Chained market" after the chains that mark its borders.

Zmaj Jovina Street leads one to the Republic Square (*Trg Republike*). Here lies the **Town Museum** (*Gradski muzej, Trg Republike 4, 025/22-728, www.gms.co.yu, open Mon-Fri 8 a.m. – 6 p.m., Saturdays 9 a.m. – 1 p.m.*). The museum presents the history of Sombor and its vicinity. To the right of it stands the **National Theatre** built in 1882. It has an original, preserved neo-baroque interior.

Traditional dress in North Bačka

To the back of the Town Hall stands Trg Svetog Djordja, named after the Serbian Orthodox **Church dedicated to St George**. The church is not in line with the street but is orientated towards the East. It was finished in 1761 in a combination of baroque and rococo styles. The new iconostasis was painted in 1866 by Pavle Simić and is considered one of his best works. At the address of house **No. 6** in this square lived the famous Serbian romanticist poet Laza Kostić (1841-1901). During the last ten years of his life he was the president of the **Serbian reading room** (*Srpska čitaonica*) whose edifice can be seen just few metres away, on the corner of Čitaonička St. At the end of this street one reaches the Kronić house, a small neo-baroque palace, erected according to the plans of Vladimir Nikolić in 1906.

At the end of Kralja Petra Prvog Street there is a large park that surrounds the **Županija** building. The representative front part was finished in 1808 in the late baroque style to house the seat of Bač-Bordrog County. It was remodeled in 1882 with the addition of a new part that gave the edifice its square ground plan with a large atrium inside and two towers

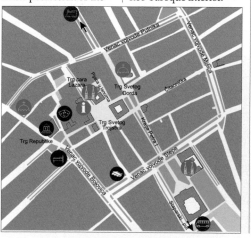

Spires of the Carmelite Church in Sombor

on the sides. In the main hall is the large (7 by 4 metres) **painting "The Battle of Senta"** by Ferenc Ajzenhut from 1896. It commemorates the 200th anniversary of the Christian victory that sealed the destiny of Bačka and in which the Sombor militia took part. On the ceiling, coats-of-arms of noble families who made up the County assembly are depicted.

To the left of the Županija building is the **Carmelite church**. This imposing edifice with two bell-towers took around 45 years to complete, between 1860 to 1905. Inside it, one can see the largest organ in Serbia.

❻ Kikinda

🏠	43.200
ℹ️	Srpskih dobrovoljaca 12 23300 Kikinda 0230/26-300
🚌	0230/423-770
🅿️	0230/22-114
	50 km - Zrenjanin

Kikinda was just a prosperous village until 1774 when it was declared as the seat of the Kikinda District (*Kikindski distrikt*), a predominantly Serb area enjoying certain autonomy and excluded from the feudal order of the rest of the state. After that date, it grew into an important town within northern Banat. It held its seat for about a hundred years when it was abolished, however Kikinda managed to obtain the status of a free royal city soon after. The economy of the town grew fast in the 19th century, especially after it was connected to Szeged by the railway built in 1857, the oldest railway line in Serbia. Today the town is best known for its tiles and bricks factory.

The tower of the **Town Hall** marks the centre of town. It was built in 1894 to house the town's newly instated representatives. The edifice looks like it is made out of the joining of three buildings; this is a deceitful impression that comes from the various styles in which it was designed. On the tower one can see the coat-of-arms of the town and a Latin inscription: *Attendite!*, the town's motto, a warning to the citizens to stand united.

Next to the Town Hall is the tall **"Narvik" hotel** (from 1980) named after the north Norwegian seaport in which a number of people from Kikinda were sent to work by force during WWII. For a many years Norwegians were the regular guests of this once prestigious hotel.

Across the hotel is the **"Kurija" building**, the District's seat of administration and the courthouse but also a prison. It was built between 1836 to 1839 in the classicist style. It has stood witness to many events of Kikinda's history: the beginning of the upheaval in 1848, the visits of Franz Josef (1872) and Aleksandar of Jugoslavija (1919), and the shooting of thirty innocent hostages by the Nazis in 1942. Today it houses a **Museum** (*tel. 0230/21-239*) that has an especially rich archeological collection from nearby localities, aswell as the works of local 18th and 19th century painters and an ethnographical section. Among the items exhibited one can find the well-preserved skeleton of a mammoth.

Nearby is the **Serbian Orthodox Church** dedicated to St Nicholas, built in 1769 on the site of an old wooden church. The paintings of the iconostasis are attributed to Teodor Ilić Češljar who also painted the two compositions on the sidewalls, "The Ascension of Christ" and "The Last Supper". On the southern church wall, there is a sundial.

An exhibitor at the Ludaja Pumpkin Fair in Kikinda

Further along the elongated Trg srpskih dobrovoljaca Square, one can see the **Roman Catholic Church**. It was built between1808-11 in the classicist style after Emperor Francis I visited the town and donated funds for the building of the edifice.

In Kikinda there is also an old mill powered by horses (*Suvača*). Once an ordinary sight in Vojvodina, today it is one of only two surviving in the whole of Europe. It was used to mill wheat and peppers while today the building is mainly used for concerts and theatrical performances.

ENVIRONS:

14 km north of the town is **Mokrin**, a large Serbian village from which many prominent men of culture originated. There are two interesting manifestations that take place here, these being, in February, the "Gusanijada", a gander-fighting competition and at Easter, the World Championship in egg-cracking (called simply "Tucanijada"). Apart from these, there is not much to see. The **Orthodox Church** built in 1762 has an iconostasis painted by Teodor Ilić Češljar in the Rococo style and wall paintings from 1857, the work of Nikola Aleksić.

A bathing gander, Mokrin village

❼ Bečej

🏛 22.300
🚌 021/811-060
51 km - Novi Sad

Bečej was originally a 12th century Hungarian castle located on the Tisa river island. It was conquered by the Turks in 1551 and stayed under their rule for 150 years. According to the peace treaty of Carlowitz in 1699, the Tisa became the border line between the Habsburg and Ottoman Empire and the old castle had to be pulled down. In 1701, with the organization of military frontier, a Serbian military camp was formed and named Bečej. When the border was abolished in 1749, Bečej became the seat of a privileged district, which enabled it to develop faster. The Serbs lost their soldier status, moved away while the Hungarians were inhabited in this territory. The town suffered badly in the clashes between these two ethnic groups in 1848 and almost no buildings originate prior to this period.

Most important monuments of Bečej are on its main square – **Trg Oslobodjenja**, known among people as **Pogača** (sort of round bread) because of its shape. A line of two buildings joined together is on the west side of the square. The left one is **Town Hall**, built in 1884 with the tower, which was the usual feature for such edifices at that time. **The endowment of Baroness Eufemija Jović**, the work of a famous architect Vladimir Nikolić, is on the right hand side.

Opposite to these buildings is the **Orthodox Church** built from

Drummer at the Tisa Military Frontier (18th c.)

1851 to 1858 where the old church used to be before it was burnt down in the clashes of 1848. With its three towers, classical portico and gothic details it represents the mixture of styles that achieved great success at the time of its construction. The iconostasis was carved by Viennese masters, while the paintings were the work of a respectable Uroš Predić, painted in 1889-93. This was Predić's first major order by the Church and its quality brought him work for many years to come.

On the right hand side from the church, there is the **Serbian primary school** from 1861. A small **monument of King Petar Karadjordjević** on the lawn in front of it used to stand in the middle of the square between the two World Wars.

The **Roman-Catholic church** from 1830 is in the northern side of the square. It was thoroughly restored in 1875 after being damaged in 1848. Inside there are two large paintings by a well known Hungarian painter Ferenc Tan

Mor, a native of Bečej: "Ascension of the Mother of God" and "St Joseph". The so-called **"Yellow Well"** (*Žuti bunar*) named after the colour of its hot thermal water lays by the temple.

The south side is occupied by three nice buildings from the turn of the 20th century: on

Serbian Orthodox Church in Bečej's "Pogača" Square

the left the edifice of the Potiska Savings Bank, than the offices of the Eiffel Company and (on the right) the house of the wealthy landowner Bogdan Dundjerski.

The **Town Museum** (*Maršala Tita Street 43, 021/6915-765*) is very well known for its archaeological collection, mainly artefacts from the Sarmatians and Avars, and the gallery containing many works of local painters from the XIX and the XX century.

The southern side of Bečej lays on the Danube-Tisa-Danube canal. There is the conduit on it, called by a German word **"Šlajz"** on the canal, an interesting construction from the beginning of the XX century which is also protected as an important technical monument.

❽ Fantast

ℹ️ 021/813-531
14 km - Bečej

At the 14th kilometer on Bečej – Bačka Topola road is the "Fantast" castle, the most famous summerhouse of Bogdan Dundjerski, a landowner and one of the richest Serbs in the 19th century. It was built at the beginning of the 20th century as the centre of the 65-acre-large estate. The castle itself is a mixture of many different styles, but on the whole it resembles the medieval structures with round towers on corners and a dominating "keep". Today it is turned into a luxurious hotel that preserved a good deal of the old furnishing. Close by is a family chapel in neo-Byzantine style with an iconostasis done by the great painter Uroš Predić. Bogdan Dundjerski is buried there.

Most of the estate is a nicely maintained park, with lakes and small woods scattered around, wandered by ostriches. Dundjerski's large horse-farm, that at one point had more than 1400 horses, has been functional ever since and

offers a riding school, horse renting and carriage and sledge riding. The arranged footpaths enable visitors to enjoy the park and its beauties both by foot or bicycle. In the surroundings are the copious hunting grounds and a fish pond with a restaurant.

❾ Arača

🚊 12 km - Bečej

Arača, the ruins of a medieval Benedictine abbey, is well hidden in the midst of the endless fields of Banat. It is however, one of the most interesting monuments in Vojvodina and lies 8 kilometres south of the village of Novo Miloševo, on the Kikinda-Novi Bečej road. The first monastery that stood here was recorded in the 11th century and was most probably Eastern Christian. It was situated on a hillock (82m) that safeguarded it from floods. On the same site the present church was built around 1228. It was then destroyed by the Cumans some half a century later, after which the abbey remained in a bad state until the famous Hungarian Queen Elisabeth reconstructed it in 1370. A settlement developed around the

Fantast Castle on the Vojvodinan plain

monastery that over time grew into a small town with a protective wall. In the 15th century, it came under the possession of Serbian despots and Serbs settled here. Pillaged during the Turkish takeover of Banat in 1551, the abbey perished for good. The Serb village moved away in 1720, unwilling to adhere to the feudal lords. The three-nave basilica was built out of bricks in the Romanesque style.

Ruins of the Arača Benedictine Abbey

More expensive materials were used for the modeling of details; for instance, red marble was used for the western portal and grey sandstone for the columns. The capitals of the columns are especially well done, adorned with floral motifs and a representation of Adam picking an apple from the Tree of Knowledge. The most well preserved part of the church is the middle apse with its three windows. The gothic tower was erected next to the apse in the 1370 renovation.

⑩ Zrenjanin

> 🏙 132.300
>
> ℹ Koče Kolara 68
> 23000 Zrenjanin
> 023/523-160
>
> ☎ 023/541-000
>
> 📠 023/530-388
>
> 50 km - Novi Sad

Zrenjanin is made up of several smaller settlements that evolved around the meandering path of the Begej River which formed here several peninsulas and islands. These settlements later united under the name Bečkerek. Its medieval fortress was conquered by the Turks in 1552 and remained in their hands until 1716 when Prince Eugene of Savoy brought it under the rule of the Habsburgs. Shortly afterwards it became one of the centres for the colonisation of Banat. Apart from the Germans, the authorities also tried to settle Italians and Catalans here. The latter even formed their district here called New Barcelona. All of these efforts failed when the Turks reached the city once again in 1739. During most of the 18th century the city developed at a slow pace however this all changed, when in the 19th century, it became the seat of the Torontal

County. In Yugoslavia it changed its name to Petrovgrad after King Peter Karadjodjević; this name was discarded immediately after WWII and changed to Zrenjanin after the "National Hero" Žarko Zrenjanin, a local communist. Today Zrenjanin is the most important town in Banat and, in many economic and cultural aspects it competes with its larger neighbours.

Trg slobode is the main town square. Once again, sixty years after having been destroyed by the occupying forces, the square is adorned with a **monument to King Peter**, originally designed in 1926 by Rudolf Valdec.

The principal building in Trg slobode is the **Town Hall**, built in 1820 as the seat of Torontal County. It obtained its present day neo-baroque decoration in 1897 by the plans of a famous architectural duo: Djula Partoš and Eden Lehner. The main staircase and hall are opulently decorated with painted ceilings and stained glass windows. Behind it lays the **Gradska bašta** ("Municipal garden"), a pleasant area of greenery with a musical pavilion, fountain, many sculptures and even cages with rare bird species! At the edge of this park stands the **Russian Orthodox Church**; formerly a prison, it was adapted in 1922 to suite the needs of the colony of Russian émigrés.

To the right of the town hall stands the **Roman-Catholic Cathedral** built in 1864-68 by the design of Jovan Djordjević in a somewhat naïve Romanesque style. In contrast with

Town Hall in Zrenjanin

Zrenjanin's Catholic Cathedral

Courts of Justice Palace built in 1906-8 by architects from Budapest.

From the fourth side of Trg slobode Square begins **Kralja Aleksandra I Karadjordjevića Street**, the centre of the commercial district in Zrenjanin. At its start lies the richly ornamented **Bukovac Building** from 1905 leading towards an attractive row of houses from the turn of the turn of the century.

At the first intersection, Svetosavska Street takes one to the left towards the orthodox church, **Uspenska crkva**. Built in 1746 out of bricks and covered with tiles, it was one of only a few buildings that managed to survive the great 1807 fire that devastated the town centre. The iconostasis was created in 1815 and the wall paintings in 1924.

Kralja Aleksandra I Karadjordjevića Street ends at Trg Republike in front of the **Great Pedestrian Bridge** (*Veliki pešački most*) over the Begej. The bridge, named in reference to its width, was constructed in 1971 in place of the 1904 Iron Bridge made by the Eiffel Company. The old bridge was described in a popular local

song as being "as narrow as a box".

Taking Svetosavska St. and then Nemanjina St. further to the north one reaches **Karadjordjev Park**, a vast green common and in which there is a row of busts and monuments to the great men of Zrenjanin, called **"Alley of Great Men"**, ("Aleja velikana").

Another point of interest is the area along Cara Dušana Street, north of Trg Slobode. This part of town is known as Gradnulica, and was once a separate settlement. Here lies the Serbian Orthodox **Vavedenjska Church** (otherwise known as Gradnulička Church) built in 1777 on the site of a monastery that is well known to to the fact that Saint Rafailo of Banat had lived there. The new church has become a place of pilgrimage due to holding the Saint's relics. The legend says that after Rafailo's death a spring emerged from a nearby elm tree whose water could cure illness, especially eye diseases that were endemic in the area. When it was hit by lightning some 30 years ago, the five hundred year old elm tree was almost completely burnt down in a fire. Its trunk however is still visible and is venerated, although the miraculous water is long gone.

the austere exterior, the inner decoration is exceptional. It was executed by a local artisan, Jožef Gojgner, following the designs of the famous graphic artist Gustav Dore. It is also influenced by Leonardo da Vinci ("The Last Supper") and certain Hungarian painters. Facing the Church stands the corner edifice (1906) of the former financial department. Today it houses the **Town Museum** (*Subotićeva 1, tel. 023/61-841*) containing several interesting departments (archeological, ethnographical and fine arts). Next to it is the **Theatre** whose performance hall dates from 1839 making it the oldest operating stage in Serbia.

Subotićeva St. leads to **Mali most** ("Small Bridge"). The latter stands over the former stream of the Begej River, now just an elongated lake, having been cut off from both sides. On the other bank stand the neo-gothic **Reformist Temple** with its high spire (1891) and the large

Merry band of men at the Zrenjanin Beer Days Festival

Wetlands of Carska Bara are a heaven for birdwatchers

⓫ Carska Bara

17 km- Zrenjanin

A special natural resort "Stari Begej – Carska Bara", is 17 km away from Zrenjanin. On the Belgrade-Zrenjanin road, you need to turn left towards village Belo Blato and continue straight to the nice "Sibila" Hotel, which is located on the north side of the pond and which serves as the usual staring point for all the activities in the reservation area. The reservation covers the floodable area between the Tisa and Begej rivers, and consists of ponds, swamps, channels between them and the rivers, marshy terrain, meadows, as well as woods. Among the water surfaces, Carska bara stands out as a pond that hosts 140 species of resident birds, and in summer, 110 species of migratory birds, the most distinguished of which are white-tailed eagle, marsh harrier and hen harrier, buzzard, sparrow-hawk, spoonbill. The Carska bara Pond can be reached through a pathway which branches off to the left after the "Sibila"

Hotel, wherefrom the tourist boat also goes and the most common walking route, so-called "Health Path" (Staza zdravlja) begins. The pond is rich in flora as well, recognizable for the abundance in white water lilies and water fern. Various animal species can also be found at the resort territory, such as wild boar and cats, roe deers, foxes, pond turtles and multicolored salamander.

The visitors are offered a wide range of services: tourist boat rounds, rowing-boat or motorboat rounds with or without a guide, bird watching, hockney-carriage rides, walking paths, sightseeing from a powered paraglider and bike renting. The wider area of the resort offers

conditions for hunting (wild ducks and geese, quails, roe deer, wild boar) and fishing (carp, pike, perch, catfish).

⓬ Bač

11.300

Trg Zorana Đinđića 2
21420 Bač
021/770-075

021/770-189

62 km - Novi Sad

Bač is one of the oldest settlements in Vojvodina: it is mentioned as early as 535. A.D. in a letter of Byzantine Emperor Justinian. The history of Bač is directly connected with the fate of its fortress, around which the settlement grew. It was built in the 11th c. by Hungarian King Stephen I on a bend of the river Mostonga that filled its moat with water making it inaccessible from all sides. The fortress became the seat of the county and of the Catholic Bishop. Due to its importance, the whole region under its jurisdiction became known as Bačka ("of the Bač"), the name still used for one of the three sub regions of Vojvodina. In the 12th c. it played an important role in the war against Byzantium when, in 1164 the advance of Emperor Manuel I Comnenus was stopped at its walls. The present day fortress was built between 1338-42, under the auspices of King Charles Robert and was modeled on the similar flatland structures of western Europe. In the 15th c. the river Mostonga was broadened so that ships from the Danube could now sail to Bač itself. In the confusion that followed the demise of the Hungarian state in 1526, Bač was held by various sides until the Turks took it in 1529. After the expulsion of the Turks it maintained its military

The keep of the Bač Fortress

significance until it was destroyed in 1704 so that it could not be taken during Hungarian Rakoczi rebellion against the Habsburgs.

Franciscan Monastery with its gothic features

Despite that destruction, it is still the best preserved medieval fortress in Vojvodina. It is located in the western part of this little town, within its now dry circular moat. The **Fortress** was built in the form of an asymmetrical rectangle with towers on each corner. The tall keep in the centre is the only part that has been restored to its former grandeur. On the north side one can still see the remains of a gothic chapel. All the constructions are brick except the details, such as frames and balconies that are made of stone.

Approaching the town of Bač, one reaches the footbridge over the Mostonga and crossing it finds the **"Šiljak" ("Spike") Gate**, named for its gothic looks. It dates from the same period as the fortress and was once part of the defensive walls of the town. Still closer to the town we pass the ruin of the **Turkish Baths** dating from the 16th c.

The most interesting site in Bač is the **Franciscan Monastery** in the middle of the town. It was established in 1169 by the Knights Templar; later it was turned over to the Franciscans who inhabited it from 1301. The knights, and later the monks, operated one of the first hospitals in

this part of the Europe. The Turks turned the monastery church into a mosque, while the rest of the complex lived to see the liberation from the Ottomans in a very bad state, only to be burned in the Rakoczi uprising. Its present day appearance dates from a 1743 reconstruction. The oldest preserved part of the monastery is the romanesque apse flanked by a tall gothic tower. In the apse there is a fragment of a gothic fresco. The altars are the work of an unknown baroque master and the most revered relic is an icon of the Virgin Mary, painted in the manner of the Italo-Cretan school. In the refectory is a painting of The Last Supper dating from 1737.

In the center of the town stands the **Gebauer House** which housed the oldest pharmacy in Serbia. The original entrance with a shop window and staircase are preserved.

Bodjani Monastery Church

⓭ Bođani

14 km - Bač

Bodjani was founded in 1478 by a tradesman Bogdan from Dalmatia, who, thanks to the engagement of a nobleman Dmitar Jakšić, was granted the building permission from the Hungarian king Mathias Corvinus It was built next to the miraculous spring where Bogdan cured his eye disease. Present day church dates from 1722 and was built by donations of Mihailo Temišvarlija a Serb tradesman from Szeged, Hungary. It is a single nave edifice with a massive dome that copies the architecture of the previous 15th century temple that stood here.

The wall paintings were done in 1739 by Hristifor Žefarović, one of the most important Serbian painters of the mid 18th century. Žefarović introduced new and less traditional forms, coloring and light in his paintings and, for these unconventionalities and novelties, he is considered to be the first modern Serbian painter. He transformed the traditional iconographic scenes into lively, decorative and highly descriptive compositions with special love for ornaments. Of a special interest are the contemporary details (clothes, furniture etc.) from the 18th century society, that he depicted in his frescoes, as well as more presentations of Serbian rulers who were canonised the saints, which was an obvious response to the proselytism of the Habsburg Empire. The icons at the iconostasis were done by Jov Vasiljevič and date from the 1740's.

⓮ Novi Sad

🏛 302.400

ℹ️ Bul. Mihaila Pupina 9
21000 Novi Sad
021/421-811, 421-812

🚌 021/444-021, 444-022

📱 021/443-200

82 km - Beograd

Despite the fact that Novi Sad can be labeled as a young town, even its relatively short history wasn't spared of the twists and turns of events in this turbulent region.

Before the 18th c. there was no settlement in the area of the present day town. The Roman Empire had the Danube as its border and the northern bank of the river was merely a military outpost that could be abandoned if the barbarians attacked in greater numbers. In the Middle Ages, Petrovaradin developed on the south bank, with its castle and abbey, while on the other side of the Danube a few minor villages were scattered.

What was to become Novi Sad started to evolve when, at the end of the 17th c., the newly conquered Petrovaradin was converted into the most important fortress on the southern borders of the Habsburg Empire. On the other side of the river was the bridgehead of a fortress and around it grew a small Serb village named *Varadinci* or *Varadinski Šanac* ("Varadin Trench"). As non-Catholics weren't tolerated in the fortress, they settled

Novi Sad Coat-of-Arms

across the Danube. Since many among them were capable Serb, Greek or Jewish tradesmen, they soon turned the Trench into an important trading post, as opposed to the purely military Petrovaradin. A new impulse came in 1739 when Belgrade fell back into Turkish hands and Serb and German inhabitants fled northwards along the Danube. Many of them decided to settle here and, with their links to Turkey, they almost immediately turned the town into one of the most important trading centers in the Habsburg Empire. The small town grew so fast that in 1748 it managed to buy itself the status of the Royal Free City. With its independence from Petrovaradin the town got the new name – *Novi Sad* ("Newly Planted"). The town prospered until 1849, when, in the civil war that raged across the Empire the Hungarian controlled Petrovaradin responded to the attempt by the Serb forces loyal to the Habsburgs to take the fortress by firing on the town below. The cannon fire from hundreds of guns turned the town to rubble and what was left perished in a huge fire. Only a few houses survived and when the citizens returned they had to start all over again. During the rebuilding in the second half of the 19th c. the town took on

Statue of the "Iron Man" in the building of the same name

its present day appearance and grew again to be the most important cultural, educational and artistic center of Serbs outside Serbia, earning it the nickname "Serb Athens".

In 1918 Novi Sad became part of the Kingdom of Serbs, Croats and Slovenes and the administrative seat of the region of Vojvodina. The growing importance of the city was reflected by the opening of new wide boulevards and the construction of many large buildings. Between 1941-44 the city lived through one more ordeal when it was occupied by Hungary; several thousand Serbs and almost all the Jews perished as victims of the terror. After World War Two, Novi Sad became the seat of the Autonomous Province of Vojvodina as part of the Republic of Serbia and started a rapid growth that continues to the present day. In 1999 the town fell victim to the heavy NATO bombing that, amongst other things, destroyed all three bridges across the Danube. The wreckage

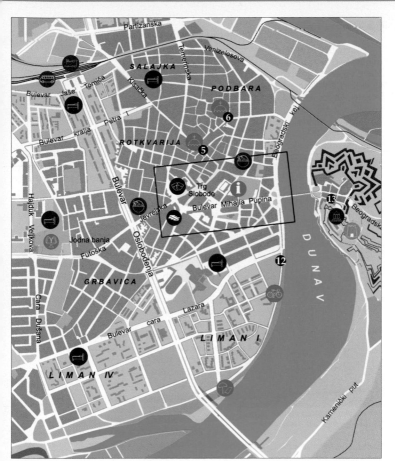

1. Trg Slobode
2. Bishop's Palace and Ortodox Cathedral
3. Dunavska Street
4. Museum of Vojvodina
5. St Nicholas Church
6. Almaš church
7. Serb National Theatre
8. Newlyweds Square
9. The Synagogue
10. Mihailo Pupin Boulevard
11. Galleries Square
12. Banks and Bridges
13. Petrovaradin

closed the river to traffic, all of which was a huge setback for a town of this size.

In spite of all the hard times, Novi Sad is best known as a town of open-mindedness and tolerance where Serbs from all parts of ex-Yugoslavia, Hungarians, Slovaks, Ukrainians and many other nations live side by side. Since 2001 the city has organized a large international summer music festival "Exit" that attracts hundreds of thousands of visitors and which has placed Novi Sad on the musical map of Europe.

Novi Sad's central square Trg Slobode with the Town Hall on the left

❶ Trg Slobode

The central city square once served as a shared market place for both the Catholic community, which resided to the west of it, and the Orthodox community to the east.

In the middle

Parish church often mistakingly known as the Cathedral

stands the **Monument to Svetozar Miletić** (1826-1901), lawyer and politician, leader of the Serbs and their Liberal party in Vojvodina and ultimately the Mayor of Novi Sad. It is the work of the great sculptor Ivan Meštrović from 1939, who represented Miletić in a dramatic and threatening pose. Standing five metres high, it is the largest monument in the city. It was hidden during the Hungarian occupation but regained its place in 1944.

Behind the monument stands the **Town Hall** (*Gradska kuća*), a neo-baroque edifice designed by well-known architect Djerdj Molnar, in 1895. Its most beautiful features are the 16 allegorical sculptures

and the high bell tower with the popular bell called "Matilda", once used to raise the alarm in case of fire.

Facing the Town Hall stands the Catholic parish church of the Name of Mary which, from its size and appearance became known as the **"Cathedral"**, although the seat of the Bishop is actually in Subotica. The old 18th c. church that stood here was quite large but unattractive and was therefore replaced with the present-day edifice. It was finished in the same year as the Town Hall by the same architect but in a completely different style, more appropriate for a Catholic church. It is an imposing neo-gothic building with a 76 meter high bell tower and a clock that can be seen for miles around. The steep multicolored roof is covered in famous *Zsolnai* ceramics. Inside there are three altars and an organ; especially striking are the stained-glass windows created by Czech and Hungarian masters. To the left of the entrance is the plaque commemorat-

ing the architect, Djerdj Molnar, who left here one of his best works.

On the north side of the square there are three significant buildings: the two-storied building on the left was once the **Hotel "Majer"**, next to it stands the **Novi Sad Savings Bank**. Across the small Njegoševa Street stands the **"Iron Man" Building** which takes its name from the figure of a knight standing on its roof. The building dates from 1909, while the knight is much older and was retained from the building that previously stood here.

On the south side stretches the long green-yellow façade of the **Hotel "Vojvodina"** previously known as "Empress Elisabeth". Modena Street (named after the town's twin city in Italy) with its popular row of cafés was set out between the two world wars. Opposite the hotel is the long red **Tanurdžić Palace**, the ambitiously envisioned modernistic edifice of architect Djordje Tabaković from 1933.

Immediately to the left of the "Cathedral" entrance is one of the most charming spots in the town. Standing on the place of an ancient Catholic graveyard and enclosed by the

Hotel "Vojvodina" previously known as "The Empress Elisabeth"

buildings once belonging to this community, this small courtyard is unsurprisingly called the Catholic Churchyard (*Katolička porta*). On the north side of this quiet

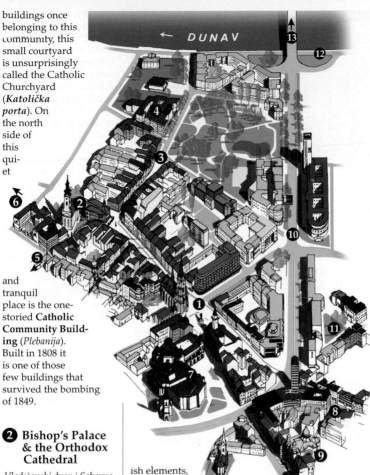

and tranquil place is the one-storied **Catholic Community Building** (*Plebanija*). Built in 1808 it is one of those few buildings that survived the bombing of 1849.

❷ Bishop's Palace & the Orthodox Cathedral

Vladičanski dvor i Saborna crkva

The palace of the Orthodox Bishop of Bačka is found where Zmaj Jovina Street splits into two. Behind the palace stands the Orthodox Cathedral with which it shares a courtyard. There was originally a small palace next to this cathedral, and the architect Vladimir Nikolić made the best of the location when building the new palace, which is now one of the city's notable landmarks. Erected in 1901 it is designed in an eclectic mix of styles among which the most obvious are the romanesque and the pseudo-Moorish elements, immensely popular at the time. Especially attractive is the polychrome red and orange façade with its small garden in front filled with flowers.

In front of the palace is the **Monument to Jovan Jovanović "Zmaj"** (1833-1904), physician, humanist and one of the most popular Serb poets. This prolific writer is best known among kids for his children's songs and magazines. He earned his nickname "Dragon" after a Novi Sad satirical magazine of the same name that he edited for a number of years.

The street bearing his name has always been what it remains today: a lively artery, commercial center of the town and a promenade, a place to see and to be seen. The story goes that if you want to meet someone in Novi Sad just sit back in one of the cafés and wait until he strolls past.

The **Serb Orthodox Cathedral** lies at the very beginning of Pašićeva Street. The old 18th c. church was almost totally destroyed in the bombing of 1849 and a renovation had to be undertaken almost from the foundations. It was built from 1860 to 1880,

Bishop's Court and the Orthodox Cathedral

while the belfry and some other details were completed only at the beginning of the 20th c. The decoration of the interior was entrusted to the most prominent Serb academic painters of the time: Paja Jovanović painted the pictures on the iconostasis and contributed sketches for the stained-glass windows while Stevan Aleksić produced the frescoes. In the churchyard there is the old **Oath-Cross** made of red stone, which until 1945 stood in front of the Bishop's palace. Dating from the second half of the 18th century, it was the first public monument in Novi Sad.

In the same block of houses, behind the Bishop's palace, is the **"Jovan Jovanović Zmaj" High School** (*Gimnazija*). Founded in 1810 it was the second Serb high school in the Austrian-Hungarian Empire, the first being the one in Sremski Karlovci. The old building was declared unsuitable for use by the Hungarian authorities that wanted to close down this important Serb institution. Fund-raising achieved little and just as the high school seemed doomed it was saved by a large donation from Baron Miloš Bajić.

The neo-renaissance edifice was constructed in 1900, again following the plans of Vladimir Nikolić. The present-day building stands on the site of the birth-place of Jovanović Zmaj, which influenced the naming of the high school.

❸ Dunavska Street

This commercial street starts from the very heart of the city and runs to the shore of the Danube. When it was first laid out it was much shorter because the Danube and the pools of water around it stood closer to the city. Since it was the only street that stood amidst these marshes, all the goods brought by the Danube had to pass through this street - a fact that determined its fate. Nowadays it is lined with shops, many of them still run by the descendants of the original owners.

At the beginning of the street, the right hand corner is occupied by the house known as **"At the White Lion's"**. With a ground floor dateing from

1720, it is considered to be the oldest house in the town. On the left corner stands the **City Library**. It was here that Emanuilo Janković, the first Serb to hold a doctorate in philosophy, opened the first Serb printing house in the town, in 1790.

The **Collection of Foreign Art** (*Dunavska 29; tel. 021/451-239; open 9a.m.-4p.m., closed on Mondays*) is located in a mansion which dates from 1903 designed by local architect Franz Voruda. The main part of the collection was donated to Matica srpska by zealous collector Dr Branko Ilić. It consists of artworks by European painters from the Renaissance to the 20th c., as well as containing period furniture and other household objects from Germany, Austria and Turkey (18th – 19th c.). The most valuable exhibits are Rembrandt's "Portrait of the father" and Rubens' "Seneca".

Danube Park is certainly the most beautiful commons in the town. The old swampy ground was cultivated into a neatly-arranged park and opened in 1895.

Foreign art collection in Dunavska St.

A favorite recreational area for the townsfolk, it has been consistently improved. In 1912 the corner to Dunavska St. was adorned by the first sculptural monument in the town – "The Nymph" by Djordje Jovanović. A lake with ducks and swans stands in the middle of the park; in it is a tiny island with a weeping willow

Spring in the Danube Park

that was planted in remembrance of Empress Elisabeth, wife of Franz Joseph, who was shot in 1898 in Geneva by an anarchist. Nearby is an unusual sculpture of a Russian hermit Sergius of Radonezh, a gift from the city of Moscow.

❹ Museum of Vojvodina

Muzej Vojvodine

Dunavska 35-37,
tel. 021/420-566,

Facing the Danube Park stands the long façade of a building erected in 1909 as a district court. The Museum of Vojvodina, now housed there, evolved from the Museum of Matica Srpska founded in 1847. After WWII it became an independent institution and in 1966 it moved to its present location.

The Museum traces the cultures of the region of Vojvodina and illustrates its history from the Paleolithic age to the 20th century. It is divided into two parts: the one at No. 35 covers the archeology, ethnology and medieval history while the other (at No. 37) deals with the more recent history.

The archeological collection is well known for its items from the archeological site of Gomoglava, antique frescoes from the necropolis in Beška and late Roman ceremonial helmets. *Open workdays 9a.m.-4p.m., Sat & Sun only for the prearranged groups*

❺ St Nicholas Church

Nikolajevska crkva

This, the oldest church in the town, is located in the churchyard of the same name (Nikolajevska porta) in the old Serbian quarter. The church is mentioned as early as 1730 when the wealthy merchant Nedeljko Bogdanović renovated it. The services were held in Serb and in Greek, the language of many of the tradesmen. Severely damaged in the 1849 bombardment, it was rebuilt thanks to the donations of Jovan Trandafil and his wife Marija, who was later to become the biggest Serb benefactress. Both were buried in the church. The church is of small proportions and has onion-shaped cupola. Inside there is a valuable iconostasis by Pavle Simić. On one of the gravestones built into the outer church walls the name of Novi Sad receives its earliest recorded mention. It is interesting to note that the sons of Albert and Mileva Einstein were baptized in this church.

At the end of Nikole Pašića St. is the building of **"Matica Srpska"** society. This edifice owes its existence to yet another donation by Marija Trandafil and was built in 1912 to house the Institute for the Orthodox orphans. Curiously, it was designed by archi-

---

Mileva Marić-Einstein

Mileva Marić (1875-1948) and Albert Einstein met in 1897 during their studies in physics at Zurich university. The quiet but talented girl who got all the best marks, and her curious curly haired boyfriend were already collaborating on projects before they were married in 1902. Together they worked on research in a totally new field of physics that was to become the world famous theory of relativity. She gave her husband strong, vital support in a time when women were regarded mothers not scientists. The couple visited Mileva's family in Novi Sad twice, the first time being in 1905 just before Einstein first made his theories public. A number of his biographers insist that a great part of its formulation was the work of Mileva, a story further supported by a number of facts such as passages from his letters mentioning „our work" and the giving of all the money from his Nobel prize award to Mileva. Mileva and Albert had three children but divorced in 1918. Her life and an intriguing role in Einstein's scientific work were the inspiration for many books, dramas and films.

tect Momčilo Tapavica, the first Serb to take part in an Olympics, back in 1896. "Matica Srpska" is the oldest cultural institution of the Serbs. It was founded in 1826 in Pest (today Budapest) with the aim of developing and nourishing Serb culture in

Serb National Theatre

the Habsburg Empire. In time it grew into a huge cultural center initiating the founding of almost all the cultural institutions in Vojvodina. It moved to Novi Sad in 1864, meeting with great approval from the local Serbs. In front of the building stand the busts of some of the leading personages in its long history.

❻ Almaš Church
Almaška crkva

The Almaš quarter (Almaški kraj) is a picturesque part of the old town stretching to the east of the center. It got its name from the Serb village of Almaš that used to lie to the north of the town and which was resettled here in the first half of the 18th c. The agrarian population kept their ways for a long time, which can be seen from the style of small houses lining the narrow winding streets that had to avoid the swampy ground. In the middle

of the quarter stands the parish church. Built between 1797 and 1808 in a mix of empire style and early classicism, it is the largest of the four old Serb orthodox churches in the town. Its high tower is recognizable for its uncharacteristic mound-shaped roof. The tall nave preserves the iconostasis painted by distinguished artists Aksentije Marković and Arsa Teodorović and the skillfully carved seats and thrones.

❼ Serb National Theatre
Srpsko narodno pozorište (SNP)

The Serb National Theatre was founded in 1861 and was the first Serb theatre to have a permanent ensemble. Its opera section was founded in 1920 and ballet in 1950. In 1981 it moved into the innovative modernistic building with three stages, that dominates the recently developed Theatre Square. In front of the Theatre stands the elongated **Statue of Jovan Sterija-Popović**, a 19th c. dramatist after whom is named "Sterijino pozorje" the best known drama festival in

the country that takes place here every year during the last week of April and the first week of May.

Behind this edifice stands the Orthodox **Church of the Holy Ascension** (*Uspenska crkva*) from 1731 with an elegant baroque belfry. It was formerly surrounded by a large cemetery on which site the present day theatre building was constructed.

❽ Newlyweds Square
Trg mladenaca

The square got its unusual name from the Registry Office that is located there, and where all couples that want to solemnize their marriage must come. In its center is a nicely arranged area with a symbolic arch; it is customary for the newlyweds to take their wedding photos here. Facing the gate stands the old **Post Office** building, originally Hotel "Central". The most striking edifice in the square is the large **Adamović Palace**. It has a long indented façade, many terraces of various sizes and a high roof with intriguing chimneys. It was built in 1911 for Stevan Adamović, a rich industrialist and

Newlyweds' Arch

Entrance to the Novi Sad Synagogue

9 The Synagogue
Sinagoga

The Jewish community erected this large temple as the fifth one on this site. Two of the buildings flanking it on either side housed the Jewish Community center and the Jewish School. The whole complex was created in 1909 by Lipot Bauman in the recognizable Hungarian variant of Art Noveau style particularly noteworthy for the skilled use of bricks for decoration. Following the Second World War almost all the Jews that survived the Holocaust left for Israel. Because of the small number of worshippers, the Synagogue was given to the municipality in 1991 and is now used as a concert hall for classical and jazz performances.

10 Mihailo Pupin Boulevard

This 777 m long boulevard, starting from the bridge over the Danube and passing through the center, was laid out in the 1920's, as the first of the grand traffic arteries of the town. To construct it a lot of old buildings had to be demolished and at its lower end, around the intersection with Kralja Aleksandra, it still has a somewhat unfinished look.

At the beginning is the **Main Post Office**, the work of renowned modernistic architect Dragiša Brašovan. It is the last-built of his three great architectural masterpieces in this street. In front of the underground passage facing the Post Office building are two unusual monuments, reminders of the old Armenian population in the town. The older one is the **Tombstone of the Čenazi Family** (1790), a remnant of the old cemetery that stood by the Armenian church prior to the construction of the boulevard. Constructed of red marble, the tombstone is characterized by skulls holding a block with four hearts merging together. Opposite, stands the **Monument to Serb-Armenian Friendship**, carved from a block of volcanic stone

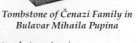

Tombstone of Čenazi Family in Bulavar Mihaila Pupina

and donated to Novi Sad in gratitude for the help provided after the 1989 earthquake which shook Armenia.

In the middle of the boulevard is the magnificent **"Banovina"** building, another work by Brašovan. It was built between 1935-40 to house the administration of the regional government headed by the governor or *ban*, hence the name. Today it is the seat of the executive council of the Autonomous Province of Vojvodina, the highest authority in the province. The long building covered in shining white marble dazzles, while its tranquil rhythm of windows leads to a contrasting 42 m-high square tower. To the back of it stands the smaller edifice of an unusual shape intended for the governor's office. The larger building was bombed in 1999 but was soon repaired.

Two streets down, on the right-hand side is the red and white building of the **Workers Centre** (*Radnički dom*) again the work of Brašovan. It was built in 1931 and was the last building before the riverfront. The sculpture of a worker is by Toma Rosandić.

11 Galleries Square
Trg galerija

Just off the Mihailo Pupin Boulevard, this small hidden square was formed by the construction of the building

Mihailo (Michael Idvorsky) Pupin (Idvor 1854 – New York 1935) was born to illiterate parents in a small Banat village. Although in his childhood he spent as much time herding sheep as he did in school, his gift for science was noticed and he was sent away to continue his education. As an ardent Slavophile he had problems with the Austrian authorities in both Pančevo and Prague high schools. Outraged, he decided to try his luck across the ocean. Pupin arrived in the US in 1874 on an immigrant boat with just a few dollars in his pocket and spent the next five years as a labourer. He managed to enrol in Columbia University and soon proved to be one of the best and most talented students. He got his PhD in Berlin and became a professor of electro mechanics at Columbia. His most important scientific achievements are the invention of the "Pupin coil" which enabled long distance telephony and of short exposure X-ray photographs that could be safely used in medicine. During WWI he acted as the Serbian Consul General. His great influence on the American public and politics enabled him to help explain the positions of Serbia and Yugoslavia at the Versailles peace conference in 1919. He was a prolific writer popularizing science and in 1924 he got the Pulitzer Prize for his autobiography "From Immigrant to Inventor".

neded to house the Pavle Beljanski collection. Today, in the space of several meters are three superb collections of art.

The Gallery of Matica Srpska

Galerija Matice Srpske, Trg Galerija 1, tel. 021/48-99-000, open 10 a.m. to 6 p.m. on Tue, Wed, Thu & Sat, 12 a.m. to 8 p.m. on Fridays, closed on Sun & Mon;; www.galerijamaticesrpske.org.yu; e-mail: galmats@eunet.yu

The Gallery of Matica Srpska was founded back in 1847 in Pest, as part of the Matica Srpska Museum intended to collect and preserve items important for the history of Serbs. This Museum in Novi Sad opened in 1933 and after WWII the artistic works were singled out to form a separate collection. The Gallery opened to the public in 1958 in the former Commodities Exchange building, which dates from 1926.

The exhibition presents the works of Serb artists from Vojvodina starting from the 16th c. onwards and showing the process of the

"Europeanization" of Serb art. The ground floor contains copies of frescoes from monasteries, such as those of Hristifor Žefarović done in Bođani. On the first floor there are several older icons (17th c.) and a large number of 18th c. works, mostly with religious themes as well as portraits of nobles and citizens. Most notable among these are the baroque icons by Teodor Kračun, a fantastic icon "Neversleeping Eye" by an unknown artist and a self-portrait of Stefan Tenecki. Exhibited on the same floor are woodprints and copperplates from the same period. On the second floor are exhibited works of the 19th and the first half

of the 20th c. There are several large paintings with historic and religious themes, such as the small version of "Dušan's crowning" by Paja Jovanović, "St George" by Uroš Predić, Novak Radonjić's gloomy "Death of Marko Kraljević" and "Montenegrins in battle" by Djura Jakšić. As well as numerous portraits, landscapes and the like, there are also the bizarre self-portraits of Stevan Aleksić and the dreamlike "Allegory on the First and Second Serb Uprisings" by Djordje Krstić as well as several sculptures. The central room of the second floor is dedicated to 20th c. art with works by Sava Šumanović, Milenko Šerban and others.

The Memorial Collection of Pavle Beljanski

Spomen-zbirka Pavla Beljanskog), Trg Galerija 2, 021/528-185; open Wed, Fri and weekends from 10 a.m. to 6 p.m., on Thu from 1 p.m. to 9 p.m., closed on Mondays and Tuesdays; e-mail: pbelj@eunet.yu

In 1957 Pavle Beljanski, lawyer and diplomat but also a keen art collector, donated his collection as a gift to the Serb people. The Gallery bearing his name was opened in 1961 in an interested building by architect Ivo Kurtović.

Mališa Glišić's "Borovi" in the Memorial Collection of Pavle Beljanski

It contains paintings of the most important Serb artists of the 20th c., starting with the first generation of modernists and continuing with the eminent representatives of the interwar and post-WWII scene.

The Memorial Collection of Rajko Mamuzić

Spomen-zbirka Rajka Mamuzića, Vase Stajića 1, tel. 021/520-467, open Wed-Sun

big river is the crucial reason why Novi Sad is located here.

Mihailo Pupin Boulevard will take you to **Varadinska Duga Bridge** ("The Rainbow of Varadin") that leads to the old Lower Town of Petrovaradin. This was where in 1928 the first bridge for cart transportation was built across the Danube. It was named "Prince Tomislav's Bridge", after the middle son

the residents of Novi Sad used to call all bridges in this place, was added the word rainbow to poetically describe its shape. On a small square by the bridge, there is a little sculpture, a monument to a famous violinist, Janika Balaž.

Further down the river (i.e. to the left, observing from the Novi Sad side) there is a so-called **Temporary Bridge**, whose full name explains its purpose

Nightview of the Varadin Rainbow Bridge

9a.m.-5p.m., closed on Mondays and Tuesdays, ticket price 50Din, e-mail: glurm@eunet.yu

Opened in 1974, the Gallery is based on the donation of fine art collector Rajko Mamuzić. The collection consists of works by 35 Yugoslav painters belonging to the first post-WWII generation.

⑫ Banks and Bridges

There is a beautifully arranged strand along the whole northern bank of the Danube and taking a walk there is something you shouldn't miss in Novi Sad, because this

of King Aleksandar Karađorđević. This bridge was destroyed in 1941 during the retreat of Yugoslav Army but the new one was built in the same place five years later by the name of "The Bridge of Marshal Tito". This bridge was then bombed in the 1999 Bombing Campaign, but was quickly rebuilt and reopened in the tempestuous days just before the fall of Milošević's regime. Contrary to earlier examples, no name with an ideological conotation was given, but to the name Varadin Bridge, as

– "Patent bridge for road and railway traffic". This bridge was installed right after the NATO bombing to enable, to some degree, a functioning of the town that lost its entire links to Srem and Belgrade. It is alternately used for road and railway traffic. The Temporary Bridge is next to the remains of former **Žeželj's Bridge**, built in 1961 and named after its constructor. To the joy of Novi Sad residents, it resisted American missiles for a long time during the Bombing Campaign, but was inevitably destroyed.

If you take a walk upstream from Varadinska duga Bridge, you will first come across **Monument "The Family"** by Jovan Soldatović. The monument was erected in the memory of Novi Sad Raid victims in 1942, when from 21st to 23rd of January the Hungarian occupying forces arrested everyone to their dislike in town. Most of the arrestees were brought to this place, killed and thrown under the ice. 1246 people, mostly Jews and Serbs, lost their lives in the Raid.

A little further behind the monument, you can see the pillars of the old railway bridge from 1883, the first permanent bridge on the river. After crossing the bridge, the trains would go through the tunnel in Petrovaradin rock and continue further through Srem. It is interesting to mention that this was the longest lasting of all the Novi Sad bridges, since it was demolished only in 1941, when it celebrated 58 years of its existence.

Yet further down the riverbank is the **Štrand Beach**, the most famous swimming place of Novi Sad. When you pass Štrand, you come to the **Liberty Bridge** (*Most Slobode*), just recently renewed after having been lying in impressive ruins since 1999. This elegant, 1321-metre-long technical construction was first built in 1981, by the designs of an engineer Nikola Hajdin.

Petrovaradin Fortress, nicknamed the "Gibraltar on the Danube"

⑬ Petrovaradin

If it wasn't for the Danube separating it from the rest of Novi Sad, Petrovaradin, now a mere district of the town, would be almost totally merged into it. The river and the mighty fortress still fill Petrovaradin with a notion of being different from its younger sibling across the river, making it more so proud of its history. The key to Petrovaradin's existence is a high rock above the Danube; from it one could easily control the river traffic and thus it was inhabited from ancient times. During Roman rule a settlement and fort named *Cusum* stood here safeguarding the frontier. In the 11th and 12th centuries, the castle named Petrikon (*petros* in Greek means "rock") stood on the high rock above the Danube while the Byzantine Empire fought with the Hungarian Kingdom for the dominance of the

Clock Tower of Petrovaradin Fortress, a symbol of Novi Sad

region. The Hungarians prevailed and in 1237 King Bela IV donated the castle and the monastery beneath it to the Cistercian monastic order. The Hungarians called the castle *Petervarad* or "Peter's castle" which is also the origin of the Serbian name. In 1526 about 1000 Hungarian and Serbian defenders, although greatly outnumbered, resisted the army of Suleyman the Magnificent until they all met their end. In Turkish days Petrovaradin was too far from their borders to signify more than a port on the Danube. A change of fortunes came with the collapse of the Turkish Empire on the Pannonian plain. In 1688 the Austrians took the small fort and defended it from Turkish attack two years later. The new masters realized the potential of the position right away and decided to make it the strongest point of defense against the Turks. Large scale work started right away, even

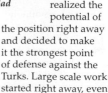

before the peace treaty was signed, and lasted for almost the whole century turning Petrovaradin into the greatest fortification on the whole of the river, earning it the nickname "Gibraltar on the Danube". In the next war with Turks, Eugene of Savoy won a

Beogradska (Belgrade) Street leading from what used to be the Novi Sad gate (at the place now occupied by the bridge) to the Belgrade gate on the other side of the Lower Town. The second house on the right, with the two relief lions protecting the gate, used to

House of Graf Josip Jelačić (1801-1859), Austrian field marshal, later ban (governor) of Croatia and Croatian national hero. By a twist of fate, Jelačić led the Serbian army in an unsuccessful attempt to seize Petrovaradin that was followed by the catastrophe of 1849. The house was built in 1745 and has an interesting second floor with a high gable.

Belgrade Gate in Petrovaradin's Lower Town

crucial victory here in 1716. During the 18th century, the fort and the town of Petrovaradin acquired their present day appearance. The army was stationed in the barracks and the officers lived in the small Lower Town. In the 19th c, with the disappearance of the Turkish danger, the town spread out of its walls to the south.

Lower Town
Podgradje

Surrounded by the strong battlements and trenches that were filled with water, the Lower Town used to be the administrative center of the fort. With just five streets and a square it is squeezed between the fort's mighty bastions and filled with buildings of historic and artistic value, presenting a unique urban whole.

Coming from the Varadinska duga ("Petrovaradin Rainbow"), the bridge from Novi Sad center, you enter the long

be the **Seat of the Šajkaš Battalion**. *Šajkaši* were sailors who mastered the Danube, maneuvering their light-weight ships against the Turks and their fleets. In a first-floor niche stands an interesting image: atop a globe the Virgin Mary holds the infant Jesus, who with a lance, pierces the snake wrapped around the globe. This allegorical group symbolizes the Christian fight against the Turkish danger, represented as a snake.

On the first corner to the right stands a white house with green ornaments around the openings and a rounded bow window on the corner. Originally the seat of the **Town Magistracy**, during the interwar period it housed the archive of Vojvodina while today it is an ordinary residential building.

On the next corner stands the **Birth**

Passing several more military edifices we reach the **Belgrade Gate** that gave the street its name. This fine monument of the baroque period was constructed in 1745; it is 20 m long and has a central carriage way and two smaller pedestrian passage-ways on the sides. The dungeons of the gate and the neighboring bastions represented the heart of a notorious prison in which many a famous person spent time, amongst them Ljuben Karavelov, a Bulgarian poet and patriot and young Josip Broz, future Marshal Tito, imprisoned for communist agitation during the First World War.

Around the corner in Štrosmajerova Street stands the **Jesuit**

Stairway leading to the Upper Town

Monastery of St George
(*Samostan Svetog Jurja*). Its church stands out as the best baroque monument in both Petrovaradin and the whole of Novi Sad. The typically baroque façade is decorated with three doors and statues of St Francis Xavier, the Virgin with Christ and St John of Nepomuk. Inside, the main and four side altars are all richly decorated. Josip Juraj Štrosmajer, future bishop and one of the promoters of the Yugoslav ideology served here for two years in his youth.

Upper Town
Gornji grad

The Upper Town of the fortress was constructed between 1694 and 1780. It spreads over 112 acres, has three large barracks and 16 km of underground passages. It was used for military purposes until 1951 when it was opened to public. Today the former barracks host the Municipal museum, a hotel, ateliers of Novi Sad artists and a dormitory of the fine arts academy. Every summer the fortress, and its moats and bastions host the "Exit" music festival.

There are four ways to reach the fortress: following a steep path from the side of Sremska Kamenica, by car from

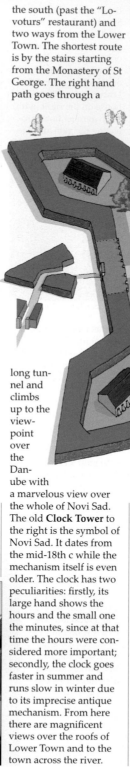

the south (past the "Lovoturs" restaurant) and two ways from the Lower Town. The shortest route is by the stairs starting from the Monastery of St George. The right hand path goes through a long tunnel and climbs up to the viewpoint over the Danube with a marvelous view over the whole of Novi Sad. The old **Clock Tower** to the right is the symbol of Novi Sad. It dates from the mid-18th c while the mechanism itself is even older. The clock has two peculiarities: firstly, its large hand shows the hours and the small one the minutes, since at that time the hours were considered more important; secondly, the clock goes faster in summer and runs slow in winter due to its imprecise antique mechanism. From here there are magnificent views over the roofs of Lower Town and to the town across the river.

Behind the Clock tower is the **Officers Pavilion** (*Oficirski paviljon*) with arched windows and a pleasant terrace. Now a restaurant, it has hosted eminent visiting personalities. In 1813/14 the leader of the suppressed Serb uprising, Djordje Petrović - Karadjordje and several Serb leaders lived here under the house-arrest.

Nearby is the **Long Barracks** (*Duga kasarna*), running parallel with the river for about 200 meters. The ateliers and galleries of local artists are found here. A somewhat longer

Štrosmajerova Street in Petrovaradin's Lower Town

Suburbium

path up to the fortress is the one continuing past the Monastery and winding three times until it reaches the most beautiful gate of the fortress – **Leopold's Gate** (*Leopoldova kapija*), named after the emperor who started its construction. Passing through it will lead you to the high plateau where the main buildings and former barracks, are found.

To the south of the main plateau stretches the larger part of the fortress with many more interesting gates, bastions, passages, and more artists' ateliers.

Municipal Museum of Novi Sad

Muzej grada Novog Sada, Petrovaradinska tvrdjava 4, tel. 021/433-145, 433-613; open every day 9 a.m. – 5 p.m.; entrance 70 din; muzgns@eunet.yu

The central edifice of the Fortress's upper plateau is the Mamula or Gunners' Barracks (*Topovnjača*), home to the Municipal museum. The museum displays archeological material from the vicinity of the town from the prehistoric period to present day, following the develop-

ment of both Petrovaradin and Novi Sad. Its prime exhibits are a large Celtic ship pulled from the bottom of the Danube and interesting artefacts from the medieval Avar necropolis in Čelarevo with Judaistic symbols. A collection of period furniture, icons, portraits and old instruments represent life in the two cities in the 18th and 19th centuries. By prior arrangement here you can tour the **underground passages** which are open every day (except Mondays) from 10 a.m. to 5 p.m.

⑮ Kovilj

🚌 18 km - Novi Sad

To reach this village from Novi Sad, head for the Belgrade motorway and some 10 km further get off the road. Kovilj is a large village with two baroque churches and many chimneys adorned with stork nests. Behind the village, on its southern outskirts, is the monastery of the same name. The main street, although it makes several turns, will unmistakably lead you to it.

The legend has it that this monastery was built in a place where St Sava reconciled his brother, King Stefan the First-Crowned, with the Hungarian King Andrew II, whom he also healed on the occasion and in that way got the permission to found the monastery. The first reliable data of an orthodox monastery at this territory come not sooner than 1651, but this oldest church had been destroyed by the Turks no less than four times in the war years at the end of the 17th century. The new church, still in existence today, was built in 1741. The contract between the abbot and the master builders clearly stated that the new church of Kovilj should be designed by the model of Manasija Monastery in so-called Serbia proper. The church is nevertheless far from identical to Manasija, since the builders also introduced some baroque decorative details. It has three naves and two cupolas above the central nave. The façade is in stone and decorated with blind arcades. The old church,

whose former location is marked by a cross to the right of the church, and the interior of the new church perished in fire set by the Hungarians during the civil war of 1848. The renovated church got the new iconostasis in 1870-90, a work of Aksentije Marodić, under the heavy influence of Italian Renaissance. Some valuable 18th century icons are also on display here. The monastery is currently undergoing a detailed reconstruction, with new dwellings and a high tower being added.

At the end of the 18th century, the learned Jovan Rajić, the writer of the first history of the Serbs in Serbian language (1794), resided here as an abbot. A small **Memorial Museum** dedicated in his memory is to be found within the dwellings.

By the monastery, there is a **Chapel** dedicated to St Petka. There is an old tree in the chapel that grew in its rear side, making it a rather picturesque sight.

The Danube River flows nearby, behind the wetlands called **Koviljski rit** covering over

St Petka's Chapel next to the Kovilj Monastery

5000 acres of land. It is protected by the state as a natural reserve. If you continue further, when you pass the monastery and take the second turn right, the road will lead you to the closest marsh called Arkanj. At the end of the road, there is an interesting *čarda* inn named **"At the End of the World"** (*"Na kraj sveta"*, tel. 064/12-68-280) covered in comic murals. Without any running water, electricity or other modern comforts, this famed inn offers excellent fish soup and live gypsy music every evening, that will take you back to long forgotten times. You can rent boats in this inn and further explore the marsh.

Comical murals of the "At the End of the World" čarda-inn

⑯ Sremska Kamenica

🚌 8 km - Novi Sad

In Roman times a fortified military camp called *Cusum* was sited on the grounds between Sremska Kamenica and Petrovaradin and thus it is believed that a settlement also existed here in that period. In early medieval times the Slavs that settled here named it after the quarry (*kamen* meaning stone) that still exists a bit further to the south on the slopes of Fruška Gora; the name was first mentioned in 1237 when the village was granted to the Cistercian abbey in Petrovaradin. Its flowering was interrupted by the Turkish onslaught in 1526 when Kamenica was burnt down and looted. Liberated by the Austrian army in 1687, it developed as part of the Karlovci feudal estate whose best-known lords were the Marcibanji family. Since 1957 it is administratively part of Novi Sad. Today it is best known for the Institute for Cardiovascular diseases and the School of the Ministry of the Interior.

Jovan Jovanović Zmaj Museum (*Trg Jovana Jovanovića Zmaja no. 1, tel. 021/462-810, open every day from 9 a.m. to 5 p.m.*) is in the first street to the right after passing his monument in the main square. It is situated in the house in which Zmaj, one of the greatest 19th c. Serb poets spent his last years. The property had been purchased by his brother and Zmaj then built this modest

rural house and used it as a lodge where he would spent his days of rest. On the centenary of his birth in 1933 it was converted into a museum presenting the poet's life and work. In the courtyard stands the monument "Zmaj and a Child" the work of sculptor Ivan Meštrović.

In the main square is the **Catholic Church** dating from 1746. In its chapel are the graves of the counts Karačonji.

The most interesting of the town's monuments is the **Serbian Orthodox Church**, situated in the lower part of the steep Karadjordjeva St, which starts on the left of the Catholic church. The church was constructed between 1737-44. Originally designed in the Serbian medieval

Orthodox Church in Sremska Kamenica

The "Five Heads" monument in Ribnjak Park, Sremska Kamenica

style, the Habsburg-prescribed baroque style was incorporated by adding the bell tower and pointed cupolas. The iconostasis was created by several artists throughout the 18th c. but the most valuable is

the upper level of icons (Christ's life) painted by Teodor Kračun. The icon of Archangel Michael is famous because the conspirators that killed prince Mihailo of Serbia took their oath by its side. The gilded cross (from 1854) is a gift from Russian Tsar Nikolay I.

A street running parallel with the Danube will lead you east to the **Kamenica Palace**. It was started by count Livius Marcibanji in 1790 and finished by his son-in-law Guido Karačonji. This classical edifice was their summer residence standing at the beginning of a pleasant English-style park lying alongside the Danube. It had an artificial pond that gave it the name Ribnjak ("Fishpond"). Nowadays somewhat neglected, it still has many old trees of rare and exotic species. From the surviving monuments the most striking is the one popularly called "The Five Heads" (*Pet glava*), representing the busts of heroes from classical antiquity on columns, today in a pitiful state.

⑰ Sremski Karlovci

🏠 8.800

ℹ️ Trg Branka Radičevića 7
21205 Sremski Karlovci
021/882-127

🚌 10 km - Novi Sad

For centuries Sremski Karlovci was one of the largest and most important Serbian towns, especially from 1761 to 1920, when it was the seat of the Karlovci Metropolis, an institution that was the spiritual centre of the orthodox Serbs within the Habsburg Empire. Today, it is a quiet small town not far from Novi Sad that proudly bares the heavy burden of its significant history. Karlovci was first mentioned in 1308 as *Castrum Caron*, a rather small stronghold on a hill north from the current city centre. The settlement grew with the arrival of Serbian refugees that enjoyed the surroundings of hilly Fruška Gora and gladly inhabited this area. In the 16th century, Karlovci was a prosperous town that unlike most of the Ottoman towns had a majority of Serb Orthodox population. The place was already known for its excellent wines with which it paid most of its taxes to the Sultan. The Great Viennese War that raged for the full 16 years from Vienna to

Skopje was ended here in 1699 when the famous Carlowitz peace treaty was signed by Austria, Venice and Poland on one side and Turkey on the other. It transformed the political map of Europe, and moved the borderline between the Christian and Islamic

Belfries of Sremski Karlovci

world from the suburbs of Vienna to the edge of Sremski Karlovci district. During this war, the Serb patriarch Arsenije III Čarnojević and the mass of Serbs fled to Habsburg Empire after its Emperor granted privileges for them and their church. Krušedol Monastery was appointed as the seat of the church under the rule of Habsburg Emperor but in the following war with the Turks, this monastery was burnt down and the seat of the Archbishop's residence was in 1716 moved to Sremski Karlovci. Around the Archbishop's court soon grew a circle of baroque

painters and men-of-letters, who were needed for the reconstruction of the town as well as cultural restoration of entire Serb nation. To name just one example, it was here that the first theatre performance of modern times was staged in 1733. Under the Archbishop's patronage, many important schools were established here during the 18th century. In 1791 permission was given to open the first Serb High School and in 1794 the Orthodox Theological Seminary, the second oldest school of that kind after the one in Kiev. The Serbs counted not only on their privileges for most of things they have been granted, but also on famed Karlovci wines that were unofficially used to "grease the palms" during every negotiation. In the turmoil of the revolutionary 1848, the representatives of all Serbs living in Habsburg Empire met here and pronounced the unification of Srem, Banat, Bačka and Baranja regions into a province with a Serb Duke as a ruler, named *Srpska Vojvodina* (Serbian Dukedome), a dream long dreamed by the Serbs at this territory. At the end of the 19th century, the vineyards of Karlovci were ruined by the phylloxera epidemic outbreak, which had a devastating

The "Four Lions" Drinking Well

effect on the local economy that mostly depended on wine production. The epidemic also meant a certain stagnation of Sremski Karlovci and loss of primacy in comparison to the nearby Novi Sad. After the First World War ended, the Serbian church united and moved the seat of the Patriarch to the capital city of Belgrade, which left Karlovci without any trump card. Karlovci is still remembered in the official title of the head of Serbian Orthodox church "The Archbishop of Peć, the Metropolitan of Belgrade and Karlovci, the Serbian Patriarch, etc". In the decades to follow the epidemic, the gradual recovery of vineyards never managed to increase the production to its previous level when the whole town lived off of it. However, the name of Karlovci was always identified with good wines, which at all times gave hope for the wine business to revive again. That is what happens today in Karlovci: after years and years of negligence, many residents of Karlovci have rediscovered the profession of their ancestors, creating new flavours in wine based on the confidence built throughout the centuries.

The center of Sremski Karlovci is **Trg Branka Radičevića Square** which is close to the Belgrade-Novi Sad motorway. Where this motorway is today the Danube used to be. This big river now flows some 300 m further, but its previous course was just by the square enabling the residents of Karlovci good conections to the world. The square was named after the most popular Serbian romanticist poet Branko Radičević who spent the schooldays of his short life here. **"Four Lions" Fountain** was built in 1799 to mark the completion of the first town waterworks. It was designed by the Italian architect Aprili, made of red marble and has four lion heads with pipes that spray water. The legend has it that if you drink water from this fountain, you will definitely return to Karlovci.

The **Orthodox Cathedral** (*Saborna crkva*) was built in 1762 in the place of the old wooden church used since the 16th century. The spacious church with two bell-towers was the greatest Serb church of its time and has served as a model for designing all other Serb churches throughout the Empire. The façade was somewhat modified with neo-classicist features by the architect Vladimir Nikolić in 1909/10. Cathedral's magnificent iconostasis was painted right after the construction by the leading Serb artists of the period, Teodor Kračun and Jakov Orfelin. The large oil paintings on the sidewalls are the work of Paja Jovanović, the most prominent Serb academic painter from the end of the 19th century. The church houses two significant relics: the miraculous icon of the Virgin, the work of a Russian painter from the 14th century, and the coffin with a part of the body of Archbishop Arsenije I (13th c.), originating from the Srem district, who was the first successor to Saint Sava. Almost all the heads of the Serb Orthodox Church that resided in Karlovci were buried in the church crypt.

Next to the cathedral is the **Patriarch's Palace** (*Patrijaršijski dvor*), built in 1895 in place of the old residence. As many construction enterprises of the time, the building of the Court was an order from the ambitious Patriarch Georgije Branković. The project was executed by his favourite architect Vladimir Nikolić in his eclectic architectural style that transformed the appearance of Sremski Karlovci. On the first floor of this edifice, you can find a

Trg Branka Radičevića

Edifice of the famed Sremski Karlovci High School

Chapel of St Demetrios painted by Uroš Predić, another superb painter of his day (the chapel can be seen from the rear end of the building). The valuable library and the treasury in the palace were looted in the WWII by the Croatian Nazi occupiers, and what was later found is kept today at the Museum of Serbian Orthodox Church in Belgrade. Today this beautiful palace is the residence of the Orthodox Bishop of Srem.

Northern side of the square is closed by the building of the **Church & National Funds** (*Crkveno-narodni fondovi*) from 1901, another work of the architect Vladimir Nikolić. The Church & National Funds was the institution that united the administrative work of all Serbian endowments in the Austro-Hungarian Empire. Today this building houses the Theological Seminary continuing traditions of the one established in 1794.

On the other side of the Cathedral is the **Catholic Church of Holy Trinity**. It was built in 1735 in the place where the medieval Benedictine abbey stood. The most distinctive feature is the richly carved baroque door.

The building of the famed **Sremski Karlovci High School** is on the south side of the square. The house in which the High School was originally opened in 1792 was replaced a hundred years later (1891) with the new edifice. In decorating the façade, the Hungarian architect Djula Partoš was inspired by the Serbian medieval heritage. The High School also has an exquisite library with many manuscripts and rare books in Serbian. In front of the building, there is a bust of Patriarch German Anđelić who initiated the building of this edifice, and of Branko Radičević, the most famous pupil of the School.

To the right of the High School is the classicist construction of the **Town Magistracy** dating from 1808. The Serb Dukedom was proclaimed from its balcony on the 13th of May 1848. Today it houses the town archives.

Patirjarha Rajačića Street will take you to the **Town Museum** (at number 16, *tel. 021/881637, open every day 9 a.m.-4 p.m.*). The Museum is based in the former house of Baron Rajačić from 1848. The permanent exhibition in the Museum shows the archeological collection (basement), exhibition dedicated to the High School (first floor), ethnographic collection and the collection of the paintings of famous excentric artist Milić of Mačva (second floor).

Further up the street, there is the so-called **Upper Church**. Precursor to this temple was a small orthodox monastery, given as an appendage to the famous Hilandar, which used to be there since 16th century. This church was built in 1746 in a traditional style. You enter the churchyard through the big baroque gate. The iconostasis is the work of Dimitrije Bačević from the second half of the 18th century. Many prominent citizens of Karlovci were buried here, including the patriarchs Georgije Branković and Lukijan Bogdanović.

The Mitropolita Stratimirovića Street leads to the eastern part of the town and the **Lower Church**. It was built in 1719 in place of an old temple from the 16th century. The iconostasis is the work of a not so well known painter Dimitrije Bratoglić. The ruler of Montenegro Petar I Petrović Njegoš, later to be known as St Peter of Cetinje, was consecrated to the Archbishop here in 1784. There is an ancient **plane-tree** in the church courtyard that is under

Church & National Funds building, today the Theological Seminary

the protection of state. The **House of Dimitrije Anastasijević Sabov** is across the road. He was one of the wealthiest merchants of Karlovci in the 18th century and without his financing the Karlovci Grammar School would not have been founded. His house from 1790 is the most beautiful rococo edifice in town. Especially striking are the wrought iron window bars of on the ground floor windows. At **number 76** of this street, there is a small house believed to be the home of Branko Radičević during his student days.

Further down the same street, at number 86 b, there is the **Museum of Beekeeping** (*Muzej pčelarstva, tel. 021/881-071; open workdays 10 a.m.-7 p.m., muzpcela@eunet.yu*). From times immemorial, Karlovci was famous for beekeeping. Already in 1878 beekeeping was upgraded to the scientific level when a department for the study of this ancient vocation was opened at the Theological Seminary. The Museum is maintained by the Živanović family, the descendants of Jovan Živanović, the first professor at this cathedra and the father of modern beekeeping in Serbia, whose heritage makes up the core of the museum collection.

To the south and somewhat further up the hill, is the **Chapel of Peace** (*Kapela mira*). It stands on a hill where 72-day-long negotiations took place in the winter of 1698-99 and where the peace treaty of Carlowitz was signed on the 26th

Wrought-iron bars on the windows of Sabov's House

January 1699. Since there were four parties to the agreement, they could not decide who would have the honor to enter first the log cabin where the negotiations were held, and therefore decided to make four doors that they could enter simultaneously. They also agreed to sit at a round table, for it would make them all equally significant. That is where the practice of conferring at a round table came from and became customary in diplomatic negotiations. A small chapel dedicated to Our Lady of Peace was arranged in the same log cabin by the Franciscans in 1710, as soon as they inhabited the town. The present-day edifice dates from 1808 and with its round shape resembles the celebrated table. It also has four entrances, but the eastern one that was used by the Turkish representatives was immediately bricked in as a symbolical precaution measure against their return. In the chapel yard there is the grave of a Venetian delegate who passed away during the negotiations.

ENVIRONS:

The favourite excursion site of Karlovci has always been **Stražilovo**, 4 km south from the town centre. Branko Radičević also enjoyed the nature here, so the people of Karlovci decided to bury him here and put up a monument in his honour.

The **Church at Tekije** (*Crkva na Tekijiama*) is half way (3km) to Petrovaradin. Tekija is the name for the place where the Muslim dervishes resided; here, they even had a small mosque. After the Turks were banished, the mosque was transformed to suit the needs of the Franciscans. In the memory of the victory over the Turks in 1716, every 5th August a religious procession has been held together by the Catholics, the Orthodox and the Protestants. Upon the initiative of the local abbot Ilija Okrugić the new church was built in a mixture of eastern and western styles and also three altars were placed for all three religions. Above all, at the church domes, there is a half-moon under every cross – a mark that this place of worship was also used by the Muslims.

Monument to Branko Radičević in Stražilovo

18 National Park "Fruška Gora"

i 021/813-531

22 km - Novi Sad

Fruška Gora is a rather low mountain massif standing lonely in the Panonian basin, between the Danube and Sava rivers. It spreads more than 80 km in length, from Vukovar to Belegiš, but its highest peak, Crveni Čot, is only 539 m high asl. Apart from that and the fact that it is studded with smaller and larger settlements, several locations of Fruška Gora conceeal the real wilderness of a thick forest inhabited by deers, roe deers and wild boars. Geological history of the mountain is also vey interesting, for its sediments revealed extremely versatile fossil fauna. The most famous sites, and also the unique ones in Europe, are the Čerević Potok with 164 and the steep cut by Grgeteg with 120 kinds of fosilan remnants found .

Running away from the Turks in the 15th and the 16th centuries, the Serbs moved to the north, choesing Fruška Gora and its surroundings as the most prefered location to settle down, because it reminded them of the land they had left. The orthodox monks who also came here built many monasteries, 16 of which still exist and represent the most treasured cultural and historical attraction of Fruška Gora.

1 Krušedol

The most important of the Fruška Gora monasteries is also the first one we encounter coming from the east. After 5 km on the road from Sremski Karlovci towards Belgrade there is a crossing: turn right onto a road that leads toward the village of Krušedol but before entering the village, take the road to the right that will take you to the monastery.

The monastery of Krušedol was built between 1509-15 by Belgrade metropolitan

His son Djordje was a ruler without a country but had vast estates in Southern Hungary, already settled by the Serbs who recognized him as their leader. The monastery was envisioned as a mausoleum for the Branković family and its founders were buried here. Due to its great fame Krušedol also became the seat of the Srem bishopric. In 1708 it became the seat of the autonomous Metropolis that was the spiritual and national center for the Serbs in the Habsburg Empire. In 1716, angry after the defeat at Petrovaradin, the Turks burned the relics of Bishop Maksim and his mother Angelina, seriously damaging the monastery. After this event, the seat of the metropolis was transferred to Sremski Karlovci. There followed the baroque renewal that gave its present-day appearance. The monastery was plundered by the *Ustaša* (Croatian fascists) in WWII who used it as a prison and torture chamber. Most of the items from the treasury that were saved from destruction were transferred to Belgrade.

Marked pathways for the Fruška Gora Marathon

The mountain was named after the Francs (*Fruzi* in archaic Serbian), who during the reign of Charlemagne expanded their empire all the way to Belgrade.

Maksim Branković (earlier in his secular life Depotes Djordje) and his mother Angelina, wife of the blind Despotes Jovan who was the last ruler of Serbia (1458-59).

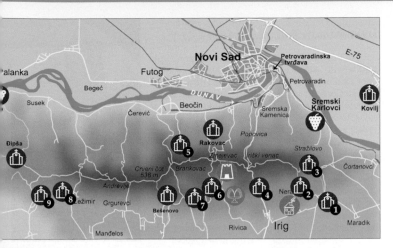

1 Krušedol 4 Novo Hopovo 7 Jazak
2 Grgeteg 5 Beočin 8 Šišatovac
3 Velika Remeta 6 Vrdnik 9 Petkovica

The church of the Annunciation has a trefoil ground plan and a dome that follows the Morava style. However, the details of the outer appearance, such as the enlarged windows with their decoration and a portico above the main entrance, owe much to the baroque renewal. The high bell tower was added in 1726 while the dwellings that close the church from all sides were finished in 1759. On the outer west wall is a depiction of the Last Judgment dating from 1654 with heaven on the left and hell on the right. Inside, the original 16th c. frescoes are preserved only on the columns under the dome and in some fragments visible beneath the newer paintings. On one of the pillars is depicted Maksim, the founder of the monastery. The new paintings were created using the new technique of oil. The earliest in the narthex, dating from around 1750, are by the Ruthenian Jov Vasilijevič

and his assistants. Of particular interest here is the gallery of the Serb medieval rulers, keeping the old traditions of statehood alive. The central space was painted by Stefan Tenecki in 1756. The traditional repertoire is in the new baroque fashion, and even includes two small landscapes beneath the choir windows.

The oldest part of the iconostasis is the upper level of icons representing the Deisis theme. This masterpiece of late Byzantine painting executed with a delicate feeling for modeling and colors, was on the first, 16th c. iconostasis. The carved high crucifix was added in 1653 while the lower line of frescoes is again the work of Jov Vasilijevič,

with the exception of the Royal door, which was created by an artist from the south of the Balkans.

This prominent monastery is a final resting place for many important personages from Serb history. At the left of the entrance stands the tablet with a two-headed eagle and a lion marking the grave of Patriarch Arsenije III Čarnojević (†1706). Immediately after entering the church, to the left is the grave of

View of the frescoes and the magnificent iconostasis of the Krušedol Monastery

King Milan Obrenović (†1901) and on the floor is a plaque covering the grave of Princess Ljubica (†1843), wife of Prince Miloš Obrenović. By the left wall Count Djordje Branković (†1711) and Duke Stevan Šupljikac (†1848) are buried, and by the right wall is the sarcophagus containing the body of Patriarch Arsenije IV (†1748).

Between the monastery and the village stands the Church of the Presentation of Our Lord. It was built in 1512 as a convent by Angelina, mother of Maksim Branković. This simple construction is notable for its frescoes from 1634 and the iconostasis painted by Dimitrije Bačević and Teodor Kračun from 1763.

❷ Grgeteg

From the Krušedol village continue westwards towards Irig and then take the turn leading to Neradin, a picturesque village that retains a lot of old world charm; the monastery lies to the north of the village.

Grgeteg is thought to have been founded by

A djeram well in front of the Grgeteg Monastery

Lord Vuk Grgurević Branković (1459-85), known in epic songs as "Fiery Dragon" Vuk (*Zmaj Ognjeni Vuk*), but its earliest documents date only from the 16th century. It has been destroyed on several occasions, the last time in the Second World War when, amongst other things, it lost its bell tower. The 18th c. church was thoroughly renovated in 1901 by architect Herman Bole during the time of the enlightened Abbot Ilarion Ruvarac, who was the founder of the critical school of Serbian historiography. The most valuable feature of Grgeteg is the iconostasis created by the great academician painter Uroš Predić between 1902-4.

❸ Velika Remeta

To reach this monastery take the same road as for Krušedol but at the first fork keep to the right. After a while there is a sign for a left turn to an unpaved road that descends steeply into a wooded dale wherein the monastery lies.

The monastery was founded in the 13th c. as a catholic convent. It was destroyed in Turkish raids and abandoned, only to be revived in the 16th c. by the Orthodox monks who arrived from the south. Little remains of the 16th c. frescoes (St Demetrios, the patron saint,

The tall belfry of the Velika Remeta Monastery

on the outer wall). In WWII Croatian fascists destroyed the church dome and burned down the iconostasis. The trademark of Velika Remeta is its tall baroque bell tower constructed in 1735. It is the tallest of all bell-towers in any Serb monastery.

❹ Novo Hopovo

The monastery lies to the east of the Novi Sad - Ruma road. It is reached by taking a turning on the left after some 2 km from Iriški Venac, at the top of Fruška Gora. The monastery was built in 1576 on the site of an earlier church, by a group of citizens from the Serb town of Gornji Kovin / Rackeve (on Csepel Island, near modern day Budapest). The new, large, monastery quickly became a center of learning and copying of books. The Turks damaged it during their retreat in 1688 and it was renovated and rebuilt in the first half of the 18th c, gaining its large monastic dwellings. The monastery was severely damaged in WWII by Croatian fascists who blew up the high belfry and the south wing of the dwellings, destroyed the iconostasis and many of the frescoes. After the war the monastery underwent radical restoration.

The monastery church is one of the largest Serb churches built under the Turks and its sheer dimensions show the enthusiasm and flourishing of arts after the renovation of the Peć Patriarchate. It has a trefoil base, continuing the architectural tradition of the Morava school, and lively façades with rows of blind arcades carved in stone and decorated with bricks. However, its most captivating feature is a graceful 12-sided dome with the same number of freestanding colonnettes supporting its roof.

The interior was fresco painted on two occasions: the nave and altar area in 1608 and the narthex in 1654. Each time the artists were

Saints depicted on walls of Hopovo

the six levels depict figures of standing saints, others show the life of Christ, celestial hierarchies, deaths of the apostles and Serb saints, predominantly rulers (on the east and the west walls). The compositions are elegantly arranged with fine, though conventional, painting in subtle, dark colors that emphasize the solemnity of the monastery The most striking compositions in the nave are the "Wedding in Kana" (north wall), "The Last Supper" and "The Mas-

dating from 1752; a small single-nave structure with a comparatively large baroque dome. It was heavily damaged in WWII and is still in a dismal state.

❺ Beočin

This monastery is located 2 km south from the center of Beočin town, on the way into the Fruška Gora Mountain.

It is not sure when exactly this orthodox monastery was founded but we find it's first mentioning in mid-16th c. Destroyed and abandoned during the course of the Great Turkish war, it was renovated in 1697 by the newly arrived monks from Rača monastery. The new church edifice was constructed in 1732-40. The main portal (1787) is decorated in the classicist style with several sculptures.

Baroque dwellings and the bell-tower of Novo Hopovo Monastery

skillful Greeks, probably from Mt Athos. The high walls of the church, interspersed by only a few small windows, allowed them to express their talent in a vast number of monumental compositions and cycles. In the narthex, two of

sacre of the Innocents" (both on the south wall).

At the exit of the monastic complex starts a path that leads through the forest to the ruins of the **Staro (Old) Hopovo** monastery (3 km away). The only remaining part of it is the church

The iconostasis is work of several famous artists: the large icons are by Janko Halkozović and the rest of the icons by Dimitrije Bačević and Teodor Kračun. Behind the south wing of the residence hall there is a park with a small harmonious chapel, work

Vrdnik Monastery, also known as "Ravanica of Srem"

gruously small cupola. The iconostasis and frescoes are the work of the classicist painter Dimitrije Avramović from 1853. Both are quite dark in colouring and solemn in expression. Most of the rich treasuries of the monastery together with the relics of St Lazar were transferred to Belgrade when faced by the destruction by Croatian fascists in WWII. Just south of the dwellings stands the monument to the romanticist poet Milica Stojadinović "Srpkinja" who spent her life here and was known as the "Fairy of Vrdnik".

leads toward the ridge of Fruška Gora, presents the only remains of the 12th c. town, which was errected on the Roman foundation.

of architect Vladimir Nikolić from 1905.

❻ Vrdnik

The monastery is situated in the outskirts of the small town of the same name, by the road that leads across Fruška Gora to Beočin.

Founded around the middle of the 16th c. the monastery was almost totally destroyed during the Great Turkish War. It was rebuilt by monks who had fled the Ravanica Monastery, bringing with them the holy relics of St Lazar (formerly Prince Lazar). Due to the great respect that the highly revered relics brought to the monastery, Vrdnik was also named "The Ravanica of Srem" (*Sremska Ravanica*). The simple old church was torn down in 1801 to allow for the new construction. It is a single nave edifice decorated in the styles of classicism and biedermeier. The only detail reminiscent of the old architecture is the incon-

Although it seems as a slightly larger then the rest of villages in Fruška Gora, the **town of Vrdnik** was from 1804 until 1968 a rather well known mine. A few streets with purposely built houses for mine workers are reminders of these past times. During the ore explatation, a mineral water spring was descovered, which after the mine was closed, enabled transformation of Vrdnik into the health spa and resort.

The isolated **Vrdnik Tower** (*Vrdnička kula*), situated in the dense deciduous forest, above the road which

❼ Jazak

The village of Jazak is some 15km north of Ruma. The monastery of Jazak lies two kilometres beyond the village.

Not far from the old monastery (*see below*) a new one was constructed in 1736-58 thanks to donations from several well-to-do Serb merchants of the region. Although built in the heyday of the baroque era, the structure of Jazak follows strictly the principles of Serbian medieval architecture: the trefoil base, the walls of alternate rows of brick and stone, and the cupola. The tall belfry, which contrasts with the traditional forms, was finished in 1803. After its completion, the new

Detail from Fruška Gora

monastery took over the assets from the old one including the relics of St Uroš, the second Serbian Emperor, which have been brought to Jazak from Kosovo in 1706, and were the basis of monastery's fame. The rich iconostasis was created by Dimitrije Bačević in 1769 in a mixture of traditional post-Byzantine painting and the new trends coming from the West. Also of interest are the skilfully crafted thrones at the sides.

To the south lie the ruins of the original Jazak monastery (*Stari Jazak*). It was founded at the end of the 15th or the beginning of the 16th c. The traditionally modelled church was abandoned in 1778 and damaged in a later earthquake.

Immediately to the east of Jazak is the **Mala Remeta** village with the monastery of the same name. It was established in the late 15th c. on the site of the abandoned Catholic Pauline monastery. Its church, dedicated to the Shroud of Mother of God, dates from 1739. It was constructed by two master-craftsmen from Macedonia who used patterns of traditional church-building such as double windows and blind arcades running all around the church. The humble quarters, added in 1758 were seriously damaged in WWII. The well-preserved iconostasis boasts four large icons by the famed Janko Halkozović.

❽ Šišatovac

The monastery church dedicated to the Birth of the Virgin Mary was founded around 1520 by monks who had fled from the Žiča Monastery and settled here on the ruins of a Catholic hermitage. In 1543 it

Nobleman's gravestone in Šišatovac Monastery

grew in importance when the remains of St Stevan Štiljanović were brought here. These were the principle assets of the monastery over the next centuries, until they were relocated to Belgrade during WWII. The new church was constructed from 1758 until 1778 but retained its trefoil ground plan and a cupola from the older edifice. The facade was enlivened by the tall pilasters and alternating rows of bricks and stone which imitate the medieval building. Also reminiscent of Serb medieval architecture are

Serb officers from the Petrovaradin regiment. It is also well-known for its liberal abbot Lukijan Mušicki (1777-1837), a pseudo-classical poet and friend of Vuk Karadžić. Šišatovac suffered badly in WWII but has been renovated recently.

❾ Petkovica

This small 16th c. monastery was subordinate to the nearby Šišatovac with which it shared an abbot. The name of the monastery comes from its Patron Saint, Petka. The architecture of its church is strictly traditional. The only valuable feature that survived the looting and damage caused in the Second World War are its fine frescoes dating from 1588.

Many of the monasteries produce very good wine

the pointed arches of the windows. Šišatovac was a favourite burial place of the prominent

⓳ Irig

🏛 7.500

ℹ Ribarski trg 17
22404 Irig
022/461-126

12 km - Ruma

Already a substantial settlement in the 13th c, in late Middle Ages Irig was an important fort in the hands of the Branković family. In 18th c. it was the biggest town in the region of Srem but in 1795 a disastrous plague epidemic killed half of its population. Since then it has slumbered, known only for being the center of a famous winegrowing area.

Irig has three 18th c. Orthodox churches. Just to the east of the main town square and park is the oldest and most important of the three, dedicated to St Nicholas (*Nikolajevska crkva*). Built in 1732, its architecture copies almost exactly the model of the nearby Hopovo monastery. The carvings of the iconostasis dating from 1760 are among the most interesting of the period; the icons are the work of painter Vasa Ostojić, from the same period. The church dedicated to the Virgin (*Bogorodičina crkva*) lies at the southern approach to the town. It has a late baroque iconostasis and frescoes from 1863. The third church celebrates St Theodore (*Teodoro-vska crkva*) and lies at the western end of Irig. It is the youngest of the three – it was built and got its iconostasis shortly before the devastating plague.

ENVIRONS:
7 km to the north of Irig, on the ridge of Mt Fruška Gora is **Iriški venac** (451 m), one of the best-loved

Partially destroyed TV Tower at Iriški venac

excursion points on this mountain. The focal point here is a huge **Monument**, created by the sculptor Sreten Stojanović in 1951 to commemorate the victims who fell in the fight against fascism. Nearby you will find the hotel "Norcev" (tel. 021/621-172), the motel "Vojvodina" (with a restaurant, tel. 021/463-008) and the restaurant "Venac" (tel. 021/463-023). A short walk through the woods to the east will bring you to the **TV Tower**. Damaged in the 1999 bombing it still stands, perhaps even more imposing than before.

St Nicholas' Church in Irig

⓴ Ruma

🏛 45.300

📠 022/422-544

📱 022/429-130

60 km - Beograd

Although there are numerous traces of human dwellings throughout prehistoric and historic times in the vicinity of Ruma, the present-day town developed only in the mid 18th c. as an artisan and commercial center in the feudal possession of Baron Marko Pejačević. In 1747 it was granted a privileged status and a new town plan was laid. With the collapse of the Austro-Hungarian Emprire, on 24th of November 1918 the representatives of the Srem region gathered in Ruma and proclaimed the unification of Srem with Serbia. Today this pleasant town is best known as the most important road and railway junction in this part of the country.

There are three Serb Orthodox Churches in the town. The most interesting one is the so-called **Greek Church** (*Grčka crkva*, officially the Descent of the Holy Spirit church) in Glavna ("Main") Street. It was built in 1840 by local Greek and Cincar tradesmen and renovated in 1903 by the Marković family whose mausoleum lies behind the apse. At the time of the renovation several important Serb artists left their mark here. The famed academician Uroš Predić painted the iconostasis; in the mausoleum there is an epitaph by poet Laza Kostić; texts on two memorial plaques are by writer Simo Matavulj and there is the only fresco made by Uroš Predić, whose usual medium was oil on canvas. **Nikolajevska Church** is the oldest in town, dating from 1758, although its classicist iconostasis was done only in 1847. **Vaznesenska Church** was built in 1761 and has a very good baroque iconostasis with icons by Stefan Tenecki.

Back in the Main Street is the large **Roman-Catholic Church** (*Katolička crkva*) built in 1813 in classical style with a splendid main altar and two smaller ones.

The **Local Museum** (*Zavičajni muzej, Glavna 182, tel. 022/424-888, zavmuzejruma@ptt.yu,* open Mon-Fri 9 a.m. – 8 p.m, Sat 9 a.m. – 1 p.m.) is in the building of the former Franciscan high school which dates from 1772. There you can see the archeological, historical and ethnographic collections.

ENVIRONS:
17 km south-east of Ruma lies the **village of Pećinci** (follow the freeway to Belgrade and then take the exit to Pećinci) with an interesting **Museum of Bread** (*Srpski muzej hleba "Jeremija", tel. 022/86-141,* open only on weekend 10 a.m.-5 p.m., e-mail: *mhleba@eunet.yu*) maintained by its creator and owner Jeremija who will guide you personally through the history and

Types of bread to be seen in the Bread Museum in Pećinci

processes of bread making, as well as traditional and ceremonial types of Serb bread.

21 Šid

- 24.800
- Svetog Save 40
  22240 Šid
  022/710-661
- 022/714-147
- 022/712-422

  41 km - Sr. Mitrovica

An insignificant village until the 18th c, Šid developed when it was granted the right to hold annual fairs. As it was a possession of the Uniate (Greek-Catholic) bishop of Križevci (Croatia) it was settled by Ruthenians (Ukrainians) whose church stands together with the Serb Orthodox one in the center of the municipality.

Šid is best known for the painter Sava Šumanović (1896-1942). Born here, Šumanovic also tragically ended his life here when he was shot by Croatian fascists. Some of his most famous landscapes depict the town and its vicinity. The **Sava Šumanović Gallery** (*Svetog Save 7, 022/712-614*) holds 417 of his paintings presenting all phases of his work and all themes he worked on.

Ilijanum Naïve-Art Gallery (*Školska 2, tel. 022/712-614*) was created from the endowed works of Ilija Bašičević-Bosilj (1895-1972), a farmer from Šid whose original paintings of fantastic creatures and interpretations of characters from Serb epic poetry are as puzzling as they are visually exciting. In it are

Painting of Sava Šumanović, "Shepardess" (National Museum Belgrade)

also to be seen works of other naïve artists from Serbia.

ENVIRONS:

5 km away lays the Privina Glava monastery. Take the road to Ilok and after passing Berkasovo village take a right turn to **Privina Glava** village; the **monastery** is at the end of the village. Probably founded in the 15th

Privina Glava Monastery

c. by brothers Jovan and Maksim of the Branković dynasty, the present day church was constructed between 1741 and 1760. The direct model for the architect was the famous Hopovo monastery, hence the unusual columns supporting the cupola and the medieval style trefoil base. The iconostasis is carved in rococo style and was painted by Andrej Sartist in 1786. The frescoes in the central part of the church are work of Kuzman Kolarić from the end of the 18th c. The whole of the monastery's treasure

was destroyed in World War Two.

7 km further, at the very border with Croatia, lies the tiny village of **Molovin**. To reach it go back on the Ilok road and at the next village, Sot, turn left to Molovin. In the small Serb Orthodox church there is a stunning **iconostasis**. It was carved around 1770 by an artist from the south in his own interpretation of the dominant baroque style. Its decorative elements consist of a large number of floral ornaments, animal and human figures. Brothers Jovan and Georgije Četirević-Grabovan from Macedonia painted the icons in 1772.

15 km to the south of Šid lies **Morović** village on the confluence of the marshy Bosut and Studva rivers. Approaching the village one finds the Catholic **Church of St Mary** (*Crkva svete Marije*) dating from the 13th c, with its cemetery surrounding. The original Romanesque structure visible only in the apse was later extended in the gothic style. The bell tower has unusual cross-like windows.

Sarcophagus from Roman Sirmium

23 Sremska Mitrovica

45.600

022/221-143

022/221-444

67 km - Beograd

Lying on the left bank of the Sava River, the town is better known for the name it bore in antiquity – *Sirmium*. Already at the time of the Roman conquest (around 10 AD) there was a settlement here that quickly grew in importance and obtained the status of Roman colony under Emperor Domentian (81-96 AD). It was used as a temporary seat of emperors during their wars with the barbarians over the Danube. The 3rd and 4th centuries were the glory days of Sirmium: emperors such as Trajan Decius, Aurelian, Probus or Maximian were born in the town or its vicinity and many more Roman rulers spent time here. The town had public baths, an opulent imperial palace and a hippodrome, considered to be one of the largest in Roman world. In the time of Diocletian's partition of the Empire it became one of the four capitals and the seat of caesar Galerius. The town was also famous for its Christian martyrs such as Bishop Irenaeus and his Deacon Demetrios who were beheaded on the bridge over the Sava in 304. During this century, in which Orthodox Christianity fought for predominance against paganism and the

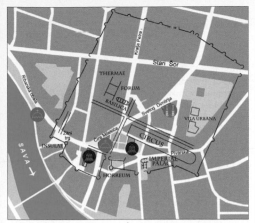

Arian heresy, several councils were convoked here to discuss the controversies. Although well fortified, Sirmium was soon afterwards taken by barbaric Goths and then in 441 it was plundered by Huns. While diminished in importance, the town survived and in the next century it became the capital of the Gepid state. After a short time spent back in Byzantine hands, Sirmium saw its final doom in 582 when it was captured and destroyed by Avars and Slavs after a three-year siege. Over the next three hundred years the town fell into obscurity; one thing was preserved, however: the Latin *Sirmium* was transformed by Slavs to *Srem* and the whole surrounding region took the name. With the conversion of the Slavs to Christianity in the 9th c. this prestigious place once again became the seat of an eparchy with a monastery dedicated to St Demetrios. In the 11th and 12th centuries it changed hands between Byzantines and Hungarians who were ultimately victorious. Although Hungary was a Catholic state, the Orthodox monastery, sustained by Greek and

Slav monks, held its own here well into the 14th c. The rise of *Civitas Sancti Demetri* (or Dmitrovci in Serbian), that had also obtained the privileges of a free royal town, and had a flourishing colony of merchants from Dubrovnik, was suddenly put to an end in 1396 when the Turks plundered it in a raid following their victory over the Crusaders at Nicopolis. Destroyed, the town deteriorated until it fell into Turkish hands in 1521. Under the Ottoman rule

it flourished once again, the best testimony being its 17 mosques. During the Austrian times in the 18th and 19th centuries it hosted the headquarters of the border regiment but also developed intensive trade with the Turkish regions on the other side of the river.

Being on the front line, Sremska Mitrovica was severely damaged in the First World War especially during the failed Serb counter-offensive in early 1915. Between the two world wars Sremska Mitrovica was famous for its prison where many of the future communist rulers served their sentences for anti-state activities. In the Second World War it fell to Croatia and the Serb majority lived through difficult times; especially horrible was the pogrom of 1942 when over 7000 civilians from the town and surrounding villages were brutally murdered here.

The heart of Sremska Mitrovica lies over the remains of its famed predecessor Sirmium. The excavated sites can be seen at several places; one of the most interesting is the grounds of the imperial palace located at the corner of Pivarska and Branka Radičevića Streets. In Nikole Pašića Square, there is another

Archeological site in Žitni trg

archeological site with the foundations of living quarters (*insulae*) and part of the city walls. The Square, better known as the **Žitni trg** ("Grain Market") for the main merchandise sold here, is surrounded by the finest examples of merchants' houses,

Marble antique head, Sremska Mitrovica Museum

mostly from the 19th century.

Nearby lies the old Serb **Church of St Steven** (*stara crkva Svetog Stefana*). This interesting building dates back to the 16th c. and is the oldest place of worship in the town. Since it was built during the Turkish reign it had to keep a low profile and modest exterior. The small wooden baroque bell tower was added later. After WWII it was turned into a Museum of Church Art, but is now again serving as a church. Apart for its meticulously carved iconostasis from the 18th c. with paintings by Teodor Kračun, it also boasts a collection of icons, books and other church artifacts.

The **Museum of Srem** is located in two sites. The first one is in 2, Pinkijeva St, opposite the hotel "Sirmium" and houses a collection of applied art, icons and paintings (18th-20th c.). The other part, which encloses the most interesting, Roman collection is in a fine 18th c. mansion that once belonged to the Bajić family (*15, Svetog Stefana St, tel. 022/223-245, open Tue-*

Fri from 8 a.m. to 8 p.m., weekends 9 a.m.-1 p.m.).

Next to the museum building stands the **Old Customs House** dating from 1729; one of the oldest edifices in Sremska Mitrovica. Facing the museum stands the monumental **new Orthodox Church of St Steven** (*nova crkva Svetog Stefana*), with a lavish iconostasis painted in 1815 by Arsa Teodorović, but later retouched. Behind it lies the corner edifice known as the **Serbian Home** (*Srpski dom*). It is the work of the famous architect Vladimir Nikolić, from 1895, and was partially renovated following its destruction in the World War One.

There are several interesting edifices built in the late 18th and early 19th c. nearby. The **Lieutenant Colonel's Quarters** at the corner of Svetozara Markovića St. and Ćire Miletića Square has an austere, military look typical for buildings of the period when the town was under military jurisdiction. The 18th c. **Court** building and the

building of the **Main Guards** in Pinkijeva St. are built in the similar style with somewhat more decoration of the façades.

22 Zasavica

022/226-089

10 km - Sremska Mitrovica

Zasavica natural resort lies in the northern part of Mačva county. It is a lowland river whose flow often resembles the stagnant waters of an elongated lake. It flows almost parallely to the Sava River, with which it is linked by a channel. Around this small river, there are swamps, preserved in their wilderness, floodable meadows and forests inhabited with a large number of plant, fish, mammal and insect species, some of which are very rare and relict. Riches in endangered autochthonous fish species, such as bream, bitterling, crucian carp and weatherfish, are something to be emphasized. 180 species of birds can also be found, some of which nest here, then the Balkan amphibian - the miraculous Danube triton, as well as otters, wild cats and the European beaver that was brought back to this area in 2004 and has accommodated well in this environment ever since. On the surrounding pastures, old species of domestic animals can be found, the Mangulitsa pig and the autohtonous podolian cow, that once used to be a usual sight all over Serbia.

Orthodox Church of St Demetrios

A scene from Zasavica wildlife reserve

The visitors are also offered tourist boat trips, sports fishing, lectures for students and other interested parties, as well as the ecollogical products of this area.

24 Obedska bara

46 km - Beograda

The Obedska bara Pond is a special natural resort whose territory is under the protection of home laws, but is also marked on the Ramsar List of World important wetland habitats and is considered to be an internationally significant bird area. This pond is in fact a former riverbed of the Sava that, after the river changed its flow and turned to the south, remained as a oxbow lake. The Sava floods this pond frequently, supplying it with enough water, but also with fish that find its spawning conditions more than convenient. It is interesting that the Obedska bara was already put under protection in 1874! It is well known for its old English oak forests, swampy vegetation and great riches in birds, some 220 species. It is also rich in mammals (the beavers were brought back recently), amphibians, reptiles and mushrooms that live in its waters, reed-beds and wet meadows. Among the birds, we can emphasize eagles, great white herons, bitterns, shovelers and above all ibis, also known as "the paradise bird".

The easiest way to reach the Pond from Belgrade is taking the motorway to Zagreb, exit for Šimanovci and continue to Kupinovo village. There is the "Obedska bara" Hotel in the nearby Obrež village (*tel. 022/886-22*).

There are several interesting historical monuments in **Kupinovo**. From the former castle, the residence of several despotes of Branković family, only the foundations remained, but the plain **Church of St. Luke** (*crkva Svetog Luke*) from the same period was preserved better. As this church has been continuously used since the middle of the 15th century, it is also the oldest preserved church in Vojvodina province. The iconostasis was painted by Jakov Orfelin. Kupinovo is one of the best preserved villages in Srem county and many of its houses depict the atmosphere of the past times. The visitors are recommended to see the houses and stables at the end of B. Mađarevića street, numbers 127, then 137 to 150. The house of the Putnik family distinguishes the most (no. 142) – it is from the end of the 18th century, with many nicely carved ornaments.

26 Pančevo

84.400

Sokače 2
26000 Pančevo
013/351-366

013/510-455
013/341-111

21 km - Beograd

As early as the 9th century the settlement at the confluence of the Tamiš River and the Danube was known to have been frequented by traders. During Turkish times (1552-1716) Pančevo was a little fort with only one mosque but surprisingly there was a Serbian majority. During Habsburg monarchy it became part of the military border and German and Romanian settlers were brought in. Pančevo lived through the ordeal of Turkish destruction again with

A stork above the old houses of Kupinovo village

Town Magistracy, today housing the National Museum

the badly administered war of 1789-91. In 1794 the Emperor granted the town the status of a "free military community" which enabled it to become a lively commercial and cultural centre in the 19th century. However, the town kept a somewhat rigid military appearance and was therefore nicknamed "Serb Sparta". After WWII it was heavily industrialised and the population grew to 100,000 inhabitants. The petrol and chemistry factories make it notorious for pollution that is often over critical measurements.

The old town, earlier encircled by battlements, stretches around the main square in its centre. The square, Trg kralja Petra I, is covered in extensive greenery giving it the appearance of a park. The most important building here is the former **Town Magistrate**, a classicist edifice from 1833 carried out by the plans of a local officer, Major Hajman. The central part of this sturdy building is emphasised by columns and a terrace that is crowned by a gable in which two geniuses hold a clock. Today it serves as the **Town Museum** (*Trg kralja Petra 7, tel.*

013/42-666, open Tue –Sat 10 a.m. – 1 p.m. and 4 – 7 p.m.) notable for its collection of items from the neolith Starčevo culture and a smaller version of the famous painting "The Migration of the Serbs" (*"Seoba Srbalja"*) by Paja Jovanović.

Towards Tamiš is the Catholic **Church of St Charles Borromeo**, a modest edifice from mid 18th century used from the beginning as a Franciscan monastery. When the Turks took the town in 1790 they pillaged the dwellings and used the church as a stable. In 1858 it was renovated and obtained the slim, unornamented

bell tower. By it stands an attractive Trinity column.

Towards the north one heads to the one-time Serbian quarter where there are two fine churches. **Uspenska crkva** in Dimitrija Tucovića Street is a lavish edifice dating from 1810 whose two high baroque towers represent the city's landmark. The material was donated by Karadjordje from the insurrectionist Serbia across the Danube. The iconostasis is the work of the great classicist Konstantin Danil, while the wall paintings (from 1928) are the work of the academic painter Živorad Nastasijević, the leader of the "Zograf" group, pioneers in the revival of Serbian medieval painting.

Four blocks away, up this street, one reaches the **Preobraženska**

"The Migration of the Serbs"
("Seoba Srbalja") by Paja Jovanović

The painting was commissioned by Patriarch Georgije Branković, to be exhibited at the Hungarian celebration of the 1000 year anniversary of their arrival to Pannonia which was to take place in 1896. The idea was to demonstrate that the Serbs came to Hungary on a call from the Habsburg Emperor as an organized nation, with soldiers and their Patriarch as their leader. In this way the picture would ward off attacks on Serbian religious and educational autonomy in Austro-Hungary. The young yet brilliant Jovanović was chosen for the assignment and spent some months in meticulous preparation with Ilarion Ruvarac, the greatest Serbian historian of the time. This enabled him to include many interesting details in the painting. However, the first, smaller version (as can be seen in Pančevo) did not satisfy the Patriarch who found it weak: the boy in the middle looked too meek while the woman carrying a baby and the sheep were demeaning to the honour of the church leaders. In the new, larger version, the boy carries a gun on his shoulder, the standard-bearer took the place of the woman and the Bishop riding by the Patriarch carries the diploma with the "Privileges" in his hand. Through a twist of fate, it was the smaller version that was reproduced in large numbers and became a favorite image in almost every Serbian home.

Colourful detail from the facade of the People's Bank

Church. It was constructed in 1878 by young Svetozar Ivačković, a pupil of the famous Viennese Teophil von Hansen. Its design won Ivačković fame and many more commissions for new churches. Unlike the Vaznesenska church, this is a neo-Byzantine structure with a large central dome and a detached bell tower that, in its day, represented a specific symbol of religious and artistic freedom. The Iconostasis (1908-11) was painted by Uroš Predić and the wall paintings, mostly historical compositions, were executed by Stevan Aleksić, both well-known artists of their time.

Just south off the main square stands the Trg Slobode Square with an interesting Art Noveau building of the **People's Bank** (*Pučka banka*) built in 1903 by the designs of the Budapest architects Kalman and Ulman.

At the corner of Nikole Tesle St that leads to Tamiš is the **"Sundial House"** built in 1792 for the seat of the Banat military frontier. On the ceiling of the entrance is depicted General Mihaljević, its first commander. At the lower end of the street is the **Brewery** (*Pivara*). Established in 1722, only six years after the expulsion of the Turks, it is one of the oldest industrial objects in Serbia. It obtained wide fame when managed by the famous brewers, the Vajfert family (from 1847 to 1944) who later spread their business to Belgrade. Last year it was badly damaged in a fire and is waiting for renovation.

A German majority once inhabited the south part of the town. The **Evangelical Church** in Svetislava Kasapinovića Street is the finest remaining monument of their presence. It is a neo-gothic edifice from 1905 built with a brick façade and has a high belfry crowned by a clock.

South of Pančevo lies the village of Vojlovica inhabited by Slovaks. Today it merged with the town and is closed off from the other side by the Oil Refinery. By the entrance to the refinery stands the medieval orthodox **Vojlovica Monastery** (one can reach it by taking bus 11, 12 or 14). Enclosed in a small yard and encircled with pipelines, it is living testament to the communist negligence of historical and religious monuments. Monks fleeing from the south of Serbia founded Vojlovica in 1405. In the 18th century it was torched twice by the Turks and took a long period of time to be reconstructed. During the First World War, the Austro-Hungarian authorities took the monks to prison camps, looted the monastery and melted the bells for military usage. In WWII it was used by the Germans to imprison the Serb Patriarch Gavrilo Dožić before sending him to Dachau. The monastery was closed down and stood in pitiful state until its reconstruction in 1987. The church is built in the style of the Serbian Raška School; a slightly taller narthex was added, in the same style, in 1752, while the last addition was the unproportionately tall bell tower in the first part of the 19th century. Wall paintings from 15th, 17th and 18th century are preserved only in fragments. The Iconostasis (1798) is the work of a lesser painter from Pančevo.

Quiet flow of the Tamiš River by Pančevo

㉕ Kovačica

🏠 11.800
🚌 29 km - Pančevo

This predominantly Slovak village is known throughout the world for its naïve painters. The tradition was started in 1939 and advanced in

Naive-art being made

the 1950's when several peasants took to painting scenes from their daily lives. Zuzana Halupova and Martin Jonaš were the first to be recognised in the wider world and since then many others followed in their steps. Today, almost every house is home to a painter and works by artists from Kovačica are to be found in many museums and private collections worldwide (Dali's and Picasso's for instance).

Slovaks were settled in Vojvodina since the 18th century as hard and modest workers. Not only did they live up to expectations but also managed to keep their culture alive to the present day. The Slovaks arrived in the small Serbian village of Kovačica in 1802 and transformed it completely. Some of the Slovak houses are still painted or tiled in the traditional light blue colour with the name of the family in the gable. One can also observe older women

in fluffy dresses sitting in front of their houses or riding bicycles. The **Evangelist Protestant Church** in the centre of the village dates back to 1829. The paintings on the main altar are by a famous Serbian painter, Konstantin Danil. Today the village is bursting with living traditions and original arts and crafts aswell as several collections.

The **Gallery of Naïve Art** (*Galerija naivne umetnosti, Masarikova 65, tel. 013/661-157, www.artkovacica.co.yu, office@artkovacica.co.yu*) is the oldest and has the broadest range of art for sale on and display. Just around the corner is the **Ethno Centre "Babka"** (*Vinogradska 7, tel. 661-522, www.babka-center.com, office@babka-center.com*) where one can take a peak into several of the artists' ateliers. Apart from the paintings,

Painted squash from Kovačica

handicrafts are also on sale here such as painted plates and squashes or corn-husk dolls.

㉖ Vršac

🏠 48.200
ℹ️ Trg Pobede 1
26300 Vršac
013/822-554
🚌 013/822-866, 839-917
🚕 013/823-305
86 km - Beograd

The settlement evolved below the castle that lies at the hilltop (*vrh* in Serbian), built at the beginning of the 15th century by the Hungarian King Sigismund to protect his southern border from persistent Turkish attacks. The fort was given to the Serbian ruler Djuradj, whose main strongholds were directly opposite, on the other side of the Danube. In 1425 Serbian refugees from the south came here and founded the settlement called Podvršac, "Under Vršac". In those days, Vršac was already famous for its wine production and its local wines were amongst the most sought after (and the most expensive!) at the Hungarian royal court. After a long period of pillaging of the vicinity, the Turks conquered the town in 1552 yet most of the population remained Serbian. This changed when the Serbs of Banat, hopeful of liberation with the help of the Habsburg army, took to their arms in the spring of 1594. The rebellion was successful at first and Vršac, aswell as other towns, were in Serbian hands. However, by the end of the summer the Turks regained control. Most of the Serbs fled to Tran-

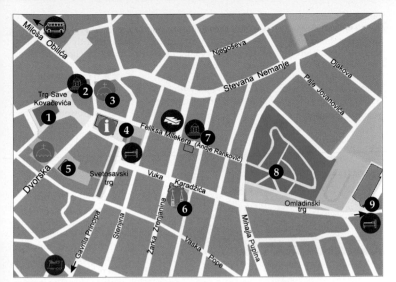

1. Trg Save Kovačevića
2. Old Pharmacy
3. Romanian church
4. Trg Pobede
5. Metropolitain's Court
6. Cathollic Church
7. Natonal Museum
8. City Park
9. Vršac Tower

sylvania after which the town obtained oriental appearance. Eugene of Savoy expelled the Turks from Vršac in 1716 when a new era began for the town. Germans from the river Moselle were collonised in the town bringing with them new techniques in wine cultivation that again made Vršac one of the main wine producing areas. After the fast economic growth of the 18th century, Vršac managed to obtain the status of Free Royal City in 1817. The town suffered in the 1848 revolution when fighting occurred between Serbs and Hungarians. The rest of the 19th century passed by quietly and the town prospered until the phylloxera disease struck the vineyards. The results of this catastrophic illness were gradually reversed with the planting of American grapes that first began here. The end of the Second World War saw a grave ethnic change when the ethnic Germans were forced to flee ahead of the advancing Red Army. Their absence was soon felt in the fields of culture and economics. In recent years the main drive of the city became the concern of its medical industry "Hemofarm", the most important of its kind in Serbia.

❶ Trg Save Kovačevića

Once the centre for the town's tradesmen, the square is today a pleasant pedestrian zone with several interesting buildings. At no. 15 stands the house called **"Two pistols"**. Built at the end of the 18th century as a guesthouse, it received its most important guest in 1813 when the leader of the failed Serbian insurrection Karadjordje spent some time here before leaving for Russia. To cover his expenses he gave the owner two of his finest guns that later became the distinctive sign of this inn. Of interest is the inner courtyard with a fine vaulted porch. **No. 11** of the same square, dates from 1868 and was

Panorama of Vršac as seen from the hill above it

built by Djordje, brother to the famous Serbian dramatist, Jovan Sterija Popović, on the site of the older house where they were both born. Sterija (1806-1856) was a lawyer, a poet, the

Cafes in Trg Save Kovaćevića

founder of the National museum in Belgrade and the Serbian Academy of Arts and Sciences. However, he is best known for his comedies that wittily portray the hypocrisy and other faults of Vojvodinian society.

❷ Old Pharmacy
Stara apoteka

At the corner of Kumanovska and Stevana Nemanje Street, stands the building of the Old Pharmacy, also known as the "Pharmacy on the Steps". It was built in the mid 18th century and in 1784, the "At the Savior" pharmacy, the first one in the town, was opened here . It was used for this purpose until 1965 when

it was bestowed to the local museum. The original façade was changed to classicist style in the 19th century but its other characteristics remain: the high roof with two levels (used to dry medicinal herbs), a large cellar to house the stock in a cool place and, of course, its unusual entrance. Today it houses two exhibitions: one of the Medical Museum of Banat and the other in memory of the great painter Paja Jovanović, whose brother was one of the pharmacists here. This includes several great paintings amongst which is a large portrait of King Aleksandar of Yugoslavia. Unfortunately, both exhibitions are open only on Sundays, from 10 a.m. to 1 p.m. and again from 3 to 7 p.m.

❸ Romanian Church
Rumunska crkva

On the next corner stands the small but picturesque Romanian church dedicated to the

Ascension of Christ. It was built in 1911-13 in a predominantly Byzantine style but with clinker bricks.

❹ Trg Pobede

The tall new hotel "Srbija" towers over the middle of this square. However, historically the most important edifice here is the Town Magistracy. Facing the square stands its new part, the so-called **"Gothic Edifice"**, built in 1860 by the German masters. The main facade is highlighted by its balcony, a municipal coat of arms in a medallion and a gothic gable. The interior is embellished by wall paintings from the end of the 19th century. To the left, in the side street stands the smaller and older part, built at the very beginning of the 19th century and immediately purchased to be used as Magistrate offices. The ornament is late baroque and its most striking feature is the corner bay window.

❺ Metropolitain's Court
Vladičanski dvor

This palace is located in 20, Dvorska ("Court") Street and surrounded by a well-kept French park enclosed by an ornamented fence in the Baroque style. It was constructed between 1750 and 1757, by the metropolitan Jovan Georgijević, as the residence for the Orthodox Bishops of Banat. It still serves as such today. The final touch to the old façade was given in 1904 when it obtained richer, neo-renaissance and neo-baroque elements. The chapel dedicated to Saints Gabriel and

"Gothic Edifice" facing Trg Pobede Square

Michael date from the 18th century aswell. It has a baroque iconostasis with icons by Nikola Nešković. Moreover, the court keeps an impressive collection of portraits of church dignitaries, icons and other religious paintings, old books and vessels.

Facing the court stands the **Orthodox Cathedral** of St Nicolas with an unusual tower featuring a narrow terrace. It was constructed in 1785 in the place of an older temple. Inside one can find works by various prominent Serbian artists such as Pavel Djurković (who painted the icons on the iconostasis), Nikola Nešković (the free-standing icons) and Paja Jovanović (the wall paintings). At the end of this street stands the smaller **Church of the Dormition** (*Uspenska crkva*) from 1766. This Serbian Orthodox Church has an impressive 1809 iconostasis whose icons were executed by Arsa Todorović.

Continuing further in this direction one reaches the **Railway Station**. Built in 1900, it is one of the most impressive station edifices in Serbia. The exterior is covered in clinker bricks and, inside the main hall, the original wooden decoration still exists.

Imposing neo-gothic catholic church of Vršac

❻ Catholic Church
Katolička crkva

The tallest and most impressive edifice in the town is the Catholic Church easily located by its twin towers. This beautiful neo-gothic structure dedicated to St Gerhard was constructed in 1860-63 by the plans of a local architect, Franc Brandajs. Rich sculptural decoration is to be found mainly in the upper parts of the towers, around the windows and the portals. The three naves finish with three altars, the main one being painted by Karl Geiger, a professor at the Viennese Academy, in 1863.

The architect Brandajs also signed the plans of the **"Concordia" Building** standing just a hundred meters to the north of here at 20, Žarka Zrenjanina St. This classicist building with a central tract emphasized by four Corinthian pilasters was built in 1847 for the hotel of the same name, but was later adapted to be used as a high school.

❼ National Museum
Narodni muzej

Feliksa Milekera 19,
tel. 013/822-569

On permanent exhibition at the museum are archeological findings from the rich localities around Vršac, an ethnographic collection, as well as a large number of artworks from the 19th and 20th centuries. Special sections of the museum are dedicated to the life and work of Paja Jovanović and Jovan Sterija Popović.

❽ City Park
Gradski park

At the foothill of Vršački breg lies the town's common land which had once belonged to the Šerbl family estate. The town magistrate bought the estate in 1797 and half a century later it was developed as a park with a firing range, an ice rink and tennis courts. Meticulously maintained by the citizens, the large park was one of the lovliest in the region. Today it has lost a lot of its

Vršac Hill with its famous vinyards in the foreground

beauty yet one can still admire its old trees or the fountain with allegorical representations of the seasons.

9 Vršac Tower
Vršačka kula

The easiest and most popular route to climbing up Vršac hill (*Vršački breg*), the westernmost reach of the Carpathians, is by the elongated Omladinski trg. Above the City Park is a new sports complex with a hall called "Millennium", home of the "Hemo-farm" basketball team. The climb upwards starts at Mate Matejića St. that after some time turns into a winding stairway. Past the **Calvary Church** (1728), one reaches the top, crowned by the Vršac Tower. Dating from the 15th century, the keep is the only part of the castle that remains; other parts can only be vaguely identifed. The castle was torn down in the 18th century when it lost its military importance. Built of stone and brick, it had the characteristics of Byzantine and Serbian fortifications and was therefore probably constructed by the Serbian Despotes Djuradj. The outer steps lead to the

second of three floors that reach a total height of 20 metres. Continuing to the east there are several magnificent panoramic views of the entire city. The road leads to a mountain hut at Široko bilo (*open only*

Gudurica village in the Vršac Mountains

on weekends, tel. 013/820-708), the starting point for tours around the Vršac Mountains.

27 Mesić

9 km - Vršac

The monastery was first mentioned in the 16th century. Its architecture, based on medieval patterns, has been connected to the Branković dynasty or even with St. Sava. The modest church has a cross-ground plan and an eight-sided dome. During the course of the 18th century the monastery was damaged by the Turks and then restored three times. In the last restoration it obtained the outer narthex with a closed dome. The wall paintings were executed in 1743 yet look considerably older as they follow the patterns associated with

traditional painting, strongly resisting the baroque innovations of the epoch. In some places, older frescoes can be seen showing through from under the surface of the more recent ones. The monastic residences, dating from 1841-43, are in classicist style.

28 Bela Crkva

🏘 16.600

☎ 023/541-000
   35 km - Vršac

The medieval settlement in the valley of Nera was abandoned during the reign of the Turks and needed to be repopulated by the Habsburg authorities at the beginning of the 18th century. One group of settlers were the Serbs from the vicinity and the other the Germans from the area of the Moselle River who were known as skilful viticulturists. The city was the seat of the Illyrian (i.e. Serbian)–German regiment, but enjoyed a privileged status since 1777. In the WWII, it was the first city in Vojvodina to be liberated by the Red Army (on 1 October 1944) and one of the first to loose its German populace, the fact that

Vršac Tower rising above the town

greatly depreciated the town in terms of economy.

The main street, Prvog oktobra (the 1st October St), which was named after the liberation date, runs from the central park towards the north. Most of the town institutions and the monuments are in this street. **Romanian Orthodox Church** from the late 19th century is a romanticist building whose entrance is flanked by two symmetrical commercial facilities decorated with strong pillars and arcades. Next to a modern police station, there is the **"Golden Stag"** building (10, Prvog oktobra St.), the oldest one-story building in town, today in a pitiful state and waiting to be reconstructed. It was built in 1785, with massive walls and baroque decoration and used as an inn. Next to it can be seen, a small Russian church, built to serve the needs of refugees from Russia after the October revolution. Facing this church is a large white-painted **Catholic Church**, used as a symbol on coat-of-arms of the town, which can be seen carved on

its doors. Left from the church stands the town magistrate building from 1830, still used for the same purpose today. The best panoramic view of the town can be enjoyed from **Kalvarija (Calvary) Hill**, the first slope of the Carpathians, which rises above the Catholic church. From here, one can

Mesić Monastery

see the whole of Bela Crkva, the plains north from the gold-rich Nera River and the hills of the neighboring Romania. In the eastern part of the town is situated the **Serbian Orthodox Church** from 1780. It has a nice iconostasis painted by Pavel Djurković in 1793, considered to be one of

his best achievements, and wall paintings from 1810. The gravestones of Serbs from the 18th and the 19th century are within the church courtyard.

Bela Crkva Lakes (*Belocrkvanska jezera*) are scattered along the road to Belgrade. They emerged from holes where the gravel was once dug up for industrial purposes. Later on, the lakes became a tourist attraction primarily because of their crystal clear greenish water filtrated through the soil and for their sand beaches. On the shores of the lakes there are several tourist facilities.

One of the lakes near Bela Crkva

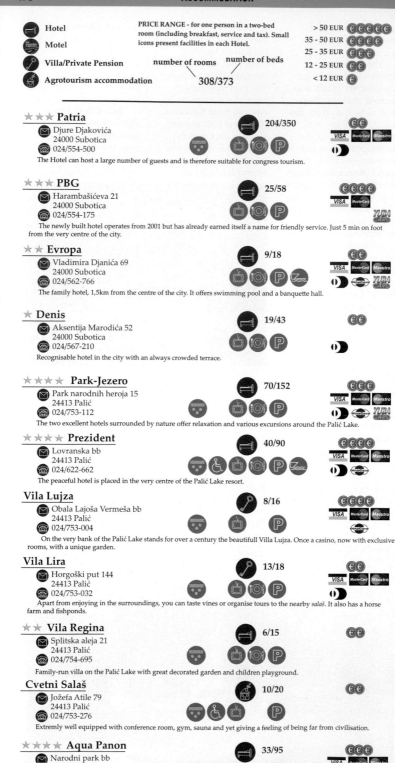

Hotel

Motel

Villa/Private Pension

Agrotourism accommodation

PRICE RANGE - for one person in a two-bed room (including breakfast, service and tax). Small icons present facilities in each Hotel.

number of rooms   number of beds
308/373

> 50 EUR €€€€€
35 - 50 EUR €€€€
25 - 35 EUR €€€
12 - 25 EUR €€
< 12 EUR €

★ ★ ★ Patria
Djure Djakovića
24000 Subotica
024/554-500

204/350

The Hotel can host a large number of guests and is therefore suitable for congress tourism.

★ ★ ★ PBG
Harambašićeva 21
24000 Subotica
024/554-175

25/58

The newly built hotel operates from 2001 but has already earned itself a name for friendly service. Just 5 min on foot from the very centre of the city.

★ ★ Evropa
Vladimira Djanića 69
24000 Subotica
024/562-766

9/18

The family hotel, 1,5km from the centre of the city. It offers swimming pool and a banquette hall.

★ Denis
Aksentija Marodića 52
24000 Subotica
024/567-210

19/43

Recognisable hotel in the city with an always crowded terrace.

★ ★ ★ ★ Park-Jezero
Park narodnih heroja 15
24413 Palić
024/753-112

70/152

The two excellent hotels surrounded by nature offer relaxation and various excursions around the Palić Lake.

★ ★ ★ ★ Prezident
Lovranska bb
24413 Palić
024/622-662

40/90

The peaceful hotel is placed in the very centre of the Palić Lake resort.

Vila Lujza
Obala Lajoša Vermeša bb
24413 Palić
024/753-004

8/16

On the very bank of the Palić Lake stands for over a century the beautifull Vila Lujza. Once a casino, now with exclusive rooms, with a unique garden.

Vila Lira
Horgoški put 144
24413 Palić
024/753-032

13/18

Apart from enjoying in the surroundings, you can taste vines or organise tours to the nearby *salaš*. It also has a horse farm and fishponds.

★ ★ Vila Regina
Splitska aleja 21
24413 Palić
024/754-695

6/15

Family-run villa on the Palić Lake with great decorated garden and children playground.

Cvetni Salaš
Jožefa Atile 79
24413 Palić
024/753-276

10/20

Extremly well equipped with conference room, gym, sauna and yet giving a feeling of being far from civilisation.

★ ★ ★ ★ Aqua Panon
Narodni park bb
24420 Kanjiža
024/876-600

33/95

An excellent new hotel in Kanjizha spa, suitable for medically supervised exercise training and recreation.

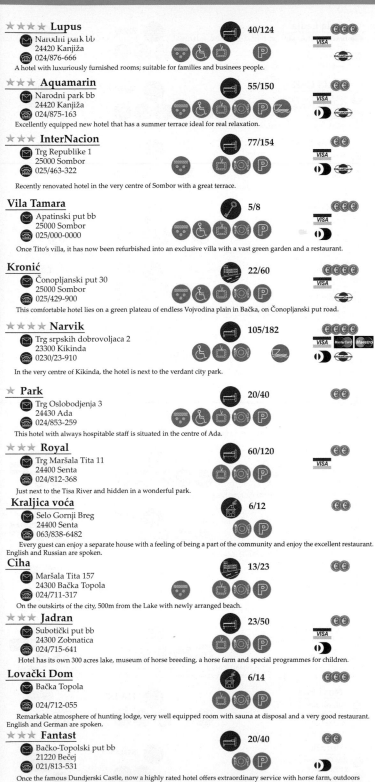

★★★★ Lupus
✉ Narodni park bb
24420 Kanjiža
☎ 024/876-666

40/124

A hotel with luxuriously furnished rooms; suitable for families and businees people.

★★★ Aquamarin
✉ Narodni park bb
24420 Kanjiža
☎ 024/875-163

55/150

Excellently equipped new hotel that has a summer terrace ideal for real relaxation.

★★★ InterNacion
✉ Trg Republike 1
25000 Sombor
☎ 025/463-322

77/154

Recently renovated hotel in the very centre of Sombor with a great terrace.

Vila Tamara
✉ Apatinski put bb
25000 Sombor
☎ 025/000-0000

5/8

Once Tito's villa, it has now been refurbished into an exclusive villa with a vast green garden and a restaurant.

Kronić
✉ Čonopljanski put 30
25000 Sombor
☎ 025/429-900

22/60

This comfortable hotel lies on a green plateau of endless Vojvodina plain in Bačka, on Čonopljanski put road.

★★★★ Narvik
✉ Trg srpskih dobrovoljaca 2
23300 Kikinda
☎ 0230/23-910

105/182

In the very centre of Kikinda, the hotel is next to the verdant city park.

★ Park
✉ Trg Oslobodjenja 3
24430 Ada
☎ 024/853-259

20/40

This hotel with always hospitable staff is situated in the centre of Ada.

★★★ Royal
✉ Trg Maršala Tita 11
24400 Senta
☎ 024/812-368

60/120

Just next to the Tisa River and hidden in a wonderful park.

Kraljica voća
✉ Selo Gornji Breg
24400 Senta
☎ 063/838-6482

6/12

Every guest can enjoy a separate house with a feeling of being a part of the community and enjoy the excellent restaurant. English and Russian are spoken.

Ciha
✉ Maršala Tita 157
24300 Bačka Topola
☎ 024/711-317

13/23

On the outskirts of the city, 500m from the Lake with newly arranged beach.

★★★ Jadran
✉ Subotički put bb
24300 Zobnatica
☎ 024/715-641

23/50

Hotel has its own 300 acres lake, museum of horse breeding, a horse farm and special programmes for children.

Lovački Dom
✉ Bačka Topola

☎ 024/712-055

6/14

Remarkable atmosphere of hunting lodge, very well equipped room with sauna at disposal and a very good restaurant. English and German are spoken.

★★★ Fantast
✉ Bačko-Topolski put bb
21220 Bečej
☎ 021/813-531

20/40

Once the famous Dundjerski Castle, now a highly rated hotel offers extraordinary service with horse farm, outdoors swimming pool, ostrich farm and finely arranged park surrounding it.

★★★ Bela Ladja

✉ Borisa Kidriča bb
21220 Bečej
☎ 021/815-608

30/90

Situated on the Tisa riverbank, the hotel offers quiet atmosphere with walking area and sport courts.

★★★ Tiski Cvet

✉ Trg Oslobodjenja 1
23272 Novi Bečej
☎ 023/773-424

36/80

The only hotel in Novi Bečej is situated in the centre of the city at the Tisa riverbank.

★★★ Lipov Cvet

✉ 23270 Melenci
☎ 023/731-220

20/50

Quiet place near the Rusanda Spa, with music over weekends and everyday during summer.

★★★ Vojvodina

✉ Trg Slobode 5
23000 Zrenjanin
☎ 023/61-233

72/140

Recently renovated hotel in the very centre of the city, just across the Town Hall known for high quality service.

★★ Kastel

✉ Novosadska 7
23203 Ečka
☎ 023/881-013

20/40

Once the summer house of Prince Ferdinand where famous Franz Liszt held his concert when he was 8 is now famous for hunters with extraordinary garden decorated with sculptures of old times.

★★★ Sibila

✉ Lukino Selo
23203 Ečka
☎ 023/884-023

16/26

Surrounded with numerous fishponds the hotel in the heart of Carska Bara wetlands has also a wonderful terrace .

Sneža

✉ Beogradski put bb
23203 Ečka
☎ 023/881-201

11/19

Quiet and isolated place for guests seeking for a rest on the road to Belgrade.

★★★ Fontana

✉ Jugoslovenske armije 15
21400 Bačka Palanka
☎ 021/742-022

21/59

Surrounded with numerous fishponds the hotel has a wonderful terrace in the heart of Carska Bara.

Poloj

✉ Čelarevska Šuma bb
21400 Bačka Palanka
☎ 021/745-370

20/40

A quiet place in the woods, 3 km from the Dundjerski Castle in Čelarevo.

★★★★★ Park

✉ Novosadskog sajma 35
21000 Novi Sad
☎ 021/480-4444

225/380

The only 5 stars hotel in Novi Sad. Recently renovated and with remarkable service, next to the Novi Sad fairgrounds.

★★★★ Aleksandar

✉ Bulevar Cara Lazara 79
21000 Novi Sad
☎ 021/480-4444

131/227

Designed to meet the highest world standards. Contemporary styled and elegant furniture. Hotel that, with its refined style and its business charm goes hand in hand with you or, just like you, one step further.

★★★ Novi Sad

✉ Bulevar Jaše Tomića bb
21000 Novi Sad
☎ 021/442-511

116/270

Hotel is next to bus and railway stations.

★★★ Putnik

✉ Ilije Ognjanovića 26
21000 Novi Sad
☎ 021/615-555

84/146

Excellent hotel with very good restaurant.

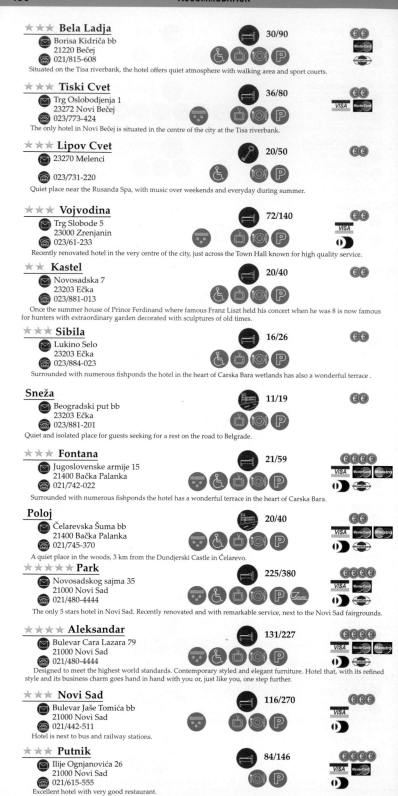

SUITES
A creative combination of comfort, elegance and high level of technical equipment.

ROOMS
Elegance and style, sophisticated details and calm colours create the necessary measure of warmth in our rooms.

CONGRESS HALL
A modern Congress Hall with the latest equipment for presentations and simultaneous translation.

TV SALON
A cosy space with a large plasma screen and Internet point.

APERITIF BAR
Turned towards the boulevard, living in the rhythm of the city, the most attractive part of the hotel lobby was designed as the place for exchange of ideas, business consultations or informal chatting.

RESTAURANT
A cosy ambience of the restaurant becomes an ideal place where you can enjoy in a wide selection of top class wines while you listen to the sounds of piano.

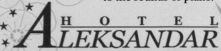

HOTEL ALEKSANDAR

Welcome to Novi Sad

000 Novi Sad , Bul. Cara Lazara 79 , Hotel : +381 (21) 480 - 4444 , Uprava : +381 (21) 543 - 222
e-mail : office@aleksandar-hotel.co.yu , www.aleksandar-hotel.co.yu

★★★ Sajam
Hajduk Veljkova 11
21000 Novi Sad
021/420-266

71/138

Just across the Novi Sad Fairgrounds. The guests are required to make reservations in advance.

★★★ Vojvodina
Trg Slobode 2
21000 Novi Sad
021/622-122

61/110

Hotel is situated in the very centre of the city, right across the Town Hall and the "Cathedral".

★★★ Zenit
Zmaj Jovina 8
21000 Novi Sad
021/621-444

20/50

Very good hotel in the most congestive street in the city offering a high quality service.

Voyager
Stražilovska 16
21000 Novi Sad
021/453-711

20/45

"Voyager" has 20 exclusively furnished apartments offering bed and breakfast accommodation. Breakfast is served in a restaurant 10 metres away.

Fitness Gymnas
Teodora Pavlovića 28
21000 Novi Sad
021/469-285

22/44

Luxury sport hotel is in a quiet part of the city, 15 minutes walk from the centre.

Rimski
Jovana Cvijića 26
21000 Novi Sad
021/443-237

23/49

New private hotel with wonderfully decorated garden for the exclusive use of guests. Smoking and non-smoking areas.

Jet-Set
Temerinski put 44
21000 Novi Sad
021/414-511

24/47

Small hotel in the very centre of the city providing family atmosphere.

Fontana
Nikole Pašića 27
21000 Novi Sad
021/662-1779

12/24

Attractive place in the centre, with a garage and fine terrace.

Salaš 137
Medjunarodni put bb
21233 Čenej
021/714-501

14/32

Just as it was decades ago, guests may enjoy the beautiful nature, very good equipped rooms, restaurant and the nearby paddock. French and Italian are spoken.

Salaš 84
Stari Žabaljski drum bb
21000 Novi Sad
021/445-993

2/4

Beautiful house and excellent restaurant next to a small pond, perfect for unforgettable experience.

★★ Boem
Branka Radičevića 5
21205 Sremski Karlovci
021/881-038

6/13

In the centre of Sremski Karlovci, 1 km from Stražilovo, close to botanic garden, open-air garden in the very centre.

Olimp
Miloša Obilića 8
21208 Sremska Kamenica
021/463-295

5/16

In a quiet neighbourhood, 100 meters from Danube and near the palace in Kamenica. It has its own bowling alley.

Vila Evangelina
Branislava Bukurova 2
21208 Sremska Kamenica
021/464-111

16/32

Very quiet place, not far from Novi Sad, with internet connection.

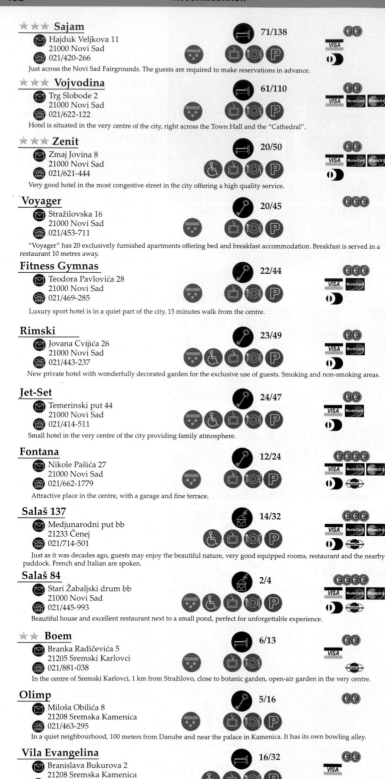

★ ★ Norcev
✉ Iriški venac

☎ 021/480-0222

🛏 43/100

In the woods of Mt Fruška Gora, lying on the altitude of 506 meters asl. Ideal both for family vacation and congresses. It has several duplex rooms, a gym, table tennis, swimming pool and sauna.

★ ★ Termal
✉ 22408 Vrdnik

☎ 022/465-102

🛏 99/102

Surrounded by forest the hotel has an adequately decorated garden. It stands below the medieval Vrdnik Tower.

★ ★ ★ MV Ruma
✉ Autoput bb
22400 Ruma
☎ 021/636-400

32/72

On the Belgrade-Zagreb motorway, ideal for spending a night after a long journey.

★ ★ Tamiš
✉ Moše Pijade bb
13000 Pančevo
☎ 013/342-622

🛏 116/180

In the very centre of the city the hotel is very suitable for business people.

Uzon
✉ Bratstva i jedinstva 30
26228 Skorenovac
☎ 013/764-066

2/6

Guests can enjoy a hospitable atmosphere of an ethnic Hungarian homestead.

★ ★ ★ ★ ★ Vila Breg
✉ Goranska bb
26300 Vršac
☎ 013/831-000

🛏 48/105

Just opened modern hotel on the slope of the Vršac Hill situated in beautiful environment. Excellent chice for business people.

★ ★ ★ Srbija
✉ Svetosavski trg 12
26300 Vršac
☎ 013/815-545

🛏 72/135

Recently renovated hotel stands in the very centre of the city. Suitable for congress tourism.

JAT
✉ Podvršanska 146
26300 Vršac
☎ 013/823-033

🔑 56/80

This is a small hotel off the beaten track - next to the Vršac Airport.

Rustical ambiance of Salaš 137

Fish restaurant    National restaurant    International restaurant

Mala Gostiona
✉ Park Narodnih heroja 9
24413 Palić
☎ 024/753-447

      06-01

On the shore of the lake, inside the Hotel Elit Palić complex; has a congress hall; live tambourine music on Sundays.

Majkin Salaš
✉ 24413 Palić

☎ 024/753-032

     10.00-01.00

Furnished in the style of the old Vojvodina salaš. It promotes characteristical cuisube of the region. Live tambourine music.

Guljaš Čarda
✉ Ludoški šor 208
24413 Palić
☎ 024/758-093

      07.00-0.00

In čarda-inn style, has its own ostrich farm and a ZOO garden, a playground, a fish pond in which guests can fish. Music on weekends.

Vinski Dvor
✉ selo Hajdukovo
24413 Palić
☎ 024/754-762

      11.00-0.00

A national restaurant with more than one hundred Serbian, Hungarian and international dishes served with a buttery for wine tasting; surrounded by vinyards.

Baron
✉ Borisa Kidriča 4
24000 Suborica
☎ 024/557-800

      11.00-23.00

In the very centre of the city, on the town promenade. Pleasant and traditional atmosphere. Excellent regional cuisine.

Pod Tornjem
✉ Trg Slobode bb
24000 Subotica
☎ 024/557-800

     10.00-22.00

Located in the Town Hall, the heart of the Subotica. Hungarian and Vojvodinian cuisine. Live piano and violine music every day.

Nepker
✉ Trg Lajoša Košuta 11
24000 Subotica
☎ 024/555-480

      10.00-22.00

A restaurant is a part of the Hungarian Folklore Society "Nepker". One must sample a delicious Perkelt Goulash. Lunch on self-service basis. On Sundays there is a gypsy orchestra playing.

Majur
✉ 24104 Kelebija

☎ 024/789-007

     11.00-0.00

Just next to the border-crossin and 500 m away from a horse farm. Tambourine music performed everyday. Try the superb *majušnica*.

Riblja Čarda Andrić
✉ Veliki Bački kanal
25000 Sombor
☎ 011/23-055

     09.00-0.00

A fish čarda on the Veliki Bački Canal, serving excellent stews. Welcoming green garden on two levels. Live tambourine music on weekends.

Čarda Kod Srećka
✉ Bezdan
25000 Sombor
☎ 011/810-200

     10.00-0.00

In Bezdan, 190 km from Belgrade. This establishment has its own fishing and hunting grounds. It serves excellent stew.

Čarda Pikec
✉ naselje Baračka, Bezdan
25000 Sombor
☎ 011/81-909

      09.00-0.00

A Danubian, fishermen's atmosphere, with an excellent fish stew served.

Largoš
✉ Bačko-Topolski put bb
21220 Bečej
☎ 021/810-085

     12.00-22.00

This fine restaurant is situated in a cellar not far from the centre of Bečej. Founded 10 years ago; pleasant and quiet.

Citadela
✉ Novosadski put bb
23000 Zrenjanin
☎ 023/536-782

    09.00-0.00

Just after you passenter Zrenjanin lies this touristy place. Reasonably priced.

Trofej
✉ Stajićevo, Beogradski put bb
23000 Zrenjanin
☎ 023/884-122

    09.00-0.00

On the entrance to the Carska Bara bog, it has a small ZOO Garden; venison specialties.

Žal za mladost
✉ Futošku put 99a
21000 Novi Sad
☎ 021/400-934

    10.00-23.00

On the outskirts of Novi Sad, but everything in this restaurant originates from the South of Serbia: waistcoats, woven table cloths etc.

Alaska barka
✉ Ribarsko ostrvo 4
21000 Novi Sad
☎ 021/6365-683

 07.00-01.00

An excellent restaurant, 3 km from the city centre, on the very bank of Danube, in a large garden; wide choice of wines.

Arhiv
✉ Ilije Ognjanovića 16
21000 Novi Sad
☎ 021/472-2176

 09.00-0.00

In the very heart of Novi Sad, in a pleasant and intimate atmosphere; excellent choice of European dishes.

Ognjište
✉ Dimitrija Tucovića 3
21000 Novi Sad
☎ 021/450-594

 09.00-23.00

In a unique atmosphere, you can enjoy old national specialties.

Dukat
✉ Đorđa Rajkovića 12
21000 Novi Sad
☎ 021/525-190

 12.00-23.00

A typical Vojvodina restaurant serving good food at reasonable prices.

Ribarska noć
✉ Podunavska 2 (Kamenjar)
21000 Novi Sad
☎ 021/6364-664

 12.00-01.00

Experience the true atmosphere of salaš; a large garden is open during the summer.

Čarda Aqua Doria
✉ Kamenicki put bb
Petrovaradin, 21000 Novi Sad
☎ 021/6433-111

 08.00-0.00

A fish čarda, made of woods, on the Danube riverbank; tambourine music; and a stunning view to the town on the other side of the river.

Ribarac
✉ Ribarsko ostrvo 4
21000 Novi Sad
☎ 011/466-977, 466-978

 10.00-0.00

On the Danube, set in a large garden. This exclusive restaurant serves good food has an excellent choice of wines.

Četiri lava
✉ Trg Branka Radičevića 3
21205 Sremski Karlovci
☎ 063/524-456

 07.00-01.00

The oldest tavern in Sremski Karlovci (200 years) serves regional cuisine and quality home-made wines.

Dunav
✉ Dunavska 5
21205 Sremski Karlovci
☎ 021/881-666

 07.00-0.00

This restaurant lying on the bank of the Danube and has a large terrace just above the water. A Gypsy tambourine orchestra performs music.

Točak
✉ Novosadska 72
St. Pazova
☎ 022/311-719

 07.00-23.00

A small restaurant along the Belgrade – Novi Sad motorway. Calm and quiet with intimate, informal atmosphere.

Ribarska Čarda Kečiga
✉ Vodna bb
22000 Sremska Mitrovica
☎ 022/613-835

 08.00-23.00

On the Sava River bank, made in woods with a beautiful view; all sorts of fish and grill specialties are served; ordering service; ready-to-eat meals; a great choice of all sorts of drinks.

Kajakaški klub
✉ Veslački klub, Obala Tamiša
13000 Pančevo
☎ 013/351-543

 10.00-0.00

The restaurant is on the other bank of Tamiš River, facing the centre of Pančevo. Go to the end of Žarka Fograša St. Ring a bell on a dock and wait for a boat to transport you cost-free to the other side.

Fontana
✉ Trg S. Kovačevića bb
26300 Vršac
☎ 013/822-556

 08.00-23.00

In the very city centre, with clientele of business people and other well-to-do.

Restoran M
✉ Omladinski trg 17
26300 Vršac
☎ 013/800-158

 11.00-0.00

In the Milenijum Mall on a hill facing the town. It is very popular with businessmen and members of various delegations.

Ikar
✉ Podvršanska 146
26300 Vršac
☎ 013/830-650

 12.00-20.00

A restaurant in the Flight Academy with two large halls. Surrounded by pine and birch trees.

WESTERN SERBIA

Western Serbia's landscape is one of many different shapes and colours. Starting with the fertile plain Mačva, over the low Cer Mountain, up to the first mountains of Povlen and Maljen from where the land rises to the higher peaks of the Tara, Zlatibor and Zlatar mountains. In contrast to this geographical diversity, the people of this region are nearly all the sons and daughters of settlers that came centuries before from the west - from Bosnia, Herzegovina or Montenegro. The winding river Drina and narrow valleys could not stop the traditional migration pathways from the heart of the Dinaric Alps towards its edges and flatlands, and so the cattle-breed-

reminders of which can be frequently seen throughout the Cer and Suvobor mountains where monuments and tombs are scattered over the landscape marking the Serbian victories in 1914 and 1915. Moving south one comes across monuments to the uprisings against the German invaders. The city of Užice is known as the centre of the territory called "Užička Republika" ("Republic of Užice") freed in the autumn of 1941. This included nearly the entire region of Western Serbia and was much celebrated in postwar communistic ideology. In the last decade, the royalist call for an uprising in May 1941 is regularly celebrated on Ravna Gora Mountain.

Enjoying a quiet afternoon in Guča

ing population constantly spread to the more fertile areas. The Ijekavian dialect used here has been influenced and transformed over the decades by the literary Ekavian dialect. The heroic tradition of battling against the Turks continued into the 20th century with fierce fighting against the Austro-Hungarians and then the Germans. These parts sacrificed much for freedom in both the World Wars,

Yet some good has come out of all these horrific wars. The tradition of military bands from 19th and 20th century wars created trumpet orchestras that played folk songs on trumpets in the days of peace Today, the small town of Guča is called the "trumpet capital of the world". Every year in early August, famous trumpet players gather here at a festival that attracts tens of thousands of visitors. Tradition playing of gusle, the Serb national string instrument, is well worth experiencing for its archaic sounding melodies that date back to the Middle Ages when they accompanied epic poetry reciting. Of musical interest too are the groups of elderly men singing in the traditional style.

The daily lives and gruff spirit of Western Serbia is unimaginable without mentioning local brandy rakija, primarily *šljivovica*, plum brandy that accompanies a Serbian from morning till night, or juniper brandy (*klekovača*), made in the high mountains. The area is still predominantly used for cattle breeding and thus famous for its cheeses, a cream called *kajmak*, smoked ham (*pršuta*), and also potatoes, the best one being considered the one from Ivanjica and the vicinity.

Nature to be found in Western Serbia deserves special attention. Green meadows stretch for kilometres alongside dense forests. Lowland clearings are spattered with steep-roofed wooden houses that are then replaced by rocky peaks over which soar eagles and hawks. The cultivated land around scattered villages quickly transforms into unexplored wilderness such as the primeval forests of Tara and Zlatar, where bears and wolves are still a common phenomenon.

1 Šabac

2 Banja Koviljača

3 Valjevo

4 Pustinja

5 Struganik

6 Rajac

7 Ravna Gora

8 Koštunići

9 Bajina Bašta

10 "Tara" National Park

11 Mokra Gora

12 Užice

13 Zlatibor

14 Arilje

15 Ivanjica

16 Guča

17 Ovčarsko-Kablarska klisura

18 Čačak

Trbušnica

Loznica

Banja Koviljača

Mali Zvornik

SARAJEVO
144km

BiH

SARAJEVO
147km

Traditional wooden house in Zlatibor

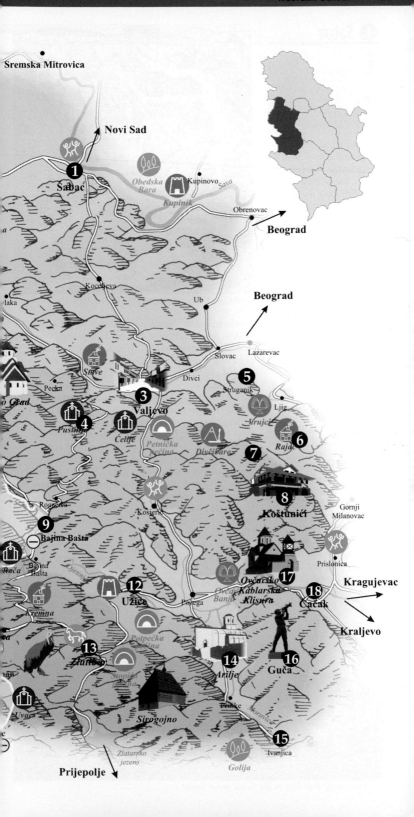

Sremska Mitrovica

Novi Sad

① Šabac

Obedska Bara

Kupinik

Kupinovo

Sava

Obrenovac

Beograd

Kočeljeva

Ub

Beograd

laka

Slovac

Lazarevac

Pecka

Struve

Divci

Struganik

⑤

Ljig

o Grad

④

Pušina

Valjevo

Ćelije

Petnička Pećina

Divčibare

Vrujci

Rajac

⑥

⑦

Rogačica

Kosjerić

⑧

Koštunići

Gornji Milanovac

Bajina Bašta

⑨

Prislonica

Rača

Bajina Bašta

Đetinja

Kremna

⑫

Užice

Požega

Ovčar Banja

Ovčarsko Kablarska Klisura

⑰

⑱

Čačak

Kragujevac

sa

Potpećka Pećina

Zlatibor

⑬

Mokra Gora

⑭

Arilje

⑯

Guča

Kraljevo

Uvac

Sirogojno

Trnke

Moravica

ijn

Zlatarsko jezero

Golija

Ivanjica

⑮

Prijepolje

❶ Šabac

👥 82.300

ℹ️ Karađorđeva 5
15000 Šabac
015/347-383

🚌 015/347-065

📱 015/341-384

84 km - Beograd

The first record of a town on the river Sava in the fertile plain of Mačva comes from the mid 15th century. The town, then called *Zaslon*, was frequented by merchants from all over the region. It fell to the Turks in 1459, who built a fort that they used for frequent incursions into Hungary. For that reason the fort was overtaken by the despotes Vuk Grgurevic in the name of the Hungarian king Mathias Corvinus.

Under Hungarian rule between 1475-1521, the new name of the town, derived from the name *Savac*, was mentioned for the first time. The town flourished After the Second Serbian uprising (1815) the town flourished under the governance of Jevrem Obrenović, the enlightened brother of Prince Miloš. During his reign, the first hospital, pharmacy and secondary school in Serbia came into being. It was

Šabac at the beginning of the 16th century

also here, more specifically in Jevrem's house, that the first piano was obtained. The city was further modernized after the Turkish garrison left the fort in 1867. As it lay on the frontline, Šabac suffered heavily in the First World War. It was bombed and changed hands between Austrians and Serbs several times (1914 and 1915) never again to recover its former glory. The town that was known as "Little Paris" before the war was now nicknamed "Serbian Verdun". Furthermore, Šabac and its vicinity was the site of

some of the worst Austro-Hungarian atrocities against civilians. The Second World War brought new destruction as 7000 inhabitants lost their lives and a further 5000 were resettled by the Nazis.

The **fortress** lies by the riverfront some 1.5 km from the town centre, on the banks of the Sava. Today there is a charming beach here that is delightful in the summer months. The fortress was built in 1471 by the Turks on flat terrain protected by the moats that the river flooded. The fort has a

Krsmanović Building in the Šabac main street

Gingerbread hearts - Licidersko srce, on sale in Šabac famous fair

rectangular base plan and a round tower on every corner. The walls rise to the height of 8 metres. Sadly only one tower remains today.

The **Church of SS Peter and Paul** dates back to 1831. It has an impressive bell tower that was added a decade later. Noteworthy is the tall Iconostasis painted in 1855 by Pavle Simić. Heavily damaged in WWI, the frescoes were repainted in 1932 by Andrej Bisenko. In the courtyard of the church stands the **Monument to the fallen soldiers of the 1912-1918 wars** by F. Menegelo-Dinčić from 1934.

To the left of the church stands the **museum** (*Narodni muzej, Masarikova 13, 015/324-245, muzejsabac@ptt.yu, open Monday to Friday 8 a.m.-2 p.m. and 4 p.m.-6 p.m., on Saturdays 9 a.m.-3 p.m.*) situated in the old high school. It is a simple, Romanesque style building constructed in 1856.

The **Bishop's Residence** (*Vladičin dvor*) is an interesting edifice that shows a mixture of traditional architectonic forms (the arches) and classical style. Today it houses the city library.

The main town promenade is **Karadjordjeva Street** along which are

situated some of the finest buildings of Šabac including the corner **Krsmanović house** and the two-storied edifice of the **District Court** with its symmetrical wings, both dating back to the beginning of the 20th century.

❷ Banja Koviljača

6 km - Loznica

Located in a plane and bordered with the Drina River on one side and Gučevo Mountain on the other, Koviljača Spa is known for its many springs rich in sulphur and iron. Records exist that the Turks used it in the 17th century as a picnic location and called it *Smrdan bara* ("Stinky Pond") because of the awkward smell of its waters. The facilities were first opened for

the visitors in 1858, but the spa was not widely known until King Peter visited it at the beginning of the 20th century. After being successfully healed, the King ordered the construction of several edifices with the park in the middle. The Spa was given a more appealing name, Koviljača, after a nearby village and plant kovilj (feather grass) believed to be the favorite sleeping place for fairies. The Spa prospered until the First World War when it found itself in the front lines of battle. After the Great War, several modern hotels and sanatoriums were built, but the spa suffered damage again in the next war.

The central point of the Spa is a nice park from the turn of the 20th century around which there are villas and hotels. The park has a fine fountain with colorful lights at night. The main building in the park is the **Kursalon** edifice from 1934 with its pointed towers, which has been turned into a high-class hotel with a conference hall and a casino.

Baths at the Banja Koviljača Spa

❸ Valjevo

🏛 76.700

ℹ️ Prote Mateje 1
14000 Valjevo
014/221-138

☎ 014/221-482

📠 014/221-697

90 km - Beograd

Houses of the old Tešnjar quarter

Mentioned for the first time in 1393 when it was an important staging post on the trading route from Bosnia to Belgrade, Valjevo became significant only during the stable Turkish rule which spanned the 16th and 17th centuries. Severely damaged in the Austro-Turkish wars of the 18th century, it became one of the key towns connected with the First Serbian Uprising thanks to several prominent personalities among which stands out the Nenadović family from nearby Brankovina: knez ("duke") Aleksa Nenadović was one of the first to be executed by the Turks, Jakov became one of the leading military commanders and his brother Mateja, the president of the Governing Council of Serbia. After the liberation, the town started to blossom again. Its centre was transferred in 1855 from the constricted right bank of the Kolubara River to the other bank where the town expanded with broad tree-lined streets. At the beginning of the 20th century this was one of the most prosperous cities in Serbia. For instance, electric street lights were introduced in 1899 after the construction of the dam on the Gradac River. During the 1999 NATO bombing, the city's economy was crippled when the "Krušik" factory was destroyed creating severe unemployment.

Valjevo lies in a position of outstanding natural beauty: there are no less than five waterways (Kolubara, Gradac, Jablanica, Obnica and Ljubostinja) at the foot of the wooded hills supplying the town with fresh air at all times. The oldest part of Valjevo is situated on the right bank of the Kolubara River under Vidrak hill. Between them lies the old trading quarter **Tešnjar**, one of the most picturesque in Serbia with its cobblestone streets, traditional 19th century houses and inns, some of which carry inscriptions from local craftsman. From Tešnjar one can climb up **Vidrak hill** to the park surrounding the colossal **monument to Stjepan Filipović**, a partisan fighter who was hanged by the Nazis during WWII and later granted the highest honors with the title of "National Hero". The monument, work of sculptor Vojin Bakić, takes a bold leap away from the usual social-realism style in depictions of communist martyrdom in the "Struggle for Natioanl Liberation" as it was called back then.

There are several bridges that lead across the river. The central one takes you to **Vojvoda Mišić Square** (*Trg vojvode Mišića*), on which stands the monument to this revered World War I commander of the Serbian army. In Živojina Mišića St there are several attractive buildings such as the **Valjevo Savings Bank** and the **District Court**, both dating from the turn of the 20th century.

To the right of the old **"Grand"**, still the best

Watermills by the Gradac River, Valjevo

hotel in the town, is the street that leads to the interesting building of the **old school**, dating from 1870. Today it houses the **Town Museum** *(tel. 014/221-041; www.museum.org.yu, open Mon-Fri 9.30 a.m. - 2 p.m.)*. Part of the museum is also the **Muselim's residence** *(Muselimov konak,,* situated behind the museum building on the left), the small residence of the Turkish governor of the town in which Ilija Birčanin, Aleksa Nenadović and other Serb leaders from the vicinity were imprisoned prior to their execution in 1804. Today it houses exhibitions on local episodes of the First and Second Serbian Uprisings.

Continuing up the short Čika Ljubina St, we reach the bridge which marks the place of the famous execution that stirred Serbia to rebellion. The occasion is commemorated by a small red stone **pyramid**. Behind the corner to the left stands the **High school**, a twin building to the Third Belgrade High school, the style of which proved to be such a success.

Facing Vidrak on this side of the river rises the squat **Kličevac hill** and on it the oldest landmark in the town – the **Nenadović tower**. It was originally built by the Jajić family of Turkish landowners, to guard the northern approach to the town. It was renovated by Jakov Nenadović in 1813, thus the new name. It is a three storey structure

with one meter thick stone walls and openings of various shapes and sizes – windows and loop holes. There are two stone plaques from that period built into the walls featuring the Serbian coat-of-arms.

Downstream from Tešnjar, the Kolubara river is joined by the immaculately clean **River Gradac**. Along its last few kilometres it flows past old mills, wooden bridges, restaurants and fish ponds, and is crossed by the railway line heading further south towards the river gorge. The 30 kilometres of the Gradac is itself a beautiful area of considerable ecological importance. The source of the river is made from three streams that flow into each other to form the Gradac. Nearby is the **Hut of the "Gradac" Ecological Society** *(014/225-188)*, where an overnight stay can be booked. Down river there are several beaches frequented by fisher-

man and a succession of small ravines. There is also Sava's mill *(Savina vodenica)*, named after Sava Savanović, the first known Serbian

Nenadović Tower on Kličevac Hill

vampire whose name and representation were immortalized by the writer Milovan Glišić (1847-1908), himself a native of this region.

West of the Tešnjar quarter one can take a pleasant walk along Birčaninova Street to the **Pećina** locality and Valjevo brewery surrounded by a dense wooded landscape. Not far from here the rivers Obnica and Jablanica join up to form the Kolubara.

ENVIRONS:

10 km down the road to Šabac, a left turn takes one to the **village of Brankovina**. The church marks the old centre of this rambling village whose habitats are spread widely about the surrounding area. Almost everything here is connected with the famous Nenadović family whose birthplace this is and several of whom were celebrated in the 18th and 19th centuries. In a field crossed by a stream there are several smaller buildings, the smallest of which are the wooden *sobrašice*, which were shelters built by wealthy families used for feasts on church feast days . The **Church of Holy Archangels** was built in 1830 from the

Playing the bagpipes in Valjevo

funds donated by the priest Matija Nenadović, one of the leaders of the First Uprising, who became the president of the Governing Council and wrote the famed "Memoirs". The graves of this prominent family stand by the north wall of the temple as well as the monument by Djordje Jovanović to the soldiers of Brankovina and other neighboring villages who fell in the 1912-18 wars. Items exhibited in the church treasury include a 10th century cross and the Gospel on which the members of the Governing Council took their oath. On a small mound left of the church lies the grave of the much admired poetess Desanka Maksimović, one of the leading Serbian lyricists of the 20th century, who was born here. On the other side of the stream stand two school buildings. The **Old school** was constructed as early as 1834 and was one of the first schools to be established in the newly autonomous Serbia. This was built on the initiative of the already mentioned Matija Nenadović, who was one of the few men who could read and write in Serbia at that time. Today its unchanged classrooms house an exhibition on the school

system in 19th century Serbia.

In the **village of Petnica**, 8 kilometres south east of Valjevo there is an underground **cavern**. Visitors are welcome to visit 414 metres into its depths. Found in the cavern were a number of

Vojvoda Mišić's House in Struganik village

human remains whose origins date back to paleolithic times. In the 3rd century AD this site was a place of pagan worship. Out of several of its chambers, the most beautiful are those of Koncertna, naturally lit by two openings in the roof, and Zmajeva with a pool of water 20 metres deep.

❹ Pustinja

23 km - Valjevo

23 km west of Valjevo lies the village of Poćuta. 4 km to the north of the village the Pustinja monastery is to be found. Its name, pustinja, meaning

"desert" which was derived from its earlier seclusion in the picturesque landscape of the Jablanica River gorge. In the early 17th century, the ruins of the medieval monastery were used as the foundations for a new building. This newer construction is in a somewhat unusual and distorted variety of the Raška style. The white painted narthex with a bell tower was added in 1848.

The interior was painted in 1622 thanks to a donation from the Abbot Jovan Bitojević, who is depicted with a model of the church. The painters Jovan and Nikola were both well skilled, however one of them was clearly more talented than the other. Still, the lavish frescoes are among the most valuable examples of 17th century Serbian art. The monastery prides itself on a relic that purports to be the hand of St John the Baptist.

❺ Struganik

7 km - Mionica

Struganik is a birth place of Field-marshal (*vojvoda*) Živojin Mišić, where his family house still exists. The village was named after the dark stone struganik

Pustinja Monastery

that is even nowadays being extracted. It is easily broken into flagstones and widely used for decorative purposes. It is interesting to mention that the stone from this area was used to decorate the Opera House in Vienna.

After some 15 km down the Ljig-Mionica road, turn left and you will reach this village. If you continue straight forward through the scattered village, you will come to **Mišić's house**, which is on the right from the main road. The house is maintained by his descendants, who will gladly give you a tour through his memorial home. For its distinguishing architectural style of this region, the house of the Mišić family would still be considered a monument, even if there weren't for the interesting exibition of life and wars of Živojin Mišić (1855-1921), a great army commander who was among the most deserving people for the Serbian victories in the First World War. The wooden part of the house, where the fireside is and where the whole family used to gather, together with its preserved enterier and household furniture

gives an insight into life of a Serbian village from the 19th century.

Also, not far from here, is **Vrujci Spa** with its thermal springs (28°C).

❻ Rajac

5 km - Ljig

Rajac is a peak (848 m) on the eastern side of Suvobor Mountain, but it is also the name of the whole area that surrounds the summit. Thanks to its mountain hut "Čika Duško Jovanović" (tel. 014/800-06) built in 1952/3, Rajac is an old and well-known mountaineering destination. The Hut, named after the diligent naturalist and devoted climber, is still the largest in Serbia. There is a **monument** in front of it, in the memory of 1300 corporals who died there fighting in the famous Kolubara Battle which outcome was decided at Suvobor. Right behind the hut, there is a Resort Centre owned by „Poštanska štedionica" (tel. 014/800-22).

The Home and the Resort Centre can be reached by an asphalt road from Slavkovica village which was built two years ago.

❼ Ravna Gora

30 km - Gornji Milanovac

Every year in mid July, the manifestation Haymaking at Rajac (Kosidba na Rajcu) is held in the surrounding of the Hut, when skillful haymakers show their artistry. Rajac is a tame and extremely pleasant mountain of preserved

Rakija infused with herbs

beauty, with a lot of marked paths enabling longer and shorter walks.

Ravna Gora ("Flat Hill") is a wide mountain plateau stretching in a westward direction from the high peak of Suvobor (864 m).

On 13th of May 1941 the officers of the defeated Yugoslav army and other patriots led by Colonel Dragoljub "Draža" Mihailović gathered here and pronounced the beginning of the uprising against the German occupiers and their accomplices. This telling of events was prohibited after the war as it clashed with the prevailing communist ideology. Since 1990 and the relaxation of communist restraints, Ravna Gora has become the Mecca for Serbian nationalists celebrating "Uncle Draža" (Čiča

Reaping on Mt Rajac

Church in the Ravna Gora plateau

Draža) especially on the first Saturday following the 13th of May when tens of thousands gather together at the focal manifestation.

In the centre of the plateau stands the **monument to General Mihailović**, the **church of St George** and a conference hall. Further to the west is a fine viewpoint from the **Babina glava hill** behind which are two small **caves** – Suva and Mokra pećina.

❽ Koštunići

27 km - Čačak

Koštunići village is on the southern hillside of Suvobor Mountain. Mostly old, little houses are scattered around the beautiful mountain area interlaced with meadows, forests and fields. With its preserved nature, untouched by modern life, the village attracted enthusiasts who launched a project in 1996 of creating an existing ethno-village that would produce organic food and traditional handiworks, at the same time accommodating the visitors in the local houses. That was when the centre of the village was built, with a few counstructions in a harmonious combination of the traditional and the modern. By the side of the road is a **church** whose frescoes are painted from the donations of the local residents. A small **museum** in the memory of Kolubara Battle is next to the church. The **Ethno-house "Anđelija Mišić"** is the centre of clothes production on old weaver frames in traditional techniques.

"Ravna gora" restaurant is above it, and behind it the **Ethno-museum Prodanovića magaza**, a 120-year-old large building made of wood, where you can still see objects used once in village households. Accommodation facilities by the name „Vajati", built to resemble log cabins of this area, are also near.

❾ Bajina Bašta

🏠 23.500

ℹ️ Milana Obrenovića 34/II 31250 Bajina Bašta 031/865-370

✉️ 031/865-485

💻 031/863-485

🚗 29 km - Užice

In 1834, the old village of Pljeskovo practically vanished when the local Muslims had to move away in accordance with the Serbian-Turkish agreement. This convenient location, the fertile plain close to the Drina River, was soon inhabited by people from nearby villages. The new settlement was named Bajina Bašta ("Baja's Garden") for its floral surroundings and soon became widely known for its tobacco *bajinac*. The new town plan for Bajina Bašta was adopted in 1882 and a rectangular street plan was introduced with a large square that still exists today. There are several interesting houses by provincial builders in this lively small town and a beach on the bank of the Drina, beneath the bridge to Bosnia. The bridge is also used as the border crossing.

ENVIRONS:

Some 6km to the south, at the foot of the beautiful Tara Mountain, there is **Rača Monastery**.

Sowing folk-inspired costumes in Koštunići

An idyllic afternoon in high summer on Lake Perućac

An endowment attributed to King Dragutin (13th century), Rača was rebuilt from the ruins in the 16th century. It reached its peak during the next century, as a transcribing centre where transcripts and manuscripts were kept. Its monks became well known men-of-letters and as transcribers from this monastery, at one point even called *Račani*! Deserted and destroyed in 1690, the activities of the monastery were reactivated in 1795. The existing church was built in 1835 on the foundations of the older one. The wall paintings and iconostasis are from the mid 19th century.

⑩ "Tara" National Park

The territory of the Tara National Park consists of Tara Mountain and, west from it, Zvijezda Mountain, separated with the gorge of the Derventa River. Rising sharply above the Drina River, Tara Mountain goes up from 1000 to 1200 m asl, where it is flattened in a wooded plateau without any higher peaks - the highest point is Smiljevac, 1444 m. Tara is known to be very rich in water: many springs make streams and rivers that run down to the Drina, creating on the way several waterfalls, the best known being Veliki Skakavac and Mali Skakavac.

Forests of Tara are well known to be intact by human factor and they are considered to be among the richest in flora in the whole Europe. The most common species are groups of juniper, fir tree and birch. Pančić's spruce (lat. *Picea omorica*), a rare endemic species, stands out among more than a thousand species of plants. It was named after a well-known Serbian naturalist Josif Pančić who discovered it in 1871. This very rare species exists only in the middle course of the Drina and is under the protection of the state. The tree grows up to 30-35 m, but is very thin and with short branches, which visually makes it higher and more attractive. The best place to observe this tree, spread today over the mountain in small groups, is Bilješka stijena above the Perućac Lake.

Thick forests and deep gorges were convenient for the survival of many animal species, so you can also find here brown bears, the "trade mark" of this mountain, then mountain goats, martens, wild cats, large grouses and golden eagles. What Pančić's spruce stands for flora that is a Pančić's grasshopper for fauna. The territory of the Tara National Park registers over 100 species of birds. On the western and northern side, the Tara National Park is fringed with a slower course of the Drina which is dammed at Perućac. You can raft and go fishing on the Drina, while there is a popular beach on the Perućac Lake.

Tourist capacities are grouped in several locations. A group of big hotels, such as the "Omorika" and "Beli bor", are at the **Kaludjerske bare**, as well as the information centre. A children recreational centre and several taverns are located at **Mitrovac**. A small isolated wood house is at **Predov krst**, while the "Jezero" hotel is, as its name says, at the Perućac Lake.

View of the Drina from Mt Tara

⑪ Mokra Gora

50 km - Užice

The road to Mokra Gora passes through the **village of Kremna** which is located in a valley that divides the areas of Tara and Zlatibor. Kremna is famous for its prophets, one such example being Miloš Tarabić (1809-1854) and his better known nephew Mitar Tarabić (1829-1899), both of whose house and graves in the village cemetery can be visited. Another site of interest here is the **Moljkovića Han**, an attractive example of Balkan style architecture.

Mokra Gora ("Wet Hill") is a picturesque mountain village (altitude 600m) which in recent years has opened itself to tourism. The main attraction here is the old **narrow gauge railway** (760 mm) that takes a wonderful route up the hill towards Kremna. It is a part of the old railway line that ran from Užice to Sarajevo and was launched in 1925. The construction of the railway immediately allowed ready access to the rest of the world for many mountain villages. It closed down in 1974 due to its state of disrepair and mounting losses. But starting in 1999, it has undergone a slow process of renovation and expansion, mainly

Houses from Kusturica's ethno-village

thanks to the efforts of the villagers themselves. The most interesting feature of this railway route, that earned it fame and the name "The Šargan Eight" (*Šarganska osmica*), is the remarkable feat of engineering which spans a height of 300 metres with an extraordinary loop in the shape of a figure 8. The 15 km line from Mokra Gora to the Šargan-Vitasi station takes one down a zigzag route through 22 tunnels and over 10 bridges with impressive views. Operated by steam locomotives fitted with old wood-panelled passenger cars, the line passes through lovely scenery and a series of small, romantic stations making this a delightful worthwhile journey.

The film director Emir Kusturica filmed his "Life Is a Miracle" in Mokra Gora. Fascinated by the scenery, he constructed a small "ethno-village" with a school for film direc-

tors on **Mećavnik Hill** above the centre of the village. The entire school complex was built in a style corresponding to the local rural architecture, mainly in wood, earning it the nickname of Drvengrad ("Wooden town").

Proceeding by road towards Višegrad and the border with Bosnia-Herzegovina, one reaches **Markovo Polje** with its **mediaeval necropolis** adorned with stećak (serb. *stećci*). There are 38 of them in all of different shapes and sizes and adorned with ornaments such as circles, crosses, crescents, shields, swords, bows and arrows.

⑫ Užice

🏛 71.300

ℹ Trg Partizana 10
31000 Užice
031/513-485

☎ 031/520-521

☎ 031/513-165

59 km - Čačak

Town Užice is on the river Djetinja, in a narrow valley from all sides surrounded by hills and high rocks. The town itself has today substantially expanded to the steep hillsides, turning some of the streets into serpentines, whereas some suburbs are entirely in the hills separated from the town.

Station on the "Šargan Eight" narrow-gauge railway, filmed by Kusturica in his "Life is a Miracle"

The town Uzice was mentioned for the first time in relation to a colony of merchants from Dubrovnik settled at this territory in 1392, and the fortress above it - half of the century later. At the end of 14th century, it was a solid stronghold of Nikola Altomanović, a young arrogant nobleman, who turned his neighbours against him. In 1373, prince Lazar and ban Tvrtko allied against Altomanović and besieged him in Užice fortress, imprisoned him, blinded him and sent him off to a monastery. The Turks overrun the managed to take the town and the fortress during the First Serbian Insurrection, but the Turkish troops later returned and stayed in the fortress until 1867. Freed from the threats of Turkish canons, the town developed fast as the centre of the mountain region, where the peasants from the surroundings brought *kajmak* (thick cream), ham, kindling wood and tar, products that were then passed on from here all over Serbia. In 1941 the town was liberated by partisans and proclaimed to be the centre of the free terri- the Djetinja River makes an "S" curve. When the Turkish troops left the citadel in 1867, the angry people tore the fortress down and used most of its material for their own private purposes. The inaccessible fort is triangular in shape and protected by five towers. The narrower part ends with the remains of the Water Tower overlooking the river. Gradska Street and walking paths lead from the river to the fortress.

Below the fortress, in picturesque scenery with a lovely small waterfall, there is a miniature **old**

Ruins of Užice Fortress standing near the town

town in 1456 and turned it into a centre of a district. The town developed fast and became known for its craftsmen, especially those who manufactured leather, so in reference to the number of inhabitants, at the end of the 16th century Užice fell behind Belgrade only a little. With the wars of the 18th century the importance of the fortress increased while the settlement was frequently burnt down by armies. The Serbs tory, called the "Republic of Užice". The partisans managed to maintain control over town for 67 days, when the Germans invaded it with severe revenge. Because of all these events, in 1946 Užice was named Titovo ("Tito's") Užice and it kept this name until 1992.

Certainly the most appealing monument in town is the **fortress**. Its remains are west from the town centre, on a high rock under which **hydropower plant** from 1900. This was the second constructed power plant in the world, on which Tesla's polyphase current principle was applied. Today, the old machines are still in function, but only as a part of the small **Technical Museum**. Not far from there is a town beach with a promenade leading to the town centre.

The main town square was built after the WWII and named **Trg Partizana**; on it predominates the **National Theatre** built in 1968. Until the beginning of the 1990s, when it was moved to the Museum, a huge statue of Tito, the work of Frane Kršinić from 1961, was representing the centre of the square. This was one of the only two statues of Tito in the whole of former Yugoslavia, the other one being his native village Kumrovec, Croatia.

The old **Church of St Mark** was built in 1828 in post and petrail construction and with a steep roof characteristic for the western Serbia. There is a three-storey bell-tower from 1890 next to it. The church houses the collection of ancient engravings and works of town silversmiths.

The **House of the Jokanović family** is a fine example of the town house from the 19th century in oriental-Balkan style, standing out from the local architecture. It belonged to the respectable Užice family of merchants, who also owned several inns. Rakija that was served in these inns was made in this house so that people of Užice popularly called it Pecara ("Distillery"). In the house today there is the **Ethnographic Museum** (*10 Slanuška St, tel 031/513-035*) with the permanent display "The town house of Užice in the 19th and the beginning of the 20th century".

About to enjoy Užice's famous rakija

Not far from the Museum, at the Svetog Save Square, there is the **Church of St. George** from 1842 and the beautiful **High School** building. The **National Museum** (*8 Dimitrija Tucovica St, tel. 031/521360, closed on Mondays, open on working days 9 a..m.-5 p.m. and on Saturdays 9 a.m.-2 p.m.*) is located in the house where the Headquarters of the partisan "National Liberation Movement of Yugoslavia" was together with the Central Committee of the Communist Party of Yugoslavia, as well as a partisan weapons and ammunition factory which was in the cellar. The Museum has three parts: one on the origin and development of Užice, the second on the Republic of Užice, while the third one exhibits the legacy of Mihailo Milovanović, the first academically educated painter in town.

ENVIRONS:

Potpeć Cave, a remarkable monument of nature, is in village Potpeć, 14 km from Užice, on the road to Požega. Cut into the calcareous cliff, the entrance of the cave is the most monumental one in Serbia: 50 m high, 12 m wide at the bottom and 20 wide on top. The Petnica River springs from the cave, whose waters gouged out the rock. The arranged part of the cave opened for tourist purposes is 555 m long.

15 km north of Užice there is the village of Karan with a medieval church dedicated to the Mother of God, **White Church of Karan** (*Bela crkva karanska*) named after the color of its exterior. This edifice of simple shape is an endowment of a lesser noble Brajan and dates from 1335, during the reign of King Dušan (1331-1355), later known as the Emperor Dušan, who was portrayed on the interior walls together with his wife Jelena and son Uroš. The wall paintings show also the portraits of the endower (holding the church in his hands) and his numerous family, mainly women in elaborately decorated attires, head garments with veils and large earrings.

White Church in the Karan village

⓭ Zlatibor

24 km - Užice

Zlatibor is a ruffled plateau 25 km south from Užice, with a settlement of the same name being the centre of this touristy region. Known for its exquisite landscapes and clean air, Zlatibor has recently developed substantially into a leading location of mountain tourism in Serbia. However, with urbanization, commercialization and popularization, its tourism at the same time lost much of its purity.

Up to the middle of the 19th century, this mountain was known as Rujno by the lustre of its vast fields filled with flocks of sheep. The area was poor, but also a place where a number of different routes in-

more. A reputation of an untached beauty of this plateau was spreading fast, so that King Alexander Obrenović visited it in 1893. There is a well commemorating King's visit in the centre of the settlement, which was from then named Kraljeve Vode ("King's Waters"). At that time, there were only a few houses there to accom-

the war, larger holiday resorts were built here and since the 1960s, Zlatibor became one of the most popular vacation destinations in the mountains.

Zlatibor owes its popularity first of all to its tamed looks in the middle of the beautiful wilderness of the mountains. Zlatibor town, (until recently known as Partizanske Vode and even earlier as Kraljeve Vode) is in the centre of the plateau at the average 1000 m asl, surrounded by Čigota, Murtenica, Tornik and Gruda mountains. The Crni Rzav river, with lots of tributaries and perfectly

Beautiful scenery around Mt Zlatibor

clear waters, flows south from the plateau. On the other hand, Zlatibor has amiable climate, with over 2000 sunny hours (i.e. 200 days) a year, whereas the snow in long and cold winters settles for over 100 days a year owing to the temperature that stays below zero from October till April. This makes Zlatibor a very convenient

tersected, so the natives were known as shippers who transported heavy load on small donkies over their own mountain and the rest of Serbia. Zlatibor ("Golden Pine") was named after a magnificent tree of the same name (lat. *Pinus Silvestris v. Zlatiborica*) which unfortunatelly cannot be found in this area any

modate the passengers and rare tourists who followed the King's example. The real progress of Zlatibor began only after 1927 with the construction of the road from Užice, when small villas were built first by well-off people from this town and later by other nature-lovers. After

Pony rides in the snow

skiing destination. In summer months – June, July and August – days are warm although nights are chilly.

The centre of the town is next to a small lake – a swimming place in summer and skating rink in winter. By the lake, there are lined up wooden kiosks with shops, cafés and restaurants, and at the other end of these rows, there is the town bus station. This is where the focus of both day and night life is. There are many accommodation facilities and big hotels all around the lake, especially private pensions whose number increased rapidly over the last few years.

Zlatibor offers re-markable conditions for taking different kinds of walks, from leisure and recreational walks to serious mountaineering ventures. Equally popular is biking either in the town area or outside it. The least strenuous walk is to **Glavudža**, where you can find a monument to the victims of the German retaliation in 1941. Further to the south-west, many people decide to walk to the first major

peak – **Čuker** (1358 m). It takes about one hour to reach it. Further on, **Čigota** ridge leads to the peak of the same name of some 1422 m, which is a few hours walk in one direction. Southwest form the town, there is a vast **Ribničko lake**. Since the town and the surrounding area is sup-plied with water from this lake, swimming is

forbiden. Nonetheless, you can still go fishing here for dace, trout, carp, etc. The highest peak of Zlatibor, **Tornik** (1496 m), rises above the lake, covered with coniferous forests. A ski centre is at the foot of the mountain, with two ski lifts frequently used in winter. On the way to the railway station, some

12 kms away form the town, there is a resort complex "Kod komša", with a small swimming area in a dammed part of a stream. The town itself has a number of basketball, football and volleyball grounds, and tennis courts, as well as outdoor and indoor swimming pools.

ENVIRONS:
There are a few destinations around Zlatibor that should not be missed.

The famous **Sirogojno village** can be reached through villages Rudine and Rožanstvo. In 1979, the best preserved part of the village was put under protection for the buildings typical of the southwestern Serbia. A few other construc-tions were transferred from the surrounding villages to complete the picture of the national

Smoked ham from Mačkat village

architecture of this area. The whole complex is today known as the **Open-Air Museum "The Old Village"** (*Muzej na otvorenom "Staro selo", tel 031/802-291, www.sirogojno.org. yu, office@sirogojno.org. yu*). It consists of some fifty buildings designed, furnished and filled with other home "applianc-es" evoking the life from the previous centuries of this part of Serbia. The houses here are specific for the whole Dinaric Alps region stretching over the whole Bosnia and a substantial part of Croatia, inhabited in the past almost solely by the Serbs. Although these houses were mostly built in the 19th and at the beginning of the 20th century, they are very archaic in design that did not change much over the centuries. Each of the family cooperatives had a central build-ing, "the house" (*kuća*), where the head of the cooperative lived and where everyone gath-ered. Each of the sons had his own "building" (*zgrada*), where he lived with his own family. Around it were various constructions, such as dairy, corn and grain cribs, the barn, etc. Houses were built on the hillside, with stone base used as cellar, half of which is dug into the hillside. The upper part of the house, used for habitation, was all made of wood, without any binding materials, not even nails. Very steep roofs covered with shingle had chimneys of particular type. All

this and much more about the life of people in this area can be learned in this museum, where you can also find a shop abundant with souve-nirs, from the famous Sirogojno sweaters to other home made prod-ucts – jam and rakija. Some of the cottages were redecorated to accommodate visitors, and there is also an herb-al pharmacy and a tav-ern in an old-fashioned ethno-ambience. At the top of the hill, above all the houses, there is the **Church of SS Peter and Paul**, which was built in 1764. The massive bell-tower was added some hundred years later. The iconostasis is the work of the famous Simeon Lazović and there are also old gravestones from the 18th and the 19th century around the church.

Not far from Sirogo-jno, there is **Stopića cave** (*Stopića pećina*), the most significant of many that adorn the area of

Gostilje waterfall

Zlatibor. It is right below Užice-Rožanstvo-Sirogo-jno road on the 19th km from Zlatibor town. The Trnavski stream runs through 1651 meters long cave. It is interest-ing to mention that the temperature inside the cave varies as the one outside. The impressive entrance to the cave is 35m wide and 18m high. The cave consists of five parts and, although it is not particularly rich in cave ornaments, it has interesting travertine tubs, quite distinctive in size and depth (up to 7 m) compared to others in Serbia.

Somewhat more to the south from Sirogojno, there is **Gostilje village**, known for village tour-ism and even more for its impressive waterfall (*vodopad*). The village also has a small camp and a trout farm. A few kilometers to the south, you can find charming **Ljubiš** village where-from the road leads back around Čigota to Zlatibor.

Open-air Museum in Sirogojno

⑭ Arilje

🏛 13.700

☎ 031/891-475

13 km - Požega

Local ceramics

Thanks to St Sava the Serbian Church was granted autocephaly in 1219, when he established bishoprics network throughout Serbia. One of the bishoprics was located here, at the monastery of St Achilles, where his relics were kept. A prosperous settlement soon emerged around the bishop's seat. After being destructed by the Cuman invasion in 1258, the monastery was rebuilt by the Serbian king Dragutin who ruled the northern part of Serbia independently from his brother, king Milutin who governed a larger and more important part of the Kingdom. The new church, preserved up to the present day, was finished around 1290 and fresco-painted in 1296. In the 14th century, the bishopric was promoted to the rank of metropolis but in the 15th century its seat was relocated to Čačak. After the Turkish occupation, the town deteriorated rapidly. In 1690, during the mass exodus of Serbs in an attempt to avoid the Turkish retaliation the whole area was deserted, the town ceased to exist and the monastery lay in ruins until the war with Austria in 1739. The new residents came from Raška, Herzegovina and Montenegro at the beginning of the 19th c. The town slowly grew bigger and the church was restored to serve as the parish church.

The 13th c. church dedicated to St Achilles is the last significant monument of the architectural style of Raška school. It is a single nave basilica with a narthex. The whole facade (excluding the narthex) is segmented with the arcades and pilaster stripes representing the distinctive features of the exterior. The part without them originates from the later period, but blends in harmoniously with the older part. In centuries to come, the architecture of this church greatly influenced the style of church building in the Western Serbia.

The most valuable feature of the church are its frescoes. Although painted by the Greek artists, the frescoes had the pattern typical of Serbian churches. In the endower's composition, both Serbian kings are depicted on the southern wall, but king Dragutin, with the model of the church in his hands, stands in the hierarchically lower place – to the left of his brother Milutin. Dragutin's wife, Katelina (daughter of the Hungarian king) is by his side with their two sons, Vladislav and the younger Urošic, who died young and was buried there. Then, the monks of the Nemanjić dynasty led by the founder of the dynasty, Stefan Nemanja, are depicted and the Serbian archbishops are opposite them. Nemanja's church council is also portrayed on the northern wall. For the first time in Serbian painting, the life of St. Nicholas was depicted

St Achilles that gave its name to Arilje

in this very church. The style of the paintings follows the brilliant example of Sopoćani church, but more vividly.

The house of serdar Jovan Micić from 1823 and the Old School from 1834 are the oldest and of the most interesting buildings in town itself.

ENVIRONS:

The **Klisura monastery** stands 12 km to the south of Arilje. The monastery is also known as Dobrača by the name of the village where it is located. Built in the Middle Ages in a simplified form of Raška style, it resembles Arilje church, but its upper portions were rebuilt during the Turkish rule. In 1789, an open wooden porch and the new ornamentally carved doors were added. The wall paintings are the 20th century work of Jaroslav Kratina.

⑮ Ivanjica

🏛 12.500

ℹ Milinka Kušića 47
32250 Ivanjica
032/665-085

🚗 31 km - Čačak

Although it is the main town of the upper Moravica region, Ivanjica (alt. 468 m) is just sleepy and small and is best known for its clean air and the beauty of its mountainous surroundings. Until the early 19th century this whole area was a blank on the map – with no towns at all and just a few caravan routes across the rough terrain.

In 1833 the area was conquered by Prince Miloš who decided to found a town around a Turkish inn - Kušića han. The town takes its name from the herb *iva*, much praised for its healing powers, which grew around the inn. Ivanjica's remoteness from any major road or town became proverbial over many years, when government clerks who were denoted for some reason would be penalized by being transferred here. Now the town's surroundings are better known for its potatoes – *Ivanjički krompir* – a brand name of itself, growing best at high altitudes.

Kušića han still stands in the middle of the town. It was built at the start of 19th century in the usual style of the Dinaric alpine wooden cottage. Next to it stands the newly erected **monument to Dragoljub "Draža" Mihailović** who was the commander of the royalist anti-Nazi forces during the German occupation in WWII and a native of the town.

Kušića Han in Ivanjica

Facing the han is the **Old Church** (dedicated to Saints Emperor Constantine and Empress Helen), built in 1836-38 on the orders of Prince Miloš. Although it possesses a high belfry, the church gives an impression of serene, rural beauty. Most of the icons and the wall-paintings are the work of Dimitrije Posinković from 1862.

The town park is to be found behind the church. The **old electric plant** built in 1911 stands across the river Moravica creating artificial waterfall, one of the town's landmarks. Though the plant today has been made into a technical museum, it still produces enough energy to light up the park.

South of the town rises the beautiful and unspoilt **Mt Golija** (1833 m) protected by UNESCO and famed for its lovely forests and small mountain lakes.

The villages around Ivanjica are well known locations for rural tourism. The most celebrated among them is **Kušići** (900 m), 12 km southwest from the town, with a hotel, boarding houses and a small ski track. Lisa, Devići and Katići also offer suitable accommodation in local households.

Lake on Mt Golija, listed by UNESCO as a place of outstanding natural beauty

16 Guča

ℹ️ Trg Slobode bb
32230 Guča
032/854-110

Three generations enjoying the Guča Festival

Once a year, during the last weekend in August, tens of thousands of people from all over Serbia and the world head for Guča to take part in a celebration of loud brass band music called "Dragačevski sabor trubača" ("The Dragačevo meeting of trumpeters"). The event was organized for the first time in 1961 as a review of orchestras from the vicinity in which only four bands took part. In more than 40 years of existence the manifestation has grown to become the largest festival in Serbia that, for many trumpeters, has become the starting point towards fame, glory and success. During these couple of days in August Guča becomes indeed "the trumpet capital of the world".

In the last few years, the festival has gone through many changes: much of its local character has been lost, the dates have been moved, its duration has been extended from four to seven days, the main events are charged however it is also better organized and adapted to the much larger number of visitors. The whole of this small town, no bigger than a large village, is turned into a fairground where all the rules of usual behavior are broken with much music, alcohol and dancing on tables aswell as the traditional *kolo*. Although the main events are staged at night, during the day there are many traditional happenings (exhibitions, arts and crafts, competitions and such like.) All the main concerts are held at the city's sport grounds across the River Bjelica.

Visiting Guča at any other time is rather odd. The little town returns to its unhurried daily routine that nevertheless, offers several interesting sights for the visitor. Guča is the centre of the region of Dragačevo, a lovely valley set amid hills covered by woods. It is best known for fruit cultivation, especially raspberries that are considered to be amongst the best in the world, as well as for its hospitality and village tourism. Excellent home made food and drink, clean air and water, forests and great excursion points are the primary enjoyments in this beautiful region.

The **Cultural Centre** (*Dom kulture*) in Guča's main square possesses a gallery of self-taught painters and sculptors. In front of the elementary school (*osnovna škola*) there is an open-air exhibition of extraordinary **wooden sculptures** by Bogosav Živković. Just behind the school is a **collection of**

Most of the visitors to the festival prefer to arrive from Čačak (20 km) and Lučani (16 km). As most people come by car, on all days and especially at weekends, the roads are very busy. The centre of Guča is closed to cars. There are no parking lots around and most people park by the road; many villagers open their yards and charge for parking. Even during the height of the festival local buses operate. Two small hotels and most private houses are likely to be fully booked and therefore making arrangements for accommodation prior to arriving is highly recommended. There is also a campsite behind the sport grounds.

On stage in Guča

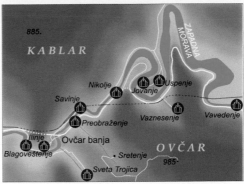

krajputaši ("roadsiders"), gravestones of those who died far from home. Most are in memory of soldiers who could not be brought back to their native town. This Western Serbian local artform dating from the 19th and early 20th centuries, is unique in the diversity of folkloric symbols representing the status and profession of the deceased, as well as the fine verses engraved in soft sandstone.

In the centre of the town stands a **church** on whose memorial tablets is inscribed a gruesomely long list of villagers who died in 1912-18 wars, a painful reminder of Serbia's losses. The small square in front of the church is where the entire first trumpet festival took place.

Trumpet and other brass instrument music is very much present in the area. Nearly all of the villages of Dragačevo have a brass band or two that play when they are asked. All the important occasions in the life of local people, from the birth of a child to the burial ceremony is unimaginable without their presence.

There are also several interesting **village graveyards** with some remarkable gravestones, for example those in the Puhovo or Dostanića groblje in Turica. **Kaona** is the biggest of the villages in Dragačevo and has a small ethnographic museum, a swimming pool and a lake. In the village of Rti there is an interesting cave – Rćanska pećina.

Ovčarsko-Kablarska klisura

22 km - Čačak

The basins of Požega and Čačak are connected by a gorge created by the West (*Zapadna*) Morava River passing between Mt Ovčar (986m) and Mt Kablar (885m). The twenty kilometre long gorge is one of the most scenic regions in Serbia:

the river snakes between the wooded foothills rich in springs, whose steep sides are up to 550 m deep and dotted with caves. At its narrowest, the gorge is only hundred metres wide. The beauty of the region is heightened by ten small, but nonetheless interesting, monasteries, which lie alongside the river or higher up in the mountains. The monasteries sprang up in the 15th and 16th centuries, the dark ages in Serbian history, as many monks looked for secluded places away from the main roads, far from Turkish towns. Being very poor, looted by Turks or rebuilt in the past two centuries, they have little artistic value; yet they are nonetheless worth visiting as, with the gorge, they form part of the idyllic scenery, perfect for hiking, moun-

West Morava River near Ovčar-Kablar Gorge

A chapel tucked between the rocks

taineering and other sorts of activities.

The **Monastery of Nikolje** is the oldest of the ten, and probably dates back to the middle of the 15th century. It is a modest edifice with preserved wall paintings from 1587 that have, sadly, lost most of their colour during a fire. The monastery was renewed with the help of Prince Miloš in 1817, and an attractive iconostasis was added in 1826. Soon afterwards, a fine building for the monastic dwellings was also added, a good example of 19th century folk architecture.

Blagoveštenje is certainly the prettiest of the ten monasteries. It was built on the foundations of an older monastery in 1601 as a small but proportional building with a wooden porch in front of the entrance that protects the paintings on the outer wall. The frescoes were made in 1632 by a local painter who showed a lot of skill in the modeling of his naively simplified figures and the choice of calm, harmonic colours. Of special interest is the iconostasis from the same period with interesting icons, and carvings with distinctive decorative dragons at the side of the cross.

Situated near this monastery is the **Ovčar Banja Spa**. The motel "Dom" is the most common stop for travellers on the road through the gorge. The spa is known for curative properties such as the healing of rheumatism and bone fractures.

The **Sveta Trojica Monastery** was built at the very end of the 16th century though its antique shape, good proportions and a narthex with a blind calotte and stone portals make it look much older. It possesses a well-carved iconostasis painted in 1868 and fine dwellings.

Sretenje is located under the very top of Mt Ovčar. It also dates from the end of 16th century; peculiarly, the first mention of the monastery from 1623 tells us about its destruction! It remained in ruins until 1818 when, thanks to the efforts of its Abbot, Nićifor Maksimović, a one-nave church with a deep apse and a tall belfry was constructed. The frescoes were created in 1844 in the conservative tradition of the previous centuries due to the deeply religious Abbot Nićifor, who did not want any novelties in his monastery.

Both Ovčar and Kablar are covered in dense woods, oak dominating in the lower regions and birch in the upper. The gorge is widely known for the large number of bird species inhabiting it (as much as 104!) as well as for medical and aromatic herbs. The Zapadna Morava is blocked in two places by damns creating two artificial lakes that offer great conditions for fishing. The shore of one of these, the **Medjuvršje Lake** is equipped for fishermen and is a favourite destination in Serbia.

⑱ Čačak

👥	89.500
ℹ	Trg Ustanka 4 32000 Čačak 032/342-360, 343-721
🚌	032/222-461
🚌	032/222-518
	140 km - Beograd

Formerly called Gradac, the town evolved in the Middle Ages around the monastery that was the seat of the bishop. Its new name is first mentioned in 1405. During the Second Serbian rebellion in 1815, a decisive victory was won over the Turkish forces on the hill Ljubić above the town. After the liberation, Čačak grew as a residence of

Blagoveštenje Monastery

prince Miloš Obrenović's brother Jovan and, later on, as the seat of the district. In recent years the town developed due to the large number of small entrepreneurs. Opposition party sympathizers from Čačak led the way in the line of events on 5th of October 2000 when the regime of Slobodan Milošević was overthrown.

The **Ascension church** (*Crkva Vaznesenja Gospodnjeg*) was once part of Gradac Monastery. Built in the late 12th century, it was an endowment of prince Stracimir, brother of Stefan Nemanja. During the Turkish reign it served as a mosque and the upper parts of the church with atypically wide dome remained from those days. It changed denomination several times until 1834 when it was finally re-established as an orthodox shrine. Some parts of the original decoration can still be seen on the façades. Inside the church, there is an exquisite high iconostasis dating from 1846.

The **Manor of Master Jovan** (*Gospodar Jovanov konak*) is a fine example of Balkan architecture dating from 1835. On the front wall, there is a large painting of Obrenović dynasty coat-of-arms. Today it serves as a **museum** (*Narodni muzej, 1 Cara Dušana St, tel. 032/22-169, camuzej@eunet.yu*). It is divided into three parts: archeology and classical antiquity, churches and monasteries of the region, the development of Čačak and surroundings from 1804 till 1941. The **art gallery** dedicated to Nadežda Petrović is nearby (*Umetnčka galerija*

The old facade of Hotel "Belgrade"

"*Nadežda Petrović*", *6 Cara Dušana St, tel. 032/22-375*). Petrović (1873-1915) was a leading impressionist and fauvist painter in Serbia. The gallery treasures her works as well as the paintings of other Yugoslav painters from 1950s onward.

The construction of the monumental **High School** started in 1910 by the plans of Dragutin Maslać, but was finished only fifteen years later due to three wars waged in the meantime. This largest pre-WWII edifice is decorated in national style and enlivened by rhythmicaly arranged openings. There is a **monument to Nadežda Petrović** in a small square in front of the High School, presenting her in a seated position.

The old part of the **"Beograd" Hotel** from 1900 stands as a nice example of the Art Nouveau style of provincial art in Serbia.

Ljubić Hill is today a popular jaunt venue with a monument to a famous hero Tanasko Rajić who died here in 1815 defending his cannons.

ENVIRONS:
Ježevica monastery is situated in a village of the same name, 15 km to the south of Čačak. Founded in the 14th c, it was reconstructed several times, the last time in the 19th century, leaving the mark in a shape of narthex and a large bell tower with a baroque spire. The wall paintings were started twice: first in 1609 and then in 1636, all due to the lack of finance in those gloomy days. Apart from the cycle of paintings depicting the life of St Nicholas to whom the temple is dedicated, there are also representations of Serbian Saints such as Sava, archbishop Arsenije I and prince Lazar.

Church of the Ascension in the centre of Čačak

Hotel	PRICE RANGE - for one person in a two-bed room (including breakfast, service and tax). Small icons present facilities in each Hotel.	> 50 EUR €€€€€
Motel		35 - 50 EUR €€€€
Villa/Private Pension	number of rooms number of beds	25 - 35 EUR €€€
Agrotourism accommodation	308/373	12 - 25 EUR €€
		< 12 EUR €

★ ★ Dvor

✉ Miloša Pocerca 11
15000 Šabac
☎ 015/346-390

24/50

€€€
VISA MasterCard Maestro

Just after you enter the city, in its urban part, near to a leisure centre, 1 km away from the city centre.

★ ★ Galeb

✉ Koste Abraševića
15000 Šabac
☎ 015/347-700, 367-720

10/17

€€
VISA

Excellent small family hotel in the very centre of Šabac near the pedestrian zone.

★ ★ Bogatić

✉ Vojvode Stepe 35
15350 Bogatić
☎ 015/411-062, 411-003

20/50

€€

Also a restaurant-tavern and a confectionary, near to Spa, thermal waters; 2 km from Šabac.

★ ★ Borač

✉ Đulim 2
15314 Krupanj
☎ 015/681-891

54/120

€€

A beautiful conference hall, fully equipped, guests are allowed to use a swimming pool nearby, the 14th century Dobri Potok Church is 1.5 km away.

★ ★ Podrinje

✉ Park br. 4
15316 Banja Koviljača
☎ 015/818-275

76/245

€€
VISA MasterCard Maestro

On the Gučevo Mountain, 2 km from Drina River, a quiet place, close to forest, healing sulphur springs.

★ ★ ★ Grand

✉ Vojvode Mišića 2
14000 Valjevo
☎ 014/227-133

35/58

€€€€
VISA MasterCard

In the centre of Valjevo, at the riverbank, this hotel witrh a long tradition is a famous symbol of the city.

★ Beli Narcis

✉ Zikice Jovanovica 1
14000 Valjevo
☎ 014/221-140

35/68

€

Inexpensive hotel in the centre of Valjevo.

Stave

✉ Dragutin Živanović
selo Stave, 14000 Valjevo
☎ 014/271-136

5/10

€

Very good accommodation in an ethno style excellent for taking break from urban life.

Popučke

✉ Jovanović
selo Popučke, 14000 Valjevo
☎ 014/283-317

3/8

€

Very good atmosphere in a family house and restaurant just right to it, offering Internet access, mini bar in rooms and telephone. English language is spoken.

Valjevska Kamenica - Maletić

✉ Branko Rakić
selo Valjevska Kamenica, 14000 Valjevo
☎ 014/254-407

6/12

€

Excellent opportunity to experience the real life of countryside, exploring at the same time the Internet. Rooms are well equipped and French is spoken.

Pepa

✉ 14204 Divčibare
☎ 014/277-323, 277-652

63/140

€€
VISA

In the centre of Divčibare, next to a ski piste, surrounded by forest, with pool tables and a pizzeria; group visits organized.

★ Maljen

✉ 14204 Divčibare

☎ 015/277-234

53/150

200 m from a ski piste, in a forest near the centre of the resort, a quiet place in the centre of Divčibare.

Izvor

✉ Karadjordjeva 14
31260 Kosjerić

☎ 031/783-331

12/30

With an open garden, this motel lies close to the main road to the sea, with many coaches stoping here for rest.

★ ★ Skrapež

✉ Jose Bruha 1
31260 Kosjerić

☎ 031/881-651, 881-328

46/94

Well-known hotel in the centre of Kosjeric with numerous sport courts nearby.

★ ★ ★ Drina

✉ Vojvode Mišića 5
31250 Bajina Bašta

☎ 031/862-451, 862-452

85/175

Hotel is situated in the very centre of the city, beneath the Tara mountain

★ ★ ★ Jezero

✉ Perućac bb
31250 Bajina Bašta,

☎ 031/859-081

30/80

Fully equipped studio houses with a TV set and a kitchen, next to a admirable view at the lake and its surroundings; offers swimming, fishing and rides across the lake; also sightseeing of the Drina Canyon.

An old country house in the vicinity of Mionica

★ ★ ★ Omorika

Tara
31250 Bajina Bašta
031/862-566, 593-530

166/345

Beautiful hotel on the Tara mountain, offering splendid holiday and in addition sauna, beauty salon, gym, bowling alley, table tennis, library, with sport courts and cross-country track nearby.

★ ★ ★ ★ Zeleni čardaci

Tara

031/859-423

5/25

Both outdoors and indoors are beautifully decorated, exclusive rooms equipped with mini bar, DVD and TV set. It also has a lovely restaurant. English is spoken.

Kremna

Ruža Ivanović
selo Kremna
031/808-287, 064/340-2989

2/4

Perfect for family of four or couples, perfectly preserved in the well-known ethno-style. English language is spoken.

Potpeć

Guskić Miloš
selo Potpeć
031/546-140

3/6

Very fine accommodation, just near the Potpećka Cave. English language is spoken.

Matogi

Slavenka Stojić
Mokra Gora
031/800-386

1/2

Very beautiful house for two persons with all facilities needed for calmness and enjoyment.

Mokra Gora

Mokra Gora

031/800-505

7/11

Nice small motel near the border with Bosnia and Herzegovina.

★ ★ ★ Zlatibor

Dimitrija Tucovića
31000 Užice
031/516-188

166/280

Beautiful hotel in the centre of the town with big terrace.

★ ★ Palas

Trg Svetog Save 3
31000 Užice
031/512-752

38/84

Small Pleasant hotel for budget tourists.

★ ★ ★ Jele Ježevica

31213 Ježevica

031/829-078

13/35

In the centre of Ježevica, on the foundations of a family-run tavern from 1930's, a stylish and unique three star De Lux Apartments Jela Ježevica have been built. Rooms have a mini-bar and satellite TV; accommodating congress tours; pool tables, fitness, sauna, Jacuzzi, sports grounds and a football ground nearby. Spring water and and healing herbs.

★ ★ ★ ★ Palisad

31315 Zlatibor

031/841-151, 841-161

328/652

Exceptional hotel in the centre of Zlatibor used as a direction point to most people with beautiful summer terrace.

★ ★ ★ ★ Jugopetrol

Kamelj bb
31315 Zlatibor
031/841-467, 841-493

60/136

Hotel is in the very centre of Zlatibor with excellent atmosphere and friendly staff.

★ ★ ★ ★ Zelenkada

Gajevi 1
31315 Zlatibor
031/841-051

50/100

Very good hotel a bit relocated from the Zlatibor urban zone of Zlatibor.

Hotel Olimp on Mt Zlatibor

Čigota

✉ 31315 Zlatibor

☎ 031/841-141

127/248

Staying in this hotel is beneficial for stressed and exhausted persons. It offers saunas, swimming pool, fitness programmes etc.

★ ★ Dunav

✉ 31315 Zlatibor

☎ 031/841-181, 841-172

39/91

Hotel is located in the very centre of Zlatibor mountain, surrounded by extraordinary picturesque pine-tree forest.

★ ★ ★ ★ Olimp

✉ Naselje Sloboda bb
31315 Zlatibor

☎ 031/842-555

23/60

Ideal for weekend breaks; frequently visited by sportsmen.

Club Satelit

✉ Obudojevica bb
31315 Zlatibor

☎ 031/841-188

18/48

Close to a ski-lift, sauna and jacuzzi, fitness centre, hairdresser 200 m from the centre, surrounded by villas, with a nice view, a ski resort and an ice hockey pitch are near.

Novakov Dvor

✉ Obudojevica bb
31315 Zlatibor

☎ 031/845-095

9/28

Newly-built and, very modern, satisfied all European standards and customer friendly.

★ ★ Zlatibor

✉ Naselje Jezero bb
31315 Zlatibor

☎ 031/841-021

80/215

A national restaurant within, rooms have mini-bar; in the very centre of Zlatibor, suitable for congress tours; fitness programmes.

Kraljevi konaci

✉ 31315 Zlatibor

☎ 031/841-230

80/240

The beautiful flowered avenues and arranged places and the harmonious lines of the apartment in the pine woods make an indivisible joint of the nature, the human knowledge and the love.

Rožanstvo

✉ Melović Dragan
selo Rožanstvo

☎ 031/835-023

2/5

Very good villa with a small swimming pool, just perfect for hot summer days.

Sirogojno

Milić Dobrivoje
selo Sirogojno
031/802-010

2/7

With nicely decorated rooms and good service, the Pension offers remarkable holiday at one of the most visited mountains of Serbia.

Simex

Ljubiš
31209 Zlatibor
031/801-113

12/30

Newly built accommodation, gym, sauna, Jacuzzi, indoor playground, mini DVD rental, sleighing, aperitif bar, fish-pond, fresh trout; 20 km from the centre of Zlatibor.

Muzej Sirogojno

selo Sirogojno

031/802-291, 802-586

7/29

Old styled houses with interiors adapted to serve the needs of modern living standards. The buildings are located nearby the inn. Every cabin is furnished with small kitchen, living room with fireplace, bedrooms and bathroom.

★ ★ ★ Šumadija

Svetog Arhilija 1
343000 Arilje
031/891-357

60/167

The open-air garden is one of the most visited and most beautiful gardens in Serbia; live music during the summer.

★ ★ ★ Zlatna truba

Trg Slobode bb
32230 Guča
032/854-459

32/95

In the centre of Guča, offers an ideal accommodation during the Guča Festival, otherwise quiet.

Guča

Božanići
32230 Guča
032/854-403

2/5

A small pension with a beautiful garden and kitchen at disposal for practicing new recipes. English is spoken.

Kole

Konjevići
32000 Čačak
032/356-501, 381-804

38/88

This motel is placed in Konjevići, offers pleasant and relaxing atmosphere with rich menu and climatized area. Our chefs will present you specialities of domestic and foreign cuisines.

★ ★ ★ President

Bulevar oslobodjenja bb
32000 Čačak
032/371-401

52/108

Very good hotel with aperitif bar, excellent Italian cuisine restaurant and fitness club with 24h medical service.

★ ★ Beograd

Gradsko šetalište 20
32000 Čačak
032/224-593, 224-594

38/94

Placed in the very centre of the city, next to the main square, the hotel is known of its long tradition.

★ ★ Fontana

Banja Gornja Trepča
3232215 Čačak
032/822-313

12/27

In the centre of the Spa with beautiful surroundings offering rest and relaxation.

★ ★ ★ Park

Milana Kušića 106
32250 Ivanjica
032/661-397

65/136

Unique biosphere surrounding this hotel is under UNESCO protection.

Katići

Obradović
selo Katići
032/873-307, 873-663

6/16

Very good offer – well equipped rooms with Internet access, mini library and a nearby restaurant. English is spoken.

Lisa

Milićević
selo Lisa
032/652-092

4/8

Good accommodation with internet access and very good restaurant. German language is spoken.

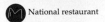 Fish restaurant National restaurant  International restaurant

Stari most
 Savska bb,
15000 Šabac
015/341-705

 10-23

The restaurant is situated on the Sava riverbank, some 3 km away from the city centre, when you turn left to the road that leads you along the city beach. A huge new garden in the shadow provides a real escape from a city jam.

Čardak
 Vojvode Putnika 109, selo Majur, 15000 Šabac
015/377-453

 09-23

In only 5 km from the Šabac city centre is a village Majur, where an excellent national restaurant is situated. It was built from old bricks in the 19th century Serbian village style. It offers a real national cuisine dishes baked in clay pots.

Tadića mlin
Miše Dudića 1
14000 Valjevo
014/238-028

 11-01

Old-fashioned, a river runs through the restaurant, so guest can fish!

Šofer bar
Vuka Karadžića 56
14000 Valjevo
014/221-476

  07-24

In the city centre, over 500 seats, guests are mainly businessmen, but with a corner for young people; girl's tress, and specialties are on offer; early 20th century Serbian urban music is played.

Jefimija
Birčaninova 40
14000 Valjevo
011/24165

 08-24

In old part of Valjevo, interior is rather old-fashion, guests are mainly businessmen and travellers; early 20th century Serbian urban music is played.

Srpska kruna
Trg Jovana Cvijića bb
Loznica
015/875-016

 08-23

In the centre of Loznica, with a view at the park and the square; 60 – 70 seats, built in the western-european style; business-urban type of a restaurant; quite music.

Brvnara
Kneza Vase Popovića 15
32000 Čačak
032/349-132

 09-23

Ethnic styled, decorated approximately to its old times look, wooden tables and cutlery made in baked clay.

Konak
Kralja Petra I 16
31000 Užice
031/510-207

 09-24

Ethnic styled, 100 metres from a square, two summer terraces, home-made dishes, unplugged live music.

Tabana
Medjaj 3
31000 Užice
031/510-207

 08-24

Old-fashion styled, 120 years old building, home-made dishes (beef with honeycomb recommended), live tambourine music every day (except Sundays).

Kod Novice
31315 Zlatibor
031/841-818

 08-24

A mix of traditional and modern, the restaurant lies in a nice natural setting secluded from the centre of Zlatibor.

Krčma Gaj
31315 Zlatibor
031/841-962

 12-24

A national restaurant, 2 km from the Zlatibor Mountain centre, with a beautiful view of Čigota peak.

Mona
31315 Zlatibor
031/841-021

 12-01

A modern restaurant, built in woods; grill specialties, green surroundings; open terrace.

Mećavnik
Mokra Gora,
selo Mećavnik
031/800-686

 09-21

The restaurant is situated in a very pleasant surroundings, whereas it offers a large number of national dishes.

Kurta
Tara
031/859-433

 08-21

The restaurant is situated on the Tara Mountain, surrounded by nature and a forest; a terrace is also open on sunny days.

ŠUMADIJA AND POMORAVLJE

This region is deservedly called "the heart of Serbia", the most obvious reason being due to its geographical position in the very centre of the land far from all borders. Heading northwards is a mountain range called the Šumadija ridge that descends gently towards Belgrade. The peaks of these mountains are still covered with dense woods, the relic of once much greater forests that gave Šumadija its name (*šuma* = wood). To the south and to the east a patchwork quilt of fields covers the rolling plains. Different types of crops such as corn, wheat and various fruits are grown here. By the village of Stalać, the Western and Southern Morava meet and continue to flow together, from here on known as the Great (Velika) Morava, on its winding route northwards into the Danube.

decorative style in which they were built consequently became known as the Morava style. In 1459 Smederevo fell to the Turks, a date that identifies the end of Serbian mediaeval statehood. Yet this is also where the Serbian state was to emerge once again: both the 1804 and the 1815 Serbian rebellions started here and this is where their leaders had their strongholds. The population of Šumadija and the Morava region, who had, since those times, many occasions on which to go to war, are made up less of a local populace than of those who have moved here from the south, east and west during the 18th century. At this time, the region had autonomous status within the Ottoman Empire making it attractive to the inhabitants of neighbouring areas. This was the case again in the 19th century when it

Ostrovica peak on Mt Rudnik

The plain of the Morava River is the largest in Serbia on which several important towns are to be found.

In historical terms this region also strongly represents the heartland of Serbia. It first came into focus in the 14th century as the southern regions of the medieval Serbian state fell to the Turks and the centre of the state shifted northwards. Serbia's 15th century revival took place here marked by the building of prominent monasteries such as Ravanica, Manasija or Kalenić, constructed by the South and Great Morava. The new

was no longer under Turkish rule and it became a magnet to Christians from the surrounding provinces.

In Šumadija the villages are divided into hamlets which are spread over wide areas. Once they were hidden amongst the thick woods that disappeared during the 19th century. Reminders of these times and of the centuries of slavery under the Turks are the modest wooden churches that can be found here in abundance. In the Morava valley (or Pomoravlje) villages are grouped together which enables them to make better use of the fertile land. To the north, Smederevo and the surrounding region is famous for its vineyards, while the neighboring Grocka area is renown for its fruit plantations. The local plum variety, Ranka, comes from the village of Darosava that lies in the very centre of Šumadija. These plums are therefore also known as "Darosavka". Not far from here is Topola, Karadordje's town where lies the Oplenac hill on which Karadjordje's grandson King Peter continued the tradition of the medieval rulers by building his endowment, the mausoleum church of Karadjordjević dynasty. To the south lies Kruševac, the capital city during the time of Prince Lazar. It was from here that in 1389 he left with his troops to fight the celebrated but fated Battle of Kosovo that brought him death and eternal glory. Aleksandrovac is the centre of a closed valley named simply Župa. Here there are perfect conditions for vast vineyards that can be found all the way up to the town of Kruševac. In the southwest corner of this region, in a beautiful setting underneath the Goč mountain, lies Vrnjačka Banja, the most beautiful spa in Serbia with its various thermal springs, parks and old villas. Mineral springs are found in many other places notably Bukovička banja where the widely used "Knjaz Miloš" mineral water is produced.

BEOGR

Stepojevac

Lazarevac   Bukovička

Valjevo

Ar

Ljig

Rajac   Ost

Rudnik

7 **6**

Gornji
Milanova

Prislonica

Gor

Čačak

Children in traditional dress of Šumadija

1 Smederevo

2 Koporin

3 Aranđelovac

4 Orašac

5 Topola

6 Gornji Milanovac

7 Takovo

8 Vraćevšnica

9 Borač

10 Kragujevac

11 Jagodina

12 Manasija

13 Resavska pećina

14 Ravanica

15 Kalenić

16 Ljubostinja

17 Kruševac

18 Naupare

19 Vrnjačka Banja

❶ Smederevo

🏠 74.900

ℹ️ Karađorđevićeva 5-7
11300 Smederevo
026/ 222-952

📠 026/222-245

📱 026/221-222

45 km - Beograd

Walls of the Smederevo Fortress

The first reference to Smederevo dates back to 1019 as one of the bishoprics of the newly established Ohrid Archbishopric. The city gained in importance in the 15th c. when the centre of the Serbian state was retreating north ahead of Turkish attacks. In 1427, after the death of Despotes Stefan Lazarević, his successor Despotes Djuradj Branković, acting on a previously prepared agreement, handed over Belgrade to the Hungarian King. Left without the capital and the strongest of his forts, Djuradj turned his atentions to the immediate construction of a new fort to become the Serbian capital. He opted for Smederevo, a site protected by the Danube River and the Jezava stream. The rapid

Apples for sale at the Smederevska jesen festival

construction turned out to be a heavy burden on the peasants who, in turn, shifted all the blame to the Despotes' Greek wife Jerina nicknaming her "Damned". The largest medieval fort

on the Danube did not manage to stop the Turks and, its second fall, in 1459 marked the end of Serbian statehood in the Middle Ages. Smederevo, however, remained an important merchants' town and the seat of the Turkish province (sanjak) that commanded the north of Serbia until the capture of Belgrade in 1521. In the 18th c. the city changed hands several times between the Austrians and the Turks, destroying its economy. From 1805 to 1807 the city was the seat of the Governing Council of Serbian Insurrectionists. On July the 5th 1941 a great tragedy befell the occupied city: an explosion of the German ammunition train located in the town claimed around 2000 lives and caused great destruction to the city and the antique fortress.

After the war, the newly constructed steel industry became the motor of the city's development.

With 1.5 km of outer walls, the Smederevo **fortress** is the biggest in Serbia and one of the largest in Europe. This lowland fortification has a triangular base plan and is separated into two parts. The **Citadel**, protected by six towers and a moat, was the seat of the ruler and his court. Its construction was completed in 1430 as stated on the inscription made of red brick on the Cross Tower. Of interest here are the keep with its 4 metre thick walls as well as the four bifore windows, all that remains of the ceremonial hall. The larger, outer part of the fort took several more years to finish, and its walls, with 19 massive towers, sheltered the seat of the Bishop and the burghers. The walls and the towers are modeled on those found in Constantinople. At the corners of the fort stand three more polygonal towers, smaller in height and suited for defense against firearms, which were built by the Turks around 1480.

Not far from the fortress is the central town square – Trg Republike, dominated by the large

Smederevo's Main Square

Church of St George. It was built in 1851-55 by the renowned Andreja Damjanov of Macedonia, who came from a family of talented builders. He left the tower built in the ruling European styles of the period, but overall modeled the edifice in the style of the church of the Manasija monastery, thereby creating the first leap towards a national style in Serbian ecclesiastical architecture. The frescoes to be found inside the church are the work of Andrej Bicenko. In the same square one can also find the lofty **District Seat** building, the work of Aleksandar Bugarski from 1884 and the squat **Municipal Hall** (N. Krasnov, 1928) crowned by four antique looking sculptures.

At the edge of downtown Smederevo, with the entrance at Narodnog fronta St., lies the Old Cemetery (the easiest approach is via Karadjordjeva St. then take a left to Narodnog fronta). In it stands the modest, early 15th c. **Church of the Dormition of the Virgin Mary** executed in a mixture of the Morava and Byzantine styles. After the fall of the city to the Turks, the church was used as the seat of Orthodox Bishops. The wall paintings date from the end of the 16th c. but are of lesser artistic value and quite badly damaged. By the outer church wall one can find the grave of Dimitrije Davidović, "the father of Serbian journalism" and the writer of the first constitution of Serbia. Facing the church is the **Memorial Ossuary** of the victims of the 1942 explosion, designed by Aleksandar Deroko.

ENVIRONS:
Some 10 km east of the town is the village of Šalinac. Between the village and the winding stream of the Velika Morava River approaching its confluence lies the **Šalinački lug**, a rare reminder of Serbia's lowland oak forests. Here one can see over 300 imposing trees, some of which are several hundred years old.

A few kilometres up the road to Belgrade is the **Jugovo** excursion point, which has a stone beach on the Danube.

❷ Koporin

110 km - Beograd

This monastery lies 5 km west of Velika Plana on the road to Smederevska Palanka. Despotes Stefan Lazarević donated the funds for its construction at the beginning of the 15th c. With a modest rectangular stone church, Koporin does not have the usual characteristics of the architecture and decoration of its time. It lay in ruins until 1880, after which it obtained a western narthex. The frescoes date from the period when the monastery was founded and are done in a style which emphasis on the linear. A grave found beneath the donor's portrait is believed to be the final resting place of Despotes Stefan.

ENVIRONS:
Just south of Velika Plana, in a place called Radovanjski Lug, lays the **Pokajnica Log**

Old oaks in Šalinački lug

Church. It was here that Karadjordje, the leader of the First Serbian insurrection was killed in 1817 under the orders of Prince Miloš Obrenović, who led the Second Insurrection and secured a concessional peace and his power afterwards. The church was built in 1818 by the remorseful Prince in penitence (to penitent – *pokajati se*, therefore the name) for the sin he committed and which saved Serbia from another clash with the Turks. Karadjordje was his ex-commander and best man but also a man who wanted to expel the Turks once and for all, no matter what the price.

Except for the stone foundations, the rest of the church is made entirely out of oak in the rural architectural style of the time. Inside, there is an iconostasis from the same period, several attractive carvings and a few valuable pictures and icons.

❸ Aranđelovac

 36.900

 Kneza Miloša 243
34300 Aranđelovac
034/ 724-097, 725-575

034/711-152

72 km - Beograd

In 1837 prince Miloš Obrenović ordered that scattered villages of Vrbica and Orašac should merge and form a new settlement along the main road. The long Knjaza Miloša Street in which almost every single important institution is to be found is still a living evidence of this regulation. There, in 1859 the same ruler started building

"Staro zdanje" Hotel in Arandjelovac

a church dedicated to St Archangel Michael and therefore renamed Vrbica to Arandjelovac, "the city of the Archangel". The growing Arandjelovac soon absorbed the neighboring Bukovička Spa and became known as a health resort. Miloš's son and successor Mihailo visited it regularly and helped the prosperity of the spa. Today it is best known for "Knjaz Miloš" mineral water, that was first bottled at the turn of the 20th century, and which was named after prince Miloš who used it abundantly at his court.

The center of the town is the hub of the Spa as well, with a large **park** spreading on some 40 acres. There are several hotels within the park and amongst them **Hotel "Staro Zdanje"** ("Old Edifice") holds a special place. This massive romanticist edifice was initially erected by prince Mihailo who intended it for his summer residence. It was finished

in 1872, after Mihailo's death and never met the initial purpose and became a spa resort right away. Not only did its construction mark the beginning of the organized spa resort life but its distinctive look also became the symbol of the town. Five thermal springs are scattered in the park along with the open-air pool but its main attraction are its 66 **sculptures** of contemporary artists, all of them carved in white marble taken from the nearby Venčac Mountain.

ENVIRONS:

In the vicinity of the city is located **Risovac cave** (*Risovačka pećina*) in which an important archeological and paleontology finds from Older Stone Age were made. The cave has been turned into a museum testifying on the life in this prehistoric era.

Turn of the century commercial for "Knjaz Miloš" mineral water

❹ Orašac

70 km - Beograd

This village, just north of Aranđelovac holds an important place in Serbian history. It was here, in 1804, that the First Serbian Uprising, also known as the "Serbian Revolution", was started. After the Turkish janissaries had massacred all the prominent Serbs they could lay their cold hands on, those who remained alive gathered here secretly on the feast of the Meeting of Our Lord (Sretenje Gospodnje) on February 15th 1804. A local elder of the community, Teodosije Marićević, summoned the meeting in a ravine on his estate, where Turkish spies could not see them. The gathered haiduks, elders and priests elected Đorđe Petrović as their leader, better known by the nickname "Black George" (Karadjorjde)

Statue of Karadjordje and Memorial School in Orašac

who immediatley led the rebels in battle against the local Turks. The site of this historical meeting became known as the Marićević Ravine (Marićevića jaruga) as Teodosije was buried there in 1807. In 1954, for the commemoration of the 150th anniversary of the insurrection, a memorial well was built here. Immediately above the ravine lies a small church built between 1868 and 1878. The church is a modest structure however, its iconostasis is notable as the work of Steva Todorović, one of the best Serbian painters of the second half of the 19th century. In 1932, thanks to donations from Karađorđe's great-greatson King Aleksandar of Yugoslavia, a memorial school was built in a mix of the romanticist and folklore style, dominating the centre of this small village. In 2004, on the grand celebration of the 200th aniversary of the First Serbian Uprising, a white marble monument to Karadjordje was erected in front of the school. At the back of the school there is an excellent souvenir shop.

Djordje Petrović (1762-1817), better known by his nickname **Karađorđe** ("Black George") is regarded as the founder of modern Serbia. From his early age Đorđe became known as a brave and harsh man, feared by the Turkish oppressors. During the Austro-Ottoman war (1788-91) he became an officer in the Austrian army and led the Serbian volunteer troops (Freikorps). After the Turkish janissary leaders usurped authority in the Province of Belgrade in 1801, Đorđe joined the Serbian outlaws. In 1804 he was elected as a popular leader against the Turkish tyranny and headed a revolt that would last for nine years. As a gifted general Karađorđe led his men in several glorious battles such as Ivankovac (1805) and Mišar (1806) and his military talents were praised even by Napoleon. After the first successful battles, Serbia gained a position of *de facto* independent principality and Karađorđe became its ruler, adopting the title of *Vožd* ("The Leader"). Short-tempered and fierce, he was a righteous ruler who didn't hesitate to personally shoot dozens of men for disobedience or plunder. Although a clumsy diplomat, Karađorđe managed to win Russia's support for the cause of Serbia, especially during the Russo-Ottoman war (1806-1812). Napoleon's invasion in 1812 forced Russia to conclude a peace treaty with the Ottomans regardless of Serbia's position. Attempts to organise a defence against the sweeping Turkish attacks failed and in 1813, together with other refugees, Karađorđe escaped from Belgrade to the Austrian territory. There he was first arrested as a notorius revolutionary, but was later sent to Russia. In 1817, Karađorđe's secret return to Serbia threatened to ruin the favourable peace agreement that had been concluded with the Ottomans by his best man, Miloš Obrenović in 1815. Under Turkish pressure, Miloš ordered the execution of Karađorđe. Soon after this act, Karađorđe's reputation reached legendary heights, and he is still remembered as a hero to this day.

❺ Topola

🏔 23.400

ℹ Kneginje Zorke 13
34310 Topola
034/ 811-172

72 km - Beograd

Karadjordje, the leader of the First Serbian Insurrection, was born in the nearby village of Viševac and later settled down in Topola. After the vengeful Turks set his house on fire in 1804, he ordered a new fortified residence to be built on the same site. Consequently Topola became a sort of his residence. However his new dwelling was also destroyed in 1813, when the victorious Turks entered Topola. During the times when the Obrenović dynasty, in constant rivalry with the Karadjordjevićs, were in power, Karadjordje's residence was deliberately neglected. The village lived through hard times in 1877 when disgruntled soldiers and supporters of the rival Karadjordjević dynasty rebeled; the rebellion was crushed by the regular army and the fortified residence was destroyed. The village was in decline for some time until its luck changed in 1903 when Petar Karadjordjević was crowned the King of Serbia. The place of his burial, the church of St George on Oplenac hill became the mausoleum for all the members of this royal family and Topola today still has a special place in the hearts of all Serbian monarchists.

After 1877 all that remained of Karadjordje's fortified residence were a few objects in a park that was once the courtyard of the fort. The

Karadjordje's Church in Topola

main entrance to the complex is from Kraljice Marije Street. In the middle of it stands a monument to Karadjordje, the work of Petar Palavičini from the year 1938. Behind it is the manor (*konak*) today turned into a **Museum** dedicated to Karadjordje and the First Insurrection. Its outer side built of stone once constituted the south wall of the fort. Next to it stands the only remaining tower, with its thick walls and small windows. One of the most interesting objects in the museum is Karadjordje's cannon. Molded in 1812 it was called "Aberdar" (The Messenger) since it was

fired only when some important news were announced to the people. Its right handle was taken off in 1903 to be used as material for the crown of the new king, Petar Karadjordjević.

Next to the Museum stands the **church** dedicated to the Birth of Virgin Mary, the endowment of Karadjordje. It was constructed in 1811-13 in the simple and sturdy manner common during those challenging times. Nevertheless, it was the most important ecclesiastical object built in the revolutionary Serbia. In the adjusted defense tower stood the first church bells in the country since the practice of bell ringing was forbidden under the Turks. Burned in 1813 just after it was completed, the church was later renovated by Karadjordje's son prince Aleksandar (1842-1858). To the right of the entrance stands the tomb of the church's endower. His headless body (the head was presented to the sultan after his murder) laid there from 1820 to 1930. The inscription

Crypt of the Oplenac Mausoleum

above the tomb charges the Turks with the crime, concealing the fact that the murder was ordered by Miloš Obrenović. In the church are the gravestones of several members of Karadjordjević family and other prominent personalitites from Topola, including Petar Jokić, commander of Karadjordje's personal guard unit. Original wall paintings, today saved only in fragments, are the work of Petar Nikolajević-Moler, who was also one of the leading commanders of Karadjorjde's army. Fantastically carved iconostas was done in 1928 by Nestor Aleksijev and presents one of the last important works of the Mijak clan of woodcarvers from Macedonia.

Starting from the entrance in Kraljice Marije Street and heading up the Oplenac Hill one arrives at King Petar's endowment. Facing the church stands the small **Petar's House** built in 1910, wherefrom the king overlooked the construction works and which soon became also his favourite residence. Today it serves as a gallery and is the seat of the local cultural center.

The Mausoleum **Church of St George** was built in 1911-12 based on a plan by a young architect Kosta J. Jovanović. It is covered with white marble from the nearby Mt Venčac. Under the Austro-Hungarian occupation in 1915-18 the temple was desecrated and looted. The interior decoration was finished in 1930. Above the monumental portal stands a mosaic depicting St George killing the dragon, based on a drawing by Paja Jovanović. Interestingly, St George has the face

of Karadjordje, therefore symbolically representing the liberation of the Serbian people initiated by the First Serbian Uprising. Above it stands the family coat-of-arms of Karadjordjević dynasty. The inner wall surfaces of the church are completely covered in mosaics. To the right of the entrance stands the endower composition: St George presenting King Petar to the Virgin Mary. Other frescoes are all copies from over 60 Serb medieval monasteries. Especially interesting are the portraits of all the rulers of Serbia in the Middle Ages, each one with a representation of his principal endowment in his hands. The columns holding the main dome are adorned with scenes from the life of St Sava while in the arches underneath the smaller domes stand the medallions of all Serb saints. The two tombs are of Karadjordje (to the south) and King Petar (north). In the crypt (stairway to the left of the entrance) are buried almost all the members of Karadjordjević family, amongst them four

Karadjordje's Grave

rulers. The crypt walls depict the life of St Peter.

Further down the road that leads away from the church stand the **villas** of King Aleksandar (to the left), dating from 1923, and of Queen Mary (from 1924). Around them are laid the famous vineyards of Oplenac.

❻ Gornji Milanovac

🏠 27.400

ℹ️ Vojvode Milana 13
32300 Gornji Milanovac
032/ 720-565

🚌 032/711-630

23 km - Čačak

The ancient village of Brusnica, nested in a deep and narrow valley that was considered inappropriate for its development, was

Barrels from royal wine-cellars

Church in Gornji Milanovac

moved in 1853 to a field several miles to the west. First called Despotovica, after the river of the same name, the newly established town was laid according to a rectangular street plan with wide streets and a central square. In 1859 it adopted a new name in memory of prince Miloš's brother Milan. Most of the old Gornji Milanovac was destroyed in late 1941 in a heavy Nazi bombing which targeted rebel forces that were fighting the occupation.

On the main square stands the unattractive former District Administration building. In front of it there are busts representing different figures of Serbian history: prince Aleksandar, during whose reign the town was founded, prince Milan and field marshal Živojin Mišić, who victoriously led the Serbian army at the battles of Suvobor and Kolubara during WWI. In the same square stands the old **Church of Holy Trinity**, built in

1862 by prince Miloš in sign of gratitude for the renaming of the town. Its architecture is romantcist but some details are inspired by the medieval school of Morava.

Above the town stands the so-called **"Norwegian house"** (*Norveška kuća*, A. Djokić, 1981) designed to resemble both the bow of a Viking ship and a traditional house of Šumadija. It's a tribute to the friendship established with Norway during WWII when thousands of war prisoners worked in Nazi camps in the north of that country. It houses a small museum documenting daily life in the camps, and a pleasant restaurant.

⑦ Takovo

9 km - Gornji Milanovac

Taking advantage of the local county fair on *Cveti* (Palm Sunday), village's saint patron's day, Serbian dukes and other prominent men led by Miloš Obrenović, gathered here on 23rd

of April 1815 and decided to start another uprising against an unbearable Turkish occupation. Today, there are several monuments that remind us on the event that eventually brought liberation of Serbia from the Ottoman rule.

Just by the road, 9 kilometres west from Gornji Milanovac, is the **Museum of Takovo Uprising**. The highlights of this well-kept museum are the oil on canvas of Paja Jovanović depicting the famous event, then also Prince Miloš's vestment, and part of the original "Takovo Oak" (*see below*).

Next turn to the right will get you to the main entrance of the old **Log Church**. In this graceful small church dating from 1795, after the service the rebel leaders sworn to each other and announced the start of the fight to the gathered people. On its west side is a delicately carved door, and inside even more precisely carved iconostasis. Behind the church lay collected the old tomb-stones, previously scattered round the churchyard.

On an open field, left from the main

Paja Jovanović, "Takovo Uprising",

Obelisk and the famous Takovo oak trees

8 Vraćevšnica

30 km - Kragujevac

road, is a monument to the Uprising, work of Petar Ubavkić from 1902, which represents Prince Miloš and abbot Melentije Pavlović. The legendary "Takovo Bush" (*Takovski grm*), actually an oak tree under which the leaders of the uprising held the last council before they made their final move, stood in this field. When the original tree fell down in 1901, an adjacent tree was proclaimed its "successor"; the dead log of this second tree still stands tall today. Several young oak trees have grown from original Oak's acorns, but it is still uncertain which one will be "crowned" the "successor". Next to the dead log stands the old **Obelisk** from 1887, with famous verses: "This bush will die, and the stone pillar will crumble, but Serbia will stand eternally and remember Miloš's name".

Going south about 3 km, following the Dičina river you will arive to the Savinac hamlet, named after its **Church of St Sava**. Prince Miloš had it built in 1819, as the first

stone church in liberated Serbia. The story says that, on his way to the Battle of Ljubić, Miloš had on this spot a dreem foresawing his victory. He therefore pledged that if he dream comes true he would have a church built here. This is the burial church of the members of Miloš's wife's Ljubica family (Vukomanovićs), which originate from neighbouring Srezojevac. The church is not decorated on the outside, except around doors and windows. Inside is a fine iconostasis from the time when the church was built. Here also lies the grave of Mina Vukomanović, the daughter of a Vuk Karadžić and also a painter and a poet, who was buried alongside her husband.

Near the church are several tomb-stones and an old tower-house (*čardak*). On the place where the Dičina River makes one of its cascades a healing spring sprangs out.

Vraćevšnica monastery was founded by Radič Postupović, one of the mightiest nobles in realm of Despotes Stefan. The legend goes that the young man Radič prayed to St George for his safe return from the battle of Kosovo. As his prayers were fullfiled, he built a monastery dedicated to his protector. According to tradition, the monastery was named after Radič's return (in Serbian *vratiti se* - to return). From the founder's inscription we learn that the monastery was terminated in 1431 while the frescoes were painted soon afterwards. Vraćevšnica was demolished in 1438 during the Turkish seizure of this part of Serbia. It was to be destroyed by the Turks three more times, in the 16th,18th and19th centuries.

During the First Serbian Insurrection the mon-

Church of Vraćevšnica Monastery

astery was important as the meeting point for the assembly, but it earned its real glory during the Second Insurrection. On the 11th of April 1815 Miloš Obrenović, one of the most distinguished Serbian leaders, arrived

Old dwellings in the Vraćevšnica

at the monastery with his troops and recieved a blessing from the monks. The next morning, along with the monastery's Abbot Melentije Pavlović, they bravely went to Takovo where they initiated the insurrection. Miloš, the future Prince of Serbia, never forgot the monastery: he buried his mother Višnja there and then helped in its renovation with the intention of turning it into a mausoleum for himself and his family. Melentije Pavlović in 1831 became the first Serbian Bishop after almost a century of Greek Phanariotes domination.

Today Vraćevšnica is a nunnery. The monastery's church is a single nave building built of skillfully modelled yellow stone blocks. The façades are decorated with a series of blind arches that run all the way around the church. The open narthex with a small attractive cupola dates from Miloš's renovation in 1860. The original medieval frescoes inside the church were heavily retouched in 1737. Nevertheless, there are several interesting ones, amidst them the endower's portrait. The iconostasis also dates from the 18th century.

The **Old Dwellings** is an imposing two storey-high edifice executed in a traditional style. The first floor has a long wooden porch facing the

courtyard which creates the impression that the second floor is flying above it. The **New Dwellings**, with a small tower, date from 1860 and were designed in the romanticist style imitating the church's architectural style.

Vraćevšnica has also a small but impressive **treasury**. Among other things here, one can see a small cross that used to belong to the 18th century Serbian Patriarch, Arsenije IV. One can also observe late 19th century furniture and the belongings of King Milan Obrenović and his wife Natalija.

❾ Borač

14 km - Gruža

This old village is situated on the western rim of the Gruža River valley. Turn right on 7th kilometre from Knić for the village of Radmilović, and then left for Borač at the T-crossroad. Already

after a couple of hundred metres in front of you opens the view of the magnificent Borački krš, a group of high pointy rocks emerging from the wavy valleys. One can often see eagles as they circle, around the peaks, contributing to the exceptional atmosphere of the place.

After passing through the centre of the village, you are at the foothill of the Karst, where the most interesting sights lie. Just under the granite rock is an old **church**, reachable only by stairways cut through the very rock. This small stone church dates from middle of the 14th century and was renovated in 1553, when it got its present-day looks. In 19th century it received its outer narthex and a wooden steeple.

Near the church stand several gigantic lime trees, of which one has 6 metres in circumference!

To the right of the churchyard gate starts a pathway by which you can climb up to the top of the Borački krš, where, a long time ago, stood the castle Borač, which belonged to Radič Postupović, one of the Serbian feudal lords, and after which the whole district was named. At the very start of that pathway is an **Old Cemetery** with its variated tomb-stones originating from 17th to 19th century.

View on Gruža from Borački krš

⑩ Kragujevac

🏛 175.800

ℹ Kralja Aleksandra 98
34000 Kragujevac
034/332-172

🚌 034/9802

🚊 034/9803

72 km - Beograd

Lying in the very centre of the Šumadija, Kragujevac is the region's biggest and most important city. Already during the 18th c., it was one of the main towns in Serbia but it really soared after prince Miloš chose it as the first capital of free Serbia in 1818. One of the reasons for this choice was the fact that it stood in the middle of the country and far away from any Turkish garrison or settlement. Kragujevac saw the birth of some institutions that changed the face of Serbia: the first printing-house and the first theatre (both in 1833), newspapers (1834), a military academy (1837), the first high school (1838), the seat of Metropolitan of Serbia etc. The town was also the young state's political centre, where important decisions were reached, where proclamations were made public, where National Assemblies met and where rebellions started. Viewed as the stronghold of the Obrenović dynasty, Kragujevac was abandoned in 1841 by the Constitutionalists and Belgrade became the capital. The town, still very small, lost its cultural and political importance but continued to rise steadily as a regional centre. A new impulse came when the first Serbian industrial

plant, a cannon factory, opened here. It soon started to produce all kinds of armament and greatly contributed to the town's development, while at the same time creating the first working class in the country. The demonstration known as the "Red Flag of Kragujevac", held after the socialist victory at the local elections in 1876, made Kragujevac the pride of the Serbian communists. The town's population suffered heavily during WWI

The Kragujevac coat-of-arms

and WWII: on 21st October 1941, the Germans shot some 3000 civilians in reprisal to the attacks suffered by their forces. After the war, Kragujevac stood as a symbol of the communist regime's values with its workers, strikes and war sufferings. While fast development destroyed most of the old town, the armament factory, now

called "Crvena Zastava" (Red Flag), started to produce automobiles, first copies of Fiat and then its own Zastava and Yugo, which became Yugoslavia's national means of transport. During the Milošević years, all industrial activity was brought to a halt and the town quickly declined until becoming one of the poorest and most economically problematic cities in Serbia.

The core of the old town was situated around the Lepenica River, but all that's left today of the old princely compound in oriental style is the **Amidžin konak**. This modest Balkans style construction was one of the first administrative buildings built when Kragujevac became the capital. It was named after Sima Paštrmac, nicknamed "Amidža" (Uncle), the main administrator of the princely office. Next to it stands Prince Mihailo's Manor built in 1860. Today both buildings house the local **Museum** (*Narodni muzej, Vuka Karadžića 1, tel. 034/33-302*), focusing on history but also showing a collection of 17th -19th c. artworks. In the modern edifice connecting the two buildings we find the Gallery of Contemporary Painting.

Amidžin konak, part of old Kragujevac

Kragujevac High School

Next to this complex is the **Monument to the Fallen 1804-1912**, an interesting work executed by Antun Augustničić in 1937.

Across the small river stands the **Old Church** built as well by prince Miloš in 1818. Despite its small size, it was actually bigger than what the Turkish regulations allowed and Miloš had to use all his diplomatic skills to secure its completion. The bell tower was added during the reconstruction works at the beginning of the 20th c. In the churchyard, the National Assemblies used to meet and it was there that the first Serbian constitution was proclaimed in 1835, making it one of the first European constitutions. The unpretentious ground-floor edifice is actually the first Serbian **Parliament Building**, dating from 1859. In 1878 the declarations of the Berlin Congress that gave Serbia its independence were read to the MPs in this place.

The factory grounds of "Crvena Zastava" start near the church. The **Monument to a Kragujevac Worker** is situated in front of its old administra-

tion building. On its pediment there is a flag with the inscription Samouprava – "Self-management", one of the demands of the workers in 1876 which coincided well with the policy of socialist Yugoslavia at the time when the monumwn was erected.

Back on the other bank, just behind Amidžin Konak stands the building of the High School (*Gimnazija*). Constructed in 1884 in a neo-classical style, it is regarded as the most

attractive school edifice of 19th c. Serbia.

The **New Church** is located across the tiny Erdoglijski potok stream. Designed in 1866 by Andreja Andrejević, it presents one of the cornerstones of Serbian architecture since it categorically breaks with the

baroque and classicism in favour of the romantic Byzantine-Romanesque style, closer to medieval tradition. The new iconostasis was made in 1926 by two Russian émigrés – Aleksandar Redkin who carved it and Andrej Bicenko who painted the icons.

The church faces Kralja Aleksandra I Karadjordjevića Street, the town's old commercial centre. The street continues further as the pedestrian Kralja Petra St. with several fine houses that managed to survive the rapid industrialization of the town. On the first left corner opens the view to the imposing **Local County** building (N. Nestorović, 1902) following a calm academic style. In 1915 the Serbian high command led the celebrated Kolubara Battle from here.

Two corners north up Karadjordjeva St. is

Pedestrian area in Kralja Petra Street

Svetozara Markovića Street. Along this street, you will find several old houses dating back to the early 19th c. At number 5 you will see the house of the above-mentioned Amidža, Nos. 9 and 11 are attractive examples of middle class domiciles from the

Old bridge in Kragujevac

period, No. 19 is the large house of Vojvoda Dena. As for No. 23, it was occupied for some time by Svetozar Marković (1846-1875), a leading figure amongst early socialists.

Leaving the town centre through Kralja Aleksandra I Karadjordjevića St. and further on through Kragujevačkog Oktobra St., you will reach after 1.5 km **Šumarice Memorial Park**. It commemorates the tragic events of 1941 when German occupiers shot innocent civilians and amongst them many schoolchildren. The **"21. oktobar" Museum** (*Desankin venac bb, tel. 034/336-112, open Mon-Fri 8 a.m.-6 p.m., weekends to 1 p.m.*), located to the right of the park, is an impressive edifice built in 1968 by the plans of Ivan Antić and Ivanka Raspopović. The large park has several monuments dedicated to the victims of the executions, and among them the V-shaped **"Broken Wing"** (M. Živković, 1963), one of the symbols of the town. On the same grounds, a memorial graveyard pays tribute to the Czech and Slovak soldiers shot at the end of WWI for refusing to fight their Serbian brothers.

⑪ Jagodina

🏨	32.500
ℹ️	Hotel Jagodina
	35000 Jagodina
	035/220-052
☎	035/220-205
📠	035/221-003
	135 km - Beograd

Despite the fact that it lies in the fertile Morava valley, this region developed rather slowly during the Middle Ages due to its location close to the borderline. The town emerged in the 14th c. but held no real importance until the 16th c. when it became a prominent station on the Belgrade-Istanbul road. During the first Serbian Insurrection, it was the stronghold of the Turkish outlaw Kučuk Alija and his mercenaries, against whom the Serbs led two battles. In 1830 the Turks left Jagodina for good and the town started its speedy development, mostly due to its position on the still busy road from the capital to the south. From 1946 to 1992 the town was renamed Svetozarevo in memory of Svetozar Marković, the first Serbian socialist, who lived in the town for some time.

In the centre of the town lies the large Church of SS Peter &

Paul, colloquially called the **New Church**. It was erected in 1899, according to the plans of Dušan Živanović's as a five-domed structure with a separate bell tower, in the style of academic historicism, following the spirit of Byzantine tradition.

The **Old Church** (*Stara crkva*), dedicated to Archangels Michael & Gabriel is a modest building from 1815. Its 1822 iconostasis is the work of painters who followed the tradition of medieval painting.

Not far from the Old Church stands the **Hajduk-Veljko's Manor** (*Hajduk Veljkov konak*), a typical example of 18th c. oriental house in the Balkans. It was named after the famous hero of the first Serbian uprising, Hajduk-Veljko Petrović who once resided here.

The **Museum of Naïve Art** (*Boška Djuričića 10, tel. 223-419, www.naiveart.org.yu*) is located in a noteworthy villa built in 1929. The museum was founded in 1960 in order to collect and exhibit the works of self-taught artists from all over Yugoslavia. It

Uroš Knežević, "Hajduk Veljko" (National Museum Belgrade)

was established in Jagodina because its collection originally gathered many works of painter Janko

Brašić, who lived in a nearby village. Today its permanent exhibition shows 200 works and the stockrooms hold about 2500 more works of art, making it one of the biggest collections of naïve art in the world. The most famous artists to be found here are Ilija Bašičević Bosilj, Janko Brašić, Milosav Jovanović, Sava Sekulić and Emerik Feješ.

Battlements of the Manasija Monastery

 ⑫ **Manasija**

2 km - Despotovac

In the vicinity of Despotovac stands the last of the grand, endowments of the Serbian rulers of the Middle Ages. The Manasija monastery was built between 1407 and 1418 by despotes Stefan Lazarević (1377-1427) who wanted it to be his final resting place. The monastery was initially known as Resava, after the river that runs nearby. After its creation, it gathered many well-taught monks who fostered writing and literature. The number of works produced and their excellence contributed to change the history of South Slavic literature and languages, spread-

ing its influence all over the orthodox Balkans. The most famous local scholar was Constantine the Philosopher (Konstantin Filozof), an influential writer and also biographer of despotes Stefan. The monastery is protected by massive walls with eleven towers and ditches in front of them. The importance given to the protection of the monastery is related to the atmosphere of danger created by the increasing number of Turkish raids. However, not even these battlements could save Mansija and it was taken by the Turks for the first time in 1439. After that, in 1456, the complex was again looted and burnt. In the following centuries, it served more as a fortress than as a place of worship. During the

Austrian occupation, gunpowder was stored in the church, and in 1718 its explosion blew up most of the narthex. At the beginning of the 19th c. the enterprising monks started the restoration and, in 1845, the first state-funded conservation works were concluded.

The only entrance to the interior of the battlements is in front of the parking lot. To the right of the church, you can see the ruins of the **Old Refectory**. In the first tower to the left of the entrance are the steps leading to the walls from which you will get a nice view of the yard.

Although it shares most of the features of the Morava school of religious architecture that prevailed at that time, the **church** dedicated to the Holy Trinity is quite singular as far as decoration is concerned. The façades are covered by ashlars and thin mortar beds arranged in a tidy order, very different from the playfulness observed in other churches of the period. The flat walls are decorated only with colonnades, arcaded cornice and windows with

Manasija monastery church alongside the keep

pointed arches. This church brings together architectural elements peculiar to the edifices built by the Nemanjić dynasty and others that characterise the new dynasty started by Stefan's father, Prince Lazar. The church was also praised for its height (25.6 m), which makes it the second tallest church ater Dečani monastery in Kosovo. Also of interest are the elongated domes, the element that will continue to live after the fall of Serbia in

red-haired ruler appears dressed in an elaborate vestment adorned with two-headed eagles. He is holding a scale model of the church and the founding charter while the Christ crowns him and the angels offer him a sword and a scepter. Above the entrance door stands an interesting composition of the Souls of the righteous in the Divine Hand flanked by Kings Solomon and David. Manasija's most famous painting is one of the Holy Warriors

⓭ Resavska pećina

23 km - Ćuprija

From the depths of Mt Beljanica, some 10 km east of the Manasija monastery, emerges the entrance of Resava cave. Due to the thick bushes that were covering it, the entrance was only discovered in 1962. A decade later, it was the first cave in Serbia to be arranged for tourist visits. The cave has three levels and its length totals 2830m. The two upper levels are partially open for visitors and a 800m long path has been set up for tourists. Through the lowest floor flows an underground river. Resava is a very rich and colourful cave and it boasts several impressive halls. The cave has a constant temperaure of 14°C.

There is a permanent guide service that can arrange a 40 minute tour of the cave (*tel. 035/611-110*). From 1st April to 31st October visiting hours are 8 a.m.-6.30 p.m., during the rest of the year 10 a.m.-5 p.m.

Holy Warriors

the architecture of the Romanian monasteries in the north, founded by Serbian monks.

The narthex, rebuilt in 1735, has an original 15th c. floor, made of red, blue and yellowish marble tiles arranged in a rosette shape.

Mansija's frescoes rank among the most beautiful medieval works of art in Serbia and art lovers visited the monastery to see them already in the days of its completion. Unfortunately, the ravages of time spared only about half of the original compositions. To the left of the entrance stands what is considered to be the best and most faithful portrait of despot Stefan: the tall,

in the north choir. The warrior saints appear gold-clad and armored with realistic representations of their weapons. Manasija is also famous for the busts of saints in medallions woven in rainbow-coloured stripes to be found there. The master-painter who worked here skillfully handled the space: his figures are classically proportioned and have natural motions, while the balance between gold and blue surfaces creates a unique luminosity.

Warm colours of cave interior

⑭ Ravanica

11 km - Ćuprija

11 km east of Ćuprija, after the village of Senje, stands the principal and the largest endowment church of Prince Lazar which he intended to be his burial place. This church, dedicated to the Ascension, was constructed between 1375 and 1381. In the following years were added the refectory, the monastic cells and the ramparts with seven towers. After Lazar's death at Kosovo Polje battle in 1389, his body was brought there. With the rise of his cult as a martyr the church gained more and more significance. Destroyed several times during the Turkish conquest, it was reconstructed in the 16th c., but during the First great migration (end of 17th c.) it befell even greater misfortunes as it was burnt and fell into ruin for the next 30 years. During the occupation of Serbia by the Habsburg (1717-39) it was rebuilt: a new, low narthex was added and new frescoes were painted.

Relics of Prince Lazar

The design of the church is one of the cornerstones of the new Morava school of architecture. Its ground-plan is a combination of the cross-in-square, popular with the previ-

Yellow and red facades of Ravanica Monastery

ous edifices of the 14th c, and the trefoil base, characteristic of the Mount Athos monasteries. The slender main cupola reaches unprecedented heights and is surrounded by four smaller ones at the corners. The façade abounds in decoration: the usual Byzantine principle of combining layers of bricks and stones is here applied but it is further enlivened by a large rose window above the western portal and by checked semi-circular fields. Additionally, the frames of the windows

are richly carved. This generous decoration of the façade was a totally new feature that later became the standard in other churches of northern Serbia and even in present-day Romania, where it continued to spread in the following centuries.

The original frescoes, finished in 1385-1387, also set examples for subsequent painters, both because of their iconographic choices and because of their refined style. We find some new motifs that can also be observed in later Morava churches: the Holy Warriors, a large number of hermits, medallions surrounded by rainbow-coloured strips etc. The style is characterized by a new sense of movement, individual portraits and the importance of colour. To the left of the entrance is a portrait depicting Lazar with his wife Milica and sons Stefan and Vuk. The most famous paintings here are the "Virgin

The Odyssey of the Decapitated Prince

After he was beheaded in the Battle of Kosovo Polje, Lazar's body was initially kept in the parish church of Priština. After being proclaimed a saint, his relics were transferred in 1392 to Ravanica, where the cult of the martyr prince developed. In 1690, while running away from the atrocities performed by the Turks, the monks took with them their most sacred relic and carried it all the way to Szentendre, north of Budapest, where the Serbian Patriarch and the mass of refugees finally stopped. After the end of the war, the relics were taken to the monastery of Vrdink, on Mt Fruška Gora, from then on called "Ravanica of Srem" that kept alive the traditions of the old monastery. During the savage destruction of Serbian shrines by Croatian Nazis in WWII, the holy remnants had to be moved again: they were carried to Belgrade and placed in the Cathedral. In 1989, on the 600th anniversary of his death, Lazar's body was finaly returned to his temple.

with the Infant Jesus" and the Cycle of Christ's Miracles. The paintings in the narthex date from the 18th and 19th c.

⓯ Kalenić

37 km - Varvarin

To reach this monastery secluded in the heart of Šumadija you need to go to the village of Oparić from Trstenik, Ćićevac, Jagodina or Kragujevac. From Oparić continue westwards for 12km, through the village of Prevešt, until you reach Kalenićki Prnjavor, which lies next to the monastery.

With its harmonious architecture and exquisite decoration, Kalenić is considered to be the best work of the Morava school of architecture. The only remaining part of the monastery is the church dedicated to the Presentation of the Virgin and built in 1407 by nobleman, Bogdan, treasurer of the court under despotes Stefan Lazarević. The mon-

astery was burnt by the Turks in 1690 and again in 1789, when it was being used as a military base by captain Koča Andjelković, the commander of the Serbian troops in the Austro-Turkish war. From 1815 to 1839, the church hosted the holy relics of King Stefan the First-Crowned. Renovated several times in the 19th c, the monastery recovered its original appearance after meticulous renovation in 1928-1930.

The style and refinement of the works of art in medieval Serbia depended mainly on the education and wealth of the patron. Bogdan, a high court official, judging on the perfection of his endowment, was obviously both educated and wealthy. The architecture of the church reminds one of Lazarica Church in Kruševac, but Kalenić excels its architectural predecessor both with its proportions and refined decoration. Arches, pillars and colonnades, the alternation of sandstone and bricks, the high central dome, all contribute to its unparalleled beauty. Pay special attention to the stunning carving of the western portal, to the various shapes of rose windows and to the reliefs above the windows depicting biblical, allegorical and mythical scenes.

The fresco decoration of the interior is a worthy match to the outside looks. It is the work of one of the greatest Serbian artists of the first part of the 15th c, master Radoslav, and

Kalenić Monastery, the peak of the Morava School

his troupe. The paintings are colourful and seem to radiate diffuse light, with figures and scenes more intimate than decorative, all of which makes them a masterpiece of Byzantine painting of the period. The most famous amongst the frescoes are "Wedding in Cana", "Adoration of the Magi" and "Flight to Egypt".

16 Ljubostinja

7 km - Trstenik

This monastery is the endowment of princess Milica. wife of prince Lazar. It was built immediately before the Battle of Kosovo (1389), where Lazar met his end. With her son Stefan still a child, Milica had to run the state, but she later decided to take her monastic vow and retreat in this monastery. Around her gathered a circle of noble women that were widowed in the past wars. In later centuries, the monastery fell into relative seclusion and the only thing we know is that it was destroyed and renovated at least three times.

Ljubostinja is one of the pearls of the Morava School and it follows all its characteristic features: a trefoil base plan, an outer narthex built at the same time as the rest of the church, abundantly decorated façades of stone and bricks etc. From the inscription found on the threshold between the narthex and the nave (chosen as the most humble place), we know that Ljubostinja was built by Rade Borojević, widely know in folk songs by the name of Rade Neimar ("Rade the Mason"). The exterior is especially rich in decoration with its

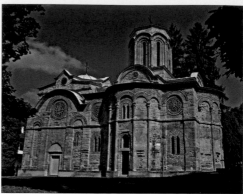

Ljubostinja Monastery

rose windows, archivolts, twisted columns... In addition, the façades were once painted with even more motives, but none of these survived.

The interior was painted with frescoes on two occasions: first the cupola in 1388/1389 and later the rest of the church in 1402-1405. The paintings on the cupola are marked by an unusual liveliness. Frescoes from the second phase of painting are of varying quality. It is interesting that they were executed by Makarije, brother of Metropolitan Jovan, a very able painter himself. To the left of the entrance, on the western wall, stand the portraits of the patrons: prince Lazar, princess Milica and their sons Stefan and Vuk. The church holds the graves of Milica herself and of the nun Jefimija, author of the "Eulogy to Prince Lazar", one of the best literary works of the period.

17 Kruševac

🏛 132.300

ℹ️ Miloja Zakića 3
37000 Kruševac
037/440-332

▭ 037/21-706

▭ 037/28-888

195 km - Beograd

After 1371 Prince Lazar emerged as the most powerful nobleman across the Serbian lands controling most of the valleys of Western and Southern Morava as well north Serbia. At that time he decided to put up a new capital for his land. The ideal place for the new town was found in Kruševac, on top of a hill, near the confluence of the two Moravas and close to the centre of Lazar's state. There he built a strong fortress and soon afterwards a court church. After his death in 1389, Kruševac remained the capital of

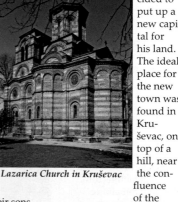

Lazarica Church in Kruševac

Serbia until Lazar's son Stefan transferred it northwards to Belgrade in 1403. The Turkish danger soon lurked over and the town became one of their prime targets. It was taken and retaken twice until the Hungarian army, raiding against this Turkish stronghold, set the town on fire in 1437, ruining its prestige forever. In 1454 the Ottomans took it for good and turned it into the provincal capital. They renamed it *Aladža Hisar* or "Dappled Town", due to the colour of its battlements that were constructed from various kinds of stones. The town was freed in 1833 and kept its importance as a regional centre.

Downtown shows a rather austere face since it was almost completely rebuilt after WWII. The black marble **Monument to the Kosovo Warriors** stands on the main intersection. It

Monument to Kosovo Warriors

here before heading to Kosovo and their glorious end. A winged victory stands above a Serbian soldier while on the sides we see a seated young woman, a personification of Serbia and a *guslar* fiddler, who traditionally sang

retains an air of the 19th c. with its small houses tucked in greenery.

Kruševac's main sites are the remains of Lazar's fortress and Lazarica Church inside of it. To reach these, head right through Pana Djukića Street. On your way you will pass by the fine **Okružno načelstvo** (State County) edifice, built by Nikola Nestorović in the year 1900. Its main hall is decorated with Mladen Srbinović's colourful mosaics representing the Kosovo Battle. Cara Lazara Street was the old commercial street of the Turkish town called Stara čaršija. One of the interesting houses on this street is **Menzulana**, the old oriental Post

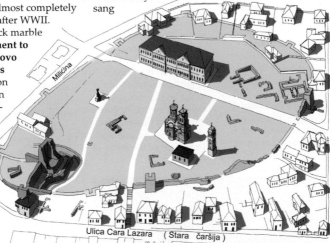

is the work of Djordje Jovanović, commissioned for the celebration of the 500th anniversary of the Kosovo Battle (1889). This site was chosen because Lazar and his army originally assembled

about the deeds related to this essential part pf the Serbian epic cycle.

Part of Vuka Karadžića Street is called **Grčki šor** or Greek Lane ("Greek" was a colloquial name for a merchant) and it

Office, which is situated in a 18th c. building and still in use for the same purpose today.

Further up appear the remains of the massive **keep** of Lazar's Castle. With its 15 m of height it was the last refuge for the assaulted and is nowadays the castle's best preserved part.

Kruševac's most important monument is certainly the beautiful Lazarica Church. This masterpiece of Serbian religious architecture was built around 1377. It represents the beginning of the Morava school of architecture with its bold new conception of masses, its attempt to reach new heights and its curious decoration. The façades are enlivened by the alternation of stone and red brick, by the reliefs around the windows, rose windows and red-white checkers that all blend into a sparkling whole. The interior, with no remaining frescoes, is of no interest.

Behind the church is the **Monument to Prince Lazar** by Nebojša Mitrić in his easily recognisable style. The **Museum** (*tel. 037/29-172, open Tue-Sat 8 a.m.-6 p.m., Sundays and holidays 9 a.m.-2 p.m.*) is located in the 1863 building of the old Grammar School. Among its interesting pieces stands out prince Lazar's apparel, a richly ornamented dress that one can see

in old frescoes. On the first floor, you will find a permanent 20th c. art exhibition, mainly concerned with the Kosovo Battle. The most interesting item here is the model of the never executed Vidovdan Temple designed by Ivan Meštrović in 1912, just after the liberation of Kosovo.

ENVIRONS:
The village of Stalać is located on the 14th kilometer towards Ćićevac and the Belgrade-Niš highway. The scenic ruins of a castle known as **"Kula Todora od Stalaća"** stand on the hill above the point where Southern and Western Morava meet. Not much is left except for one large keep and the walls around the entry gate. Konstantin the Philosopher, despot Stefan's biographer, wrote that in 1413 the castle's commander fought the Turks with the "valour of antique heroes" and in the end perished surrounded by fire. According to local tradition the commander's name was Todor, hence the name of the tower.

⑱ Naupare

20 km - Kruševac

After a 10 km drive south of Kruševac on the Blace road, you will reach the village of Gornji Stepoš. Take left towards Naupare,

Naupare church with its large rose windows

where you will find a monastery of the same name. It is the endowment of monk Dorotej and his son Danilo, also a monk, who later became a Serbian Patriarch. Built before 1382, it wasn't originally intended for a monastery but for a court church for Dorotej, a nobleman of Prince Lazar whose estate was on these grounds. The church copies the structure of Lazarica church with a small narthex and a bell-tower above it. Its most interesting details are two large rose windows above the western entrance and several smaller ones on the sides. The wall paintings and iconostasis date from the 19th c.

Monument to Prince Lazar

⑲ Vrnjačka Banja

🏛 9.300

ℹ Vrnjačka 6/2
36210 Vrnjačka Banja
036/611-106, 611-107

📠 036/612-652

🖥 036/662-035

27 km - Kraljevo

This capital of Serbian spa tourism lies in the valleys of the small but picturesque rivers Vrnjačka and Lipovačka reka. At approximately 230m of altitude, it is sit-

Modernistic touch to the old Spa

uated on the north slope of Goč Mountain, from which it gets a constant flux of fresh air. The spa was known allready to the Romans who made use of it until the 4th c. AD. The Turks used it abundantly, forcing the local peasants to provide them free shelter and food. This is why the locals tried to keep the spa as little known as possible. It was "discovered" again in 1835 by Baron Herder who was looking for potential mining sites, following prince Miloš's orders. In 1860, the first spa installations were built, and in 1868, the "Founders' Society for Curative Thermal-Mineral

Water" was organized, thus marking the beginning of spa tourism. In 1882, the state became conscious of the spa's potential impact and it posted a seasonal medic to advise people on their medical problems. The 20th c. saw rapid development of the spa: from small houses to villas, from small family hotels to record tourist frequentation - 163 thousand people in 1985, making it the biggest health resort in Serbia.

Today, Vrnajčka Banja is a place where people enjoy themselves and relax in the various parks, thermal springs and pleasant natural surroundings. It has six springs, out of which the best known are

"Jezero" (25,7°C) and "Topli izvor" (36,5°C) for hot springs and "Slatina" (14°C) and "Snežnik" (17,5°C) for cold ones.

Aside from the spa, the most interesting sight is the complex of residential houses on **Čajkino brdo Hill**. A small parish church stands on top of it. It was founded in 1856 by priest Jeftimije Popović, who regulated the first thermal spring in the Spa that very same year.

One should not forget to visit the **Belimarković Manor**, situated above the main walkway. It was built in 1886 as a summer residence for General Jovan Belimarković in the style of the country villas of Northern Italy. Today the manor hosts a cultural centre with an art gallery.

Several walkways and bicycle roads cut across the whole resort and there are several sport fields and pools. **Mount Goč** (1124 m) is perfect for trekking and has ski tracks and lifts operating in winters. During the summertime the Spa has a rich cultural and entertainment program.

Flower beds in one of the parks in Vrnjačka Banja

Hotel

Motel

Villa/Private Pension

Agrotourism accommodation

PRICE RANGE - for one person in a two-bed room (including breakfast, service and tax). Small icons present facilities in each Hotel.

number of rooms   number of beds

308/373

> 50 EUR €€€€€
35 - 50 EUR €€€€
25 - 35 EUR €€€
12 - 25 EUR €€
< 12 EUR €

★★★ Country club - Babe

Milovana Milenkovića 3
11233 Babe
011/826-0077

69/194

€€€€
VISA MasterCard Maestro

Because of the excellent climate and 350m height above sea level, hotel complex is an ideal environment for all who are desirous of peace and fresh air.

★★★ Plana

Pokajnički put bb
11320 Velika Plana
026/521-406, 521-416

106/260

€€

Hotel is surrounded with forest and very easy to get to.

★★ Stari hrast

11325 Markovac

026/861-021, 861-022

48/96

€€€€€
VISA MasterCard Maestro

Along the motorway, but not exactly next to it. A legend says that the oak that it was named after is over 600 years old; 101 km from Belgrade.

★ Jerina

Autoput bb
11330 Malo Orašje
011/330-5300

30/60

€€

Near Smederevo on the motorway, 45 km from Belgrade; mini-bar, an open-air garden (during the summer); a good option for campers.

★★ Staro Zdanje

Ilije Garašanina bb
34300 Arandjelovac
034/711-981, 711-904

58/146

€€
VISA MasterCard

This family hotel is just 1,5km from the centre of the city. Besides the terrace with a swimming pool and great banquet hall.

★★ Oplenac

34310 Topola

034/811-430, /811-980

31/43

€€

Beautiful hotel very close to the Karadjordjevic mausoleum. There is a great restaurant and wonderful garden hidden in shadow during hot days, particularly recommended for drinking coffee.

★★ Ljig

Ibarski put bb
14240 Ljig
014/85-380, 85-015

48/100

€€

A lovely hotel in the very heart of the Ljig, with organized excursions to nearby mountains.

★★★ Vrujci

Banja Vrujci
14243 Gornja toplica
014/66-118 , 66-271, 66-287

103/217

€€
VISA MasterCard

The hotel is situated in the centre of this Spa; Convenient for all sorts of sport and cultural events.

Kod Uče

Radojko Radisavljević
14240 Ljig
014/85-840, 83-760

7/14

€

The Pension offers good accommodation, with a beautiful lawn – ideal for morning coffee or tea.

★★ Šumadija

Vojvode Milana 1
32300 Gornji Milanovac
032/711-151, 717-231, 717-230

73/102

€€

The hotel is situated in the centre of Gornji Milanovac.

★★ Neda

Karadjordjeva 35
32313 Rudnik
032/741-303

45/150

€€€€€
VISA MasterCard

Beneath the top of the Rudnik Mountain this beautiful family hotel is situated at 600 m, surrounded with forest will enrich your health, pleasure and holiday.

Bogdanica

✉ Veselin Čolović
selo Bogdanica, Gorjni Milanovac
☎ 032/846-012

2/4 €

Good accommodation, best for family holidays, rooms are equipped with telephone and TV set. Spoken language is English.

Gojna Gora

✉ Boško Mijailović
selo Gojna Gora, Gornji Milanovac
☎ 032/846-266

6/12 €

Guests can enjoy a friendly atmosphere in TV room, the hospitable staff speaks French.

Pranjani

✉ Stojka Obradović
selo Pranjani, Gornji Milanovac
☎ 032/844-073

2/4 €

The Pension has a beautiful garden and ethno-style rooms, the staff speaks Russian.

Lovačke priče

✉ selo Rajac, Gornji Milanovac

☎ 014/80-441

5/10 €

With a very good 'old-style' dinning room and a big yard, guests can enjoy both indoors and outdoors. In the Pension, English is spoken.

Ravni Gaj

✉ 34240 Knić

☎ 034/891-140

31/50 €€

Situated at the crossroads of Kragujevac – Kraljevo and Kragujevac – Čačak routes, 15 km from Kragujevac. Šumadija village-house styled

Knić

✉ Dragana Arsenijević
34240 Knić
☎ 034/510-836

2/3 €

Fine accommodation with beautiful garden and a small swimming pool. English language is spoken.

Ruža Gruže

✉ selo Bare
34240 Knić
☎ 034/592-247

7/13 €

Very nice countryside house equipped with, amongst others, internet access. Many languages spoken – English, French, Spanish, Portuguese and Czech.

★ ★ ★ ★ Stari Grad

✉ Karadjordjeva 10
34000 Kragujevac
☎ 034/330-591

16/26 €€€

A business hotel in the very centre of Kragujevac offers extraordinary service.

★ ★ ★ ★ Zelengora

✉ Branka Radičevića 22
34000 Kragujevac
☎ 034/336-254

29/46 €€€

The Hotel is placed in the very centre of the city, at the five street junctions.

★ ★ Kragujevac

✉ Kralja Petra I 26
34000 Kragujevac
☎ 034/335-811

106/154 €€€

This hotel with a beautiful terrace is situated in the very centre of Kragujevac.

★ ★ Šumarice

✉ Desankin venac bb
34000 Kragujevac
☎ 034/336-180, 336-181

131/227 €€

A fine hotel situated in nice location in Kragujevac.

★ ★ Jagodina

✉ Slavke Đuršević 3
35000 Jagodina
☎ 035/226-144

139/350 €€

The hotel and its botanic garden are placed in the very centre.

★ ★ Petruš

✉ Branka Krsmanovića 14
35250 Paraćin
☎ 034/336-180, 336-181

52/110 €€

This fine hotel is placed in the centre of Paraćin.

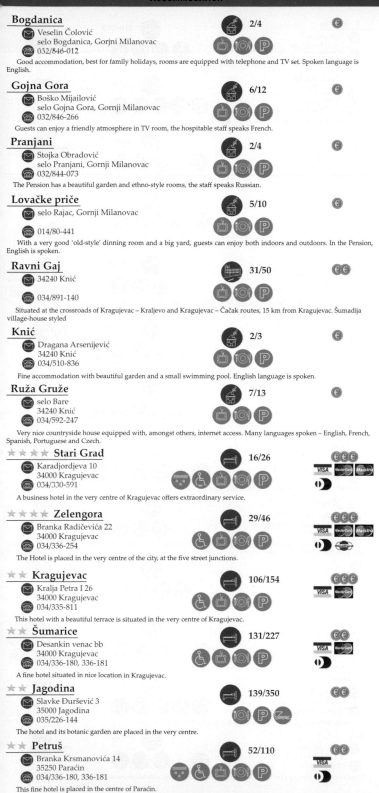

★★ Rubin

- Nemanjina 2
- 37000 Kruševac
- 037/425-535

116/200

This hotel is located in the centre of the city near the Lazarica Church.

★★★ NIS FAM

- Trg Mira 7
- 37000 Kruševac
- 037/441-981, 442-378

18/34

This family atmosphere hotel is suitable for businessmen.

★★ Golf

- Gavrila Principa 74
- 37000 Kruševac
- 037/460-563

15/30

Quiet hotel on the outskirts of the city offering an excellent service.

★★ Aleksandar

- Čajkina 7
- 36210 Vrnjačka banja
- 036/617-999

19/40

One of the most eminent hotels in Vrnjačka Banja, situated close to the central park and the main promenade. Surrounded by gorgeous park and a street with old buildings, popularly called "Vrnjački Monmartre".

★★ Slavija

- Svetog Save 2
- 36210 Vrnjačka Banja
- 036/612-679, 612-680

100/180

In the central park, aperitif bar; Merkur and Breza hotels' swimming pools are near; sport clubs frequently come here on a pre-season training

★★★ Novi Merkur

- Bulevar Srpskih ratnika 18
- 36210 Vrnjačka Banja
- 036/611-625, 611-626

448/840

Great and new hotel is just next to the river with beautiful summer outdoors café.

★★★ Breza

- Promenada bb
- 36210 Vrnjačka banja
- 036/612-400 665-969

158/386

In the very centre of Vrnjačka Banja Spa next to the main walking area is suitable for congress tourism.

★★ Fontana

- Cara Dušana 2
- 36210 Vrnjačka Banja
- 036/612-153, 612-154

219/386

The hotel is surrounded by nature, during summer there is a great restaurant with a terrace.

★★★ Zvezda

- Banjska promenada
- 36210 Vrnjačka Banja
- 036/662-202

103/217

Near the central part and with 5 congress halls this hotel is suitable for congress tourism. Guests can also enjoy in sauna, solarium, and gym and summer café.

San

- Banjska promenada
- 36210 Vrnjačka Banja
- 036/612-150

8/16

The Pension offers good accommodation, with a beautiful lawn – ideal for morning coffee or tea.

Passage

- Vrnjačka 5
- 36210 Vrnjačka Banja
- 036/616-789

7/14

On the main spa promenade with the view on the its park stand these seven modernly equiped apartments.

Garden

- Kraljevačka 8
- 36210 Vrnjačka Banja
- 036/611-067, 611-068

9/16

This house set in a large garden has nine spacious and well furnished rooms.

LUX

- Kneza Miloša 60
- 36210 Vrnjačka Banja
- 036/611-417

17/36

Good accommodation, best for family holidays, rooms are equipped with telephone and TV set.

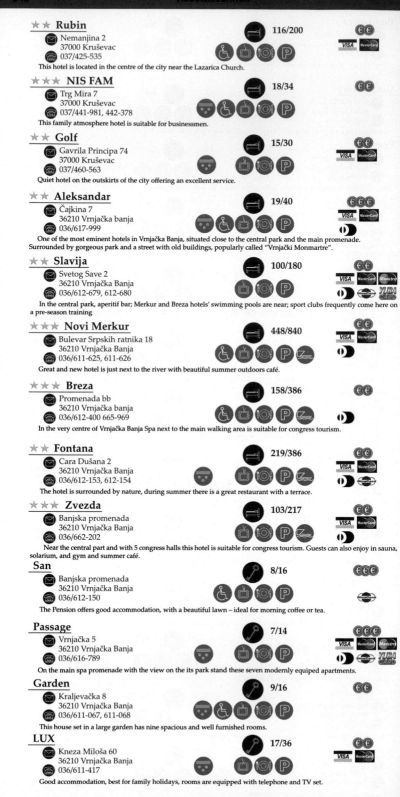

Fish restaurant    National restaurant   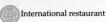 International restaurant

Djurdjevi Vajati
- Beogradski put
  26000 Smederevo
- ☎ 026/221-943

   08-24

On the river bank of the Danube; a promenade; suitable for families, 6 km from Smederevo.

Brvnara
- Beogradski put 161
  26000 Smederevo
- ☎ 026/617-064

   10-24

A typical ethnic styled restaurant, rustical, with a rattan roof. Located on the Belgrade – Smederevo road.

Zlatni kotlić
- Zanatlijska 35
  34300 Arandjelovac
- ☎ 034/723-175

   09-23

In the main street, ethno-styled; fish specialties.

Aleksandar
- Knjaza Miloša 173
  34300 Arandjelovac
- ☎ 034/725617, 714-617

   10-24

Ethnic styled, delicious national cuisine, inspired by the life and work of King Aleksandar Karadjordjević.

Vožd
- Bul. Vožda Karadjordja 90
  34310 Topola
- ☎ 034/811-365

   08-24

An ethnic styled restaurant, after you enter Topola, 500 m from Oplenac Church; a quiet atmosphere; actors, members of Serbian royal family - Karadjordjevićs, and diplomats among guests.

Jezero
- Beogradski put bb
  34310 Topola
- ☎ 034/811-528

   08-23

Just after you enter Topola, a huge restaurant with a traditional interior; you can taste old Serbian grilled specialties.

Putnik
- 34240 Knić
- ☎ 034/510-519

   07-23

Situated on the bank of the Gružansko Lake, along the Kragujevac – Čačak route, with a lovely garden, in Šumadija style. Accommodation is available as well.

Tito
- Autoput bb
  35000 Jagodina
- ☎ 035/565-406

   08-24

A restaurant on a main road, decorated with Tito souvenirs, such as his busts, relay baton in his honour, waiters dressed like *pioniri* (youth section of the Communist Party in Yugoslavia).

Konak
- Radomira Jakovljevića 5
  37000 Kruševac
- ☎ 037/443-410

   10-24

Ethnic styled, close to the city centre, a quiet place, early XX century Serbian urban music.

Kraljica
- Nemanjina 22
  36210 Vrnjačka Banja
- ☎ 036/611-565

    07-24

Contemporary styled, in the very centre of the city, recommendable for family people; quiet music.

Kruna
- Slatinski venac 3
  36210 Vrnjačka Banja
- ☎ 036/613-513

   10-23

National restaurant in beautiful surroundings with a view at the spa lake; live acoustic music, candles and a wide choice of quality drinks.

Traditional kafana "Karadjordjevi vajati" in Orašac

EASTERN SERBIA

This is one of the least explored parts of Serbia which is a great pity considering its natural beauty and interesting traditions. The landscape is dominated by a picturesque mountain range that is actually the southern tip of the Carpathian Mountains. On its west side lie the flatlands around the river Morava that finish in the great fertile plain of Stig, with Požarevac, the biggest town of the region, at its centre. West of the mountains is the Timok valley, which, due to its specific mild climate is filled with vineyards. There are many scenic views of nature to be found here. The main attraction is, of course, the Danube

remains dating back 9000 years. Next to it, one can find the *Tabula Traiana*, one of many testimonies of the Roman presence in the area. Gamzigrad, the ancient *Romuliana Felix* which is situated to the south, is an example of a late Roman locality. The Golubac castle, at the entrance to the Iron Gates gorge and Sokograd, above the famed spa-town of Sokobanja, remain as testimony to the skillful builders of the Middle Ages.

In the central mountain range most people are the descendants of the Romance-speaking Vlah population, who were settled in this secluded area

Shepherds' hut on Mt Miroč

with the famous Iron Gates gorge (serb. *Djerdapska klisura*) that forms the north border of the region. The river, the second largest in Europe, is constricted between the Carpathians forcing its way through several narrow passes. The hillsides that rise above it are home to an abundance of wildlife. For this reason it is protected as a National Park.

On the bank of the mighty Danube near Donji Milanovac is Lepenski Vir, an archeological site with cultural

in the 18th century by the Habsburg authorities. Apart from the language that is still used in some families, Vlahs are known for their interesting traditional white dress and large woolen hats. Music found here has a fast rhythm and is played tirelessly by local bands. Most interesting of all are the customs and traditions of the area, many of which come from primeval times – the region is known for its soothsaying and other kinds of peasant magic that is still practiced to this day.

This region has one of the largest émigré populations in the country due to the freer border access to the West in the 1960's during Socialist times. In many villages one can see the unnecessarily large houses embellished with peculiar decoration, built as a testament of the moneyed status of their owners living abroad.

The Timok valley is an area famous for its wine where once upon a time people drank more wine than water. Several villages like Rajac or Štubik have preserved their pimnice, wine cellars grouped in streets amidst the vineyards - a perfect setting to savor the excellent home made wines. Nearby lies the pleasant town of Negotin, that takes pride in Hajduk-Veljko its hero from the First Serbian rebellion. A bit further to the south is Zaječar, the cultural and economic centre of the Timok valley.

Pančevo

Skorenovac Kovin Dunav Viminacijum Ram
Kostolac

Smederevo Ljubičevo

Beograd ① Požarevac

Smederevska Palanka Morava

Koporin Velika Plana

Rača Svilajnac

Kragujevac

Jagodina

Jerinin Grad

① Požarevac
② Ram
③ Veliko Gradište
④ Golubac
⑤ National Park "Đerdap"
⑥ Lepenski Vir
⑦ Kladovo
⑧ Ceremošnja
⑨ Rajkova pećina
⑩ Gornjak
⑪ Zlotske pećine
⑫ Negotin
⑬ Zaječar
⑭ Gamzigrad
⑮ Sokobanja
⑯ Knjaževac
⑰ Stara Planina

Ruins in Gamzigrad

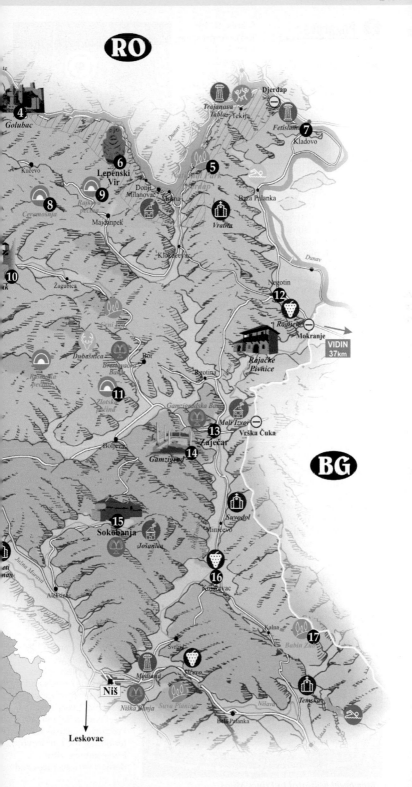

① Požarevac

74.900

Stari korzo 8
12000 Požarevac
012/ 221-941

012/211-844

012/222-051

78 km - Beograd

The town is located in the middle of the Stig plain, south from the Danube. It expanded in the 17th c. and became world famous when in 1718 the peace treaty of Passarowitz was signed there between Austria and Turkey. It played an important role during Serbian insurrections at the beginning of the XIX century and was the centre of the court of prince Miloš for some time. During that century, Požarevac became commercially important primarily because of the export of cattle into Austria and was for some time the second largest town in Serbia. In recent times it was known as the hometown of Slobodan Milošević, whose power was unmatched here until his fall in the year 2000.

In the center of town, there is a nice park in front of **County Seat building** (*Okružno načelstvo*). It was constructed in 1888 and was at the time one of the largest buildings in

Serbia. It still looks impressive with its long, academically shaped façade. In the middle of the park is the **monument to Prince Miloš**, probably the most important man for the development of the town. The bronze statue is the work of the sculptor Djordje Jovanović from 1898.

The Local **museum** (*Narodni muzej, 10 Dr Voje Dulića St, tel. 012/223597, open Tue-Sun 10 a.m. – 5 p.m.*), apart from being one of the oldest in Serbia (founded in 1895), has become known for the collection of antique Roman findings from the nearby locality in Kostolac, where the mighty Viminacium was based in the Roman times.

The **museum of the painter Milena Pavlović-Barili** is next to it. Pavlović-Barili (1909-1945) was a outstanding surrealist, who both as a painter and a poet, and a renowned fashion magazine designer, was influenced by the early renaissance masters who worked in Rome, Paris and New York.

The **old church** was constructed in 1818 by

Ljubičevo equesterian events

the orders of prince Miloš and is one of the oldest examples of constructions from the 19th century Serbia with a tower above the entrance.

On the nearby **hill Tulba** is a small open-air ethno park with eight constructions done in traditional architecture.

ENVIRONS:

Just by the road leading to Belgrade is the **horse farm Ljubičevo**. Founded in 1858 by Miloš, it was developed by his son prince Mihailo who was born here in Požarevac. Mihailo was interested in promoting horsemanship in Serbia in order to gain good cavalry for the planned war against Turkey. Therefore, he made Ljubičevo (named after his mother Ljubica), a state farm where most of the horses needed for the army and other state services were bred, but also a place where prestigious breeds and racehorses first appeared in Serbia. Every first weekend in September, Požarevac focuses its attention to the Ljubičevo horse games with defiles, various races and

Monument dedicated to Prince Miloš

*Antique fresco from **Viminacium**, at the Požarevac National Museum*

competitions in riding skills and use of antique weapons on horseback.

13 km to the north of Požarevac lies the mine town of **Kostolac**, nowadays best known for its huge power plant. In its shade lay the grounds where in Roman times stood the town of Viminacium. This city appeared in the 1st century AD around the camp of VII Claudiae legion, brought here to secure the lands of the Dacians conquered north from Danube. Viminacium was the center of Moesia Superior province. It had the right to run its own mint and later became the seat of a bishop. It was destroyed by the Huns in 441. Today it is a valuable archeological site, one of only two seats of the Ro-

man legion in the whole of Europe that lies out of urban agglomeration. Unfortunately, its biggest part lies in the grounds of the power plant and is thus restricted for most visitors. A more tolerant visiting policy will be introduced in the spring of 2006.

❷ Ram

21 km - Veliko Gradište

Ram castle is 24 km east from Kostolac, on a stumpy hill above the river Danube. It was an important strategic point in the 12th century when it was mentioned in the clashes between Hungary and Byzantium. The present-day fortification was constructed during the reign of the Turkish sultan Bayezid II (1480-

1512) in a technique that that made the fort more able to resist firearm attacks. It has a central keep and four towers at the corners of the battlements. In front of the castle there are the ruins of a Turkish **caravanserai**.

A little further to the east, one can find archeological remains of the Roman *castrum Lederata*. It is possible to cross the Danube here by ferry to Stara Palanka.

❸ Veliko Gradište

📷 11.500

ℹ️ M. Miloradovića 1
12220 V. Gradište
012/63-161

34 km - Požarevac

Veliko Gradište is a drowsy small town on the Danube, 32km east from Požarevac. It was founded in the Middle Ages on the place of the Roman settlement *Pincum*, by the river of the same name (today the Pek River), widely known for the gold that can be found in it. Veliko Gradište prospered the most in the 19th c, when it was an important point where cattle was brought from inland to

Ram Castle at sunset

be transported and sold across the river. From that period originates the **church of St Archangels** (1856) in the main square. Right after being built, it was fresco-painted by Jovan Isailović and Dimitrije Posinković, whereas the iconostas was painted in 1902. Next to it is the building of the **High School** from 1879. On the other side of the church, closer to the river, is the **City**

Gold washing in Pek river

council building. In the park by the Danube, there are **monuments** to the soldiers killed in both the First and the Second World War.

ENVIRONS:

Some 2km west from the town is the **Srebrno jezero** ("The Silver Lake") named after the bright glimpse of its surface on sunny days. It was made in 1971 when the mainland was connected with the Danube island in order to save village Ostrovica on it. Its 13 km long coast is today lined with weekend houses, cafés, pensions and a hotel. In summer months, it attracts most of the population from Veliko Gradište.

④ Golubac

🏛 3.200

ℹ️ Gorana Tošića-Mačka 1
12000 Golubac
012/ 78-145

🚌 012/211-844

55 km - Požarevac

4 km to the east of town Golubac lays the fortress of the same name. It is situated on the very entrance to the Iron Gate gorge (Serb. *Djerdap*). It was built at the beginning of the 14th c. and with its powerful ramparts it soon became the most significant fort on the Danube. Hungarians use to call it *Galambocz* and Germans *Taubenburg*. The Turks conquered it for the first time after the Kosovo battle in 1389. From 1402 to 1427 it was in Serbian hands. After the death of despot Stefan, the master of the city decided not to turn it over to the Hungarians, but to the Turks who stayed here until 1444. In 1458, it was permanently reverted to the Turkish jurisdiction. Although it was used for military purposes until the mid 19th century, with the development of the firearms it lost much

of its defensive characteristics.

The fort has an irregular base formed around the slope of the hill. Its nine towers are arranged one above the other, making it one of the most picturesque sites on the Danube. Solid towers of different shapes and sizes are further reinforced by retaining walls. The only gate was the one on the west side but today the road also goes through the other side of the fort. By the wall closest to the river can be seen the remains of the palace. The lower, polygonal tower stretching into the river was built by the Turks to strengthen the fortress against firearms.

Small town Golubac lies on the place of the earlier Roman settlement *Cuppae*. It flourished together with the trade on the Danube in the 19th century, but afterwards it ceased to grow. After the construction of the Djerdap dam, and the rise of the water level, the Danube flooded the river islands in front of the town and the river is now some 7 km wide at this spot. The width of the Danube, combined with plenty of winds, make it one of the best places for gliding. The

Golubac castle where the Danube is at its widest

"Golubački grad" hotel is on its shore.

Golubac is also associated with the story of the alleged Golubac Dragon, a three-headed water monster that is believed to have lived in the deep waters of the Danube. The story has it that after the dragon was slain its offspring shed tears from which flies were born. Unlike the dragon, the flies are very much real: *Simulium colombaschense* or the Golubac fly (*Golubačka mušica*) is a small insect that attacks cattle and whose larvae develop in rapid streams around Golubac.

⑤ National Park "Djerdap"

ℹ️ Kralja Petra I br.14a
19220 Donji Milanovac
030/ 86-788

The Djerdap National Park stretches along the right bank of the Danube River from Golubac fortress to the "Djerdap One" dam, covering the most spectacular tract of this mighty river – the Iron Gates (Serb. *Djerdap*). Some 100 kilometers long (from Golubac to Tekija), the gorge is practically a river valley made up of four ravines, Gornja klisura, Gospodjin vir, Veliki Kazan, Mali Kazan and Sipska klisura. They are separated from each other by broader sections of the river. One of the greatest river depths in the world (82 m) has been measured in Gospodjin vir. The cliffs of the canyon in Veliki Kazan are about 300 meters high, while the riverbed in this part is narrowed down to 150 meters.

However, the Iron Gates are only half of what they used to be. With the completion of the dam in 1972, the level of the water rose some 35 m, creating the biggest water accumulation in Serbia. The dangerous cliffs that made the gorge famous, but hardly passable, disappeared together with towns, allowing ships of up to 5000 tonnes to navigate upstream.

All of the natural and historical aspects unique for this area classify it as one of Europe's most interesting tourist destinations. Some 11,000 plant species and many diverse animal and fungi species make the best recommendation for the nature-lovers.

Donji Milanovac had quite a turbulent topographical past. It was once a small town located on an island in the middle of the Danube and was called Poreč. Harassed by frequent floods and without any Turks in the vicinity to worry about, its residents moved to new location on the Serbian shore in 1832 and the settlement changed the name to Donji Milanovac, in memory of the oldest son of prince Miloš who helped make

One of many lynxes in Iron Gates gorge

the new settlement. The town lived off the river trade, production of small boats and skilled captains, the only men who knew how to navigate through the dangerous gorge safely. In 1970, it had to be moved once again, this time because of the rise in water level. It was moved to a ridge above the Danube. The old town was left underneath water, except for a few monuments such as the old **house of Miša Anastasijević** (1803-1885) nicknamed Captain Miša, who was a salt merchant and the richest Serb of his day and his endowment, the old church.

Tabula Traiana ("Trajan's Plaque"), or

Veliki Kazan ravine

Old houses near Lepenski Vir

in Serbian *Trajanova tabla*, was put up to commemorate the end of the construction works on the road built in 103 AD during the reign of the Roman emperor Trajan, that went through the wilderness of the gorge. Two years later, the emperor led his armies past this road to the bridge bearing his name and conquered Dacia, the present day Romania. The ancient road and the original place of the plaque had been covered with water, but this monument was put above the level of the Danube. For this reason it cannot be seen from the coast. It is roughly 3.5 by 1.5 meters large and decorated with geniuses, dolphins and an eagle above it.

"Djerdap One" dam was a joint construction work of Yugoslavia and Romania in 1964-72 . It is 1278 m long and 34 m high and produces electricity for a considerable part of Serbia. There is a border crossing on it.

6 Lepenski Vir

i 063/206-271
19 km - Donji Milanovac

Lepenski Vir is a Mesolithic site some 19 km west from the city of Donji Milanovac. During the archeological explorations (1965-1970),

initiated before the rise of the Danube level (caused by the construction of the two large dams), the late Professor Srejović found traces of Mesolithic culture on a low-lying Danube terrace at the location of Lepenski Vir. Further excavations brought to light some dozen settlements of the same culture. From 8000 to 4500 year BC, a very complex and unique Stone Age culture flourished at Lepenski Vir, probably the most advanced in prehistoric Europe. People of this settlement built unusual, trapezoid huts with rectangular fireplaces. Figurines found behind these fireplaces show that members of the community had small sanctuaries in their homes. Lepenski Vir is best known for its stone figures of people, with large eyes and fish-like mouths, probably idols of hunters and fishermen who depended on the river Danube. Apart form the figures, archeologists discovered graves, fine examples of jewelry and tools made of bone and stone as well as tablets with letter-like symbols carved in. Somewhere around 5200 BC, the settlers of Lepenski Vir started to breed domestic animals. With the beginning of the Late Neolithic

period, the old way of life was abandoned, as was the settlement of Lepenski Vir.

The original excavation site is now under water, but the settlement has been transferred on a higher level and protected by a large cover. The **museum** (*tel. 063/206-271, open Tue-Sat 10 a.m. to 5 p.m., Sundays to 2. p.m.*) keeps the copies of the most valuable artifacts (the originals are in the Belgrade National Museum).

On the very entrance to the locality, you can see a group of old houses, nice examples of traditional architecture preserved from the flooded villages.

7 Kladovo

🏛 18.300

i Dunavska 16a
19320 Kladovo
019/801-690

🚌 019/211-844
57 km - Negotin

Kladovo is a small town opposite to the Romanian port of Drobeta Turnu Severin. In Kladovo there is the **Djerdap Archeology Museum** (*nn Kralja Aleksandra St, tel. 019/81130, open 10 a.m.-10 p.m. in summer and 10 a.m.-8 p.m. in wintertime*) where the artifacts from the archeological excavations in Iron Gates gorge are kept.

"Praroditeljka" sculpture from Lepenski Vir (National Museum, Belgrad

The fort known by the name **Fetislam** lays on the western outskirts of Kladovo. Inner walls of the fortress were erected following the shape of the Roman quadrangular castrum that used to be here. It was extensively rebuilt in the Middle Ages and again in the 18th century by the Turks who called it *Fet-Islam* or "the Rampart of the Faith". The three outer gates have inscriptions in Arabic from the renovation in 1739. the Turks did not leave the fort until 1867. Today it stands in a pitiful state.

ENVIRONS:
Several kilometers further to the west, just by the "Djerdap One" water power plant is the **Karataš excavation site**. The remains

Fetislam fortress, Kladovo

of the *Diana* fort were found here, a part of the Roman lines of defense on the Danube. Built at the beginning of the 2nd century AD, it was renovated in the 6th c. by Emperor Justinian; most of the ruins are from this period. A stone plaque commemorating the deeds of Emperor Trajan was found here, to mark the end of the construction of the channel that passed here parallel to the Danube and made the traffic much easier.

Just east of Kladovo there is the village of Kostol. When you pass this vilage, there is an unmarked dirt road leading to the Danube and the two preserved columns of the famous **Trajan's bridge**. This site is unfortunately also neglected.

Ceremošnja

> **i** Svetog Save 114
> Kučevo
> **☎** 012/850-666
>
> 13km - Kučevo

The cave is situated near Kučevo, in the heart of Homoljske Mountains. It can be reached via villages Kučajna and Bukovska. In front of the cave there is a small motel. A stream (Strugarski potok) flows through Ceremošnja cave. The length of the cave is 775.5 meters, of which 431 meters are accessible to visitors. Following the underground stream you will reach the cave's biggest hall, the so-called Arena, one of the most beautiful in Serbia. The highest ceiling point of its dome reaches 20 meters and is lined with white crystal calcite and adorned by many stalactites, transparent curtains and folds. From Arena, there is an access into another cavern nicknamed Dveri ("Gates")

Boy in Vlah costume

and through them, passing by the small waterfall of Strugarski potok, there is a path towards the exit, which is situated 100 meters away from the entrance. *Visiting hours: 9.00 a.m. to 6.00 p.m. from April 1 to October 31 and by prior appointment in winter. Guide service is available at any time during working hours.*

Rajkova pećina

> **i** TO Majdanpek
> 030/ 86-184
> **☎** 2 km - Majdanpek

The cave is located 2 km from Majdanpek, at a place where Rajkova reka ("Rajko's river") springs from the cave to join Paskova reka making thus the river by the name Mali Pek. Rajkova reka runs throughout the whole cave. The total length of the cave is 2.304 meters, which makes it the longest in Serbia, but the part open for tourists covers only a quarter of it, some 1.410 meters. It consists of two separate caverns, an underground river channel and a spring cave, both on two levels. Air temperature is constant, 8°C, and relative humidity is close to 100%. Cave ornaments in Rajkova Cave are of the highest quality. The most attractive are: "The Egyptian Goddess", "The Snail", "Stump with Mushrooms", "Sleeping Bear" etc.

The guide service offers tours that last approximately 60 minutes.

⑩ Gornjak

18 km - Petrovac

26 km - Žagubica

This monastery is situated not far from Petrovac in an interesting gorge of Mlava River called Ždrelo (literally "Pharynx"). All through the gorge there is evidence of past times: a solid fortress was here once blocking the road between the two hills with its wall. Later the gorge became known for its hermits whose cells within the caves, as well as the remains of medieval churches can be seen in several places, among which the best known locality is called Mitropolija.

Gornjak is situated in interesting scenery, leaning on a vertical rock with its north side. It is an endowment of prince Lazar, built between

Gornjak monastery

1378 and 1381 with the spiritual help of monk Grigorije from Sinai Peninsula. Once a rich monastery endowed with 240 villages, it sank to obscurity in the Turkish times. In the 18th c, it lay in the ruins; immediately after the reconstruction it was burnt down again in 1788. In the First World War, it was totally pillaged by the occupying Bulgarians and, in the Second, it was set ablaze by the Germans who sent the abbot to the concentration camp never to return. Since 1968 it has been a nunnery.

Although it was built on the medieval trefoil groundplan, the present day church construction dates back mostly from the 18th c., while the belfry and the porch are from the 19th century The fresco-paintings are from 1847 and are of considerable quality. In the small cave chapel above the church, the relics of the monastery's

co-founder St Grigorije are kept. The visitors can also see here fragments of the 14th c. frescoes.

⑪ Zlotske pećine

20 km - Bor

On the eastern side of the Kučaj Mountain, near Zlot village, there is a number of speleological sites. The most significant caves are: Stojko's ice cave, Vernjikica, Manda's cave, Vodena ("Water cave"), Hajdučica and Lazar's cave.

Lazareva pećina cave is located some 3 km from Zlot, and consists of two groups of cave canals: dry (fossilized), and wet (active). The first group of canals is abundant with cave ornaments, especially in the largest hall, and open to visitors, whereas wet canals are periodically filled with water.

Canyon of the Lazareva reka River, 4.5 km long and more than 500m deep, is one of the most spectacular canyons in Serbia and definitely not very well known. Lazareva

Medieval hermitages in Mlava gorge

New Church, Negotin

reka River, which runs through it, is almost throughout the year a small stream which dries out in summers allowing adventurers to explore the canyon by walking through the riverbed. In some segments this impassable canyon is only a few meters wide.

1.5km-long hiking trail leads from Lazar's Cave to the entrance of **Vernjikica Cave**. This dry and extraordinarily long cave has a downing cascade canal that opens towards a couple of other halls. The biggest of them is called Colosseum and is circular in shape with some 60m in diameter. The most beautiful is the Fairy-city (*Vilingrad*) hall, named after its ornaments.

 ⑫ Negotin

📷 28.700

ℹ️ Dom Kulture
19300 Negotin
019/542-255

43 km - Zaječar

Located close to the Romanian and Bulgarian border, Negotin is the centre of the lower Timok valley. It originated in the 17th century, and thanks to the fort that was used by the Austrians and the Turks, gained predominance over neighboring villages. In the 18th century it was the seat of Karapandža dukes, who governed the region ever since known as Negotinska Krajna (Negotin March), which was a semi-autonomous province of the Ottoman Empire. The town is best known for Hajduk Veljko Petrović, the hero of the First Serbian Insurrection, who fought heavy battles over it and finally met his end here in 1813.

The center of the town is recognizable for the **new church**. It was completed in 1876 in a mixture of several European styles. A nice iconostasis was done by a distinguished painter Steva Todorović and his wife Poleksija in 1901. The church is famous for its acoustics. There is a small stone **gunpowder depot** next to it, the only remains of the old rectangular fort that once occupied the whole of the main square in front of the church. In the midst of the square, stands the new **equestrian monument to Hajduk Veljko**, who resided here. There is an older one at the city outskirts marking the place of his death. In the park by the square, there is also the **monument to the soldiers of the 1912-18 wars**. The medallions depict King Petar and French general Gambetta, who liberated the town.

A small **museum** dedicated to the adventurous life of Hajduk Veljko is also close by (*17 Stanka Paunovića St*). It is located in a fine house from the middle of the 19th century, distinguished by its arcades and high gables.

The Museum of Krajina (*Muzej Krajiine, 1 Vere Radosavljević St, tel: 019/ 512-072, open Tue-Fri 8 a.m.-6 p.m, Sat 9 a.m.-5 p.m, Sun and holidays 9 a.m.-2 p.m.*) has a valuable permanent exhibition showing the development of the region from the oldest times to the present day.

The **old church** nearby was built in 1803 and, like other churches from the time of the Turkish rule, is a modest edifice. Here is the grave of Hajduk Veljko, not disovered until 1844, for he was secretly buried before the advancing Turks.

The **Mokranjac house** (*Mokranjčeva kuća, 8 Vojvode Mišića St, tel. 019/ 542-266*), named after the famous composer Stevan Stojanović Mokranjac, who was born in the vicinity of Negotin, has its interior furnished with the 19th century items reflecting the living conditions of the time.

Hajduk Veljko Museum in a fine 19th c. house

The "doors" of the Vratna canyon

ENVIRONS:

A pleasant excursion place on a walking distance south-west from the town (3 km) is **Bukovo monastery**, renovated in the 19th century but with some of the remains from the 17th century fresco paintings.

Negotin's environs are best known for their numerous vineyards and exquisite wines that were even exported to France in the late 19th century. Almost all of the villages have their wine cellars, called *pimnice*, grouped in separate formations of picturesque stone hamlets. These are not used just for storing the wine, but also have rooms for accommodating the whole family during the time of the picking, which could sometimes take weeks. In the late summer days, pimnice are livelier than their villages, but otherwise look mostly deserted. The best-preserved ones are those in Rajac (25 km south from Negotin), Štubik (20 km to the west) and Rogljevo (20 km to the south).

5 km to the north of Negotin, on the exit from the village of Miloševo, is the **Korogłaš monastery**. By its architecture, the small church is dated back as belonging to the 11th century. Allegedly, Korogłaš is known as the burial place of King Marko Kraljević, the most famous hero of Serbian epics. This presumption is not without basis: Marko died (or was deadly wounded) in the battle of Rovine at the other side of the Danube. He fought there as a Turkish vassal, but is recorded to have said: "I pray for the victory of the Christians even if that means that I die first".

25 km northwest from Negotin starts the **canyon of the river Vratna**. Take Zaječar road, then Majdanpek road and from the village of Štubik head for Jabukovac. After you have passed this village take a turn to the left. Passing the village Vratna and the small monastery of the same name one reaches the canyon and its two remarkable gates (*vrata*) carved by the erosion in limestone.

⑬ Zaječar

🏛 66.200

ℹ Trg Oslobodjenja bb
19000 Zaječar
019/421-521

🚌 019/421-545

🚆 019/421-360

233 km - Beograd

The centre of Timok valley and its biggest town, Zaječar is a rather young city. The small settlement became somewhat important only during the First Serbian Insurrection. It was annexed to princedom of Serbia definitely in 1833 and thanks to the diligence of its population and the abundance in fruit and grapevine it was soon regarded as the second wealthiest town after Belgrade. In 1876 this welfare came to an end as the region was raided by the Turks and plundered by their barbarous Cherkessk troops. It is the birthplace of two influential political leaders of the Radical Party, the first massive political organization in Serbia – Nikola Pašić and Ljuba Didić. When in 1883 the political enterprises of king Milan and his conservatives reached their peak and the government ordered the firearms to be taken from the villagers, the opposition, the Radical Party, used the dissatisfaction of the people and called them to rebel against the tyranny, thus

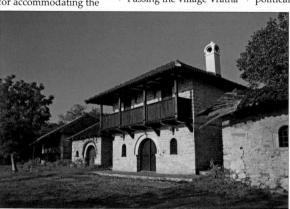

The **pimnice** *of Rajac village*

provoking a turbulent Timok Mutiny.

Trg Nikole Pašića is the central city square. The **National Museum** (*Moše Pijade 2, tel. 422-930, open 7 a.m.-6 p.m. Tue-Fri, 7 a.m.-3 p.m. Sat and Mon*) is on its north side. It owes its prominence to the nice selection of Roman artifacts brought from Gamzigrad locality, including the head of Emperor Galerius and the best of the mosaics found there. Apart from the archeological, there is also an ethnographic collection in the Museum.

Two older monuments are worth seeing.

Radul-begov konak is a typical Balkans style house from the early 19th c that belonged to a well-off family. There is a souvenir shop on the ground floor, while the upper floor is used for a permanent exhibition named "Old Zaječar" displaying furniture and furnishings (*open Mon-Fri 7 a.m.-3 p.m., closed at weekends*). The **Turkish Watermill** (*Turska vodenica*) from the same period is turned into a national cuisine restaurant.

The visitors should also see two significant edifices in the town centre both built in a fine eclectic style: the **High School** from 1882 and **Načelstvo**

Head of Emperor Galerius, Zaječar National Museum

(Municipal Authorities Building) from 1911. The **monument to the soldiers fallen in the wars of 1912-18** on the same square is a work of famous sculptor Anton Augustinčić.

Kraljevica hill is a nice excursion location covered with dense woods wherefrom a nice view spreads over the town below. The monument in commemoration of the Timok Mutiny

is on the hill. Strangely enough, it was put up during the communist era, in 1971, same time as the adjacent unusually shaped monument to the victims of the fascist terror, called "The Gallows" was erected.

⑭ Gamzigrad

11 km - Zaječar

11 km east from Zaječar, by the village of the same name, lies one of the most important late Roman sites in Europe. The first explorers believed the ancient ruins had been a Roman military camp, because of their size and numerous towers. However, the systematic archeological excavations done since 1953 revealed that it had in fact been an imperial palace. It was a project of one of the tetrarchs, Galerius (caesar from 293 and augustus from 305 till 311), the adopted son and son-in-law of the great Diocletianus. Galerius started the construction here in 289 after his victory over the Persians that brought him great admiration

*Ruins of **Romuliana Felix** palace, Gamzigrad*

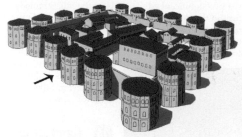

Reconstruction of the palace in **Romuliana Felix**

and glory to mark the place of his birth. It was therefore given the name *Felix Romuliana* in memory of his Queen mother Romula, a priestess of a pagan cult. This complex of temples and palaces was a place of worshiping of his mother's divine personalitiy, the monument to his deeds as an emperor, as well as an luxurious villa in which Galerius would have withdrawn after his abdication. Romuliana served its purpose until it was plundered by the Huns in the mid 5th century. Later it was turned

irregular quadrangle are guarded by 20 towers and two gates. The remaining walls and columns, as well as some marvelous mosaics, can be seen inside. Three of the mosaics depict pagan deities Dionysus, Hercules and Esculapos, which like Galerius, were born by a mortal mother. The remains of two temples can also be seen, one of which is dedicated to Jupiter, Galerius' protector. Most of the movable objects have been transferred to the museum in nearby Zaječar. 1000 meters east

 15 Sokobanja

📖 14.600

ℹ Trg Oslobodjenja 1
18230 Sokobanja
018/830-271

37 km - Knjaževac

31 km - Aleksinac

Sokobanja ("Hawk Spa") lays on the riverbanks of the Moravica between mountains Ozren and Rtanj, at the height of about 400 m above the sea level. Thanks to its thermomineral springs, air rich in oxigen from the surrounding woods and moderate continentral climate, it is one of the most frequently visited health resorts today.

Already known to the Romans, it seems that this spa first prospered in the Turkish times. Evliya Celebi, the famous Turkish traveler from the 17th century describes its hammam as a nicely kept and extremely well visited by people coming from as far as Asia to enjoy its hot baths. Prince Miloš knew this place well and after the wars with the Turks, he ordered for the Turkish bath to be renovated, and a small hospital built. Soon after, he built a summer house there. The organized tourism began in 1837 when prince Miloš sent one of his men to the spa doctor. In 19th century the spa also became a sort of cultural centre as a favorite summer holiday location of Serbian intellectuals.

The center of the Spa is located around the oldest construc-

Mosaic of Dionis and his modern day followers

into an unpretentious settlement of farmers and craftsmen, finally to be abandoned at the beginning of the 7th century with the arrival of the Slavs. The derelict complex was named Gamzigrad or "Slithertown" by the newcomers, for many snakes inhabited the ruins. The walls in a shape of

from the main gate, on a hill called Magura, stand the remains of two mausoleums where Romula and Galerius were buried.

In the village of Gamzigrad there is a spa, **Gamzigradska banja**, with springs of hot water in and around the river Crni Timok.

Old Turkish Baths at the Sokobanja Spa

tions there: the beautiful stone **Turkish hammam** that is still in use and prince **Miloš's residence** (*Milošev konak*). Also of interest are the small church from 1884 surrounded by old villas and the **local museum** (*Zavičajni muzej*) situated in an old edifice typical for the area.

The town was named after the **Soko-grad Castle** based some 2 kilometers upstream the river Moravica. It was built on Roman foundations on a high rock in late Middle Ages. It consists of two parts: the lower fort which is wider and with the water tank, and upper, smaller one, used for habitation and protected with seven towers.

Although the whole Spa looks like a big park the most beautiful part is the forest called "Čuka Dva". For people who prefer taking walks, famous excursion spots are Lepterija with its cold springs, and Kalinovica.

On the slopes of Ozren Mountain there are two sanatoriums and in their vicinity **Ripaljka waterfall** on Gradišnica stream, the tallest waterfall in Serbia.

The artificial **Bovan Lake**, one of the richest in fish in Serbia, is also near by.

Of special interest is the famous **Rtanj Mountain** that closes the Moravica valley from the north side. Its highest peak Šiljak (1560 m) is easily visible from a distance because of its volcano shape. The mountain offers a magnificent view of a large part of Serbia. It is best known for the variety of rare and medical herbs that grow on its slopes, which can be prepared into delicious "Rtanj Tea".

Soko-grad Castle above the Sokobanja Spa

16 Knjaževac

🏛 21.200

ℹ Miloša Obilića 1
19350 Knjaževac
019/731-623

📞 019/731-437

📠 019/732-914

40km - Zaječar

This town lies close to the place where the rivers Svrljiški Timok and Trgoviški Timok join together forming the Beli Timok River. This was also why the Roman settlement *Timacum Maius* was built here.

Colourful houses by the Svrljiški Timok River, Knjaževac

Villa "Džervin" on the outskirts of Knjaževac

The town of Gurgusovac was first mentioned in the 17th c. In liberated Serbia of the 19th century it was notorious for its tower used by prince Aleksandar Karadjordjević to confine political prisoners.

When prince (*knjaz*) Miloš regained control in 1859, he ordered the tower to be burned. The grateful citizens of Gurgusovac celebrated this occasion by renaming the town to Knjaževac. The centre of the town is on both banks of the Svrljiški Timok. Ace Stanojevića St runs by the river bank between two

bridges and is packed with smaller buildings of all shapes and colours. Parallel with this one is Njegoševa St and at number 6 is the **Town Museum** (*tel: 019/732-228*). It is located in the house of Aca Stanojević, a popular leader and instigator of Timok Mutiny in 1883. The interior of the Museum is in the style of a Serbian home from the turn of the 20th century.

The **Local Museum** is on the other side of the river (*Zavičajni muzej, 15 Karadjordjeva St, tel: 019/731-407*), located in the house of the wealthy Sibinović family from 1906. The museum collection offers insight into the history of the area.

ENVIRONS:

15 km to the south is the village of **Donja Kamenica**. A church was built there in the early 14th century by a Bulgarian nobleman Mihailo. The unusual features of the church are spires over two towers facing the west, that block the view of the cupola.

The frescoes come from the same period and are very valuable. Especially nice are the portraits of the patron and his family, as well as a curious painting of holy warriors Theodore Tyron and Theodore Stratilatos embraced and on horsebacks.

Some 2 km further down the road is **Gornja Kamenica** and in it the

An unusual church in the village of Donja Kamenica

endowment monastery of despotes Lazar, ruler of Serbia from 1456 to 1458. This simple edifice has no wall paintings preserved.

In **Ravna**, a village 8 km north from Knjaževac, there is an archaeological locality of Roman *Timacum Minus*, with an open-air exhibition of the monuments. Some of the preserved peasant households are transformed into an ethno exhibition. Amongst other things, there is a small **Vine Museum** and a large and interesting collection of colourful double-thread woollen socks.

⑰ Stara Planina

The borderline between Serbia and Bulgaria corresponds to the natural border of the Stara Mountain (the Old Mountain), which spreads in a slight curve over more than one hundred kilometers, from Zaječar to Pirot, and continues further into Bulgaria.

The other name for this gigantic geological formation is the Balkans Mountain and the whole peninsula was named after it. This mountain is well known for its beautiful scenery and wonderfully preserved flora and fauna, only slightly influenced by people. The Serbian side of the mountain is in a typical sub-alpine climate, with plenty of snow in winter and many sunny days in summer.

Since its ridge serves as a natural shield against north winds, there are numerous pastures on its slopes, dry and alpine grasslands, as well as deciduous and coniferous forests. Apart from the conservation area, the rest of the mountain is open for the licenced hunters. In the "Stara planina II" hunting ground at the southern side of the mountain, you can find deer, boars, wolves, wild pigeons, etc.

Children in traditional dress from the Timok region

You can get all information about the mountain and the conservation area in the mountaineering centre under the picturesque peak called Babin zub ("Grandma's Tooth", 1780 m asl), some 50 km from Knjazevac. The easiest way to get there is through villages Kalna, Balta Berilovac and Crni vrh. Local bus service operates on this route to Crni vrh. In the same village there is a Mountain Hut "Golema reka". Under the Babin zub Peak, there is a mountain hut and a hotel of the same name.

There is also a baby ski path in the vicinity and this is also the best starting point to the highest peak Midžor of 2169m asl, then to Stojkov kamen and the attractive Dojkino vrelo spring.

The Babin zub peak on Stara planina

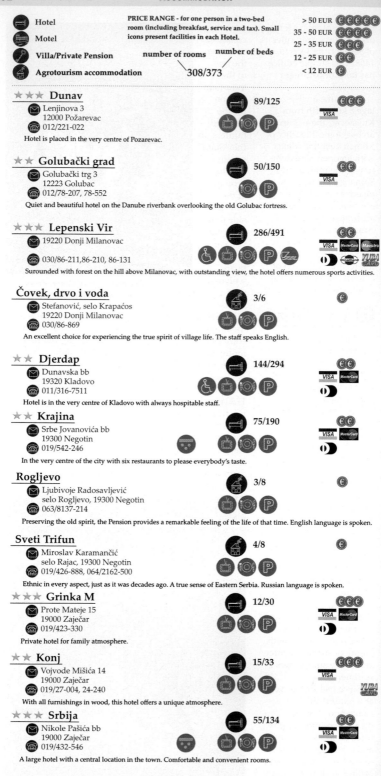

Hotel

Motel

Villa/Private Pension

Agrotourism accommodation

PRICE RANGE - for one person in a two-bed room (including breakfast, service and tax). Small icons present facilities in each Hotel.

number of rooms   number of beds

308/373

> 50 EUR €€€€€
35 - 50 EUR €€€€
25 - 35 EUR €€€
12 - 25 EUR €€
< 12 EUR €

★★★ Dunav

Lenjinova 3
12000 Požarevac
012/221-022

89/125

€€€

Hotel is placed in the very centre of Pozarevac.

★★ Golubački grad

Golubački trg 3
12223 Golubac
012/78-207, 78-552

50/150

€€

Quiet and beautiful hotel on the Danube riverbank overlooking the old Golubac fortress.

★★★ Lepenski Vir

19220 Donji Milanovac

030/86-211, 86-210, 86-131

286/491

€€

Surounded with forest on the hill above Milanovac, with outstanding view, the hotel offers numerous sports activities.

Čovek, drvo i voda

Stefanović, selo Krapaćos
19220 Donji Milanovac
030/86-869

3/6

€

An excellent choice for experiencing the true spirit of village life. The staff speaks English.

★★ Djerdap

Dunavska bb
19320 Kladovo
011/316-7511

144/294

€€

Hotel is in the very centre of Kladovo with always hospitable staff.

★★ Krajina

Srbe Jovanovića bb
19300 Negotin
019/542-246

75/190

€€

In the very centre of the city with six restaurants to please everybody's taste.

Rogljevo

Ljubivoje Radosavljević
selo Rogljevo, 19300 Negotin
063/8137-214

3/8

€

Preserving the old spirit, the Pension provides a remarkable feeling of the life of that time. English language is spoken.

Sveti Trifun

Miroslav Karamančić
selo Rajac, 19300 Negotin
019/426-888, 064/2162-500

4/8

€

Ethnic in every aspect, just as it was decades ago. A true sense of Eastern Serbia. Russian language is spoken.

★★★ Grinka M

Prote Mateje 15
19000 Zaječar
019/423-330

12/30

€€€

Private hotel for family atmosphere.

★★ Konj

Vojvode Mišića 14
19000 Zaječar
019/27-004, 24-240

15/33

€€€

With all furnishings in wood, this hotel offers a unique atmosphere.

★★★ Srbija

Nikole Pašića bb
19000 Zaječar
019/432-546

55/134

€€

A large hotel with a central location in the town. Comfortable and convenient rooms.

Zeleni zec

✉ Lidija Jovanović
19000 Zaječar
☎ 019/62-349

🛏 4/8   €

Very fine accommodation, a mixture of traditional and modern style. English, German and Russian are spoken.

★★ Jezero

✉ 19210 Borsko jezero

☎ 030/34-730, 36-778

🛏 85/250   €€

In beautiful surroundings on the Bor lakeshore guests of the hotel may enjoy in cross-country run or numerous sport courts.

★★ Srpska kruna

✉ Brestovačka Banja bb
19216 Bor
☎ 030/33-129, 441-380

🛏 24/45   €€

Just next to Miloš' Konaci in natural surroundings, hotel offers villas for accommodation and numerous healthful water swimming pools.

★★★ Rtanj

✉ Mirovo bb

☎ 030/63-088

🛏 16/32   €€

Beautifu hotel on the round just below the Rtanj mountain known for its always fresh gibanica and milk, with rooms and bungalows at disposal.

★★★ Turist

✉ Svetog Save 20
18230 Sokobanja
☎ 018/830-510

🛏 43/113   €€

Near the walking area of Sokobanja, hotel is in the very centre of the city.

★★★ Sunce

✉ Radnička 3
18230 Sokobanja
☎ 018/830-122

🛏 104/220   €€

Hotel is on the Moravica riverbank in beautiful environment.

Table set for dinner in "Markov muzej", Rogljevo village

Hotel EPS - Babin Zub, Stara Planina

★ ★ ★ Moravica
- Timočke bune 4
- 18230 Sokobanja
- 018/830-622

101/220

At very good location hotel is well equipped for congress tourism.

Banjica
- Milutina Pejovića 40
- 18230 Sokobanja
- 018/830-204, 830-224

108/270

Hotel is situated near to Moravica river with beautiful surroundings.

★ ★ ★ Zdravljak
- Miladina Živkovića bb
- 18230 Sokobanja
- 018/830-722, 830-742

270/550

Conveniently situated close to the bus station and standing on the Moravica River.

★ ★ ★ Jošanica
- Danijel Lazić
- selo Jošanica, 18230 Sokobanja
- 018/836-006

3/4

Just right for true experience of countryside life.

Vila Katarina
- Karadjordjeva
- 19230 Knjaževac
- 019/733-379

7/15

2 km from Knjaževac on the road towards Sokobanja. Exceptionaly well equiped, with a largw garden and a childrens corner.

★ ★ ★ EPS
- Babin Zub
- 19230 Knjaževac
- 019/731-780, 731-622

22/60

Hotel is on the Stara mountain slope, at 1780m above the sea level.

★ ★ ★ Gradište
- Brane Veljković
- selo Gradište, 19230 Knjaževac
- 019/738-042, 772-550

3/8

In a hidden place, near the river, ideal for those who seek privacy.

 Fish restaurant National restaurant  International restaurant

Tulba
 Hajduk Veljka bb
12000 Požarevac
012/224-560

 08-24

On the Tulba Hill, in a forest, built rustically,
with a pleasant atmosphere.

Srbija - Brka
Srebrno Jezero
12220 Veliko Gradište
012/62-025

 12-24

The restaurant is near to Danube river and a park,
opposite to the local Council building.

Tekijanka plus
Kralja Aleksandra 5
19320 Kladovo
019/800-400

 07-24

In the old city centre, has a restaurant, a confectionery, and a fast food
bar; placed in a modern, luscious building, 150 m from the river bank, with
two gardens and offering an intimate and ambient experience.

Gradska kafana
Kralja Aleksandra 30
19320 Kladovo
019/808-383

 07-24

Styled in the old fashion way, in Kladovo city centre, 500 m from
Danube.

Bela ladja
12km - Negotin
19300 Negotin
063/7500-110

 10-01

The only restaurant ship from the border to Smederevo
only 12 km from Negotin; excellent view at Danube river
banks and Romania; possible arrival by boat; marine.

Sidro
Karapandžina 1
19300 Negotin
064/1896-773

 08-23

Styled in the old fashion way, in a fishermen's manner;
situated in the city centre, 11 km from the Danube river.

Hajduk Veljkov konak
Lj. Nešića 37
19000 Zaječar
019/424-254

 11-23

An excellent Serbian national restaurant at the very heart of Zaječar, with
an interior that gets you back to the early 19th century Serbia.

Vodenica
Moše Pijade bb
19000 Zaječar
019/420-600

 12-22

The restaurant with a big open garden is situated in the street behind the
Belgrade City Museum in the surroundings of an old Ottoman mill.

Srpska kruna
19216 Brestovačka banja

030/441-380

 11-23

An excellent Serbian national restaurant, placed in a
quiet environment, in a spa from the Prince Milosh's time.
The restaurant has a terrace next to a thermal water spring.

Župan
Jabukar 1
18230 Sokobanja
018/830-325

 07-22

Right in the heart of Sokobanja, in the old Serbian style, various guests.

Splendid
Kralja Petra I 2
18230 Sokobanja
018/830-634

 08-22

In the very centre of the city, an old refurbished mansion,
with a garden and a terrace, and the intimate atmosphere

Čoka
18230 Sokobanja

018/830-905

 10-24

National cuisune as well as the specialities of the skilfull chefs are
prepared in front of the guests.

Konak park
18230 Sokobanja

018/830 710

 07-23

Founded in 1952, the restaurant is located in the pedestrian zone of the
spa across the "Park" baths, with which it formes a harmonious whole.

Isakov
Knjaza Miloša 170
19230 Knjaževac
019/732-540

 10-24

A building constructed in the classicist style, situated in the main street,
elegant, with a lovely garden, guests are predominantly businessmen and
young people; live music.

Milošev konak
Njegoševa 4
19230 Knjaževac
019/732-103

 07-23

In the city centre, under the ground, with arches,
in an archaic style, intimate atmosphere.

RAŠKA AND IBAR VALLEY

The remote southwest of Serbia has two different names used on everyday basis. The first is "Raška", the name of one of the principal rivers and of the most important Serbian medieval state. The other is "Sandžak", the Turkish word for a flag and for an administrative unit of the Ottoman Empire. These two names reflect the two characters of this region in which Orthodox and Muslim populations live alongside one another with their different traditions and customs.

This area was the heart of medieval Serbia. There are numerous beautiful examples of churches in existence from the period highlighting the importance of this mountainous region such as the old church of St

north and Raška or Ibar in the south gush their way down through the mountainous landscape cutting the steep sides of several canyons. The smaller Uvac River twists and turns creating a unique snake-like shape. Several of the larger cities in the area made good use of the wider fields and broader parts of the river valleys to be found here. The high plateau of Pešter dominates the central part. Deforested and barren, it is the perfect setting for cattle breeding which was the principle profession of this province for centuries. The sheep and cows from the district are celebrated for the delicious cheeses made from their milk, the best-known cheese being the Sjenički variety. The small town of Sjenica is also known

Cupolas of the Mileševa Monastery with the Mileševac castle in the background

Peter near Novi Pazar, or Mileševa and Sopoćani with their superb frescoes. On the other hand, this is where the Turks remained the longest, almost 500 years, and mosques are also to be found in abundance in both cities and far-flung villages. Novi Pazar, the former capital of the region and still the most important city here, bursts with oriental sights and smells.

Extreme geographic conditions unite the province and its people. Raška lies in the Dinaric Alps mountain range with several peaks rising above 1600 m. The rivers Lim in the

as the coldest spot in Serbia with an impressive record of extreme sub-zero temperatures. With its harsh climate during the long and snowy winters, many roads in the region can remain closed for weeks or even months. Yet the pleasant summer period more than makes up for the cold winters.

The rough geography and climate made people that more hospitable. In their naively modern or old wooden and stone houses one will be invited and treated to the best of all that the people here have to offer: juniper brandy *klekovača*, cheeses, thick cream kajmak or

Tičje Polje village time stands still

delicious hams and pies. For better or for worse, in many of the small hamlets high in the mountains, time appears to have stopped and in so doing many it left preserved many an old custom, ritual or song.

The River Ibar begins in Montenegro, passes through the south end of Raška and the north of Kosovo and then continues steadily northwards to Kraljevo. It has always been an important line of communication whilst also being a very beautiful one; these two reasons were ample for the Serbian kings to bestow it with many outstanding churches and monasteries, for which reason it is sometimes known as "the Valley Of the Kings". The mother of all these monasteries is the beautiful Studenica complex, the endowment of Stefan Nemanja, the founder of the Nemanjić dynasty. His son Stefan "the First-Crowned", built the Žiča monastery near Kraljevo, while queen Jelena from the Anjou family donated the Gradac monastery. The rapid waters of the Ibar River are popular for rafting which culminates at the "Veseli spust" ("Merrily Down the Ibar") event in July where hundreds of self-made rafts are sent on their merry journey accompanied by music and singing.

East of Ibar lays Kopaonik, Serbia's most well-known ski resort. This stunning mountain offers top ranking hotels and good pistes for skiers and boarders. However, Kopaonik is equally beautiful in the summertime when one can fully enjoy the flowery meadows traversed by fresh mountain streams that tumble down into dense woodland.

Čačak

Kraljevo

1

2

Žiča

Mlatarijška Banja

Bogutovačka Banja

3

Maglič

Vrnjačka Banja

Trstenik

Veluća

Kruševac

4

Studenica

Goč

Ušće

Jošanička Banja

Aleksandrovac

6

7

Koznik

8

Gradac

5

Brus

Prokuplje

Brvenik

9

National Park Kopaonik

Raška

12

Djurdjevi Stupovi

10 **11**

Lukovska Banja

14

opoćani

Novi Pazar

13

Ras

Novopazarska Banja

Ibar

Rzav

15

Crna Reka

Banjska

Gazivodsko jezero

Zvečan

Kosovska Mitrovica

Muslim village on the Pešter plateau

1 Kraljevo

2 Žiča

3 Maglič

4 Studenica

5 Kopaonik

6 Aleksandrovac

7 Koznik

8 Gradac

9 Stara and Nova Pavlica

10 Novi Pazar

11 Sveti Petar u Rasu

12 Đurđevi Stupovi

13 Ras

14 Sopoćani

15 Crna Reka

16 Mileševa

17 Prijepolje

18 Banja

19 Davidovica

❶ Kraljevo

🏠 86.300

ℹ️ Trg srpskih ratnika 25
36000 Kraljevo
036/316-000

📠 036/21-181

💻 036/22-555

170 km - Beograd

The main church of the Žiča Monastery

Earlier called Karanovac, the town lies near to the confluence of the Ibar River into West Morava. The present day name was bestowed on the city in 1882 when Milan Obrenović was crowned King (*kralj*) at the nearby Žiča monastery. In 1941 Germans shot several thousand citizens here in retaliation for the attacks on their forces.

The centre of the town is marked by a tall monument dedicated to the warriors of the 1912-18 wars standing in the middle of the circular shaped **Trg srpskih ratnika Square**. The pedestrian Omladinska Street lined with cafés begins at the Trg and leads to **Gospodar Vasin Konak**, a Balkan-style manor house with a large terrace from the early 19th c. Until 1941

Monument in Kraljevo's Trg srpskih ratnika

it was the seat of the orthodox bishopric while today the manor hosts the **National Museum** (*Tel. 036/337-960, open 7 a.m.- 8 p.m.*). Next to it is the **Old Church** built thanks to the donations of Prince Miloš in 1823.

On the other side of Trg srpskih ratnika lies Oktobarskih žrtava Street which leads one to the train and bus stations. In front of the train station stands the fascinating group of figures in a heroic socialist style, called the **Monument to Resistance and Victory** (Lojze Dolinar, 1959).

❷ Žiča

12 km - Kraljevo

On the outskirts of Kraljevo, just next to the Mataruška banja Spa, stands the Žiča monastery. It is the joint endowment of King Stefan the First-Crowned and his brother Saint Sava, started in 1208. In 1216 Stefan was crowned here as the first king of the Nemanjić dynasty and, three years later, the monastery became the seat of the first Serbian autonomous archbishopric, headed by St Sava himself. The next seven kings of Nemanjić dynasty followed Stefan's example. Legend has it that for each king a new door was opened and then walled in immediately after the crowning. Although the seat of archbishopric was soon moved to Peć in Kosovo, which was closer to the centre of the state, Žiča did not loose in its importance: state councils continued to be held here and the monastery was praised for its many relics, amongst them the body of its founder. Standing too close to the important roads and the north border of the state, Žiča has been pray to looting many times during its existence. It was looted and burnt for the first time as early as the end of 13th c. by the Bulgarian prince Šišman. Afterwards it underwent a full reconstruction by King Milutin from 1309 to 1316. During the Turkish era it was laid waste several times and sank into obscurity. Its re-emergence coincides with the renewal of Serbian statehood in the 19th c. when it was renovated and sprang back into life. In 1882 prince Milan Obrenović came

14th c. fresco from Žiča

to Žiča to be crowned as the first Serbian king of latter times. The last time the monastery was damaged was in WWII when it was bombed by the Germans.

On the walls of the passage underneath the entrance tower are preserved the early 14th c. frescoes, as well as the transcription of the founding charter of the monastery, a very important historical document.

The **main monastery church** is dedicated to the Ascension of Our Lord. The oldest, eastern part was built before it

Baptistery in the Žiča Monastery grounds

was intended by St Sava to become his seat. The adaptations he undertook, inspired by the monasteries of Mount Athos, gave it the spacious outer narthex and the bell tower in front. St Sava also ordered that it should be painted in a bright red colour, symbolizing that the Church is set up on the blood of its martyrs. When finished, the reputation of this church (called in those days "Big Church" or "Mother of Many Churches"), made it a model that was copied by all of the subsequent 13th c. churches.

The oldest layer of frescoes, painted already in the 13th c., survived only in some fragments remaining in the choir of the church, while most of the frescoes visible today date from the renovation of King Milutin. Though badly damaged, they are of interest for their still noticeable artistic quality. The most prominent composition is the one of the Dormition of Mary on the west wall.

Behind the altar of the big church stands the baptistery, reconstructed from the re-discovered fragments of the medieval one.

The **small church** dedicated to SS Peter and Paul, standing further back, was built simultaneously with the main church. In it remain a few 14th c. frescoes.

The solemn edifice of the **Bishop's Court**, left of the entrance, is the work of architect Aleksandar Deroko from 1935. The main motives here are the pointed arches, inspired by those to be seen on the cupola of the main church.

❸ Maglič

28 km - Kraljevo

This medieval castle lies on a high hill above the River Ibar, 25 km from Kraljevo on the road to Raška.

Maglič was built in the 13th c. on an outpost that enabled easy control over the Ibar valley. It was strengthened and renewed by the Archbishop Danilo II during King Milutin's reign. Danilo built the now ruined church of St George, the palaces and the monks' cells to be found here. Maglič fell into Turkish hands for the first time in 1438 and then again in 1459. It became the seat of a considerably large garrison and the centre for Turkish district that stretched from Požega and Čačak down to the Kopaonik Mountain. The castle had military importance for the last time during the Second Serbian Uprising in 1815.

Protected by the River Ibar on three sides, the castle is of rectangular shape and has seven towers and a large keep. The entry through the 2 m thick walls is possible through only one entrance on the north side. This one is reached by taking a small winding path

Maglič Castle, rising high over the Ibar Valley

churches and the dwellings enclosed by a protective wall in a shape of an almost perfect circle. The oldest and the most significant amongst them is the **Church of the Virgin Mary**, laid out as the centre point of the complex. Constructed between 1183 and 1196 it is a paragon of Serbian church architecture and an example of the burial church that has been followed by all the rulers of the Nemanjić dynasty. Combining the Byzantine notion of church space and the Romanesque treatment of the exterior, it brought to life the new independent style typical of medieval Serbia – the Raška School. The overall impression is slightly spoiled by the robust outer narthex added by Nemanja's grandson king Radoslav. The façades and the sculptural decoration of Nemanja's edifice have been executed in white marble from the neighboring Mt Radočelo by the first-rate craftsmen of the maritime town of Kotor. The most important of the outer decorations is the three-light altar window. It illustrates the beast of hell devouring a sinful man and a basilisk, surrounded by the symbolic

that begins at the pedestrian footbridge. Inside the battlements stand the ruins of a two-storey palace with high gables and of St George's church - a single nave construction showing some influence of the gothic style. From the three towers standing close to one another on the west side, a marvelous view of the Ibar valley can be seen.

❹ Studenica

12 km - Ušće

This monastery is located in the valley of the Studenica River, some 11 km from its confluence in Ibar by the village of Ušće. It was founded by Stefan Nemanja as his principal endowment in the central part of his newly enlarged state. After Nemanja's death, his body was buried here and soon became venerated as miraculous, and he was sanctified as St Simon Mirotočivi ("the one whose body exudes myrrh"). His son Sava, who established the independence of Serbian

church, became the first prior and wrote here the "Typikon of Studenica", which became a cornerstone of monastic rules for the Serbian monks. For all of this, Studenica became and remained the most important of all Serbian monasteries. Its status is best understood by the fact that the prior of this monastery was the most important one in the state, often also becoming a significant political figure. The monastery enjoyed the continual care of the Nemanjićs and of the succeeding dynasties, but it was later ravaged by Turks in 15th c. and then in each one of the following centuries. The last destruction came in 1813 after the collapse of the First Serbian Insurrection.

The monastery complex consists of three

King's Church (left) and Church of the Virgin in Studenica Monastery

Western portal enclosed by the outer narthex

Nemanja-Simeon's sarcophagus. Of great interest are also the inscriptions that are, for the first time, written not only in Greek but also in Serbian, obviously under the influence of St Sava who was preparing to make the Serbian church independent. The inner narthex was painted in 1568 by Master Longin when the church was thoroughly renovated. Frescoes in Radoslav's outer narthex are of lesser artistic value but are of utmost documentary importance, as they present contemporary historical events concerning the establishment of St Simeon's cult. In the church are also kept the relics of Nemanja's wife Anastasija and of his son Stefan the First-Crowned.

The white painted **King's Church**, with a bright red cupola, was intended to resemble the venerated older temple. It was built in 1313/14 and is named after its endower, king Milutin, who dedicated it to SS Joachim and Ann, parents of the Virgin Mary. With its graceful and skilfully proportioned architecture, clarity of style and contour, it is a simple but striking work of art. Even worthier are its frescoes, painted by Michael and Eutyches, Milutin's best loved painters from the

art school at his court. Executed immediately after the building was completed, the elegant lines and warm palette of these frescoes rank among the highest achievements of wall painting in the Byzantine world of the period. The most notable compositions, almost of unequalled excellence in contemporary painting, are the Nativity on the south wall and the Presentation of the Virgin facing it. The depictions of King Milutin, his wife Simonida, St Sava and St Simeon are counted among the finest portraits of the middle ages.

The small single-nave **Church of St Nicholas** was erected in the early 13th c. In it survive only several frescoes, but these are of considerable quality. The 17th c. iconostasis is

Crucifixion, a celebrated fresco from Studenica

believed to be the work of Georgije Mitrofanović.

The high **tower**, above the western entrance to the complex, dates from the period of the founding of the monastery. Inside is a chapel dedicated to the feast of the Transfiguration. The interesting frescoes, portraying members of Nemanja's family and a painted genealogy of the Lazarevićs, linking them with the Nemanjić dynasty, were detected only in fragments. Next to the

representations of carnal sin and indolence, as well as consoles in the shape of the obese and the humble monk. The western portal (now sheltered by Radoslav's outer narthex) shows the patroness of the temple enthroned with the Infant Christ in her lap and the bowing archangels Michael and Gabriel. The vines, with figures emerging from Satan's mouth, are the incarnations of worldly matters.

The oldest frescoes in the church date from 1208-9 and mark the beginning of a new chapter, both in medieval Serbian painting and in the the fresco-painting of the entire Byzantine world. With his wide brushstrokes and simplicity, the calm and rigor of the figures, this anonymous artist from Constantinople introduced a new and monumental stylistic expression. His frescoes are preserved in the altar area, below the dome, on the western wall and in lower zones of the other nave walls. The most praised of them all is the Crucifixion on the western wall. To the left of it is

Hermitage of St Sava above the village of Savovo near Studenica

tower is the old medieval **refectory**.

The **treasury** of the monastery, which has been looted so many times, presents only a portion of its previous wealth but is still amongst the most remarkable ones in Serbia. Prime exhibits are the pall from the reliquary of Stefan the First-Crowned (15th c.) and his ring (13th c.), a gilded silver censer (1591) etc.

❺ Kopaonik

> ℹ️ Sunčani vrhovi
> 036/71-977
>
> 70 km - Kraljevo

Kopaonik Mountain massif is the biggest one in Serbia and is positioned in the geographical centre of the Balkan Peninsula. It stretches in the north-south direction and is 70 km long but

only its north part – the plateau of Suvo Rudishte at the altitude of 1600 m - is a National Park . Several mountain peaks, mutually connected by mountain ridges, are rising from the plateau: Karaman and Gobelja (1934 m), Kukavica (1726 m), and the highest one - Pančićev vrh (2017 m) wherefrom one can see the greater part of Serbia. The peak was named after a renowned Serbian biologist, Josif Pančić (1814 – 1888), a frequent visitor of the Kopaonik, and its biggest promoter. His last wish to rest there eternally was fulfilled in 1951 when his remains were transferred to the Mountain's highest peak and buried there. The National Park also includes the northern forested slopes, descending towards Rasina and Brzećka reka

rivers. North from Suvo Rudište is the so-called Banjski Kopaonik with its highest peak - Vučak (1718 m) overhanging Jošanička Banja.

Kopaonik has a very abundant flora and fauna. Its forests are spread out in clearly distinguishable zones. At the lowest altitudes grows the oak forest, in the middle spreads beech forest, and above them the pines. Above pine forests is a zone of rich pastures, with its numerous springs and streams that descend down the mountain slopes. Wolves, foxes, rabbits, eagles as well as rare lizard and butterfly species (such as *Colias Balcanica*) also live there.

The mountain climate conditions in Kopaonik are exceptionally favourable for tourism. It is known for receiving a lot of snowfall, but since the massif is mainly south-looking it also has approximately two hundred sunny days a year. In addition, on the open plateau of Suvo Rudište cloudy weather never lasts for long.

Two roads are leading towards the tourist heart of the Kopaonik, today mostly concentrated around the splendid hotel complex of "Konaci". The first road is from Jošanička Banja and second from Brus via Brzeće. 22 ski lifts lead to 23 ski pistes: 4 of them are for children, 12 easy, 5 medium, and 2 are difficult ones. The total length of the ski lanes is 44 km, and there is also 22 km of arranged cross-country skiing lanes. During the summer walks, open tennis, football and basketball fields are at disposal.

"Konaci" hotel complex, in the centre of Kopaonik

Ski lift in Kopaonik

festivity, when the winegrowers of the region celebrate their year-long tiresome work, attracts a large number of guests who take delight in many of the wines available as well as in the wine from the Wine-well at the town's main intersection.

ENVIRONS:
In Župa there are many villages that still preserve their *poljane* (seasonal settlements) used for living in the vineyards during grape picking season. The old houses are interesting both due to their function and their architecture.

3 km north of Aleksandrovac in the village of Drenča lie the ruins of a medieval monas-

Kopaonik got it name after the iron and silver mines (serb. *kopati* - to digg) that operated here in medieval times. The mountain was known to Venetians as *Montagna dell'argento*. Just beneath the Suvo Rudište plateau springs a very attractive Samokovska River, interesting for its sudden fall with a lot of rapids which partialy also passes through a small canyon.

⑥ Aleksandrovac

🏠 14.700

ℹ️ Trg Oslobodjenja bb
37230 Aleksandrovac
037/754-404

31 km - Kruševac

Aleksandrovac is the centre of a district called Župa. The term "župa" in Serbian denotes the basin of a river closed in by hills or mountains, protected from the wind and harsh winters and therefore suitable for agriculture and specifically for vineyards. Once it was a common term for all such areas while today "Župa" stands only for the basin of the Rasina River with the centre in Aleksandrovac, one of the best wine regions in Serbia. Although vineyards have existed here since Roman times, folk tradition has it that

vines were planted here by the legendary figure of Prince Lazar himself who chose only to plant excellent quality grapes for the region around his capital of Kruševac. The legend says that the wine from Župa was the one used in Communion for Lazar's army before leaving for the Battle of Kosovo. It is said that not even the Turks, despite the restrictions imposed by their faith, could resist the temptation of the local wines and that even they never did anything to harm the vineyards here.

The geographical and administrative cenre of the region is Aleksandrovac. Earlier known as Kožetin, it is named after prince Aleksandar Obrenović when he visited it in 1882 with his father Milan who bestowed it the status of a townlet. This sleepy municipality suddenly awakes during harvest time when Aleksandrovac hosts the manifestation "Župska berba" ("The Župa Harvest"). This

Working in the vineyards of Župa

tery whose church the locals call **Dušmanica**. It was the endowment of Monk Dorotej and his son Monk Danilo. Of interest is the imaginative sculptural decoration in the Morava style, still partially preserved around the windows.

❼ Koznik

9 km - Brus

8 kilometers west of Aleksandrovac along the Rasina River a steep conical hill rises and on it lie the ruins of castle Koznik. It was built on the site

Koznik Castle on hill overlooking Rasina River

of an older Roman fort. The story goes that it obtained its name from the goats (*koza*) that, alone, could transport the materials needed for construction to this rocky point. It has an irregular base plan and five towers that are still standing today. It is known as the principal castle of Radič Postupović, one of the countries mightiest noblemen at the beginning of the 15th century From the top, a magnificent view of the surrounding area can be seen.

❽ Gradac

8 km - Raška

The monastery is located in the village of Gornji Gradac, 12 km from the Kraljevo-Raška road.

Gradac is an endowment of the wife of King Uroš I, Queen Jelena (Helen) from the illustrious French House of Anjou. The building took place between 1276 and 1279 over the ruins of an earlier church. Queen Jelena took special care of her monastery and also created here a school for the daughters from noble families here. After her death, Jelena was buried here. Sacked in the 15th c., the decayed monastery was re-established in the late 16th c. only to be destroyed again some one hundred years later. It remained in ruins until 1948 when it was reconstructed. From 1990 it has been in use as a nunnery.

In modeling her church Queen Jelena followed the examples of the most distinguished monasteries such as neighbouring Studenica or Žiča rather then solely looking towards the somewhat inovative solution of her husband's monastery at Sopoćani. For some unknown reason construction was stopped for a period of time only to be eventually completed by Serbian maritime masters who were better acquainted with western rather than Byzantine architecture. The result is a specific gothic modeling of the façades visible in the lancet arches of the windows and arcades or the buttresses built against the apse wall. The fresco decoration of the interior is almost completely destroyed but the few remaining scenes show a clear connection with the wall paintings of the Sopoćani monastery. The endower's portrait is still visible, while the most attractive of the surviving paintings is "The Flight to Egypt.

Behind the main church there is a smaller one dedicated to St Nicholas that was used for services during the construction works. The 14th c. frescoes survive only in fragments.

A mix of the Byzantine and the Gothic at Gradac Monastery

⑨ Stara and Nova Pavlica

13 km - Raška

The village of Pavlica lies 8 km north of Raška and has two important ecclesiastical monuments. Stefan and Lazar Musić, the nephews of Prince Lazar, built the monastery, called **Nova (New) Pavlica** in around 1385. Their mother Dragana was buried here after her death. The style of the church is of Morava school with

Ruins of Stara Pavlica above the Ibar River

three semicircular apses. Fragments of the original rich decoration were regrettably destroyed over the course of the centuries. Bishop Joanikije and the nobleman Mihailo Andjelović constructed the outer narthex in 1464, just five years after the fall of Serbia. Andjelović was one of the most influential nobles during the last days of the Serbian state as well as being the brother of Mahmud Pasha, the governor of all Turkish possessions in Europe, a fact that enabled him to build this structure, one of the rare artistic

projects in this troublesome time. The massive belfry was added at the end of the 19th century. The wall paintings are quite damaged but one can still see the portraits of the Musić brothers, Bishop Joanikije and the well-executed figures of saints.

On a cliff above the Ibar River stand the ruins of **Stara (Old) Pavlica**. This temple was constructed in the 12th c, later abandoned and finaly damaged due to the carelessness that occurred during the construction of the railway. It is a three nave basilica with an inscribed cross. Note the pots made of clay that were built into the walls of the altar; these were used to amplify the acoustics in the church. The remains of the 13th c frescoes are only partially preserved in the dome and on its supporting arches.

⑩ Novi Pazar

🏛 72.400
📞 036/25-963
70 km - Kraljevo

After conquering this part of Serbia, a "Turkish" noble, Ishak-beg Ishaković, founded the town of Novi Pazar (literally New Market, in Turkish *Yeni Bazaar*) around 1460, as an important stop on the trading route from Istanbul via Skopje to Bosnia and Dubrovnik. This main road brought prosperity to the town in the 16th and 17th century, when,

An elderly Muslim women in Novi Pazar

in terms of size and commercial power, it became the second most important town compared to Belgrade or Sarajevo. In 1689 and 1737, it was looted by the Austrian army and lost much of its importance. In 1809, the Serbian insurrectionists led by Karadjordje himself raided the town, but could not conquer the fort. With Karadjordje's retreat to the north, most of the orthodox population escaped as well. Although the town deteriorated in the course of the 19th century, it retained its significance as the center of sanjak (Serb. *sandžak*), an administrative unit of the Ottoman Empire. As "Sanjak of Novibazaar" was a piece of land keeping Serbia and Montenegro, the two Serbian states, divided, it therefore had great importance for both the Ottomans and the Habsburgs. It also gave name to the region, simply called Sandžak. Today, Novi Pazar is the most oriental town in inner Serbia, both in appearance and in spirit. Apart from being the hub of the Serbian speaking Muslims in the country, it is best known for its trade and especially for its jeans industry that developed in the last decade after state-owned textile factories went bankrupt.

The center of town around the Mesni trg (the Town Square) is almost entirely concentrated to trading. Here is the **Amir-agin han**, a caravanserai from the 18th century, where a traveler could take a room on the first floor while leaving his horse and merchandize on the ground floor. Actually, this was a complex of four buildings joined together with a large cobbled courtyard, a usual feature of hans and caravanserais.

"Vrbak" Hotel with its bridge over the Raška River

On the other shore of the Raška river, stands a small **Fort** (*tvrdjava*) that was constructed during the founding of the city. It was considerably reinforced and rebuilt in the 18th and 19th century as the dangers of Austria and Serbia drew nearer. Today the fort serves as

construction, called Vrbak, in neo-oriental style, with a bridge over the Raška.

The most interesting part of the town stretches south from the Raška. It is Prvog maja Street, the old merchant street dotted with jewelry shops, bakeries and coffeehouses where coffee is roasted on the spot and only men are allowed to sit. Just across the bridge, there is the small **Arap džamija** ("Arab Mosque") surrounded by small shops. The old **Turkish Baths**

Arap džamija Mosque in Novi Pazar

a park. Apart from a few sections of remaining ramparts, the best-preserved part is the high octagonal tower called **Stara izvidnica** ("Old Watchtower") dotted with loopholes. Underneath the fort there is a hotel of an interesting

(*Gazi Isa-begov hamam*) is behind it, built by the town founder Ishak-beg around 1470. With its eleven cupolas and separate departments for men and women, it is the best example of its kind in whole Serbia.

Further down Prvog maja Street, there is the most superior monument of the town, the **Altum Alem mosque**. This "Golden gemstone mosque" was built in the early 16th century by Muslihedin Abdul Gani, a wealthy and learned patron. The nicely proportioned mosque is consistent with the square plan, with the larger dome over the central space and a vestibule with two smaller domes. The interior has a nicely carved mihrab and walls painted with arabesques. The mosque is surrounded by the old graveyard and mekteb (Koran school) from the same period.

The local **Museum** (*Zavičajni muzej "Ras", 20 Stevana Nemanje St, tel: 020/25795*) has sections devoted to archeology, history and ethnography with costumes from this area. Not far from it is another fine monument, the **Lejlek (Stork) mosque**. The edifice was named after a legend that a stork landed on a church roof and started bowing as in a Muslim prayer, which was seen as a sign that the temple should be turned into a mosque. This is only a legend, since this little building was constructed in mid 15th century and is thus as old as the city itself. It was burned down and destroyed several times, renovated the last time in 1891. There are reasons to believe that sultan Mahomet the Conqueror prayed here during his campaign to conquer Bosnia in 1463.

⑪ Sveti Petar u Rasu

3 km - Novi Pazar

On the outskirts of Novi Pazar, only 3 km from the center of the town, is one of the oldest churches in Serbia. It lays above the road leading to Raška on an amazingly picturesque hill, surrounded by numerous massive tombstones.

Built in 9th or 10th century, and originally dedicated to both Peter and to Paul - the Holy Apostles, this ancient structure was the seat of the bishops of Raška, one of the Serb medieval states. It maintained its function as the bishopric seat up till 1807. The

tradition attributes it's founding to the apostle Titus, the disciple of St Paul. The location itself was thought to be sacred even earlier since the tomb of an Illyrian nobleman in the 5th century BC had been discovered under the church. The tomb contained considerable treasure which can today be seen in The National Museum in Belgrade.

The oldest part of the church is hardly visible behind the later additions. The original structure, whose shape you can grasp from the inside, is circular in construction with a central cupola and three radial apses. This unusual shape has its roots in the edifices built earlier in Armenia and Georgia and was transferred here by the influence of the Byzantine rule. The dark interior reveals three layers of frescos in pale red tones, most of which remained from the last repainting around 1250, and several tombs by the walls.

The Church of St Peter is inseparably connected with life of Stefan

The key of St Peter's Church

Nemanja, founder of the Nemanjić dynasty. After having fled to Duklja (present day Montenegro) because of the disputes in the dynasty, his father Zavida had him baptized by the Roman-Catholic rite since there were no orthodox priests around; upon his return, young Nemanja was re-baptized here by an orthodox priest. Later in his life, as the ruler of Serbia, Nemanja summoned several councils of the realm here and finally, this was where in 1196 he left the throne to his son Stefan.

In case the church doors are locked, ask for the key (*ključ*) in the nearby house.

Ancient church of St Peter in Ras

⑫ Djurdjevi Stupovi

6 km - Novi Pazar

On a hill overlooking the valley of Novi Pazar, and which was the heart of the Serbian state from the 11th to the 14th century, stand the ruins of the monastery of Djurdjevi Stupovi. When Stefan Nemanja was sent to prison by his brothers, he made a vow to St George that he would build a church dedicated to him if the saint helped him escape. Not only that Nemanja escaped and overcame his brothers, but he also managed to defeat the intervening Byzantine army, all of which he thought he did with the help of St George. Soon after, from 1167 to 1171, he kept his promise and built a monastery church. The general design is Byzantine, but, because of the war with the Empire, the builders had to be brought from the maritime lands of Serbia, therefore the Romanesque

unusual appearance and the popular name to the monastery – George's Towers. The second endower to the monastery was Nemanja's grand-grandson king Dragutin,

Frescoes in the chapel above the entrance of the monastery

who transformed the entry tower on the ramparts into a chapel where he was buried in 1316.

The monastery was destroyed after the Serbian insurrection and the consequent desertion by the monks in 1690. By the time the church authorities managed to put an end to this, the church was half torn down, and most of the material was used for the building of Novi Pazar fortress.

Ruins of Djurdjevi Stupovi Monastery

details. The location dictated the length of the church to be reduced. Two bell-towers (*stupovi* in outdated Serbian) were added to the western entrance giving the church

By the twist of fate, additional destruction was caused during the liberation of the area in 1912, when the Serbian artillery was aiming at a Turkish battery entrenched on

the hill. Later on, in the Second World War, more damage was done by the Nazi occupiers. Conservation and reconstruction works started in 1960.

Most of the 12th century frescoes in the church are destroyed, except for some of the prophets painted in cupola and some scenes beneath them. The frescoes in the chapel above the entrance are still in good condition. Painted on the orders of king Dragutin, among other scenes, they also depict all three generations of Dragutin's forefathers ending with queen-mother Jelena, the endower's composition as well as the theme of Serbian State Councils (on the ceiling). Among the councils is painted also the one held in the nearby court in Deževa in 1282, where Dragutin left the throne to his younger brother Milutin. This important decision was made after Dragutin was badly wounded in a hunt accident – therefore the medallions with saints-healers Panteleimon, Cosmas and Damian. The picture of Christ's shroud, with an air of inner illumination and nicely incorporated angels in the scene of Abraham's hospitality, are also of excellent quality.

Fortress of Ras above the road to Sopoćani

⑬ Ras

8 km - Novi Pazar

Commanding the road to the Sopoćani monastery, some 8 km from Novi Pazar, stand the ruins of the fortress of Ras. Being the most important stronghold on the eastern border of Serbian lands in the early Middle Ages, Ras gave the name to the most important of these states – Rasa or Raška. Through the Latin form *Rascia*, the term extends to include the whole of Serbia in most of the western European source texts of the Middle Ages and even later. After the expansion of Serbia to the east in the 12th c., the fortress remained in the centre of its territories and served as one of the royal residences of the Nemanjić kings, who didn't have a permanent capital but circulated constantly through their lands. It was destroyed in the Mongol onslaught of 1242, but the town that developed on this site (Trgovište or Stari Pazar, today the village of Pazarište) continued to be an important trading centre until the establishment of Novi Pazar.

Today one can see the ramparts, of irregular shape, reinforced with five towers and the foundations of several other buildings.

⑭ Sopoćani

16 km - Novi Pazar

16 km west of Novi Pazar, near the spring of the river Raška, stands the medieval monastery of Sopoćani, an endowment of king Uroš I (1243-76). From the original monastery compound remains only the church of the Holy Trinity, built during the 1260s. The outer narthex with a high bell tower was added in the first half of the 14th c. The prestige of this sanctuary was secured by the burial of the founder, his queen mother Ana Dandolo, his father Stefan, the First-Crowned and Grand Duke Djordje, Uroš's uncle. Shortly after the clash with the Turks in Kosovo Polje (1389), Sopoćani suffered serious damage and had to be restored by the Despotes Stefan who paid special attention to strengthening of its fortifications. In 16th c.

Sopoćani Monastery

Sopoćani frescoes that brought the monastery world-wide fame

in front, was built in the time of King (later Emperor) Dušan. Since it is freshly reconstructed, it has only a few traces of frescoes.

Stepping into the inner narthex we observe the magnificent ensemble of Sopoćani frescoes. On the north wall is a historical composition representing the Death of Queen mother Ana Dandolo: lying on the catafalque, she is surrounded by her son Uroš and princes Dragutin and Milutin, while Uroš's wife Jelena is seen kneeling in front; Christ and the Virgin Mary receive the queen's soul. The portraits of King Uroš's family, all standing, are to be seen once more along the east and the south walls. Side chapels are dedicated to St Steven, protector of the Nemanjićs, and to St Stefan Mirotočivi (i.e. Stefan Nemanja), the founder of the dynasty. In the latter can be seen scenes from his life.

Turkish violence forced the monks to flee to the secluded Crna Reka monastery. Brought back to life in late 16th c., the Sopoćani Monastery was finally deserted in 1689 when it was ruined and set aflame by the advancing Turks who chased the rebellious Serbs northwards. The monastery was left in a pitiful state for the next two and a half centuries until it was finally renovated in 1929.

Although from the outside it looks like a basilica with three naves, it is actually a single-nave edifice whose side chapels were incorporated to a single line in the 14th c. enlargement. The tall church, topped by a relatively small dome, with huge wall surfaces decorated only by Romanesque stone windows and arches, provides a new sense of grandeur and size that set an example for the subsequent royal endowments.

The outer open narthex, set with the tower

In the nave are the oldest frescoes (dating from 1273/4), considered to be the peak not only of Serbian but of all European painting of the time. Their expressionist strength and gracefulness, bright colours and bold compositions all keep alive the spirit of classical antiquity and predate the works of Italian Renaissance. These magnificent achievements enabled the Sopoćani monastery to be included in the UNESCO World Heritage list of protected monuments. Although damage over time has effaced almost half of these works and the former golden background has disappeared totally, one still admires the excellence of the ensemble. The compositions here are unusually large and therefore comparably few in number. The most impressive is the scene of the Dormition of the Virgin, bearing intentional similarities with the composition of the Death of Queen Ana. The central position in the painting is reserved for Christ holding in his hands Mary's soul. In the lower zone are the tall figures of prophets, that give the impression of being both physically strong and spiritually wise. In the apse one can see the Adoration of the Lamb with a line of Ser-

View of Ribariće with its mountainous surroundings

Monk from the Crna Reka Monastery

bian archbishops joining the rest of the Christian saints. The usual founder's composition is on the south wall.

15 Crna Reka

28 km - Novi Pazar

4 kilometers south from Ribariće village is this inaccessible, but incredibly spectacular monastery. It is built into the caves of a cliff above the Sovara River (otherwise known as Crna Reka, Black River) and connected with the rest of the world by a wooden bridge, thus double protected from intruders. It is not known how old the monastery is, but it was renovated and enlarged in the 16th century under the protection of an orthodox landowner Nikola (portrayed as an endower). The frescoes dating from this renewal are the work of a talented painter Longin from Peć and are regarded to be among the finest from that era. The remains of the hermit St Petar of Koriša were

brought here when his sanctuary above Prizren had been destroyed. The relics of St Stefan the First-Crowned were hidden here when the hard times befell the monastery of Studenica. These relics brought high esteem to the monastery that was the cultural and spiritual centre of the local Serbian community during the Turkish reign. In the 18th century, a school similar to the theological seminary existed here and, at the beginning of the 20th century, the first Serbian elementary school in the area was opened here.

Highlander with his dairy products

16 Mileševa

6 km - Prijepolje

Lying alongside the River Mileševka, 6 km to the east of Prijepolje, stands the principle endowment of King Vladislav (1234-43), the grandson of Stefan Nemanja and fourth in the lineage of the Nemanjić dynasty. It became the second most important monastery in the Serbian Kingdom when, in 1236, it received the body of St Sava who died during Vladislav's reign. In this way the King ensured the importance and prosperity of his endowment. In 1377, the Bosnian *Ban* Tvrtko was crowned King here above the grave of this great Serbian saint. Later on, in 1466, the Bosnian noble Stjepan Vukčić Kosača, who held this monastery in his possession, took the title of "Herzog of St Sava". From then on his province became known as Hercegovina, "Herzog's land". In the 15th c. Mileševa was the seat of the Orthodox Bishop of Bosnia. The future Grand-Vizier of the Ottoman Empire Mehmed Pasha Sokolović (1505-79) was a pupil here before he was taken from his family and enlisted into Turkish service. His relative Makarije, who in 1577 became the new Serbian Patriarch, also studied here at the time. In the same century here opened the celebrated printing-works whose liturgical books spread through Serbian lands and beyond. The next centuries saw a grave turn in fortune: in 1595 the Turks took the body of St Sava to Belgrade and burned it in a reprisal against the Serbian uprisings; in 1688 another retaliation left the monastery burnt and in ruins. During most of the 19th c. it was abandoned. The people of Prijepolje renovated it in 1863 when it obtained its present-day appearance.

The monastic church of the Holy Ascension was erected around 1225 while the outer narthex was added in 1236 to accommodate the body of St Sava. The western cupola was added in the 19th c. as a detailed copy of the older one. The original architectural style is the one of Raška School and based on the plans of the Žiča monastery (the endowment of Vladislav's father Stefan the First-Crowned) but was executed by less capable artists.

The frescoes at Mileševa represent one of the peaks of 13th c. European painting. The Greek masters who painted it skillfully adapted their program to suit the disposition of the Raška School temple. On the north wall of the narthex are depicted all the Nemanjić rulers up to King Vladislav. He stands last, on the left-hand side, holding a model of his endowment. Next to him is his older brother Radoslav followed by their father Stefan the First-Crowned with a sceptre in his hand; on the east wall can be seen the saintly figures of

The world-famous "White Angel" fresco

Vladislav's uncle Sava and his grandfather Nemanja. The latter's portrait has been cut in half due to the reconstruction works, adding to the piety of his expression. As these are contemporary portraits by painters who showed great interest in realism, these are considered to be closest to the actual images of the rulers. Furthermore, there is a clear inclination towards psychological characterisation of each portrait. This is the first representation of the lineage of the Nemanjić dynasty, later to become an obligatory representation in the endowment of each following ruler. Facing this fresco is a portrait of the endower –the Virgin Mary leads King Vladislav, holding a model of Mileševa, towards Christ. Above it stands the celebrated fresco "The Holy Chrism

Church of the Mileševa Monastery

Taking in the sights, Mileševac Castle

simultaneously guarded both the monastery and one of the most important medieval roads leading from Prijepolje towards Skopje. It has an irregular ground plan divided into upper and lower sections. Three towers and some massive walls still stand tall, while the rest lies in ruins.

⑰ Prijepolje

🏠 32.300
📠 033/24-850
📱 033/22-094
97 km - Užice

During the 13th c. the monastery of Mileševa grew into an important stopping point visited by the trade caravans that passed through the area, mainly from Dubrovnik, as they were transporting goods made on the coast further inland. The liveliness of trade and everything else that went with it bothered the monks who decided to move the trade centre away from the monastery and thus keep the monastery's peace and serenity. So, at the beginning of the 14th c. the marketplace was transferred to a narrow field at the confluence of the River Mileševka into the Lim River, the position still occupied by the town of Prijepolje

Bearers at the Tomb" with an image of the so-called White Angel that became one of the symbols of Serbia. Here again, as in the other portraits, we see the large, striking eyes, and meek, mild expressions on the faces of the otherwise imposing and clearly lit figures with balanced postures. It is interesting that this image was among those sent in the first European deep-space satellite signal. The frescoes with golden backgrounds mimic mosaics that were unsuitable for the harsh climate of Serbia.

The frescoes of the external narthex depicting the Last Judgment are barely visible as they were heavily damaged during the occupation in World War Two when the church was used as a stable.

The oldest of the preserved dwellings,

lying to the north, is a good example of 19th c. Balkan architecture.

ENVIRONS:
Two kilometres further to the east of the monastery, on a high cliff enclosing the entrance to the canyon of the Mileševka River stands **Mileševac Castle**, also known by the name of Hisardžik. It was the seat of the region of Crna Stena ("Black Crag") but more importantly it

Lim River at Prijepolje

today. Nowadays it is a scenic little city, squeezed between the green colour of the surrounding woods and the one of its gardens.

One of the town's symbols is its **Clock Tower** (*Sahat-kula*). It was built in the 18th c. and has a characteristic steep, thatched roof.

The **Orthodox Church** was built between1881 and 1894 according to the plans of a local builder Pero Ninčić. The construction of such a fine temple in the hostile Muslim surroundings was made possible only due to the constant donations from Serbian merchants as well as the steady bribing of the Ottoman authorities. The model of Mileševa and other churches in the Raška School style influenced the design of the church. In the courtyard of the church, a group of ancient tombstones can be seen, mostly from the near-by Roman site of Kolovrat (3 km southwest of the town).

There are also several attractive houses from the 18th and 19th centuries carried out in the local variation of the Balkan style. Among these, the finest one is the two-storied **Šećer-agin**

Monument to St Sava and a minaret in Prijepolje

Han, with its harmonic arrangement of wooden windows and white walls. Other Turkish monuments in the town include three square-shaped mosques of modest apearance.

On the bank of the River Lim stands a small **Catholic Chapel**, a reminder of the Austro-Hungarian military garrison stationed in the town from 1878 to 1909.

⑲ Banja

27 km - Prijepolje

The older name of the monastery is St Nicholas in Dabar, Dabar being the name of the region of the lower Lim valley, once covered in dense woods (in Old Slavonic *deb'r* meant wood). It obtained the name Banja ("Spa") after the thermal springs that erupt close by, Today these constitute the Priboj Spa.

The monastery was erected at the end of the 12th c and in 1219 it became the seat of the Dabar bishopric. The old complex was destroyed in attacks by the Bosnian Ban Stjepan. The battle ended here when Stjepan was met by the Serbian Crown Prince Dušan who defeated the Ban in a fight

The houses of Sopotnica, above Prijepolje

in which the latter only just escaped death as his horse was killed beneath him. Immediately after the battle, Dušan's father, King Stefan built the existing church. Due to the important caravan route that passed nearby, Banja amassed great wealth and was particularly important as a cultural centre after Patriarch Makarije had renovated it around 1575. The Turks destroyed it for the last time in 1875 during an uprising in Herzegovina.

Banja Monastery in wintertime

The church has an inscribed cross base plan and two atypical cupolas, both above the nave and the narthex. The pointed arches of the windows found here became frequently seen ornaments only some hundred years later. The fresco paintings from the 14th c are preserved in the altar's apse and shine out as the best from that period. Their painter had a special interest in detailing the figure's lively movements. The rest of the wall paintings are from the 16th c renewal of the church; however, those in the nave repeat the design of the ensemble lying beneath them. Especially interesting are the paintings "Transfer of the patriarchal throne of Makarije Sokolović to his nephew Antonije", commemorating the occasion that took place in this monastery, "The Victory of the Emperor Constantine the Great on Milvian Bridge" over the entrance and, the representation of the "Last Judgment".

The preserved 14th c. gravestones of nobles and church dignitaries are one of the most important paleographic monuments of the Serbian language.

The monastery **treasury** is considered as extremely opulent due to the several silver and gold artifacts that were hidden underground and found only in 1975 during reconstruction works.

⑳ Davidovica

35 km - Prijepolje

Davidovica Church is set on the Prijepolje – Bijelopolje road close to Brodarevo. It gets its name after monk David, actually *Župan* Dmitar, grandson of Stefan Nemanja by the sideline. It was built in 1281 by masters from Dubrovnik. It is interesting that the original contract is preserved being the only such document from the Serb Middle Ages. Until recently the church lay in ruins. It has a central dome and two smaller ones above side chapels while the modest decoration reflects the influences of Romanesque and Gothic art transmitted here by the builders from the seaside.

Davidovica Church near Brodarevo

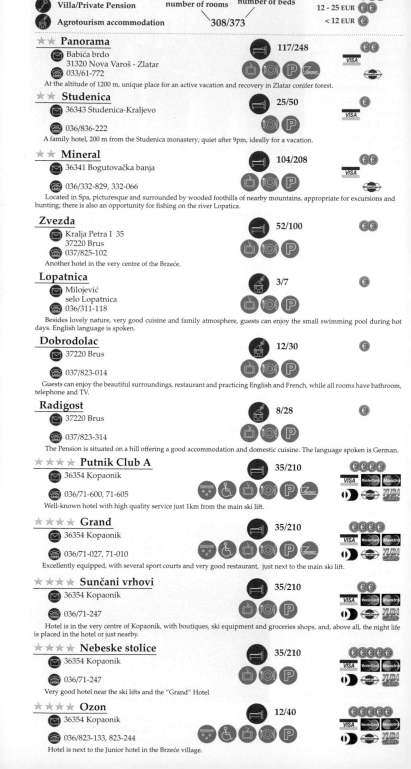

Hotel

Motel

Villa/Private Pension

Agrotourism accommodation

PRICE RANGE - for one person in a two-bed room (including breakfast, service and tax). Small icons present facilities in each Hotel.

number of rooms   number of beds
308/373

> 50 EUR
35 - 50 EUR
25 - 35 EUR
12 - 25 EUR
< 12 EUR

★★ Panorama

Babića brdo
31320 Nova Varoš - Zlatar
033/61-772

117/248

At the altitude of 1200 m, unique place for an active vacation and recovery in Zlatar conifer forest.

★★ Studenica

36343 Studenica-Kraljevo

036/836-222

25/50

A family hotel, 200 m from the Studenica monastery; quiet after 9pm, ideally for a vacation.

★★ Mineral

36341 Bogutovačka banja

036/332-829, 332-066

104/208

Located in Spa, picturesque and surrounded by wooded foothills of nearby mountains, appropriate for excursions and hunting; there is also an opportunity for fishing on the river Lopatica.

Zvezda

Kralja Petra I 35
37220 Brus
037/825-102

52/100

Another hotel in the very centre of the Brzeće.

Lopatnica

Milojević
selo Lopatnica
036/311-118

3/7

Besides lovely nature, very good cuisine and family atmosphere, guests can enjoy the small swimming pool during hot days. English language is spoken.

Dobrodolac

37220 Brus

037/823-014

12/30

Guests can enjoy the beautiful surroundings, restaurant and practicing English and French, while all rooms have bathroom, telephone and TV.

Radigost

37220 Brus

037/823-314

8/28

The Pension is situated on a hill offering a good accommodation and domestic cuisine. The language spoken is German.

★★★★ Putnik Club A

36354 Kopaonik

036/71-600, 71-605

35/210

Well-known hotel with high quality service just 1km from the main ski lift.

★★★★ Grand

36354 Kopaonik

036/71-027, 71-010

35/210

Excellently equipped, with several sport courts and very good restaurant, just next to the main ski lift.

★★★★ Sunčani vrhovi

36354 Kopaonik

036/71-247

35/210

Hotel is in the very centre of Kopaonik, with boutiques, ski equipment and groceries shops, and, above all, the night life is placed in the hotel or just nearby.

★★★★ Nebeske stolice

36354 Kopaonik

036/71-247

35/210

Very good hotel near the ski lifts and the "Grand" Hotel

★★★★ Ozon

36354 Kopaonik

036/823-133, 823-244

12/40

Hotel is next to the Junior hotel in the Brzeće village.

★ ★ ★ Olga Dedijer
✉ 36354 Kopaonik

☎ 036/ 71-033

63/226

Just 10min for the "Sunčani vrhovi", hotel as a good restaurant and ski equipment for renting.

★ ★ Junior
✉ 36354 Kopaonik

☎ 036/ 825-051, 823-355

111/450

Modern hotel with various sport grounds equally astonishing during winter and summer seasons.

★ ★ Jugobanka
✉ 36354 Kopaonik

☎ 036/71-040

49/79

Excellently placed the hotel is equally near to all the important ski slopes of Kopaonik.

★ ★ Atlas
✉ Jošanički kej BB
36300 Novi Pazar
☎ 020/316-352

36/60

A stranger when you arrive, you leave as an acquaintance, and keep coming back as a friend.

★ ★ ★ Kan
✉ Rifata Budzevića 8
36300 Novi Pazar
☎ 020/315-003

17/51

Hotel leaves a deep impression on its visitors because of its comfort, its discretion, and its warmth; you will always be served by attentive staff, the way that match this hotel's rank.

★ ★ ★ ★ Tadž
✉ Rifata Budzevića 79
36300 Novi Pazar
☎ 020/311-904, 316-838

22/50

Remarkable for it interior, made of natural materials – marble, wood and leather – hotel is very suitable for business people.

★ ★ ★ ★ Vrbak
✉ Maršala Tita bb
36300 Novi Pazar
☎ 020/314-548

50/150

Hotel in the centre with beautiful summer terrace.

Sopoćani
✉ Sopoćani bb
36300 Novi Pazar
☎ 020/313-663

24/49

Located on the spring of the Raška River, in environment of an unspoiled nature; 15 km from Novi Pazar, near the Sopoćani monastery.

★ ★ Bor
✉ Milovana Jovanovića bb
36310 Sjenica
☎ 020/741-242

40/100

In the centre of town with several halls suitable for business meetings and a casino.

 Fish restaurant   National restaurant   International restaurant

---

Potkovica
✉ selo Miločaj
36000 Kraljevo
☎ 036/855-556

11-23

In the village of Miločaj, on the Ibarska main road with interior of an old horseshoer's house; really affordable kajmak (milk cream), wedding cabbage, pogača (home-made bread), proja (corn bread).

Gurman
✉ Braće Pirić 103
36000 Kraljevo
☎ 036/355-769

07-24

On the Kraljevo – Novi Pazar route, contemporary styled

Sunce
✉ 36300 Novi Pazar

☎ 020/311-130

06-22

The restaurant is situated in the very centre of the city; open garden.

SOUTHERN SERBIA

The region of the South of Serbia is to be found alongside two of its most important rivers, the Južna Morava (South Morava) and the Nišava. Both rivers flow through the alternating scenery of wide, fertile valleys and almost impassable gorges. Bordered with high mountains on three sides, this district encompasses the roads towards the East and the South, namely Bulgaria and Greece, those ancient paths that have brought both good and evil into Serbia over the centuries. The significance of this region regarding its topography is best described by records noting that the Kunovica

In the late Roman Period, this area was the place of birth of two emperors who changed the course of European history – Constantine the Great was born in *Naisus* (Niš) in 272 A.D. and Justinian was born in the vicinity of the town of Lebane where he later built the city of Justiniana Prima (today Caričin grad). In the Middle Ages this area was the borderland between Serbia, Byzantium and Bulgaria; later on, it was invaded by the Turks in the mid 15th century, who stayed until the liberation in 1878. Turkish dominion left a deep trace on daily life here, especially in the cities. After the liberation, Niš

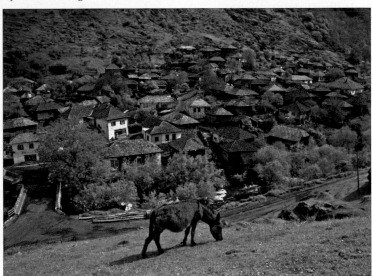

Topli Do village on Stara Planina

mountain, which finishes by the ravine of the Sićevo gorge (*Sićevačka klisura*), was known in the Classical Period and the Middle Ages as *Catena Mundi*, the "Chain of the World" on which the world was suspended! All the towns are found in valleys, each dominated by a mountain, the highest of which is the one near the city of Niš, called Suva Planina (1713 m). The secluded area surrounding the beautiful Vlasina Lake (*Vlasinsko jezero*) at over 1200 m above the sea is especially interesting for its nature and unique climate.

redeveloped into a great and important city. The cities of Pirot, Leskovac and Vranje also progressed quickly. The consequences of the Bulgarian occupation in the two World Wars were severe. All that was Serbian was under threat of destruction and all people who did not change their identity to become Bulgarians were terrorized. This was the time of the uprisings that emerged in this otherwise peaceful area: the long and bloody Rising of Toplica in 1916 was the only one to occur in an invaded Europe, and the fight against the German

al sheep farming in Sićevo Gorge

invaders 1941-44 was equally harsh. The Anglo-American bombings of 1944 were hard on the economy and stopped the rise of the most progressive city of the south, Leskovac, called the "Serbian Manchester" for its textile industry. The South has suffered greatly during these last years. The crash of large state factories was followed by the Kosovo War when this region was bombed a great deal and the population lost many soldiers in Kosovo. However, despite the ethnical problems, Albanians live in the southwest and Bulgarians in the east, alongside Serbs.

Even though the territiory of the South of Serbia is a key one due to the roads that pass through it, it seems like the inhabitants enjoy their intentionaly produced isolation. The vividness of southern landscape is reflected in the fiery temperament of Southern Serbians and their spicy local dishes. The South of Serbia is today famous for the Leskovac grill (*Leskovački roštilj*), the mother of all barbecues in the Balkans and beyond, as well as for their peppers, the tobacco produced in Niš and Vranje, and the hard cheese kačkavalj. A notable feature is the rapid and dynamic speech of the Southern Serbians, which is akin to the dialects of the neighbouring Bulgaria and Macedonia. It is the dialect that the writers Bora Stanković and Stevan Sremac enjoyed and celebrated, and of which the southerners are very proud.

Incredible scenery at Vražji kamen with its small church

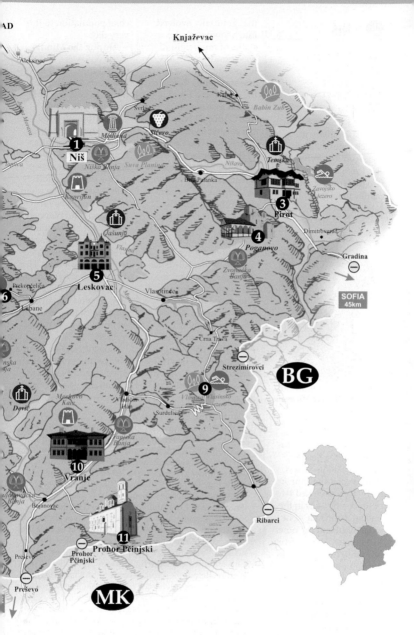

1 Niš

2 Gornji Adrovac

3 Pirot

4 Poganovo

5 Leskovac

6 Caričin grad

7 Kuršumlija

8 Đavolja Varoš

9 Vlasina

10 Vranje

11 Prohor Pčinjski

❶ Niš

📷 251.900

ℹ Voždova 7
18000 Niš
018/523-118

🚌 018/255-492

🚆 018/264-625

238 km - Beograd

Despite many wars and changes, Niš has managed to survive as a town for over two millennia chiefly thanks to its geographical position in a fertile plain. The town lies in

Head of Constantine the Great (National Museum Belgrade)

the basin of the Nišava River close to its confluence with the South Morava. Along these two rivers, from time immemorial, stretched two of the main roads in the Balkan Peninsula – one to Istanbul and the other to Salonika. Not far from Niš these two roads join continuing northwards to Belgade. These roads brought prosperity during times of peace and, destruction during wars and were thereby, the blessing or the wrath of Niš.

The name of the settlement was given by the Celtic tribe Scordisci who succumbed to Romans around the time of Christ's birth. Under Roman rule the first written evidence on *Naissus*, a small military camp on the right riverbank

that gradually evolved into a town with the status of municipium, was found. In 269 AD Emperor Claudius won an essential victory over the Goths and for that reason assumed the title Gothicus. Niš/Naissus earned its fame throughout the world as the birthplace of the Emperor Constantine the Great, the first protector of Christians. Constantine put great efforts into the town's progress, bringing new colonists and building stronger protective city walls. The celebrated Christian town saw its doom in 441 when the Huns plundered it. The town rose was again during the time of renewal under the Byzantine Emperor Justinian, yet this ended in 615 when it was sacked by the Slavs who consequently settled in the area, remaining the

chief population to this very day.

During the Middle Ages, Niš was a fort that passed from hand to hand between the states trying to gain control over the Belgrade-Constantinople road, although none of these (Byzantium, Bulgaria, Hungary, Serbia) were strong enough to keep it for a longer period. The Serbs took the town in 1183 under Stefan Nemanja who planned to make it his capital. Yet, they only managed to strengthen their hold over it in the 14th c. The Turks took it as early as 1386 but had to fight bitterly to retake it several times until they could claim it finally as theirs in 1428.

For the next two and a half centuries Niš developed steadily under the Ottomans, growing out of its battlements and

Contantine the Great

The Roman Emperor (306-337 AD) Flavius Valerius Constantinus, better known as Constantine the Great, was born in 272 in the ancient town of Naissus (modern Niš). Constantine's father, Constantius Chlorus, was a Roman general who in 293 became a member of the four Emperors' Imperial College (Tetrarchy). Constantine's mother Helena was a simple innkeeper's daughter and Constantius' concubine. Though most likely illigitimate, Constantine was the favourite son of Constantius. When in 306 Constantius died in York, his army hailed Constantine as the new Augustus. By 312 his relentless ambition and military capabilities made Constantine the ruler of the western part of the Roman Empire. Before the decisive battle at Milvian bridge (312), Constantine claimed to have seen a cross in the sky above the sun on which the words "with this sign you will be victorious" appeared. After this mystical experience the Emperor openly converted to Christianity which was, by that time, the religion of a persecuted minority. In 324 Constantine had removed the last of his rivals and became the first sole Emperor of Rome in nearly four decades. He spent the last years of his reign in his native region campaigning against Danubian barbarians. During this period he richly embelished the city of his birth Naissus and its vicinity, where, in Mediana, he built his palace. Soon after his death in 337, the first Christian Emperor was transformed into the ideal role model for the future rulers of medieval Europe. In the Orthodox Church he is regarded as a saint and the thirteenth Apostle, sharing the same feastday as his mother, St. Helen (21st May).

stretching for the first time to the left side of the River Nišava. However, with the first wind of change Niš had its share of destruction: in 1689 the Habsburg army helped by the Serbs took over the town but managed to keep hold it for only one year. The Turks prepared a stubborn defense by demolishing the old medieval walls and building the fortress according to the most up-to-date principles of the time. Austrian forces took it once more in 1739 yet with the same result as previously.

In 1809 the Serbian insurrectionist army was defeated in front of Niš and thus Turkish hold on the town was secured and the Serbian state pushed back northwards. The unbearable conditions under the Ottomans provoked several insurrections by the local

Niš at the beginning of the 20th century

especially after the railway line reached it in 1884. The royal residence in Niš was the favourite abode of the Kings Milan and Aleksandar Obrenović and several sessions of parliament were held here as the political atmosphere was much calmer than in Belgade.

During the Austro-Hungarian attacks on Belgrade in 1914 Niš served as the permanent

in front of the town, and thereby the road into the heart of the Austria-Hungary occupation was opened up for the Serbian army.

During the Second World War the town was once again occupied by Bulgarians and was ill famed for its concentration camp "Crveni Krst" where thousands of patriots died. In 1944 heavy allied bombing destroyed much of the

Nišava River bordering the Fortress

Serbs (1835, 1841) that endangered Turkish Niš. Finally, the Serbian army took the city in 1878, the year that marks a new era for the town. In the following decades the town took great steps towards modernisation, developing fast as a centre of crafts and industry,

capital of Serbia and it was here that the well-known "Niš declaration", the first official document planning the formation of Yugoslavia was made. Occupied by Bulgarians in 1915 it was to be liberated in 1918 after the last German resistance was defeated

town's centre and caused great civilian loss.

After the war, the town grew rapidly as an important industrial and university centre. Its progress stopped abruptly in the 1990's, reaching its climax in the bombing of 1999 that destroyed several factories.

❶ Fortress
Tvrdjava

The Niš Fortress was built on the territory which used to be the heart of Roman, Byzantine and Medieval town. Later when in 1717 the Habsburgs took Belgrade, the principal stronghold on the Constantinople road, the Turks were in need of another strong fortress that will protect the road leading to their capital. The works on the fortress in Niš begun in 1719 and the present day construction was finished in 1723. It has a polygonal base with seven sides and eight bastions. From the original four, two gates are now in ruins.

The principal, **Istanbul Gate** (Serb. *Stambol-kapija*), lies on the southern side, facing Nišava River and the main town square. With its niches, pyramidal parapets and Arabic inscriptions the gate is a masterpiece of Ottoman craftsmanship. The gate became the symbol of the city and is displayed on the municipal coat-of-arms.

Just past the gate on the left is the **Hammam**. Built in mid 15th c. it is the oldest remaining edifice of the Turkish times in the town. It is the endowment of

Istanbul Gate, principal entrance to the Niš Fortress

Mehmed-beg, the first administrator of the Smederevo sanjak (1459-1463). The Hammam is a symmetrical structure built out of alternate rows of brick and stone and with walls up to one meter thick. Today it houses a restaurant of the same name.

On the right hand side stands the old Turkish **Arsenal** in which the weapons needed for defence of the fortress were made and repaired. It was built in 1857 and has seven wide arches facing the promenade. Inside you can find a gallery offering a wide variety of souvenirs.

On the left is a row of cafés tucked away inside the openings in the walls and the massive **Belgrade Gate**, which remains, unfortunately, mostly closed. Continuing along central walkway one reaches the old (1902) **monument** of Prince Milan Obrenović and the liberators of Niš. It is intended to represent a bullet but is done in a very naive fashion. Further to the left is a small footway leading up the ramparts

which follow all the way back to the Stambol-gate.

Leaving behind the mound with the mountaineers' home and its reasonably priced café we reach the central part of the fortress and the one-time **Bali-beg Mosque**. Built in the 16th c., it is an excellent example of Ottoman ecclesiastical architecture: a shallow main dome rests on a hefty square base with two smaller domes above the porch, which stands on three graceful columns ending in lancet arches. The only thing missing is the minaret, torn down after the Turkish departure. By the mosque stand the unearthed remains of the Roman and Byzantine Niš.

Further along stands a fine **open-air exhibition of Roman tombstones** and other inscriptions in stone found in Niš and the vicinity.

❷ Banovina Palace

To the left of the Istanbul-Gate is a small green area dominated by an edifice called "Banovina". There are three interesting **monuments** in this open area the most remarkable of which is the covered monument to the locals who died in the 1991-99

Former Bali-beg Mosque

TVRĐAVA

Martirijum (arheo.)

Bulevar 12. oktobra

Jadranska

Bali-begova džamija

1

Letnja pozornica

Kej 14. decembra

Đuke Dinića

Beogradska kapija

Hamam

Zgrada Banovine -Univerzitet-

2 Stambol kapija

Kralja Stefana Prvovenčanog (Filipa Kljajića)

Kej Mike Paligorica

Kej Žvote Đošića

Spomenik oslobodiocima Niša

3

i

5 Vožda

Sinđelićev trg Karađorđa

7

Ćele kula Medijana →

8

Generala Milojka Lešjanina

Pobede

Nade Tomić

Narodno pozorište

4

Kuća Stambolijskih

Nikole

Pašića

Obrenovićeva

Kujundžijsko sokače

Trg kralja Aleksandra

Jovana Ristića

Trg Pavla Stojkovića

D u š a n o v a

Prijezdina

Obilićev venac

Saborna crkva

Trg 14. oktobra

6

Č A I R

1 Fortress

2 Banovina Palace

3 Trg Kralja Milana

4 Obrenovićeva Street

5 Vožda Karadjordja Street

6 The Orthodox Cathedral

7 Skull Tower

8 Mediana

wars. It was executed in a classical style but with modern materials. Next to it stands the bust of the "national hero" Djuka Dinić and, by the riverfront, is a monument commemorating the meeting of Stefan Nemanja and Friedrich Barbarossa in 1183.

The oldest part of Banovina Palace is the one facing the river, constructed in 1889 for the needs of the local administration. At the time it was the largest European-looking edifice in the still mainly oriental town. In 1914 and 1915, when Austro-Hungarian guns were threatening Belgrade,

this palace was used as a temporary seat of the Serbian government. On the 28th of July 1914, the telegram with the official declaration of war arrived here. All other diplomatic contact with the allies and with the Croat and Slovene repre-

sentatives also took place here. When in 1930 Niš became the seat of the Morava region (*banovina*, hence the name), one of the ten administrative units of the Kingdom of Yugoslavia, the old building was enlarged into a whole block. The

The monument alongside Banovina Palace

new, representative façade facing the Fortress was executed according to the designs of the architect Petar Gačić. From 1966 the building houses the seat of the chancellor of the University.

❸ Trg Kralja Milana

This square was once the meeting point of five roads along which from 16th c. onwards the town developed on the left bank of the river. At the end of that century in place of the present-day

"The Messenger of Freedom" Monument

equestrian monument the first mosque on this side of the river was built. After the liberation the mosque was torn down and in 1879 a fire cleared the rest of the future square destroying a number of small oriental shops. Thus emerged the open space that was to be transformed into the first regulated square of Niš, named after the King Milan during whose reign the town was freed. On the western side of present day square one can see a picturesque line of houses, built in the period between 1882 and 1930. Today, this is the most important square in the city, a popular promenade but also a

place where all of the big manifestations and political rallies are held.

Close to the bridge stands a small but finely modelled **monument** to the five Serb patriots from Niš, who were hanged on this spot in 1821 by the Turks on the charge of conspiracy to carry out an insurrection. It was unveiled in 1913 on the 35th anniversary of the liberation and 1600th anniversary of the Milan edict issued by Constantine the Great that proclaimed the equal rights of Christians within the Roman Empire.

The east side of the square lost its old appearance in 1959/60 when old houses were demolished to make place for the new **hotel "Ambasador"**.

In the middle of the square stands the **Monument to the Liberators of Niš**, sculpted by Antun Augustinčić and unveiled in 1938 marking the 60th anniversary of liberation from the Turks and 20th anniversary of liberation from Bulgarian occupation in World War One. The pedestal depicts scenes of battles against the Turks as well as those from First World War while on the top stands the equestrian statue called "The Messenger of Freedom".

At the top of 7. Jula St, which faces the river, stands the building of the **Major's Office**. It was built in 1924 to house the branch of the National Bank of Niš in a lavish French neo-classicist style. Previously, until it perished in flames

in 1917, the place was occupied by the Summer Residence of King Milan, the most beautiful edifice retained from the Turkish times. In the same space cleared by the fire, **Hotel "Park"**, the first truly modern hotel of Niš, was built between 1936-38 based on the design of A. Sekulić. During the Nazi occupation the hotel was home to German officers. On July the 3rd 1941, student Aleksandar Vojinović threw a bomb inside it killing several Germans – an event which marked the beginning of armed resistance against the occupiers in this region.

❹ Obrenovićeva Street

The street starts from the Kralja Milan square and continues southwards through the center of the city. Once the covered market of oriental Niš and later its principal commercial street, it got longer and longer as the town developed and grew bigger. Today it has been turned into a pedestrian zone with numerous shops and several shopping malls. There are several

Mix of old and new architecture in Obrenovićeva Street

interesting buildings in and around it, yet of far more interest is the verve you can feel here.

Starting from the square of Kralja Milana, on the right hand stands a shopping mall that incorporates a modern glass façade with much

Stambolijski Mansion, today housing Restaurant "Sindjelić"

older edifices. The most interesting is the two-storied **Building of Aleksandar Mihajlović**, a duplicate of Sme-derevo Credit Bank building in Belgrade by Milorad Ruvidić. The most representative of the merchants' palaces in this street stands a **No. 41**. It was built in 1930 for the merchant Andon Andonovic by M. Borisavljevic in a style of French neo-renaissance.

Passing the intersection with Nikole Pašića Street to the left forks out **Kujundžijsko sokače** ("Coppersmiths' Alley"), officially named Kopitareva St. Until recently this alley was a reminder of old Niš but was also totally neglected. Today it is fully renovated, yet throughout most of the year, one can hardly distinguish its small houses among the multiple cafés and their large sunshades.

Just to the right of the abovementioned intersection, at 36 Nikole Pašica St, stands the **Stambolijski Mansion**, the most attractive remaining piece of oriental architecture in Niš. The building of the mansion was started by a local Muslim Memetović in 1875 but after the liberation he decided to sell it half-completed to the well-known merchant Todor Stanković, nick-named Stambolija for his commercial relations with Istanbul (serb. *Stambol*). The house has all the feratures of late oriental style: built of wood and clay it includes a symmetrical façade with an erquer in the middle, while inside it has a central wooden staircase and carved rosettes on the ceilings. The original structure was in such bad condition that in 1981 it had to be pulled down and rebuilt from the foundations to its original appearance. Today it houses a national cuisine restaurant "Sindjelić".

Right across the street is the the **National Museum** (*tel. 018/225-32, open*

Tue-Sat 9 a.m.-8 p.m., Sundays 10 a.m.-2 p.m.). It prides itself with a fine collection of antique Roman items including a distinctive metal screen with figures of god Asclepius and the moon goddess Luna, numerous figurines and other interesting findings principally from the locality of Mediana.

5 Vožda Kara-djordja Street

This street has always been a major thorough-fare as it was actually the first part of the road leading towards Pirot and then further on to Sofia and Istanbul.

At the corner with Orlovića Pavla St lies the **Main Post Office** situated in a building constructed in 1931 for the needs of the State Mortgage Bank. The edifice has a corner part accented with strong columns, allegorical reliefs and statues, while the rest of the façade is void of decoration.

At the corner with Filipa Kljajića St, by the intersection known as Sindjelić Square, stands the modernistic **National Theatre** building opening out towards the square with its circular

District Court House in Vožda Kar-adjordja Street

National Theatre

entranceway. It was built in 1937-39 according to the plans of Vsevolod Tatarinov, a young Russian émigré living in Niš.

Diagonally across from the Theatre stands the **District Court** building. With its corner tower on which there is a clock and its rich decoration it certainly is considered as one of the most interesting edifices in Niš.

A little further along stands the **"Stevan Sremac" High School**. It was opened as the first one in the town in 1878, not a year after Niš was liberated from the Turks. It soon became one of the most important institutions in modernisation of the city. Many famous personalities from the South of Serbia were pupils or professors here: the writers Stevan Sremac (after whom the school was named), Vladislav Petković-Dis, Bora Stanković and the composer Stanislav Binički, to mention just a few. The present-day building was begun amidst much diffuclty in 1912 but due to the incoming wars, was finished only in 1922. It was executed according to the plans of the architect Milorad Ruvidić who lost his life in WWI.

❻ The Orthodox Cathedral
Saborna crkva

The largest place of worship in town, the Orhtodox Cathedral lies at the southern end of the old town in the one time Christian quarter. This was once the prettiest part of Niš with many houses done in lavish oriental style built by the rich Serb merchants, but they all perished in the Anglo-American bombings of 1944.

After in 1856 the European powers compelled the Sultan to grant religious freedom to the Christians in his Empire the Serbs of Niš decided to build a church which will reflect their number and economicla wealth. Contract was made with builder Andrija Damjanov of Veles and the works started in 1857.

However, the grand proportions of this large edifice provoked the local Turks to interrupt the building progression several times and to even at one point expell the Serb bishop. The Turks were furious particularly about the domes that rose high above the town silhouette, the mosques and their minarets, so that when they were finally finished in 1872 the authorities would not issue the permission for the running of the service. The church was consecrated only after the liberation in 1878: the first service was held by the Archbishop of Serbia Mihailo and attended by Prince Milan Obrenović.

The Cathedral is the first large scale ecclesiastical edifice built under the Turks in South Serbia and also the first one inspired by the old Byzantine traditions breaking away with the small, simple churches of the Turksih times. It is a three-nave basilica with galleries on the inside and arcades on the outside and crowned with five domes. The bell tower with a clock was added in 1937 and is done in a somewhat more modern style.

Unfortunately, in 2003 neglect caused a fire to break out, destroying the church interior together

Orthodox Cathedral

with its precious ico-nostas (Djordje Krstić and others, 1880-85) and many other valuable ecclesiastical items.

To the right of the new church is the Small or the **Old Cathedral**. Dug into the ground it stands as a testimony to the hard life of Christians under Turkish domination. This edifice was built in 1814 and dedicated to the most renowned saint of South Serbia, St Archangel Michael, popularly called "Dušovadnik" ("The Soul-Extractor"). In 1837 the church was extended with a covered terrace on three sides. Inside there is a wooden gallery with attratively carved column capitals. The iconostas was carved by a skillful master featuring icons from various periods and of varying quality.

7 Skull Tower

Ćele kula

Tel. 018/222-228

This ghastly monument is probably the best-known sight in Niš, a unique testament to the struggle for freedom. It is located some 2 km from the centre of the town on Bulevar Zorana Djindjića (the old road to Istanbul) just next to the Military Hospital. The ticket office is in front of the complex.

After the bloody battle with the Serbian insurrectionist on Čegar Hill in 1809, Huršid-pasha, the Turkish commander of Niš, ordered that the killed Serbs should be beheaded, their heads skinned and stuffed and sent to the Sultan. The remaining skulls were to be built in to the Tower so as to serve as a

Detail from the Skull Tower

warning to the rest of the population.

The tower stood exposed in the open, leading to significant deterrioration by the end of 1870s. In 1892, with the help of monetary donations gathered from all over Serbia, an elegant chapel designed by Dimitrije T. Leko was built to enclose what was left of the Tower. From the original 952 skulls only 58 remained but their sight is still a chilling reminder of the lives lost to Turkish atrocities. An account of this sight was first communicated to Europe in 1833 by the French writer Alphonse de Lamartine while on his way to Istanbul. A plaque inscribing a message from the writer in which he advises the Serbs to preserve the tower can also be found in the chapel.

In front of the chapel stands the monument to the Serbian commander on Čegar, legendary Stevan Sindjelić, and a relief depicting the battle, both from 1937. *Open Tue-Sun 8 a.m.-8 p.m., Mondays 8 a.m.-4 p.m.*

8 Mediana

Tel. 018/550-443

Still further from the centre, where Bulevar Zorana Djindjića turns into the road for Niška Banja is the archeological locality, Mediana, also known as Brzi Brod due to the village next to it. The village would have merged with Niš long ago had it not been for the prohibition of construction on some 200 acres of the protected grounds.

Mediana was built somewhere between 317 and 330 by the Roman Emperor Constantine the Great as an imperial summer residence near to his birthplace, the town of Naissus. The famous agreement on the division of the Roman Empire in to Western and Eastern parts, a cornerstone in European history, took place right here in Mediana in 364 between the brothers Valentinian I and Valens. Soon afterwards, barbaric Goths destroyed the palace complex. Mediana was soon re-established, however this time as a simple village that was to be finally abandoned after the invasion of Attila's Huns in 441.

Archeological excavations revealed the remains of the imperial palace, baptistery, granary, water tower, baths and a church. Here one can see mosaic floors, such as the one portraying the mythological monster Medusa and a water deity, as well as those with floral and geometrical patterns. Although most of the items found here are today kept in the National Museum in Niš, there is a small museum on the premises. *Open Tue-Sat 9 a.m.-4 p.m., Sundays 10 a.m.-2 p.m., Mondays 9 a.m.-4 p.m.*

AROUND NIŠ

Čegar & Kamenički Vis

To the north of Niš, past the village Kamenica, is the Čegar Hill

Monument at the site of the Čegar Battle

where, on 31st of May 1809, the Serbian insurrectionist army suffered its greatest defeat. The offensive towards Niš suffered due to discordance amongst the commanders, giving time for the Turks to regroup and assemble far greater forces. The Turkish attack on Serbian trenches finished with the heroic act of one of the Serbian commanders, the legendary Stevan Sindjelić, who fired at his gunpowder depot in order not to turn it over to the Turks thereby killing himself, the rest of his men and the advancing Turks. The monument, in the shape of a tower, commemorating the event was built in 1927 by Julijan Djupon. The lower part is made out of stone from the Niš fortress. In a niche beneath the tower stands the bust of Sindjelić.

Above the village of Kamenica lies the Kamenički Vis Top (825m), a well-known excursion point set in dense woodland.

Latinska crkva

8 km northeast from Niš, not far from Kamenica village, lays the village of Gornji Matejevac. Above it, on a hill by the name of Metoh, stands the so-called Latinska crkva ("Latin Church"). It was built in the 12th c. when Niš prospered under the rule of Byzantine emperor Manuel I Comnenus. It is the oldest surviving sacral buliding in Niš and its vicinity. In the 16th c. it was used by a colony of Dubrovnik merchants and served as the only catholic ("Latin") church in Niš. Afterwards it was in use by the villagers until the construction of their new church in 1838. During the 19th century it was the gathering place for anti-Turk brigands.

It is a modest brick and stone building with a dome done in the Byzantine architectural style. There is an older Roman monument built in the north wall. The church was painted in the 19th century by local painters of modest capabilities though its icons are somewhat more interesting.

Niška Banja Spa

Only 7 kilometres to the east of the town and connected to it with a frequent bus line, lies Niška Banja, a pleasant oasis of greenery and rest.

The spa has three springs: two hot ones (37-39°C) and a cold one (sometimes below 20°C), all of them with a radioactive component. Niška banja is also characterised by its pleasant climate with higher temperatures than Niš and a much lower rain fall average. The spa was first used by the Romans, who had several large bathing facilities here. Some of the 4th c. ruins are to be seen in the Hotel "Radon". Renovated, these ruins were later also used by the Turks. The spa changed its appearance between the two World Wars when wealthy merchants from Niš and Belgrade were attracted by the healing reputation of the springs and built their villas

Latinska Church in Gornji Matejevac village

here. King Aleksandar sent a car from Belgrade here every day to fetch him fresh water from the local springs. Today the spa is quite shabby and the old villas are hard to find and recognise. There are a couple of attractive promenades, several cafés and a restaurant, as well as a path to the spring higher up in the forest.

Sićevo

A picturesque village that has given its name to the whole gorge near it is just the place for a small excursion. One gets there by taking an asphalt road forking suddenly off the main Niš – Sofia route, just after Vine depot of Sićevo winery cooperative and heading uphill. The best view of the gorge can be enjoyed from the rocks next to village's sport fields, reachable by a pathway that goes off the road, just next to a power transformer. From here one can see a large part of the gorge, with a winding road that goes through it, as well as an old power station on the Nišava River.

Suva planina

If you like long walks and mountain climbing, then the Suva Planina massif must have drawn your attention immediately on your arrival in Nish. It rises up just south-east from the city and stretches further south in the total length of some 35 km. There are some remarkable peaks on it, such as Trem (1810 metres high), Sokolov Kamen (1552 m), and Kolov Kamen (1361 m). Under the Sokolov Kamen is a ski

Sićevo Rooftops

lift and a piste which have recently been put back into service. As many as three mountain halls are situated on the slopes of this charming mountain: "Studenac" (*tel. 064/6174-96-46*) just beneath the Sokolov Kamen, "Ploče" on the old road to Bela Palanka; and "Donja Studena" in the village of the same name. For more information see www.planina. info or contact Niš Mountaineering Association (*tel. 018/22-813*) or personally at their office in Niš fortress.

Koprijan

The remains of this medieval castle lie on the old road to Leskovac, directly above the village of Malošište; follow the signs to the "Katun" restaurant, the furthest point accessible by car. The strategically located hilltop fortified already

in Roman times was utilised by Nenad, son of Bogdan, the treasurer of prince Lazar, to build a castle in 1372. In 1413 it was taken by Musa, one of the contenders for the Turkish throne, who destroyed a good part of its walls and slayed local populace sheltering inside. Nevertheless, the castle was renovated and used until 1451 when it finally fell into Turkish hands.

Judging by its grand dimensions (60 by 80 meters) it was one of the largest Serbian medieval fortifications and was thus able to provide a hiding place for the people of the surrounding villages. The base is rectangular but only the west and the north walls survive along with the cistern inside. The top of the hill presents magnificent views across whole of the valley of Južna Morava.

Suva Planina Massif

❷ Gornji Adrovac

11 km - Aleksandrovac

Finding this village and its interesting church is not a piece of cake: one must take the exit for Aleksinac off the Belgrade-Niš motorway and than continue through the villages of Žitište, Prćilovica, Donji Adrovac, turn left for Gornji Adrovac (11 km in all).

At the end of the village, on Golo Brdo hill, stands the memorial church dedicated to the Holy Trinity. It was erected on the site where Colonel Count Nikolai Nikolayevich Rayevski died fighting as a volunteer in the Serbian-Turkish war of 1876. Rayevski served as a prototype for Leo Tolstoy as the character of Vronski in his celebrated novel "Anna Karenina".

A simple stone monument in front of the church stands above the heart of Rayevski while the rest of his body was taken back to Russia. In 1903, the Count's aunt Maria donated money for the construction of the church that has a large cupola and polychrome façade. Above the entrance inside stands the memorial plaque with an image of Rayevski. The wall paintings include images of Russian and Serbian saints and scenes from histories of both nations.

The key to the church (ključ od crkve) is kept in the house across the road.

An example of celebrated Pirot kilim

❸ Pirot

📷 56.700
☎ 010/321-489
☎ 010/311-852
71 km - Niš

Positioned conveniently in a broad, lush field along the Constantinople-Belgrade road, the town existed already in Roman times when it was known as *Turres* (Latin for "towers"). In 6th c. it is mentioned as *Quimedava* fortress. Under the name Pirot it is mentioned for the first time in the 14th c. when it was a sight of contest between the Ottoman Empire and Serbia. It finally fell into the hands of the Turks in 1415 who renamed it Šahirkej, which can roughly be translated as "Town-village". The tough living conditions under the Ottoman rule in the 19th c. led to two insurrections, yet the town remained in Turkish control until 1878. The Bulgarian occupation in both World Wars brought massive killings, expulsions, burning of Serbian books, bulgarization of all names, amongst other opressive and destructive actions. From those hard times and to this day the town and its vicinity remain renowned for their production of *kačkavalj* hard cheese and the famous Pirot kilims weaved from both sides.

On a small hill overlooking the town lies Pirot castle also known as **Momčilo's Castle** (*Momčilov grad*) named after vojvoda Momčilo, a hero of Serbian epic folk songs, who allegedly resided here. Most of its fortifications date back to the 14th century and are well preserved. It consists of an upper area with the keep, the mid part with two towers and a lower part surrounded by a moat once filled with water. Surprisingly, the castle was used by the army until after World War Two.

The Nišava River divides the town into two; the part on the left bank of the river is called Pazar and was populated by Turks and Serbs, while the right bank – Tijabara - had only Serbian population. Both of these quarters have old orthodox churches from the Turkish period. The

Tower in Momčilo's Castle

church in Pazar is older; it was built in 1834 on the site of an older temple in less than a year - a fact that shows the wealth of local Christian tradesmen. In Tijabara stands the **Cathedral** (*Saborna crkva*), the work of Andreja Damjanov from 1868. Like all other Christian churches in Turkey, it also had to be dug into the ground but unlike most of them this basilica has a representative western face with a gable and three small cupolas. The skillfully carved iconostasis is the work of master Stojčo of the Samokov School from 1872. Both of the churches have several icons that are regarded as miraculous.

In Tijabara is also the **Hristić House** from 1848, one of the most attractive examples of a Balkan-style city dwelling from the 19th c. Today it houses the **Museum of Ponišavlje** (*Nikole Pašića 49, open Mon-Fri 7 a.m—3 p.m., 10 a.m.-2 p.m.on weekends*) which has an excellent collection of folk costume, Pirot kilims and ceramics. Not far from here is another fine house from the period called "The White Cat" (*Bela Mačka*) named after a one-time inn.

With regards to buildings following the Serbian liberation from the Turks, there are several interesting examples in Srpskih vladara Street, actually part of the Constantinople road passing through the town. At the corner with Dragoljuba Milenkovića Street stands the neo-classicist **High School** building (Milorad Ruvidić, 1907) and the corner **Court** edifice from 1910.

Church in the grounds of the Poganovo Monastery

❹ Poganovo

29 km - Pirot

From the Pirot-Sofia road take a right turn to the village of Sukovo and then head south. The monastery lies at the side of the road.

The monastery of Poganovo was constructed around 1390 as an endowment from the mighty Serbian noble, Master (*Gospodin*) Konstantin and his daughter Jelena, who later married the Byzantine Emperor and became mother to the last two emperors - John VIII and Constantine XII. Master Konstantin, who ruled the area of Eastern Serbia and Macedonia at that time, was soon afterwards forced to fulfil his vassal duties to the Turks – he died fighting on the Turkish side against the Hungarian King in 1395 along with the legendary Marko Kraljević. Due to the following chaos and the Turkish takeover of Konstantin's lands, the temple was left unpainted until 1499.

The monastic church is dedicated to Saint John the Theologian. It is a modest edifice that follows some of the innovations of the contemporary Morava School, for instance a large bell tower above the narthex. The porch in front of the entrance dates back from the 19th century, as do all other living quarters of the monastery, some of them being excellent examples of local folk architecture. Of special interest are the fresco paintings done by masters from Northern Greece, considered to be true masterpieces of

Fresco at the Poganovo Monastery

Hotel "Mir" in the lush greenery of Zvonačka banja Spa

the time. The depicted characters are marked with distinguishing individuality, which can also be credited to the influence of late gothic painting.

ENVIRONS:

The monastery is situated at the very entrance of the impressive **canyon of the river Jerma** that finds its way between the Vlaška and Greben mountains.

On the other side of this gorge, at an altitude of 670 m, lies **Zvonačka Spa**. Out of the way of all major roads and squeezed in amidst the mountains and the Bulgarian border, it is situated in an unspoilt, wild landscape. With two indoor pools and several sports grounds the spa is a good start-

ing point for walking through the surrounding forests, inspecting small caves or peculiar shaped rocks and bumping into villages that seem to have been barely touched by the outside world at all. Zvonačka Spa's trademark is the grey eagle nesting on the rocks above it.

⑤ Leskovac

86.200

Masarikov trg bb
16000 Leskovac
016/233-361

016/244-820

016/212-790

49 km - Niš

The town lies on the Veternica River, not far from its confluence with the South Morava, in a wide field closed in from all sides. In the mid 12th c. Stefan Nemanja, while still only the brother of the ruler, obtained this area, known as Dubočica, from the Byzantine Emperor Manuel Comnenus, which greatly boosted his prestige among his brothers. The Turks conquered Leskovac in 1454, yet only after heroic defense by Nikola Skobaljić. As Leskovac became an important trading point in the 18th c. the Turkish authorities made it the centre of sanjak (an administrative unit) as well. After the Serbian Insurrections, the state of the Serbs

worsened drastically and subsequently the terror of Turkish and Albanian lords led the people to an unsuccessful rebellion in 1841. The town was freed from Muslim hands in 1877 and soon changed its appearance. Due to its prosperous textile industry that sold products worldwide, Leskovac was dubbed the "Serbian Manchester". This prosperous period came to an end in WWII mostly as an aftermath of the devastating and perfectly unnecessary Anglo-American bombings of 1944 that destroyed a large part of the old town. What remained was transformed into state owned factories, which failed to achieve the same results. However, one thing that survived and moreover managed to conquer the whole of the Balkans and beyond is the famous "Leskovac Grill" (*Leskovački roštilj*), now considered as the finest grilled meat.

Although most of the town centre was rearranged in the modernist style after the Second World War, there are still some old buildings in Bulevar Oslobodjenja that, through their architecture, are reminders of the golden age of the town. The most important surviving monuments lay however in smaller side streets. In this boulevard is located the **Šop-Djokić House**, a good example of the old civic architecture of the 19th century. Today it houses the Tourist Organization. However, the most important monuments lie in the surrounding streets. The Old and New Church are in the vicinity, on the other side

Leskovac Old Church

of the Boulevard. The **Old Church** was built at the very beginning of the 19th c. in the usual unassuming fashion of Christian shrines in Turkish cities. The hostility to the construction of any Christian temple was so great that the local Serbs had to declare deceitfully that the building was to be used only as priest's lodgings; due to this, the church had a non-functional chimney. Six steps lead to its gloomy interior lit only by a couple of small windows. The finely carved iconostasis is the work of an artist from the Samokov School.

Next to the old church stands the splendid **New Church**, a total architectural opposite to the previous one. It is a sturdy five-domed edifice with meticulous decoration inspired by different styles from Serbian medieval architecture. It was finished in 1931 with the designs of a Russian émigré Vasilij Androsov, while the inside is decorated with wall-paintings of yet another Russian, A. Bicenko.

A few metres further along, is the old early 19th c. **House of Bora Dimitrijević-Piksla**. **National Museum** (*Stojana Ljubića 2, 016/212-975, open Mon-Fri 8 a.m.-4 p.m.*). The most interesting artifact in the collection is one of the items brought from the excavations carried out in Caričin Grad.

⑥ Caričin grad

6 km - Lebane

Caričin Grad lies 32 km east from Leskovac. Take the SW road to Lebane; at the exit from Lebane to Medvedja, turn right towards Prekopčelica village (there is a sign pointing the way but it is hardly visible). The ruins lie some 8 km further. Look carefully to your left, because there is no sign pointing to the last turn.

Caričin Grad ("The Empress' Town") is a modern name for the remains of the Late Antique city Justiniana Prima. The city was established by the East Roman (Byzantine) Emperor Justinian I, near the village of Tauresium around the year 535 AD. Tauresium was the birthplace of Emperor Justin I (518-527) and of his nephew and succesor Justin-

Ruins of Justiniana Prima

ian. Justinian wanted to build a great city which would overshadow his low orgin and embelish his native region.. The Emperor turned the new founded Justiniana Prima in an administrative and ecclesiastical center of the whole Western Illyricum (the Central Balkans). Soon after Justinian's death in 565, the city was invaded by the numerous Slavic tribes and in the early 7th century it was laid to waste.

Nowdays, Caričin Grad extends over several acres of land, including a fortified upper town (Acropolis) and a lower town. The acropolis, at the highest point in town, contains the ruins of the **Cathedral**, built in a form of a three-aisled basilica with an atrium and a immersion pool for baptisms in front. To the east is a **Crypt Basilica** named for an unusually large crypt in which the important clerics and dignitaries were burried.

Down the crossroads in which once most likely stood a Forum, past the barely visible remains of colonnaded street heading south, one reaches the lower town. The approach is through remains of an imposing gate (anothter one is at the south side). Of interest here is the **Basilica** which preserves most of its old **mosaic floors**. Finely done mosaics depict a

Gradska kuća, ethnographical section of the Leskovac Museum

shephard with sheep (Good Shepard), a hunter spearing a lion, the Amazons & the Centaurs and a chase after a wounded bear.

The whole of the locality is in a fairly bad state. There are no directions around and it takes a lot of skill to find one's way through the ruins.

St Nicholas Church near Kuršumlija

⑦ Kuršumlija

 21.600

ℹ Kosovska 17
18430 Kuršumlija
027/380-963

52km - Niš

In Roman times the town was known as *Ad Fines* and, in medieval Serbia as Toplica after the river on which it lies. Its history changed its course in the 12th c. due to the young Stefan Nemanja. The future ruler of Serbia was still under the shadow of his older brothers but the region of Toplica was the part of the country he governed. In 1168 he built a monastery dedicated to St Nicholas here while his wife Ana established the nunnery dedicated to the Mother of God. Nemanja's brothers became worried about his rising influence and decided to incarcerate him on the pretext of not asking the ruler Tihomir for permission to build this church. This marked the beginning of the conflict between brothers and Nemanja's rise to power. As both churches were covered with shiny lead, the nearby settlement changed its name to Bele Crkve ("White Churches"). Later on, when the Turks took the town in the 15th c. they named it *Kuršumli*, "of lead".

The **Church of St Nicholas** (*crkva Svetog Nikole*) can still be seen north of the town, up the river Toplica. It is a one-nave building executed in the Byzantine style with a low eight-sided dome. When, in 1219, it became the seat of the Serbian Bishopric it obtained a narthex with two towers. In the 14th c. a small chapel was added on the south side. Unfortunately the wall paintings have been lost over the course of the centuries. The **Church of the Mother of God** (*Bogorodičina crkva*) is today only a picturesque ruin.

⑧ Djavolja Varoš

23km - Kuršumlija

To reach this extraordinary natural phenomenon one must take the road from Kuršumlija to Priština. After 15 km, behind the village of Rača,

The extraordinary earth formations of Djavolja Varoš

a small road splits to the left; it will lead you to the parking place. To get from here to Djavolja Varoš is a leisurely 20 minute walk.

"Devils' Town" owes its name to its unnatural and eerie looks. It lies above the bed of the Djački potok stream in which there is no life due to the high concentration of iron and sulphur. Djavolja Varoš consists of two hundred earth columns and pyramids topped with stone caps. The columns are between 2 to 20 metres high and 0.5 to 3 m wide, grouped or lined up in rows. This phenomenon appeared due the constant erosive processes: the caps on the top protect the columns while the rest of the ground is constantly washed away. The columns perpetually change in shape and as does their number – the old ones crumble and the new ones build up. There are two folk legends explaining how Djavolja Varoš emerged. The first one tells how the columns arc actually children turned to stone by devils they had outsmarted. The second explains that devils wanted to marry a brother to a sister, however in the last moment God reacted and turned this unholy wedding ceremony into stone.

The rest of the scenery is no less bizarre. Notice the trees whose crowns have been twisted by wind. Moreover, the wind makes creepy noises passing through the earth columns. Nearby are also two highly mineralised springs called Devils Waters for the red colour of their highly mineralised water.

❾ Vlasina

12 km - Surdulica

This region around Vlasina Lake (average height of 1200 m) is situated in the southeastern corner of Serbia, some 360 km from Belgrade. Vlasina Lake is artificial, made in 1949 through the construction of a dam on the river Vlasina which gradually flooded the lower parts of the land. The lush plants that were submerged under water started to decay creating the small floating peat-islands that soon became the symbol of the Lake. Today they are quite rare, but still occasionally appear.
The wet and very cold climate (the average yearly temperature is just 6°C) and the volcanic ground create special conditions for the animals and plants of the region. Plants, such as the carnivore roundleaf sundew or the downy birch,

Morning over Vlasina

which live on the floating islands, are exceptional sights to be found in Europe.
Mountain peaks, small gorges, springs and rivers

with their waterfalls – all of this can be seen on the walks in the lake's vicinity. Apart from the natural beauty, one can also visit the 17th c. churches in the villages of Božica and Palja, while the far flung villages are an ethnographic attraction in themselves.

Provisions for tourists are grouped on the west side of the lake with the hotels "Vlasina" and "Narcis", a mobile home campsite and holiday houses.

❿ Vranje

🏠 71.500

ℹ 29. novembra 2
17000 Vranje
017/417-545

☎ 017/21-201

🚉 017/21-714

106 km - Niš

The southernmost city of Serbia, Vranje lies just 35 km from the Macedonian border. Sheltered from the winds by the neighbouring hills it lies on the Gradska River and enjoys a pleasant mild climate. The town is known for its oriental monuments and the fairly well preserved spirit of days gone by.

Vranje, back then only a village lying under a castle of the same name, was first mentioned in 1093. It was then that this Byzantine possession was plundered by the Serbian ruler Vukan. It became a constituent part of Serbia at the beginning of the 13th century after the conquests of Stefan the First-Crowned. With the disappearance of central power in the Serbian state, the region of Vranje fell into the hands of the noble Vlatković family that held it until 1423 when its last member joined it to the rest of the Serbia. Pillaged badly in 1412, Vranje was conquered by the Ottoman Turks in 1455. Their long rule left a permanent imprint on the land and spirit of Vranje. In 1557 Vranje became the seat of the orthodox bishop whose presence led to

The Christians lived through troublesome times having to buy all rights from the new usurpers. The city was liberated in 1878 and from that time started to prosper and grow. Occupied in the First and Second World War by the Bulgarians, the people of Vranje suffered a lot resisting the attempts of ethnic assimilation and genocide, paying the price with hundreds of civilians shot and thousands incarcerated.

In the centre of the town, by the main square, Trg Maršala Tita, stands the **Church** dedicated to the Holy Trinity. It was finished in 1841 however its large size provoked local Turks and Albanians who burned it soon afterwards. Following the

Icon of St Michael by Dičo Zograf, Vranje Cathedral

iconostasis carved by local folk artisans with rich forms and ornaments. The most interesting artefacts here are the icons on the iconostasis created by Dimitar Krstević, called Dičo Zograf, in 1859/60. He painted the icons in the first section, the ones in the inter-columnar spaces as well as those in the second and the third sections of the church. Icons from the parapet, the Royal Doors and the cross on the top were painted by two far less skillful artists. Krstević stands as the most important and the most productive master of late Byzantine painting in the region. His works are influenced by the Italo-Cretan School as well by baroque decoration which is especially visible in the floral motives. The colours Krstević uses on the icons are vivid and bright, always in stark contrast one with the other. Though he adheres mainly to the style of traditional idealism in presenting ecclesiastical subjects, he distinguishes himself as an individual with genuine inspiration.

obtaining of a new permit, it was rebuilt in 1858 by the Kosta Damjanov, the brother of the even more famous Andrija. It is a typical example of 19th c. Christian architecture in the Ottoman Balkans: with no bell tower and low, blind domes it was hidden amongst ordinary houses; furthermore, it was dug down into the ground to look even less conspicuous. The church has portions of its walls painted in a naïve fashion and an

Dances of Vranje are known for their oriental flair

the growing importance of the municipality. In the 18th c. the town was terrorised by Albanians who even controlled the local Turkish pasha.

Front part of the Pasha's residences

In front of the church stands the modest 1922 **Obelisk** dedicated to the victims of the Bulgarian terror during their occupation in the First World War. Destroyed when the occupying Bulgarian forces returned in 1941, it was reconstructed through the donations of local people in 1951.

Down Kralja Stefana Prvovenčanog St one reaches Baba Zlatina Street starting on the left hand side. This old residential street of the Christian quarter, lined with walls enclosing courtyards in true Turkish fashion, is named after the grandmother (*baba*) of the writer Bora Stanković. Their house at No. 7 is today the **Museum of Bora Stanković**

(*tel. 017/23-073*). In the pleasant old-time courtyard filled with greenery that characterised the Balkan towns of Turkish days, stands the house in which Stanković was born in 1875. The edifice, typical for middle class families in Vranje, was built some 20 years earlier in the style of the South Morava region, with an open porch and a small terrace. It is filled with furniture and objects from the 19th c. as well as a small exhibition dedicated to the work of Stanković.

On the other side of the Orthodox Cathedral stretches the central pedestrian zone lined with shops and cafés that will lead one to the **Pasha's Residences** (*Pašini konaci*)

in Pionirska Street. The two neighbouring buildings were erected in 1765 by Raif-beg Džinić in the Ottoman style. The daughter of the last pasha sold it to the Serb bishop who then donated it for educational purposes so that in 1881 here opened the first high school in Vranje. The front edifice, called selamluk, was used by the pasha and other men, while the backside one (haremluk) was used as his wives' dwellings. Today the front building houses the local **Museum** (*Narodni muzej, tel. 017/24-018*) displaying archeological findings, Roman items, medieval coins, folk costumes and crafts. The building of Haremluk has been transformed into the "Simpo" company club with several dining halls.

The pedestrian zone ends at Trg Republike Square. In the middle of the square stands the **Monument to the Liberators of Vranje in 1878**, the work of the sculptor Simeon Roksandić from 1903. The monument shared the misfortunes of the city during the two

Bora Stanković's House

Bulgarian occupations and was pulled down twice. Therefore the figure of the Serbian solider lacks a hand and some parts are broken, but it holds a special place in the heart of all residents of Vranje who nicknamed him Čika-Mita ("Uncle Mita").

Behind the monument stands the large building of **Staro Načelstvo** (The Old District County). It is

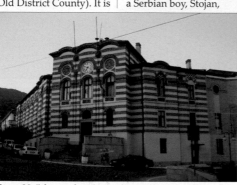

Staro Načelstvo, showing an interesting mix of Byzantine and Morava architectural schools

the most celebrated work of the architect Petar Popović, dating from the year 1908, in which he combined the influences of the Byzantine and Morava School of architecture visible in the rich decoration of the façades.

The Street V kongresa continues further north to the **Old Hammam** (*Stari amam*). This small brick and stone edifice was built at the end of the 17th c. and has only one bathtub that was used alternatively by men and women.

The upper part of the city was once mostly inhabited by the Turks while today the prevailing population here is Roma, giving it a distinctive, lively appearance. The centre of this quarter is Trg Slobode. On the left hand side is Niška St. leading into Crnogor-

ska St. that takes one to the **White Bridge** (*Beli most*). This small, graceful bridge above the Gradska River was constructed in 1844 by Lady Ajša "to repent her sins and the sins of her parents" as reads the memorial tablet in the Arabic script. The local legend tells another story: the Turkish girl Ajša fell in love with a Serbian boy, Stojan, and was mistakenly killed by her father who then decided to build a bridge in her memory.

Just by the bridge stands the **Church of St Nicolas**, the oldest one in the town. It was probably built by the noble Bagaš family. In the mid 14th c. the town of Vranje was donated to the Hilandar monastery along with this church according to the testament of Nikola

Bagaš. Torn down during the Turkish reign, it was rebuilt in 1894.

ENVIRONS:

After some 4 km along the winding road through Pržar, a picturesque northern suburb of Vranje, one reaches the ruins of a castle known as **Markovo kale** ("Marko's Fortress"). The name relates to Marko Kraljević, the most significant figure in Serbian folk poetry, though neither him nor his family ever ruled in regions this far north. The fort was built much earlier than the epoch of Marko's time, probably in the 11th c., and its name Vranje later spread to both the settlement and the whole area. Of the triangular fort, two towers and some portions of the wall still remain. From here there is a good view over the town and the Binačka Morava valley.

⓫ Prohor Pčinjski

29km - Vranje

The monastery is situated on the border with Republic of Macedonia, in the valley of the river Pčinja. To reach it, take the road from Vranje towards Skopje and the exit for the village of Ristovac. After 12 kilometres, take a right turn and then travel for another 10 km.

Markovo Kale Castle ruins

Prohor Pčinjski monastery compound

The monastery is dedicated to a South Slav saint, St Prohor (feast day: 15th January), who lived as a hermit in this secluded area. The story goes as follows: one day Roman Diogenes, a high Byzantine noble, was hunting in the area when he met Prohor who foresaw that Roman was going to become the Emperor. As the prophecy came true, the thankful Emperor (1068-1071) came back to this place to express his gratitude to the hermit but then found out that the old man had already died. On the spot of Prohor's cave the Emperor built the monastery dedicated to the saint. The 11th c. church was damaged in the Cuman onslaught but was thoroughly renovated by the Serbian King Milutin in the early 14th century. The monastery was devastated several more times, the most terrrible time being in 1371 by the Turks who almost leveled it to the ground, and the last time in 1817 by ethnic Albanians. After the liberation from the Turks, the present-day large church with six domes and a bell tower was built in 1898 enclosing the remains of the older temple within its walls.

The oldest part of the church is its NW part that has strangely orientated apse. The relics of St Prohor were held

Fresco of St Prohor

here. The frescoes of very good quality were created at the time of its renovation at the end of the 15th c. The rest of the church was painted in 1904 by T. Jovanović from Kumanovo who made several interesting compositions such as the one depicting the abbot and greatest benefactor along with people from nearby villages restoring the monastery (on the left-hand wall by the western entrance). On the south wall scenes from the history of the monastery are depicted while on the north wall the South Slav anchorites Jovan Rilski, Joakim Osogovski and Serbian saints such as St Prince Lazar can be observed.

The main building of the residence hall is one of the most monumental edifices of traditional architecture from the 18th c to be seen in the region.

In 1944 members of the communist party from Macedonia met here to proclaim Macedonia as one of the six republics of the emerging socialist Yugoslavia. In choosing this monastery they had the intention to push the boundary as far north as possible. Nevertheless, when the new borders were drawn up in 1945 the monastery was left in Serbia as it had been from 1878.

Church interior

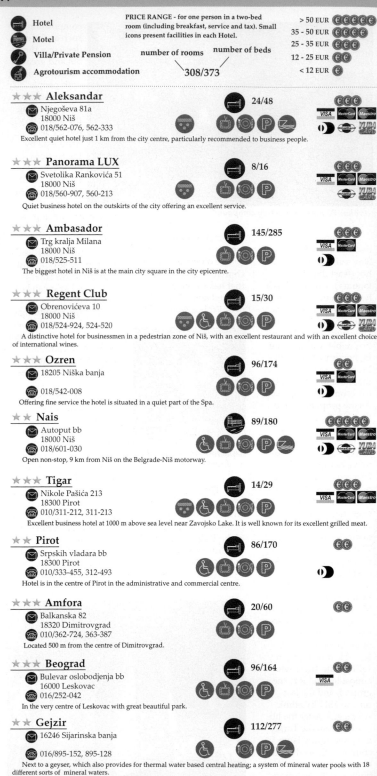

Hotel

Motel

Villa/Private Pension

Agrotourism accommodation

PRICE RANGE - for one person in a two-bed room (including breakfast, service and tax). Small icons present facilities in each Hotel.

number of rooms   number of beds

308/373

> 50 EUR
35 - 50 EUR
25 - 35 EUR
12 - 25 EUR
< 12 EUR

★ ★ ★ Aleksandar

Njegoševa 81a
18000 Niš
018/562-076, 562-333

24/48

Excellent quiet hotel just 1 km from the city centre, particularly recommended to business people.

★ ★ ★ Panorama LUX

Svetolika Rankovića 51
18000 Niš
018/560-907, 560-213

8/16

Quiet business hotel on the outskirts of the city offering an excellent service.

★ ★ ★ Ambasador

Trg kralja Milana
18000 Niš
018/525-511

145/285

The biggest hotel in Niš is at the main city square in the city epicentre.

★ ★ ★ Regent Club

Obrenovićeva 10
18000 Niš
018/524-924, 524-520

15/30

A distinctive hotel for businessmen in a pedestrian zone of Niš, with an excellent restaurant and with an excellent choice of international wines.

★ ★ ★ Ozren

18205 Niška banja

018/542-008

96/174

Offering fine service the hotel is situated in a quiet part of the Spa.

★ ★ Nais

Autoput bb
18000 Niš
018/601-030

89/180

Open non-stop, 9 km from Niš on the Belgrade-Niš motorway.

★ ★ ★ Tigar

Nikole Pašića 213
18300 Pirot
010/311-212, 311-213

14/29

Excellent business hotel at 1000 m above sea level near Zavojsko Lake. It is well known for its excellent grilled meat.

★ ★ Pirot

Srpskih vladara bb
18300 Pirot
010/333-455, 312-493

86/170

Hotel is in the centre of Pirot in the administrative and commercial centre.

★ ★ ★ Amfora

Balkanska 82
18320 Dimitrovgrad
010/362-724, 363-387

20/60

Located 500 m from the centre of Dimitrovgrad.

★ ★ ★ Beograd

Bulevar oslobodjenja bb
16000 Leskovac
016/252-042

96/164

In the very centre of Leskovac with great beautiful park.

★ ★ Gejzir

16246 Sijarinska banja

016/895-152, 895-128

112/277

Next to a geyser, which also provides for thermal water based central heating; a system of mineral water pools with 18 different sorts of mineral waters.

HOTEL

With three stars, just one kilometer from the centre of the town. Exclusive accomodation in 7 apartments, 2 semi-apartments, 2 rooms with French bed and 13 double rooms, the whole capacity of 48 beds. Each room has the top-quality equipment, including a bathroom, hairdryer, cable TV, minibar, telephone, wireless internet, air-conditioning. All hotels on the panoramic side of the hotel have a terrace.

RECEPTION DESK

At our guests' disposal 24 hours a day, equipped with a fax machine, internet, exchange office and a safe deposit box.

RESTAURANT

Capacity - 80 seats and a garden seating additional 60. It offers services of lunch on the basis of buffet, full- and half-board as well as a la carte services for hotel and external guests.

SNACK BAR

Foreign and domestic drinks, coffee and cold snacks that are basis of our room-service.

PROMOTION HALL

On the premisses of the restaurant we offer facilitating symposiums, promotions and other business gatherings of up to 80 people with the use of most up-to-date equipment - speakers, video-data beam with a screen, PC, video beam, fax- and copy-machine, videorecorder, DVD-player. If needed, the gatherings can be filmed.

SWIMMING POOL

Next to the restaurant garden lies an open pool for our guests' exclusive use.

PARKING

Large closed parking, guarded 24-hours, on the panoramic side of the hotel.

ıl. Njegoševa 81a, 18000 Niš   tel: +38118 562-333, 562-332, 562-076   fax: +38118 562-056
il: hotelaleksandar@medianis.net; info@hotel-aleksandar.com   web: www.hotel-aleksandar.com

☆ Džep
16222 Predejane
016/836154

11/29

A motel in Grdelica gorge, beautiful surroundings, international guests.

☆ ☆☆ Hammeum
Knez Mihailova 2
18400 Prokuplje
027/324-666, 324-161

40/62

Hotel of a long tradition and remarkable hospitality, famous for excellent grill.

☆ ☆ Radan
18433 Prolom banja
027/88-111, 88-162

215/440

Situated on a really beautiful spot, close to the Djavolja Varoš; numerous discounts.

☆ ☆ Srbija
Kralja Petra I bb
17530 Surdulica
017/815-043

44/80

Hotel is near to Vlasina lake.

☆ Jezero
17532 Vlasina
Vlasinsko jezero
017/86-502, 86-202

54/102

At 1260 m, hotel has a beautiful terrace overlooking the Lake.

☆ ☆ Vlasina
17533 Vlasina
Vlasinsko jezero
017/815-400

75/200

Quiet hotel at 1200 m with very good service.

☆ Han
Beogradska 71
17510 Vladičin Han
017/476-666

17/33

Situated in a forest, with a nice garden always in shade.

☆ ☆☆ Simpo Pržar
Pržanska bb
17000 Vranje
017/23-900

20/34

Just at the hill nearby, hotel overlooks the city of Vranje.

☆ ☆☆ Vranje
Trg republike 4
17500 Vranje
017/22-366

60/150

Hotel is in the very centre of the city.

☆ ☆☆ Železničar
Kralja Petra 1
17542 Vranjska Banja
017/546-432, 545-052

51/65

Due to various facilities hotel is suitable for longer stays.

Floating restaurant on Nišava River

Fish restaurant  National restaurant   International restaurant

Orač
 Knjaževačka 3
18000 Niš
018/714-124

 10-23
The restaurant with distinguished specialties of southern Serbia and with a scent of the old Niš.

Amerikanac
Kovanlučka 10
18000 Niš
018/594-489

 10-24
Built in a truly Serbian style, in the part of the city called Palilula; regular customers during the last 40 years.

Biser
Koste Stamenkovića 1
18000 Niš
018/248-205

 07-01
In the very centre of the city, ethnic styled. A lot of woodwork, tasty food.

Sindjelić
Nikole Pašića 36
18000 Niš
018/512-550, 512-548

 08-01
This restaurant in the very heart of the city in a house protected by the state. It's built in an archaic style, with a big garden and quiet atmosphere. Guests are of all ages, and live music is performed every day.

Zlatni kotlić
Koste Stamenkovića 2a
18000 Niš
018/521-909

 08-23
In the Niš city centre, 18 years old, built in woods, a small lovely garden, small benches both in the garden and inside. One of the total of two fish restaurants in Niš.

Nišlijska mehana
Prvomajska 49
18000 Niš
018/511-111

 08-24
An old house, reminding us of the building of the southern Serbia, decorated with recongnizable 19th century Serbia details such as waistcoats, national footwear *opanci*, water jugs etc. Excellent grilled meat.

Hamam
Tvrdjava Niš
18000 Niš
018/513-444

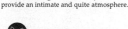 07-23
A fine looking restaurant situated in the old Turkish baths. Thick walls provide an intimate and quite atmosphere.

Krčma Ladna voda
Nikole Pašića bb
18300 Pirot
010/26-386

 10-22
This samll resturant is situated in an old-fashioned surroundings of a 19th century house, just in front of the Hristić family house. "Ladna Voda" offers a vevriety of local wines.

Mali pevac
Nikole Pašića 35
18300 Pirot
010/335-975

 08-23
Close to the Veliko Mesto, in the part of the city called Tijabara, the oldest tavern in the town, near to the Museum; pleasant ambient, many of celebrities were among its guests.

Zlatno bure
Mlinska 32
16000 Leskovac
016/242-733

 07-23
Enjoy in a pleasant atmosphere of the restaurant and in a wide range of national specialties.

Kondir
Masarikov trg 66
16000 Leskovac
016/252-506

 08-23
A small restaurant in the very centre of the city, interior in an old-fashion style with a pot as its trademark; excelent food.

Cap Cap
Južnomoravskih brigada 173
16000 Leskovac
016/55-523

 08-24
Offering great choice of grill specialties; nonetheless, pizza and other international dishes are also on offer

Boemi
Trg Republike 3
17000 Vranje
016/22-880

 08-24
Fish and national specialties in a very pleasant atmosphere.

Vranjski merak
Trg Republike 4
17000 Vranje
016/32-759

 07-23
The restaurant is placed in the very centre of the city, opposite to the City Council.

Haremluk
Pionirska bb
17000 Vranje
016/431-696

 10-24
A number of national specialties at this restaurant, situated in a unique building from the beginning of the 19th century.

KOSOVO AND METOHIJA

The southern Serbian autonomous province of Kosovo and Metohija is under UN administration since 1999 following the war in which NATO sided with the ethnic Albanian terrorists against the Serbs. Since then more than 250,000 non-Albanians have departed from the province and the Serbs are left in fear of their lives. Their existence is reduced to living in besieged enclaves and protected ghettos in the towns.

The two names of the province come from the two plains in which it is situated. In the east lies Kosovo with the rivers of Ibar, Lab and Sitnica. In the west lies Metohija where Beli Drim is the main waterway. The two are separated with the hilly area of Drenica and enclosed from all sides by high mountains. Looking towards Albania is Prokletije, whose peak Djeravica (2656m) is the highest in Serbia. To the north is Mokra Gora, to the east Kopaonik while the south side is sheltered by the imposing Šara Mountain and the Crna Gora hills north of Skopje.

The plain of Kosovo ("Field of Blackbirds") north of the regional capital Priština, gave the name to the whole region. This is where the legendary battle took place in 1389 making it the cornerstone of Serbian epic poetry. The mountains surrounding it are rich in ore: Novo Brdo was the largest silver mine in Europe until its fall to the Turks in 1455. Today, ruins, though impressive, are all that remain above the small village. By Kosovska Mitrovica, a town divided into Serbian and Albanian parts, lay the famous Trepča mines.

Metohija got its name from the large monastic estates (*metoh*) that were granted by the Nemanjić rulers in this fertile region. The Albanians use the name Dukadjin derived from one of the tribes that descended from the Albanian mountains here in the 16th century and onwards. The twin names speak loudly about the divided identity of the region. The medieval Serbian legacy although persecuted and destroyed for centuries by Muslim domination is still alive in the monasteries of Peć, the traditional seat of the Serb patriarch, and Visoki

Dečani, the largest surviving structure from the middle ages. As the monasteries needed wine, numerous vineyards embellish the landscape and local wines were well known for their excellence before the war. On the southern border lies Prizren, the main town of the Metohija region and once the city much frequented by the wandering Kings of the Nemanjić dynasty, with its many medieval churches, imposing mosques and attractive cityscape.

In most of the province all that is left from the Serbs who lived there are the names of the places and the ruins of churches: more than 93% of the names of the places and more than a thousand medieval monuments are proof of their lively ethnic and cultural presence. Since the 7th century the region has been inhabited almost exclusively by Serbs who were incorporated into the Serbian state in the early 13th century. In the following two centuries the region flourished due to its central position in Serbia. In 1455, Turkish dominance prevailed and, due to its favoring of Muslims over Christians, the influx of Albanians into Kosovo began. In spite of their utter deprivation the Serbs were the majority in the population until the mid 19th century when the real terror, funded by the Ottoman administration began. From here on the history of Kosovo is a sad story of how violence, dishonesty and money rule our world. Stripped of all their rights and property by the Albanian feudal lords, the Serbs fled in large numbers until, in 1912 Serbia managed to recover its ancient lands. However, the rich and conservative Albanian leaders that won and preserved their possessions by force were not willing to succumb to a Christian state where everyone would have equal rights. They opted for violent resistance. In both World Wars the Albanians aligned with the losing sides and suffered little consequences. After the war, the communist regime provided the Albanians with the status of an autonomous province, the equal use of language in all institutions, a university, TV and radio stations, all but total independence. From the 1960s there has been a boom in the birthrate of Kosovo Albanians. They had the highest annual growth rate in Europe – 2,68 percent in

1990. By 1981 the Serbs made up a meager 11% and the Albanians now making 82% of the populace began to make ever more vocal demands for a republic (since the autonomous provinces of Yugoslavia did not have the formal right to secession). The deprived conditions the Serbs were experiencing in Kosovo and Metohija were used by Milošević to obtain his first major political successes. The Milošević police regime that terrorized all of Serbia was made to look even worse there. As the whole world turned against this dictator, it was only the Albanians who were made to appear as the victims. In 1997 the terrorist Kosovo Liberation Army began attacks on the Serbian police, the army, Serbian civilians and on Albanians who did not approve of their methods. Legitimate reprisals against these terrorists by police were shown as ethnic cleansing and NATO intervened (without a UN resolution) by bombing Serbia in 1999. The Serb army and police withdrew and the province became occupied by NATO forces with a UN mandate. The Albanian terrorists were legalized and transformed into the Kosovo Protection Corps and the province was divided into five sectors: US, British, French, Italian and German. Since the arrival of the NATO forces more than 950 Serbs were killed (one percent of the remaining number) and hundreds of churches, graveyards and other Serb-related monuments were destroyed. The organized attack on Serbian villages and churches in March of 2004 showed clearly that no progress has been made at all. The Serbs of Kosovo are today the only people in Europe that do not have a single of their basic rights even though they live under direct UN supervision. They have no certitude for their lives outside of the UN protected enclaves, neither the right to move, nor the right to work. This disorganized province is Europe's black hole of drugs, arms and human trafficking controlled by Albanian mafia.

1 Priština

2 Gračanica

3 National Park "Šara"

4 Prizren

5 Peć

6 Pećka Patrijašija

7 Visoki Dečani

Kuršumlija

Leskovac

Kuršumlijska Banja

Prolom Banja

Prekopčelica

Caričin Grad

Lebane

Neposavac

iska

Zvečan

Kosovska Mitrovica

Vučitrn

Srbica

Devič

Podujevo

Medvedja

Sijarinska Banja

①

Priština

Gazimestan

Gračanica

②

Novo Brdo

Devič

Markovo Kale

Lapušnik

Liplian

Ulpiana

Binačka Morava

Vranje

Gnjilane

Bujanovačka Banja

Bujanovac

Kiokot Banja

Uroševac

Preševo

Preševo

④

Prizren

Devič

③

National Park Šar Planina

Tetovo

Djeneral Janković

SKOPJE 42km

MK

Zvečan castle above Kosovska Mitrovica

① Priština

750.000

125 km - Niš

Priština is the regional capital of Kosovo & Metohija and the largest city of the province. It lies at the centre of the Kosovo plain. It became part of Serbia in the late 12th century when it began developing. It was to reach its zenith in the 14th and 15th centuries as a trading town where the Nemanjić dynasty lived. Yet it remained in the shadow of the wealthy mining town Novo Brdo (20 km east of town). For a time Vuk Branković, the legendary traitor of the Serbian Kosovo epic, also resided here before in 1396 the Turks took possession of the town (though the countryside remained in Serbian hands for some time). When in 1455 the Turks conquered Novo Brdo, the already Ottoman Priština took its place and started developing into a larger town. In the 18th century it became one of the biggest cities in the region. However, in the next century it suffered seriously due to the devastating fires of 1859 and 1869. In 1874 it was connected with Skopje and Thessalonica by rail yet due to the turbulence caused by conservative Muslim Albanians the

station had to be located eight kilometres from the city. This fact largely contributed to the further decline of the city. Nevertheless, the town gradually modernised. Important development occurred after WWII when Priština became the seat of the province and the new industrial centre, both these factors quickly changing its appearance into that of a modern city with residential blocks and boomtown suburbs. During the 1980's and 1990's the town existed in two separate realities – Albanian and Serbian: both communities ignored one another and used separate schools, hospitals and cafés. After the 1999 NATO bombing that seriously destroyed much of the town buildings and monuments, and with the consequent retreat of the Serbian army and the police most of the city's 40,000 Serbs felt insecure and left for Serbia proper. Those that remained were reduced to living in several apartment blocks protected by the international forces but with no possibility of free movement. In March of 2004 the handful of remaining Serbs were forced out of their homes. Today not one Serb lives in Priština, a blatant example of the process of ethnic cleans-

ing in Kosovo.

The old centre of the town is dominated by the **Fatih Mosque** in the ancient Turkish quarter. The mosque is the most important Ottoman monument in Priština. Its many names (Fatih, Imperial, Colorful, Great) only give an idea of the

Fatih Mosque, central Priština

profound impression it creates in reality. This graceful edifice was built in 1461 during the reign of Sultan Mohamed the Conqueror, who the Turks call *el-Fatih*. As an imperial mosque it was constructed out of stone with a 13.5 m wide dome. The porch is covered by three smaller cupolas and held up by eight-sided columns. The ceilings, as well as those inside, are painted al secco with bright colored ornaments. The tall and slender minaret is extraordinarily graceful. Nearby stands the 19th century **Clock Tower**, 15 m tall with an attractive redbrick top. Close to the Fatih mosque are situated two Turkish baths. The **Large Hammam** to be found here has fifteen cupolas and dates back to the early 15th century while the smaller one is

Puzzling forms of the University Library

The legend of the battle of Kosovo is fundamental to the Serbian epic poetry that flourished from 15th to 19th centuries. The heroes of these poems quickly became widely known across the Balkans and further a field, so that by the mid 16th century Shakespeare's contemporaries were addressing the themes from these poems in their plays. During the turbulent times for the Serbs under Turkish rule, the legend of the celebrated battle became a stimulating motive for the continued struggle against the Ottomans, the goal of liberation sometimes being referred to as the "Revenge of Kosovo".

The reality behind the legend is that on the 28th of June 1389, St Vid day or Vidovdan as it is known in the traditional Serbian calendar, two vast armies clashed on the Field of Blackbirds (*Kosovo polje*) just north of Priština. One army was led by Prince Lazar and helped by his son-in-law Vuk Branković, a nobleman who controlled the region of Kosovo, and also by the troops King Tvrtko of Bosnia sent, Prince Lazar's ally who wisely preempted the approaching Turkish threat. The other army was that of Sultan Murad I whose troops included many of his Christian vassals, amongst others, several Serb feudalists. The fierce and bloody battle was a draw, ending in the death of both the commanders-in-chief and a mutual drawback. However, while Murad, who was assassinated in his tent by a Serbian knight pretending to bear important news, was succeeded by his son Bajezid I, Prince Lazar's throne was inherited by his juvenile son Stefan. Unready for further clashes Lazar's widow recognized Turkish suzerainty and began paying tributes to the Ottomans. Vuk and Tvrtko remained fully independent.

The legend however contains other aspects that have been told and retold through the ages. Once aware of the threat from the Turks – a far stronger foe than can be fought to success, Prince Lazar faces the dilemma of whether to submit at once or, regardless of the outcome, to go out and fight. He decides to fight and to lose the battle here on earth for the far greater victory of belonging to the eternal "kingdom of heaven". Vuk Branković on the eve of the battle, wishing to conceal his treason, accuses the brave and honest knight Miloš Obilić of being disloyal. In order to prove him wrong, Obilić pledges that he will kill the Sultan to prove his innocence. The legend has it that the next day Vuk Branković fled the battlefield causing Serbian defeat (historically incorrect), whilst Miloš Obilić killed the Sultan earning everlasting glory.

even older; both are out of use. An eye catching 19th century town building, the Emendžik konak, houses the **Museum of Kosovo** (*open Tue-Sat 9.30 a.m. to 5 p.m.*) with an interesting display about the local prehistory.

Another mosque to be found not far from here is the Stone or **Baazar Mosque**. It was built by Sultan Bajezid soon after the battle of Kosovo (1389), making it the oldest surviving mosque in Serbia. The women's gallery is notable for its carvings. Around the interior of the dome are beautiful, intricate, floral designs.

The Serbian church dedicated to St Nicholas was built at the beginning of the 19th century and possessed

a uniquely carved iconostasis with numerous decorations of people, animals and plants. Unfortunately, today only blackened walls remain after it was torched in March of 2004.

The city centre is dominated by modern buildings such as the tall Television and Radio building, the fantastic National and University library from 1981 or the

sports centre complex that used to be called "Boro and Ramiz", named after a Serbian and an ethnic Albanian who died together fighting the Nazis.

ENVIRONS:

North of Priština lies the legendary **Kosovo Polje** – "Field of Blackbirds". The site of the famous battle of 1389 is marked today by several monuments. **Sultan Murad's Turbe** stands close to the village of Mazgit on the left from the Mitrovica-Priština road. This is the place from which the sultan commanded the army and where he was killed. The original *turbe* (mausoleum) was built previously by Murad's son Bajezid in the late 14th century. The present day edifice is from the 19th century and is a fine example of the so-called "Turkish baroque". The sultan's bowels are kept in the turbe while the rest of his body is buried in Bursa, Turkey. On the other side of the ancient battleground stands the **"Monument to Kosovo Heroes"**, a tall tower designed by Professor Aleksandar Deroko in 1953 to be reminiscent of medieval towers. The interior has an inscription with lines of the epic poems on Kosovo battle. At the top of

Sports centre

the 25 metre tall tower there is a bronze relief with depictions of the course of the battle; from here there is a perfect view over the "Field of Blackbirds". Next to it is the reconstruction of the marble **"Kosovo Pillar"** on which are inscribed verses about the battle written by Stefan Lazarević (at the beginning of the 15th century) in old Serbian script and in the modern variant. Close by lies the octagonal **Barjaktar Turbe** built in the 15th century. Here can be found the grave of the Turkish standard-bearer, the anonymous hero of the battle. The turbe is surrounded by ornate Turkish gravestones.

On the southern outskirts of Priština the remains of **Ulpiana** can be found, the most important Roman city in Kosovo. The town prospered from the 2nd to the 4th century AD but was sacked by the Goths and then destroyed in the 518 earthquake. The site's most interesting feature is the unearthed necropolis with white marble sarcophagi.

Gračanica monastery, seen from the west

❷ Gračanica

10 km - Priština

The village of Gračanica, one of the last inhabited by the Serbs in the area, lies just 10 km East of Priština. A monastery of the same name, one of the finest examples of Byzantine architecture in the world, is situated in the village.

The present-day church of the monastery complex was built by King Milutin (1284-1321) on the site of an earlier one. It was the last great endowment of the King who, alone, commissioned and reconstructed some 42 churches and monasteries. Gračanica is the pinnacle of his construction works and indeed of the whole Serbian branch of Byzantine architecture, which king Milutin cherished in his "byzantinisation" of Serbia. It was finished in 1321 after some eight years of work and immediately became the seat of the bishopric.

The church is the only remaining part of the monastery complex as the rest fell pray to the Turkish raids already in the late 14th century. The open narthex that disturbs the harmony of the whole structure was added in 1383 to protect the frescoes on the outer wall. It was then walled up in the 16th century to provide more space for new frescoes. Gračanica is also famous as the home of one of the first printing-houses in Serbia: in 1539 the monks bought a printing press and printed valuable incunabula here.

Although the architect of the church is unknown, his work is today recognized by anyone who explores the riches of the Byzantine culture. The structure is however not typical; like the other features of Gračanica, its construction breaks many of the given conventions of the time. The cross-in-square plan and the five cupolas are usual elements as is the elaborate brick and stone arrangement of the walls. Yet, that is where the similarities end: the daring solution of the anonymous architect

Queen Simonida, King Milutin's young bride

strives for at that time yet unseen verticality, an effect achieved by the pyramidal arrangement of masses that invites the gaze upward. Note the elongated cupolas that appear here for the first time and the pointed arches under the main dome - a lesson learned from the visual effects of gothic cathedrals.

The narthex is made out of inferior material but its wide double arches follow the original pattern. Some of the frescoes from 1570 were taken off the walls and moved to the monastery's treasury, in order to give it back the original appearance. Those remaining include a row portraying the Patriarchs of the Serbian church, from St Sava to Makarije Sokolović (1557-71), and also one showing the death of a local metropolitan Dionisije.

Inside the nave of the church one finds oneself in front of an exquisite and almost entirely preserved ensemble of 14th century wall paintings. These were ordered by Milutin's trusty helper, the archbishop Danilo, who completed the arrangement of the interior in 1321-22 after Milutin's death. The artists, probably the court painters Michaelos and Eutichios, were surely the greatest masters of their time, paying close attention to the newest trends coming over Constantinople. The ingenuity of the Gračanica frescoes lies in the fact that Danilo's iconographic concept disregarded some of the traditional rules, and the skilled painters took this concept and painted in manner that was beyond the conventions of the time.

On the east wall of the outer narthex is a painting of the Last Judgment that is rich in exciting details such as the portrayals of land and sea creatures. On the entranceway arch is a depiction of the old King Milutin holding a model of the church and of his young Byzantine wife Simonida both being crowned by angels sent by Christ. There are two additional portraits of Milutin in this church. One in which he is seen with his mother Jelena, where he is represented as monk, which he never was. This was needed for his sanctification that came three years after his death. Milutin was very far from being a saint, if nothing else than for his five politically motivated marriages, but he aided the Church in many ways, not least with his endowments. Historically the most interesting fresco is the one showing the Nemanjić family tree, a composition painted here for the first time with the clear intention of promoting Milutin's supremacy over his older brother Dragutin's family in the line of descent. Iconography of the family tree imitates the Tree of Jesse, only here Stefan Nemanja is at the root and Milutin at the top. On the northern wall is written the founding charter of the monastery listing all its posses-

King Milutin with the model of the Gračanica church

sions. On the south wall of the nave is a huge composition of the Assumption of the Virgin Mary. In other parts of the church the paintings are lined in three levels: Saints (over 80 figures and 150 busts), Stories from Christ's life and Church feasts. The main cupola space is given to the monumental frescoe of "Christ the Pantokrator" ("Almighty") and the apse for the "Adoration of the Lamb" and the "Communion of the Apostles". In prothesis is depicted the life of St Nicholas; an excellent portrait of St John the Baptist can be seen in diaconicon. The last fascinating feature of the Gračanica monastery is a narrow stairway carved into the southern pier by the entrance leading to the katihumena, a royal lodge on the upper floor.

The monastery treasury keeps a valuable collection of 16th to 19th century icons.

❸ National Park "Šar-planina"

125 km - Priština

Šar-planina or more simply Šara, as it is known, is situated in the south western corner of Kosovo and Metohija. This mountain is 80km long and marks the border of the Adriatic river basin and the Vardar river basin aswell as the border between Serbia and Macedonia. The Šara massif, with 12 glacial lakes below its numerous peaks, among which the highest is Peskovi at 2651m, is a perfect example of the carst mountain relief. Due to its outstanding natural beauty, it has been declared a national park. Here one can find more than 200 species of birds (which make up to 60% of those found in Serbia), among which are the bearded vulture, the grey-haired vulture, the grey eagle and also, grouse. The mountain range is likewise known for its exceptionally beautiful butterflies of which there are 147 different kinds. There are many interesting mammals to be found here too, such as otters, pine martens, stone martens, Dinaric field voles, Balkan wildcats aswell as chamoix and bears.

Šar-planinac sheepdog

Šara is most famous for a breed of dog native to these parts called the *Šar-planinac* or Illyrian Sheepdog – celebrated for its courage, strength and reliability. One can also find several rare types of trees here such as whole woods of Bosnian and Macedoniana pine as well as of Macedonian oak.

❹ Prizren

 80.500

87 km - Priština

Set on the slopes of the imposing Šara Mountain where the river Bistrica meets the White Drim which carries with it warm air from the Mediterranean, Prizren has been inhabited since ancient times. While it was contested between the two Illyrian tribes, the Dardans and the Autariates, the Romans took the opportunity and annexed the town, naming it *Theranda*. The Serbs who settled here in the early 7th century gave it the present day name of Prizren. In the next centuries it remained in Byzantine hands but as it stood close to the hub of the Serbian state, many connections were established, not least through the local orthodox bishopric. In 1073 the Serbian Prince Konstantin Bodin was proclaimed here as the Emperor of Bulgaria and from here he led a short-lived insurrection against the Byzantines. After several shorter periods of Serbian rule, Prizren finally fell to Serbia in 1220 and immediately became one of its most important towns. In the next 150 years it was one of the favorite residences of the itinerant Nemanjić rulers. In the 14th century, it was a magnificent town, full of old and new churches, home to many craftsmen and tradesmen, including several financiers of the state. With the arrival of the Turkish threat and the insecurity of the roads, harder times were experienced

Panoramic view of Prizren from its fortress Kaljaja

Old Turkish bridge over the Bistrica River

in the 15th century. The Turks took possession of the town in 1455 and a new era began regarding its development and appearance: tall walls were built behind which were situated enclosed gardens full of greenery, while channels of clear water ran through the middle of streets and into the courtyard of every house giving it a specially attractive appearance. In the 17th century, it was again one of the Balkans' greatest cities but then suffered a lot in 1689 when it was briefly occupied by the advancing Habsburg forces including some insurgent Serbs and Catholic Albanians. Its final heyday came in the 18th century when it was again known for its crafts, such as gold and silver articles, guns and embroidery. The next century saw its fall into gradual decay like the rest of the Ottoman Empire. In 1878 the representatives of Albanians from different regions met here demanding the autonomy of the regions they inhabited. The occasion is known as the "Prizren League" marking the start of the Albanian national movement. The Serbian army liberated Prizren in 1912. Since then it developed along modern lines but nevertheless kept much charm from days gone by.

The **Fortress** crowning the town is known by its Turkish name, Kaljaja. Previous fortifications occupied the same strategic position yet, the oldest remaining parts of the fortress date back to the 11th century and form the Upper Fort. It follows the outlines of the hill and is in the shape of an ellipse. The Lower Fort was built in the 18th century and its clock tower includes a bell taken from a church in Smederevo. Several underground passages have been preserved. On a plateau half way up the hill stands the **Sveti Spas Church** built by

esque part of Prizren. Here every house has a view over the town and small streets gradually turning into steps. Since they were predominantly Serbian, both quarters were burnt to the ground in 2004.

Sinan-pasha's Mosque is the largest Muslim temple in the town. It was built in 1615 by the Albanian Sofi Sinan-pasha, partly from the material of the torn down monastery of St Archangels, an endowment of the Emperor Dušan. It is a square edifice (14 by 14 m) with a broad dome that fits harmoniously on the building. The mosque dominates the surroundings not only by its sheer height of 22 m but also by its sturdiness. The 49 m tall minaret, one of the tallest in the region, is masterfully built so that it can stand strong winds by bending slightly. In the walls one can still see the built-in ornaments of St Archangels. Inside, there is a splendidly decorated *mimbar* (pulpit) and *mihrab*

Dome of Sinan-pasha's Mosque and Sveti Spas Church

the nobleman Mladen Vladojević in the mid 14th century and further extended on two occasions. The church was heavily damaged in the pogrom of March 2004.

On the slope beneath the fort lay the Podkaljaja and Pantelej quarters, once the most pictur-

(veneration niche turned towards Mecca) from the period of construction. Not far from the mosque, the **Old Stone Bridge** stretches across the river Bistrica; built in the 16th century, it was renovated in 1989.

Just to the north of Sinan-pasha's mosque

stands the finest Christian monument of the town, the **Church of Our Lady of Ljeviš** (*Bogorodica Ljeviška*). It was first mentioned in the 11th century as the seat of the local Orthodox Bishop. The original, inner part of the church, namely, a three-nave basilica with five domes, dates back to that period. In 1307, the Serbian King Milutin added two more aisles with apses at their sides and a narthex with a bell tower at its

the Turks hammered at the frescoes, damaging them and giving them a specific appearance. There are about 650 square metres of wall paintings still surviving, made by the Greek artist Astrapas, one of the finest Byzantine painters of the

on a red background, alongside which there is a long inscription. Of interest are also the representations of female saints on the first pair of pillars, who are dressed in the contemporary

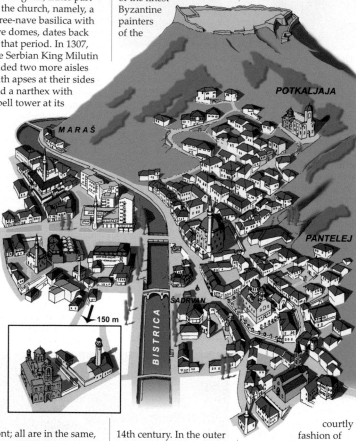

MARAŠ

POTKALJAJA

PANTELEJ

ŠADRVAN

BISTRICA

↓ 150 m

front; all are in the same, Byzantine style. On the east side of the church stands an interesting inscription in a long horizontal strip done in bricks in order not to ruin the harmony of its façades, mentioning the King and his bishop Sava. The church was converted into a mosque as soon as the town was taken in 1455 and remained so until the 20th century. The interior of the church was covered with plaster. In order for the plaster to stick better

14th century. In the outer narthex one can see the painting of the Last Judgment. In the narthex and the nave are prominent portraits of the King Milutin and other members of the Nemanjić dynasty, the Prizren Bishops and Serb Archbishops. On the first floor of the narthex are two small chapels. Especially fine is the representation of Stefan Nemanja with his sons Sava and Stefan over the doorway leading to the nave. Facing them is a portrait of King Milutin,

courtly fashion of Serbia. Other frescoes present the lives of St George, St Demetrios, St Nicholas etc. The church was set on fire in the March of 2004 and the frescoes were heavily damaged both by fire and by the destruction inflicted by the Albanian mob. One of the greatest losses was the destruction of the gracious 12th century fresco of "Our Lady of Eleusina", which was hidden by a pilaster built in 1307 and stood unseen until 1952.

-15%

TOMMY ∎ HILFIGER

STING
URBAN STORE

Mehmed-pasha's turkish baths

The Gazi Mehmet-Pasha Mosque, commonly known as **Bajrakli Mosque**, is the oldest built Islamic monument in the town. It was built in 1561 and is a simple square edifice. Alongside stand the turbe with the grave of its founder and a library building from the same period with a magnificent collection of old books in Arabic and Persian.

Mehmet-pasha also built the largest hammam or **Turkish Baths** in Serbia. Divided into different sections for men and women, this harmonious edifice with its small cupolas and many arches, is built out of stone and bricks. Today the baths serve as an art gallery.

Until the destruction that took place in Prizren in 2004, several more highly valuable Orthodox churches existed, such as the large 19th century **Cathedral**, today totally destroyed as well as the seminary, the bishop's quarters and the 15th century Church of St George in its courtyard. The same happened with the beautiful small **Church of St Nicholas**, the endowment of Dragoslav Tutić and his wife Bela (from 1331, situated in the so-called Papaz-čaršija).

❺ Peć

105.500
81 km - Priština

The town of Peć developed as a market place of the monastery. In the 15th century it became the seat of the Turkish administrator and developed quite fast. In the 1999 war the historical centre of the town was seriously damaged.

Although half-destroyed in the fighting of the last war, and much spoiled by neighboring high-rises and recent additions, the **čaršija** (trading street) of Peć is still one of the loveliest in Serbia with many old shops having been well looked after. Especially interesting are the workshops of the old craftsmen: the coppersmiths, goldsmiths, carpenters, slipper makers, saddle makers and such like all were once prominent and built a good reputation in the area. Here also lies the **Bajrakli Mosque**, the principal

Muslim temple in Peć, built in the late 15th century. Since it was torched in 1999 it has still not been fully reconstructed. It has a porch with three small cupolas and an octagonal main dome. The once beautiful interior is decorated with floral ornaments and geometrical figures painted al secco. To the right of the porch stands the impressive marble grave of Hajji Zeka decorated with floral ornamental designs.

By the river of Bistrica stands the **Jašar-pasha's Tower** dating back to the end of the 19th century. This tower-house is an excellent example of a traditional Albanian house in Metohija. It is the building of a landowner who would have protected his estate by force, therefore its height, strong walls and small windows used as loopholes were important. It was built to protect the conservative Albanian lords against the reformist Ottoman government and its army. They were used even in the last war when they made a lot of difficulties to Serb police and army. Another of the notable Peć towers is the Šeremet tower.

There are several attractive 19th century mansions that can be found near to the trading street such as Protić house, Emini Musa house or **Tahir-beg's Manor** with a stone base and a wooden floor with a large porch. The most beautiful of these is the konak of Jašar-paša in which there were private hammams.

The old trading street in Peć

❻ Pećka patrijašija

12 km - Peć

In the magnificent setting found at the entrance to the Rugovo gorge and set against a background of the Prokletije Mountains with their many caves (*pećina* in Serbian) lies the so-called Peć Patriarchate.

The Patriarchate of Peć (*Pećka patrijaršija*) is a complex of three churches and a chapel joined together by an outer narthex in one structure. The oldest of the three is the central one, dedicated to the Holy Apostles. It was built in the first half of 13th century on the land belonging to the seat of the Serbian church, the monastery of Žiča, and was intended as the burial place of Serbian archbishops. However, after a Bulgarian raid proved Žiča's vulnerability, the seat of the archbishop was transferred here, deeper inland. Peć became the most important monastery in the land and obtained its present day appearance during the first half of the 14th century. In 1346 Emperor Dušan raised this archbishopric to the level of patriarchate keeping its seat in Peć. During the Turkish onslaught the patriarch fled to the north and eventually disappeared, as did the glory days of Peć. When in 1557 the Serbian Patriarchate was re-established, the seat was again located at Peć and the monastery complex underwent extensive renovation. From here the patriarchs managed the Church and indeed the affairs of the whole Serbian nation. During the course of the Austro-Turkish wars two of the patriarchs fled to Austrian lands and both times Peć was burned down and its rich treasury looted. In the end the Turks abolished the Patriarchate altogether in 1766. In 19th century it was witness to several more atrocities delivered either by the Turks or the Albanians. Neither was the 20th century more peaceful: In 1981 Albanian extremists torched most of the dwellings. The Patriarchate of Peć still has a specific place in the hierarchical order of the Serbian Orthodox Church; for instance, it is customary for every Serbian patriarch to be ceremonially enthroned here.

To see all three churches one must go to the rear side of the complex. Of the oldest church, Holy Apostles, only the transept, three apses and a plain cupola can be seen. These were once brightly painted, as were most of the other non-ornamental sections of the façades. To the right of the Holy Apostles stands the church of St Demetrios built around 1320 and to the left lies the Virgin Hodegetria ("The one who is showing the way") with the small church of St Nicholas to its left, both some ten years younger. The exterior of both churches is quite uninteresting except for the cupolas and several gothic double windows. Along the front parts of the adjacent churches, Archbishop Danilo II added a monumental narthex that once possessed a high bell tower. The narthex was much praised for its delicacy but this was lost in the later remodeling, especially in 16th century when its arcades were walled in to secure it from collapsing and make space for new wall paintings.

The long, **Outer Narthex** is divided into two aisles by supporting columns. From the original 14th century frescoes, only a few have survived such as the Nemanjić dynasty family tree and the Virgin Mary on the south wall. Other frescoes to be found here are from the renewal of 1560, ordered by the new Patriarch Makarije Sokolović: a splendid scene of the Last Judgment and a representation of the Church calendar with a

The four churches of the Peć Patrichate Monastery

painting for each of the 365 days of the year. From here one can enter all three of the churches.

In **Holy Apostles** one first encounters the scenes from the Passion and portraits of the Nemanjić rulers painted in the 14th century and slightly retouched two centuries later. A group of paintings portraying complex theological topics follows these. The frescoes in the cupola and on the supporting arches date back to the mid 13th century making them the oldest in the complex, and bear similarities to those at the Studenica monastery. Most beautiful among these is the figure of the Virgin with outspread

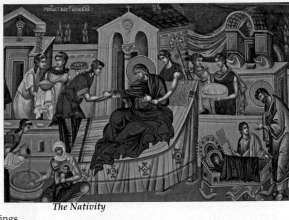

The Nativity

Christ, 13th c. fresco

arms. Three archbishops are buried in this church; over the grave of Joanikije II there is a representation of his ascension to the heavens. On the north wall, the painter Georgije Mitrofanović

made the portrait of Patriarch Jovan (c. 1620). The iconostasis dates back to 1722.

The entrance to **St Demetrios** is gained through an attractive stone portal. Here the original 14th century frescoes were extensively retouched in the 17th century. They include the life of the patron saint, portraits of Emperor Dušan with his son Uroš and the first Patriarch, Joanikije, and the Ecumenical Councils as well as two Councils of the Serbian Orthodox Church. In the Nativity of Christ, one can see the realistic representation of shepherds from that time. The monastery's treasury is also on display in this church, including some superb manuscripts, icons, liturgical objects and vestments as well as a "Rodop's bell" from 1432. Located here are the graves of the Patriarchs Jefrem and Sava IV.

The **church dedicated to the Virgin** contains some of the most revered 14th century frescoes in Serbia. The portrait of Archbishop Danilo II who commissioned the church, can be seen to the left of the entrance. He is led by the Prophet Daniel and carries the model of the monastery complex (that notably includes a representation of the original tower). The Archbishop's grave is also to be found here. Amongst other frescoes are paintings of the 23 members of the Nemanjić dynasty; the interesting "Nursing Virgin" and the Assumption of the Virgin are above the entrance. The paintings of the calendar and the Last Judgment date from the 16th century. In prothesis is the life of St Arsenius and in diaconicon life of St John the Baptist.

The small church of **St Nicholas** by the south wall of the Virgin's church contains 17th century wall paintings presenting the life of the patron saint and, on the lower level, of eminent Serbian saints. On the south wall, St Nicolas is depicted leading Patriarch Makarije Sokolović towards Christ.

❼ Visoki Dečani

97 km - Priština

15 km south of Peć lies the village of Dečane; taking the road to the west some 2 km one reaches the magnificent monastery of Visoki Dečani, the largest and most well preserved monastery in Serbia. It is situated in the pleasant valley of Bistrica stream and surrounded by wooded hills.

The monastery was endowed by King Stefan Uroš III (1321-1331) who later became commonly known as Stefan Dečanski after this grandiose building. The construction of the church of Christ the Almighty began in 1327 under the supervision of the architect, Franciscan Vito from the town of Kotor (today in Montenegro). King Dušan, although he overthrew his father from the throne and probably had him put to death, continued with the construction, finishing it in 1335 and burying his father there according to his wishes. The painting of the interior lasted for the next 13 years. The third but vital man who deserves merit for the construction was the archbishop Danilo II who probably chose the artists and gave them instructions on the program. During Turkish times the monastery escaped greater destruction and was pillaged only once, due to its relative distance from main roads and major rebellions but also due to the fact that local Albanians, though being Muslims, considered it sacred and guarded it until the 20th century. The Serbs always revered it highly and from 17th century onwards helped it by donating gifts and rebuilding the monastic dwellings. Today it is inhabited by a young and educated brotherhood and is under the constant surveillance of an Italian contingent of UN forces. The monastery is listed as a UNESCO world cultural heritage sight.

Enclosed by a strong wall, the monastery complex is entered through an impressive medieval gate. The church of Dečani, with its of length of 36 and height of 29 meters, that gave it the title "High" (*Visoki*), was one of the largest structures of medieval Serbia. It is a five-nave edifice (three-

King Stefan Dečanski holding his endowment

nave in the narthex part) with three apses and a slim cupola. The style used has been widely admired: although the base plan is Byzantine and adapted for the Orthodox service, the decoration is Romanesque with touches of Gothic, showing direct influences from the Apulia province on the other side of the Adriatic. The façade is covered in rows of white, gray and pink marble whose harmony is disturbed

Visoki Dečani Monastery exuding calm with its pale marble exterior

only by three portals, two three-light windows, 21 double-windows and several one-bay windows. The blind arches adorned with beautiful anthropo-morphic and zoomorphic heads decorate the top of the façades. In many aspects the decora-tion here imitates the one found in the Studenica monastery, the mausoleum of the founder of the dynasty, Stefan Neman-ja. This is best viewed in the large central apse three-light window that is the exact copy of the one that can be seen at Studenica. The main western doorway shows figures of Christ on the throne with two angels surrounded by zodiacal signs and two guardian lions on columns. The southern doorway has a sculpture of the baptism of Christ. Underneath it one can see a Cyrillic inscription in Serbian about the building of the church. The north portal is decorated with a representation of the flowering cross.

The interior is entirely covered with frescoes, more than a thousand of them, making it the largest surviving area of medieval fresco painting in the world. There are some 20 cycles depicted, a perfect example of the narrative style of the Paleologue dynasty from Constantinople. The paintings are distin-guished by their bright colors, lively design and attention to detail. In the narthex, scenes from the life of St George,

Emperor Dušan with his family and depic-tions from 365 days of the church calendar are

*St George rescuing the princess
(National Museum Belgrade)*

shown. The magnificent Nemanjić family tree is also well worth at-tention. One enters the nave through another beautifully carved portal revealing lions holding the heads of men at their sides, an illustra-tion of the belief that a lion cries over the head of the man he killed. Represented on the nave walls are numerous liturgical, dogmatic and biblical themes (from the book of Genesis to the Last Judgment) as well as those from the history of Christendom,

all showing the excellence of donor's theological education. The low stone iconostasis is the only preserved one in Serbia dating back to the Middle Ages. Alongside it lies the sarcophagus of the founder, minutely carved and expres-sively painted. It is thought to have healing powers. Among the scenes to be found around the altar, there is a representation of Dečanski of-fering his mon-astery to Christ. This fresco is considered the most accurate por-trayal of the King.

The **treasury** of the Visoki Dečani monastery is by far the richest in Serbia. It possesses, among other items, an abbot's throne (1335), a cross donated by Emperor Dušan himself, numerous superb icons - some of which are the old standing portraits of saints from the iconosta-sis, the 1577 icon of St Ste-fan Dečanski portraying scenes from his life, 15th -16th century liturgical objects and vestments and over 150 manuscripts from the 13th up to the 19th century.

Painting an icon

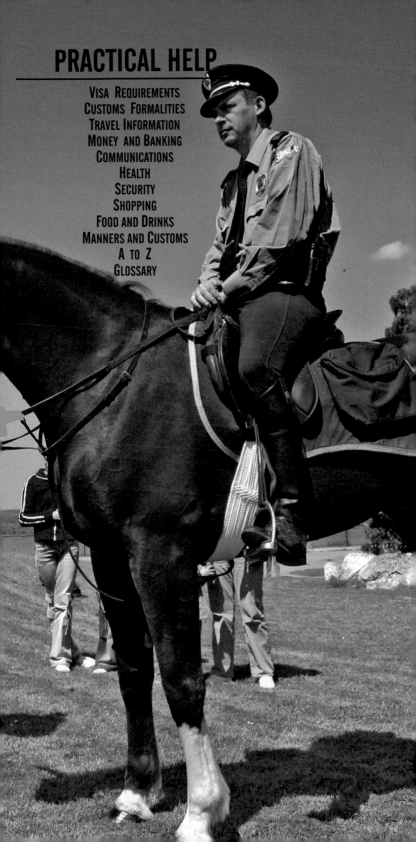

PRACTICAL HELP

VISA REQUIREMENTS

A valid passport is necessary for tourist visits to Serbia.

Citizens of the following countries don't need visas for an entry and stay in Serbia and Montenegro of up to 90 days: all EU countries, USA, Canada, Australia, New Zealand, Japan, Bulgaria, Croatia, Norway, Switzerland, Iceland, Israel etc. The full list can be checked out at www.mfa.gov.yu/Visas/f_without_visa.htm or at the nearest Diplomatic/Consular Mission of Serbia and Montenegro.

EMBASSY OF SERBIA AND MONTENEGRO

GREAT BRITAIN
28 Belgrave Square
LONDON SW1X 8QB
Tel. +44 207 235 9049
www.yugoslavembassy.org.uk

UNITED STATES OF AMERICA
2134, Kalorama Road, N.W.
WASHINGTON.D.C.20008
Tel. +1 202 / 332-0333
www.yuembusa.org

CANADA
17, Blackburn Avenue
OTTAWA Ontario K1N 8A2
Tel. +1613 / 233-62-89, 233-62-80
www.embscg.ca

Citizens of Albania, the Russian Federation and the Ukraine may enter and stay in the Republic of Montenegro for tourist visits in the territory of Montenegro individually and in organized groups on the basis of a travel document without a visa. The citizens of Bosnia and Herzegovina, Slovenia and Macedonia may enter and stay in the Republic of Montenegro for tourist visits in the territory of the Republic of Montenegro with a personal ID card plus a tourist pass issued at the border. Foreign nationals from these six countries will be issued with tourist passes at the border crossings in the Republic of Montenegro with a period of validity of up to 30 days.

Visitors who are required to obtain visas will need:
1. Valid Passport;
2. Invitation Letter (verified by a competent authority from Serbia-Montenegro) or an invitation from a company for a business visit or a receipt or an authorized tourist company certifying that the travel arrangement has been paid for (letter of credit or other payment receipt);
3. Return ticket;
4. Proof of sufficient funds in hard currency and
5. Certificate that a health fund shall cover the medical costs in Serbia and Montenegro, if any should be required.

Note: Transit visa applicants are required to obtain a visa for the country they will enter after transit through Serbia and Montenegro.

For all information related to consular matters (e.g. visas, citizenship, estates, etc.), please contact, by telephone or E-mail, the nearest Diplomatic/Consular Mission of Serbia and Montenegro in person.

CUSTOMS FORMALITIES

On entering Serbia and Montenegro (excluding Kosovo) be sure to have an entry stamp in your passport from the border police. Not having a stamp may cause problems with the police or border police.

Currency. Foreign currencies may be brought into the country freely with no restrictions as to the amount of currencies imported. Visitors may declare a foreign currency to the customs officer and receive a receipt allowing them to take it out on leaving the country. Foreigners are free to take any amount under 2000 EUR out of Serbia without proof. For a sum exceeding this, one needs to have a letter from the bank proving a withdrawal from a foreign exchange or savings account.

Art objects. Special permits are needed for the exportation of original objects of cultural,

Bright lights towards the big city

artistic, archeological, ethnographic, historical or scientific value. The permit can be obtained from the Serbian Ministry of Foreign Economic Relations.

Wildlife trophies may be exported if accompanied by: the permission of the Ministry of Foreign Economic Relations in the Republic for stuffed animals and parts thereof OR a game shooting certificate in the case of other trophies.

Car insurance. Motorised visitors are required to have an international insurance card valid in the territory of Serbia and Montenegro. If not, the competent authorities (Automobile Association – AMSS, not the customs authorities!) charge the amount of compulsory insurance on entering the country.

Note: The Serbian authorities do not recognise as official the external border crossings of Kosovo. It is therefore advised not to enter Serbia through Kosovo.

TRAVEL INFORMATION

Arriving by Air

There are two international airports in Serbia. One is in Belgrade, the other in Niš. **Belgrade airport "Nikola Tesla"** (or just "Aerodrom Beograd") is usually referred to as Surčin as is called the nearby village. It is 18 km (12 miles) from the city centre. Part of it is currently being reconstructed but not at the passengers expense. Almost all foreign travel agencies have regular flights to Belgrade, so it is well connected to all parts of Europe, Asia and Northern Africa. The national airline "Jat Airways" has scheduled daily flights from London, Paris, Frankfurt, Munich, Vienna, Zurich and Rome. The airport has a number of small shops, cafés, exchange offices, rent-a-car companies and Duty Free Shops.

EMBASSIES

AUSTRALIA
Čika Ljubina 13
Tel. 011/330-34-00

AUSTRIA
Kneza Sime Markovića 2
Tel. 011/3031-956, 3031-964

BELGIUM
Krunska 18
Tel. 011/3230-018,
3247-587

BOSNIA AND HERZEGOVINA
Milana Tankosića 8
Tel. 011/329-1277; 329-1993

BULGARIA
Birčaninova 26
Tel: 011/361-3980

CZECH REPUBLIC
Bulevar Kralja
Aleksandra 22
Tel. 011/3230-133; 3230-134

DENMARK
Neznanog Junaka 9 a
Tel. 011/367-0443

FINLAND
Birčaninova 29
Tel. 011/3065-400

FRANCE
Pariska 11
Tel: 011/302-3500

GREECE
Francuska 33
Tel. 011/3226-523

NETHERLANDS
Simina 29
Tel. 011/202-39-00

CROATIA
Kneza Miloša 62
Tel. 011/3610-535; 3610-153

ITALY
Birčaninova 11
Tel. 011/306-6100

ISRAEL
Bulevar kneza Aleksandra Karadjordjevića 47
Tel. 011/3672-400; 3672-401

JAPAN
Genex Apartments
Vladimira Popovića 6,
Tel. 011/301-2800

CANADA
Kneza Miloša 75
Tel: 011/306-3000

CHINA
Avgusta Cesarca 2V,
Tel. 011/3695-057

HUNGARY
Krunska 72
Tel. 011/244-0472; 244-7479

MACEDONIA
Gospodar Jevremova 34
Tel. 011/328-49-24

GERMANY
Kneza Miloša 74-76
Tel: 011/3064-300

NORWAY
Užička 43
Tel. 011/367 0404, 367 0405

POLAND
Ul. Kneza Miloša 38
Tel. 011/2065 301, 2065 318

PORTUGAL
Vladimira Gaćinovića 4
Tel. 011/2662-895, 2662-894

ROMANIA
Kneza Miloša 70
Tel. 011/3618-327

RUSSIAN FEDERATION
Deligradska 32:
Katićeva 8-10:
Tel: 011/361-1323;
361-1090 361-0544

UNITED STATES OF AMERICA
Kneza Miloša 50
Tel.: 011/361-9344;
361-3043 361-3909

SLOVAK REPUBLIC
Bulevar umetnosti 18,
Tel. 011/301-00-00

SLOVENIA
Zmaj Jovina 33a
Tel. 011/328-44-58, 328-26-10

SPAIN
Prote Mateje 45
Tel. 011/344-02-31/2, 3, 4, 5

SWITZERLAND
Birčaninova 27
Tel. 011/3065-820, 3065-825

UNITED KINGDOM
Resavska 46
(Generala Ždanova 46)
Tel: 011/2645-055; 3060-900

There are a number of ways to reach the city centre. A taxi should cost, depending on the location, around 800-1000 dinar (10-12 Euros). Be sure to fix the price before getting into taxi, as overcharging can occurr. "How much to the centre/hotel …" - *Koliko do centra/hotela …* Alternatively, there are a number of shuttle buses. "Jat Airways" buses are can be used from the first to the last flight, at a cost of 160 din, at time of writing. They stop at the main

Narrow-gauge railway in Mokra Gora

railway and bus stations and terminate at Slavija Square in the centre of the city. "Lasta" buses take the same route, cost 80 dinars, but run only from 5 a.m. to 10 p.m. The cheapest option is the public bus No. 72. It goes on every half hour, the first one at 5.15 a.m, the last one at midnight. The bus will take one from the airport to Zeleni venac in 40 minutes and the fare is only 40 dinars (buy the ticket from the bus driver).

Niš airport "Konstantin Veliki" operates mostly domestic flights but is also used by tour operators during the winter season as it is the closest to Kopaonik ski-centre. There are, though only infrequently, flights by "Jat Airlines" and "Montenegro Airlines" from London and Zurich.

Belgrade Airport
011/20-94-444
www.airport-belgrade.co.yu

Niš Airport
018/580-023
www.airportnis.co.yu

Belgrade railway station – 011/26-458-22
Novi Sad railway station – 021/443-200
Niš railway station – 018/264-625
Subotica railway station – 024/555-606
Kragujevac railway station – 034/366827

Arriving by Train

One can reach Belgrade directly from Venice, Zagreb, Budapest, Bucharest, Sofia, Istanbul, Thessalonica or Skopje. The main routes are from Zagreb, Budapest (via Subotica and Novi Sad) and from Sofia (via Niš) and operate at least once a day. All of these trains have sleeping carriages and couchettes, which are highly recommended as the other carriages may be overcrowded, dirty or with no heating.

Belgrade's main train station (*Glavna železnička stanica* or *Beograd centar*) is centrally located and just next to the main bus station.
Telephones: 011/2641-488, 629-400, 2645-822

Travelling by Train

Internal rail services are run by the Serbian state (Železnice Srbije). Both local and intercity (brzi voz) trains are mostly dirty, crowded and can be desperately late. Most of these points come from the fact that this is the cheapest means of transportation and is sometimes the only one people can afford. On overnight trains, sleeping berths are available.
The main lines are
- towards Subotica, via Sremski Karlovci and Novi Sad
- towards Šid, via Ruma and Sremska Mitrovica
- towards Vršac
- towards Pirot, via Jagodina and Niš
- towards Vranje, via Jagodina, Niš and Leskovac
- towards Bar (Montenegro) via Valjevo, Užice, Zlatibor and Prijepolje
Tickets can be obtained at the station ticket offices or alternatively in the train, but with an additional fee of 100 din. Timetables are posted on boards at railway stations and cannot be obtained in leaflet form.

The holders of ETC or Euro 26 card are allowed 50% discount, those of ISIC or ITC card 30%. For groups from 3 to 8 people a discount of 20% can be asked for.

Arriving by Bus

Serbia is well connected to all of Western and Northern Europe by direct bus lines. The widest choice of starting

SERBIAN RAILWAYS
present the memorable journeys...

Romantic rides with "Romantika" ("Romance") train, with its stream locomotive and original carriadges from the beginning of the last century. Every weekend from April till October a ride is offered to several destinations including Sremski Karlovci, Vršac and Vrnjačka Banja.

Informations: 011/36-16-928
Reservations: 011/36-16-855, 3616-856
e-mail: romantika@yurail.co.yu

Nostalgic rides with the old-timer Ćira on a one of the most beatuful narrow-gauge tracks in the world, the "Šargan Eight" from Mokra Gora tu Vitasi station.

Informations: 031/510-290, 031/510-690
e-mail: sarganska.osmica@yurail.co.yu

Exclusive rides with the "Blue Train" of Marshal Tito. This "Hotel on Tracks" has several saloons, restaurant etc offering a wide choice of services from catering to car transport.

Informations: 011/36-16-928
Reservations: 011/36-16-855, 36-16-856
e-mail: plavivoz@yurail.co.yu

Serbian Railways
www.yurail.co.yu
for futher informations call +381 (0)11 361 69 28
or fax us on +381 (0)11 361 67 75

Tourist boats on the Danube

tion service fee and the seat reservation (not at the Belgrade main bus station). At some of the stations one will receive a chip that enables access to the platform. Larger luggage that is stored in the trunk of the bus has an additional charge before departure (prices vary but should not exceed 60 dinars). Keep the tickets issued for the stored luggage. For tickets returned until 5 minutes before the departure one can be reimbursed up to 90% of the price, excluding the station service fee and the reservation.

Belgrade Main Bus Station, Železnička 4 (next to the Main Railway Station), tel. 011/26-36-299
Novi Sad bus station, Bulevar Jaše Tomića 6, tel. 021/444-021
Niš bus station, Bulevar 12 februara bb, tel. 018/255-492
Subotica bus station, Senćanski put 5, tel. 024/555-344
Kragujevac bus station, Šumadijska bb, tel. 034/9802

points is offered by Eurolines, which is operated in Serbia by the Lasta company (www.lasta.co.yu, head office - Belgrade, Železnička 2, tel. +381 (0)11 625-740). Another company with regular departures from around Europe is Fudeks (www.fudeks.co.yu, head office Balkanska 47, tel. +381 (0)11 3620-255).

Travelling by Bus

Bus is by far the most preferred choice of transportation in Serbia mainly because of its good network and reasonably reliable services. Almost all of the longer lines are operated by comfortable and modern buses. However, local services are mostly provided by old and quite run-down buses, though there are exceptions.

Bus tickets are purchased at the stations. The price includes the sta-

Arriving by Boat

International crossings on the rivers are the following:
- on the Tisa – Kanjiža
- on the Danube (from Hungary) – Bezdan
- on the Danube (from Romania/Bulgaria) – Prahovo

International customs points are located only on the Danube at Apatin, Novi Sad and Belgrade.

Travelling by Car

A valid international driver's license is required to drive legally in Serbia-Montenegro. If taking a car, the vehicle registration/ownership documents and a locally valid insurance policy must be available at all times. The European green card vehicle insurance is now valid in the union of Serbia and Montenegro, but not in Kosovo. Concerning other insurance policies, one will be required to purchase a month-long valid insurance policy at the price of 80 EUR.

The law requires the wearing of a seatbelt. It permits a maximum of 0,05 % alcohol in the blood – the equivalent of two glasses of wine or two bottles of beer.

The general standard of the roads is fair to poor with conditions worsening in rural areas, especially in and after bad weather. The Ibarska Magistrala road (from Belgrade via Čačak to Montenegro) is particularly notorious for its bad conditions and overcrowding which can make it dangerous.

Toll charges on the motorways depend on the size of the vehicle. One is advised to have at least 20 EUR/ 1,500 Dinars (preferred) in cash in order to pay the toll charges. The tolls can be paid in Euros. It was announced that, starting from 2006, drivers with foreign registration plates will pay the same amount as domestic drivers, which is not the case at the time of writing. For some idea of the prices, at the beginning of 2006 the toll from Belgrade to Novi Sad was 170 dinars (2 EUR), from Belgrade to Niš 500 din (6,5 EUR).

One should also be aware that some parts of the motorway between Novi Sad and Belgrade are still not fully finished and are actually a two-lane road with a hard shoulder on only one side. Some drivers use the 'middle' lane to overtake, thus forcing the ongoing traffic onto the hard shoulder. Here one needs to be even more cautious.

In case the need for towing or transport arises call the **AMSS** (Automobile & Motorists Association of Serbia) emergency number **987**. The **traffic police** number is the same as the police **92**.

MONEY AND BANKING

Currency. The Serbian currency is the Dinar (din or CSD). One Dinar is divided into 100 Para but these are so small in real value that they are near to worthless. Dinars can be occasionally purchased outside Serbia. Nevertheless, you are advised to exchange Dinars back into your own curency before leaving Serbia. Although on an everyday basis, everything is calculated in Euros, bear in mind that the Dinar is the only legal currency. However, on some occasions Euros might also be accepted.

The official currency in Kosovo is the Euro and Dinars are not accepted outside Serbian enclaves.

Please note the following: bills and coins come in two variants – one say

Narodna Banka Srbije (National Bank of Serbia) and are new, while the others say *Narodna Banka Jugoslavije* (National Bank of Yugoslavia) and are the older variant: both variants are legal tender, equally valid and equally accepted. Although the latter are being replaced by the new notes and coins (in Serbia), they remain valid for the time being - no official deadline has been set for their expiry. Old and new coins and bills are very similar but NOT identical.

Cash, credit cards, travellers cheques. International credit cards are accepted in an increasing number of places, particularly large hotels, top restaurants and stores, but, by large Serbia still has a cash economy. Obtaining Dinars is therefore advisable for everyday shopping and average restaurants. It is safest to bring money in several forms - mainly cash, some travellers cheques (which, if stolen, can be replaced), and, if possible, credit/debit cards. If bringing in cash, we suggest bringing Euros, or US Dollars, as these two currencies are the easiest to exchange. Among credit cards, best accepted are Visa, Diners Club and MasterCard/EuroCard. Travellers cheques, such as American Express, Thomas Cook, VISA, and Eurocheques can be exchanged in most Belgrade banks. If experiencing difficulty finding a place to exchange them, head to any "Komercijalna Banka" or "Raiffeisenbank" branch. For Eurocheques "ProCredit Bank" is recommended. You will not be able to use your personal or travellers cheques in shops. Bear in mind that a fee will be charged for each processed cheque.

Exchange offices and banks are numerous, particularly around business and tourist areas. All licensed exchange offices are properly signposted ("Menjačnica / Exchange"). Commission is not charged for these services. The rate is not fixed but rarely varies significantly. Always ask for a receipt and always count the money given back. One can change some money immediately after arrival: there are many exchange offices in the arrival hall of Belgrade Airport and at least one at every major railway station or chief border crossings. Try to avoid changing larger amounts of money at the motorway pay-tolls as here commission will be charged.

In Belgrade (including Belgrade airport - departures hall) and other bigger cities, one can exchange money 24 hours a day in exchange machines. Insert notes and follow the on-screen instructions. These machines can exchange up to 200 euros at a time. These machines will exchange Euros, US dollars, and British pounds.

Although it is unlikely that ine will get the opportunity to change money on the street, avoid it, as it is both illegal and risky, especially as the rates hardly differ from those in exchange offices.

Cash transfers from abroad. For fast money transfers the Western Union service is recommended. It is available at various commercial banks and Post offices. One will always receive the money in Euros, regardless of the currency that it has been sent in. Moneygram services are not available in Serbia.

If the money is not required urgently, one can open a bank account, and have the money transferred to it from any country in the world, as all Serbian banks are members of SWIFT and IBAN. Depending on the bank, the SWIFT/IBAN transfer can take between 2 to 7 business days..

COMMUNICATIONS

The place to make cheap long distance **phone calls** is the post office (*pošta*) where one is directed to a booth and charged at the end of the call. Post Offices are open 8 a.m. to 8 p.m. on workdays, on Saturdays to 3 p.m.

Many hotels have direct dial telephone facilities, some of them offer additional services: fax, internet, secretarial services. Check the unit charge as telephone charges can vary greatly.

In the central areas of all towns there are **phone booths**. A card ("Halo kartica") can be purchased in post offices or at some tobacconists/kiosks. There are 200, 300 and 500 Dinar cards. If calling locally the cheapest one will do just fine for several days.

Stamps can be purchased in post offices and at some newspaper kiosks. The postal service can be highly erratic and should not be relied upon. If you need something to arrive safely, it is advisable to use a western courier service.

Foreign newspapers can be found only in the largest of cities. Large bookstores (such as "Plato" in Belgrade) usually have available daily newspapers in several languages. English language broadcasting can be heard from the BBC World Service on short wave – 6195 kHz at morning, 12095 daytime and 9410 in the evenings. The Voice of America is broadcast on 9760 and 6040 kHz. Satellite and broadband cable TV is fast becoming a normal feature.

Internet cafés can be found in almost all of the cities. The usual charge is about 1 Euro per hour. In Belgrade and several more cities, one can find (mostly cafés) a wireless internet connection. An internet access number without an account and settings, charged via the telephone bill is 041-910-910 (username: 041, password: net).

There are two **mobile-phone operators** "Mobtel" (numbers beginning with 063 and 062) and "Telekom" (064 and 065). Phone numbers can be purchased relatively easily at the branches of these companies at the cost of 10 Euros.

To call abroad, dial:

99 + area code for the coutnry you are calling+ city code + phone number

e.g. 99-30-210-4444444
(30 for Greece, 210 for Athens)

HEALTH

Tap water is safe to drink in most regions. Caution should be taken in the regions around Ibar River (for example in Kraljevo) and in some towns in the NW of the country (such as Zrenjanin and Kikinda). Beware that water from some fountains is not safe for consumption; these are marked with a warning sign saying *Voda nije za piće*. Bottled water is available in larger markets and is advised for people known to experience stomach problems. Milk is pasteurized and dairy products are safe for consumption. Local meat, poultry, fish and vegetables are considered safe to eat.

Hygiene standards are quite high in most of the hotels and restaurants, apart from the cheapest ones. There are a number of pharmacies in all towns.

The health system in all parts of the state union of Serbia and Montenegro suffers from widespread shortage of many medicines and medical supplies. Payment in cash is normally required

VMA hospital in Belgrade

for treatment and one is advised to be covered by comprehensive travel insurance in case the need for medical evacuation arises.

Hepatitis A may occur. Tularaemia has been reported lately in Kosovo. Rabies is present and for those at high risk, vaccination before arrival should be considered. Crimean Congo Haemorrhagic Fever (CCHF) is endemic to Kosovo. CCHF is transmitted by tic bite or thorugh contact with infected blood. Anyone who has visited Kosovo and is suffering from a fever – headache, chills, muscle aches, vomiting, red rash, bleeding on the roof of the mouth – or any other unexplained symptoms should seek medical advice immediately.

SECURITY

Serbia is a remarkably safe place to be. There are always people out in the streets, even late at night or in the winter, and one will feel comfortable walking anywhere almost anytime, although it would be wise to avoid secluded places at night.

Women travelling solo will be completely safe in Serbia, as safe as any other travellers. They are unlikely to feel physically threatened, though they may have to fend off unwanted attention in bars and discotheques and other similar places, though very rarely on the streets.

There are no laws against homosexual activity but a public display of affection is highly inadvisable.

Some spots frequented by tourists are known for pickpockets so it is advisable to carry only as much money as required for the day on your person. Leave other money, airplane tickets, passport, and all other valuables in a safe deposit box at the reception desk of your hotel. Luxury vehicles might be a target for thieves and should be left only in guarded parking lots or at least in well-lit places. Never leave bags and similar items in visible places in your vehicle.

Begging is not widespread, though while sitting in open-air cafés or strolling down pedestrian zones, beggars may approach and can be irritating. Nevertheless, they are not as aggressive as their 'colleagues' in most other countries.

Do not photograph the police or military-guarded buildings nor those destroyed or damaged in the NATO air raids.

In Serbia and Montenegro (including Kosovo), carry your passport at all times. We therefore advise that you keep a photocopy of your passport in a safe place. This will help you to obtain a replacement, in case it is lost or stolen.

It is essential, when in Serbia and Montenegro (excluding Kosovo), that you register with the police within 24 hours of your arrival, unless staying in a hotel where you will be registered automatically when checking-in. For the

Traffic policeman

registration, go to the nearest police station (in Belgrade the station in Savska St.) accompanied by your host who should bring the document stating his ownership of the premises of your stay. Since all of this is fairly complicated and the police rarely check the registration papers, you might risk not putting yourself through the trouble (though you are highly advised to register).

It's better not to argue politics, as many people tend to express their political attitudes mingled with emotions. Avoid demonstrations and public gatherings.

There are a number of illegal substances present in the streets of Serbian towns. Possession (no matter how small the amount) or trafficking of drugs is met with strict penalties including prison sentences.

Stray dogs are quite a problem in large towns so one should avoid strolling in secluded places, especially alone. If you see a group of dogs act normally as attacks on people are rare.

SHOPPING

Classical tourist souvenirs ("touristy" and tacky!) are almost non-existent (so much the better) but one can find lots of genuine handicrafts, mostly embroidery, wickerwork and woodwork products, folk tapestry, knitted sweaters, needle and crochet work.

Leather is very good value. The shoe shops stock up-to-date styles at very reasonable prices. Handbags, suitcases and jackets are a good bargain. Copperware and filigree silver make good gifts, and so does good Serbian crystal or plate glass (vases, ashtrays, china tea sets).

One would probably try to find something "typically" Serbian, like traditional rustic *opanak* (pl. *opanci*) - a simple shallow leather shoe. Today there are not many craftsmen to make them (even though they continue to be worn in some rural parts of Serbia) however can occasionally be found at market places, local fairs and ethno shops.

Ethno souvenirs

A piece of the fallen regime: 500 billion-dinar-bills from 1993!

Only in Belgrade can you become an instant 'billionaire'! All you need to do is pick up a strange and non-expensive local souvenir - the biggest world's banknote in history (the highest currency denomination) that was issued in Yugoslavia on December 23, 1993 during the period of spiraling inflation. The brightly coloured bill of 500.000.000.000 dinars "was worth approximately $6 in the morning when used to pay the thousands of retirees who lined up outside post offices across the country to collect their monthly pensions. But by the time most of them had hurried to the markets it was worth only $5. By evening its value had dropped to less than $3. With it one could buy either 10 loaves of bread, or less than four ounces of poor quality pork or a gallon of milk or two dozen eggs".

When in Belgrade, ask your guide where you can find this wacky 'souvenir'. It is a great collectable item for anyone, especially someone who enjoys world currency notes. Get a piece of the fallen regime, while you can!

A few more things you will undoubtedly like to take back home: Serbian slivovitz or some other brandy, a bottle of wine, a jar of preserves, or perhaps some fine cheese.

FOOD AND DRINKS

One of the best parts of the Serbian experience is tasting the local authentic cuisine. Firstly, because there is such a thing, and secondly, as it is accessible to those with even only a modest budget. Serbians take great pride in their cooking and though most of the specialties are pan-Balkan, they are flavoured with local aroma and are prepared specifically. In recent years, with the arrival of the trend towards eating healthily, Serbian cuisine has been criticized for its abundant use of oil, fat and the extensive amount of meat eating. Certainly somewhat rough, food in Serbia offers the age-old enjoyment of being good, simple and in abundance. After sampling some of the specialties one is bound to forget the critics and nutritionists or at least consider the subject from a more epicurean point of view.

Serbian cuisine reflects the geographical and historical influences of the region. One could say that Serbs have sampled everything from German sausages, Hungarian goulash, Italian pasta and various Turkish dishes and then chose what they liked the best. The meat eating side of the culture is best noticed through the grilled dishes (*roštilj*). The distinctive taste of Serbian grill, recognised around the world, comes from the south of Serbia and is therefore sometimes referred to as *Leskovački roštilj* (Grill from Leskovac). It was from here that it spread rapidly over the rest of Yugoslavia in the 1920s. All restaurants have a menu that includes *ćevapčići* (small minced meat

rolls), *pljeskavica* (minced veal and pork spread sprinkled with spices), *ražnjicji* (grilled slices of veal and pork), *vešalica* etc. These are always a good choice – tasty and inexpensive. All come with lots of chopped onions and one should consider having potatoes and salad alongside them. Those who like cheesy and spicy fillings should order the *gurmanska* variety. Many come as *rolovani* – rolled in bacon, or *na kajmaku* prepared on the grill with kajmak cream (see below). The varieties of sausages are all quite far from the German style of sausage as in Serbia, they are almost always spicy or hot. A delicious dish similar to the Wiener schnitzel is the Karadjordjeva šnicla, rolled veal or pork steak, stuffed with bacon, white cheese and ham, breaded and fried, served with

Spicy starters

fried potatoes and tartar sauce. Another dish to try is *mućkalica* (casserole of half grilled mixed meat, peppers and tomatoes). Real connoisseurs also enjoy *beli bubrezi* (testicles) or *škembići* (bowels).

Serbian gourmets adore spit-roasts (*pečenje*). These are usually made from suckling pig (*praseće*) or lamb (*jagnjeće*), the latter being more praised for its stronger taste. It is usually ordered by kilo and consumed with horse-radish (*ren*) or grated fresh cabbage (*kupus salata*). Spit-roasts are a must have at any large celebration; a fact that can partly explain their popularity. Orders specifying *pod sačom* are also local specialties which are prepared cooked in a clay pot in hot coals.

For centuries Serbian cooking was based on corn, cabbage, peppers and potatoes. Mixed together they make some of the best known Serbian specialties. *Sarma* are stuffed cabbage rolls (a mixture of chopped meat and rice); *punjene paprike* ("Stuffed Peppers") are green peppers filled

Fresh from the fire

Stuffed peppers

with minced meat, rice and tomato, while *djuveč* is a rich casserole with meat, rice and vegetables. Probably the best known among all the dishes is *pasulj* - Serbian beans soup. A wonderfully tasty speciality is "Wedding Cabbage" (*svadbarski kupus*) named after the occasion when it is most prepared: cabbage and dried meat are prepared in huge clay pots and boiled for several hours. If one likes cabbage, try *podvarak*, a mixture of sauerkraut and rice baked in the oven and served with pork. More oriental dishes are *musaka* (moussaka) and strong *kapama* (lamb stewed with spinach, shallots and yoghurt). *Gulaš* and *paprikaš* are stews similar to those from Hungary but with their own local colouring.

Do not forget the appetisers, which are sometimes eaten on their own as snacks to accompany strong drinks. *Čvarci* are cracklings, while *duvan-čvarci* are cracklings transformed into a tobacco like shape. *Pršuta* is smoked ham; the most famous varieties are the ones from the Užice region. An unusual specialty requiring an acquired taste is *pihtije*, a jelly-like dish of pork. *Prebranac* is beans roasted with onions – a must try for any visitor. Though called a salad, *urnebes salata* is actually cheese, strongly spiced with paprika.

There are several types of porridges that can be very tasty if well prepared: *kačamak* is a kind of polenta made of corn flour and served with cream, *cicvara* is made from wheat flower and is cooked with cream, while *popara* is really basic – a mix of cooked bread and white cheese. Considering their abundant, heavy fillings, pies can be viewed eaten as meal on their own. The best known ones being *gibanica* (with eggs and cheese) and *zeljanica* (with spinach).

The range of dairy products is very rich. Creams can be light and sour such as *kiselo mleko* in comparison to the fattier and sweeter *pavlaka*. The one thing all Serbs miss a lot when far from home is *jogurt* which, though similar to yoghurt from the West is not sweet at all. A real Serbian specialty is *kajmak*, a fatty cream with a unique taste and accompaniment to many dishes. Cheeses are much preferred fresh, from the mild *švapski* ("German") to the salty *sjenički*. Of the aged cheeses the best known is *kačkavalj* (like Italian caciocavallo), especially the varieties from Mt Stara Planina or from the Krivi vir region.

Traditional summer salads include fresh vegetables. The most common combinations are *Srpska* (Serbian salad: tomato, cucumbers, green peppers and onion) and *Šopska salata* (similar but covered with grated white cheese). During the winter most people eat roasted peppers preserved in garlic and oil (some filled with cheese), *turšija* (vegetables preserved in vinegar and salt), *ajvar* (a relish made principally from red bell peppers, with eggplant, garlic and chilly peppers) or sauerkraut (*kiseli kupus*) with the inevitable touch of paprika.

Every good meal should begin with a soup. Though lighter soups are common, the local favorites are *čorba* with lots of vegetables and meat chunks in it. A most beloved starter to any meal is a delicious *teleća čorba*, a veal & vegetable concoction.

Fish is not that widely eaten except during the long feasts prescribed by the Orthodox Church which some people follow more or less strictly. It is best to order it in specialised fish restaurants though most restaurants that have it on their menus can be trusted. Freshwater and sea fish are equally available with the most popular sorts being trout (*pastrmka*), carp (*šaran*), and perch (*smudj*). A widely enjoyed dish is the *riblja čorba*, a fish soup with large quantities of paprika in it. A popular snack is *girice* - crisply fried picarels that fill the air with their

Prebranac, a delicious roasted dish

pungent scent and are therefore sometimes sold in the streets.

It is quite common to taste something sweet at the end of a meal. There are a lot of confectioners around (*poslastičarnica*) offering an excellent choice of cakes and pastries. Serbian sweets have been influenced mostly by the Turkish tradition on the one hand and the Austrian on the other

Proja corn bread

but are quite dynamic and inventive. If you want to try something local go for *baklava* (a pastry with nuts and melted sugar), *suva pita* (a pie with walnuts and raisins) or *orasnica* (a walnut pastry). There are also strudels (*štrudla*) with poppy seeds (*sa makom*), walnuts (*sa orasima*) or apples (*sa jabukama*). One can try ice creams, lemonade and *boza* (a corn meal drink, similar to Turkish but lighter). *Žito* or *koljivo* is mostly prepared ceremonially for *slava* feasts but can also tried in confectioneries. This is a kind of tasty porridge made from wheat, nuts and raisins, sometimes served with cream on top. Something that one will rarely find for sale but if lucky will be offered when visiting, is *slatko*, a sort of preserve made from various kinds of fruits from apricots to forest strawberries, usually with a walnut or two or sometimes even rose petals. Note that this is not a dish in its own; it is the custom to just take one or two spoonfuls when offered. Jams (*pekmez* or *džem*) are thicker than the ones known in the West.

Don't miss out on a visit to a Serbian bakery (*pekara*). These serve mostly salty pastries, though some include serious sweets too. There is a wide range of choice: from the traditional *burek* (pie with meat, cheese, mushrooms or on its own), which is considered to go best with yoghurt sold on the spot, *pogačice* (plain ones and those sold with crack-

ling), *pita* (pies with potatoes, spinach, meat and mushrooms), *proja* (corn bread with cheese), *mekike* (fried dough) as well as croissants, hot sandwiches and slices of pizza.

During the summer many street stalls sell boiled corn (*kuvani kukuruz*). Apart the popcorn, before going to the cinema, it is a common habit to buy peanuts (*kikiriki*) and seeds (*semenke*) – sunflower, or pumpkin, though there are also other "pastime for teeth" sold in front of theatres.

No conversation can start and no meal can finish without the almost ritual drinking of coffee, which, in consequence, is drunk in large quantities. Black coffee (*crna, turska* or *domaća kafa*) is a much praised Serbian way to prepare the drink. The fine-grounded coffee bean is boiled in small pots resulting in a strong tasting drink (therefore it is usually accompanied with the glass of cold water). It is customary to specify the degree of sweetness required - *sladja* (sweet) or *gorča* (no sugar) - otherwise one will receive the middle option (*srednja*). In old cafés one might be lucky enough to have the coffee accompanied with a piece of Turkish delight (*ratluk*), a sweet jelly. Until recently the King of coffeehouses, black coffee is now being challenged by other varieties: the espresso, cappuccino, Nescafe and others that have penetrated into all but the simplest establishments. Ordering a tea, one will be served herbal tea (usually hibiscus or chamomile). Tea the English way might not be available in many

Peppers stuffed with cheese

places, however one could try asking for *indijski čaj* (Indian) or *crni čaj sa mlekom* (black tea with milk).

Something that is synomynous with Serbia is its brandy, called by the generic name *rakija*. This drink has fueled the country's temperament for centuries and was produced in almost every home.

No two homemade rakijas are quite the same, but this does not mean that they are all good. Spending time with a brandy connoisseur will give you clues about what to look for in a good rakija. There are several variations. The basic one is slivovitz (*šljivovica*) made from plums and *lozovača* from grapes (similar to Italian grappa). There is also *kajsijevača* (apricot) and *jabukovača* (apple), however it can be made of virtually anything. Many are flavoured with aromatic herbs. Spirits consist of 40 % proof alcohol, which is considered the best in terms of taste, though one can find some that are much stronger. Strangely, good slivovitz, the country's pride, is hard to find manufactured industrially. The really good ones such as "Sokolova" or "Žuta osa" brands are too expensive for the general public, but worth every penny. In the lozovača variety, first prize indisputably goes to "Crnogorska loza" which can be widely found. *Vinjak*, the Serbian variation of cognac, is a very popular drink and the best one comes from "Rubin". *Pelinkovac* and *stomaklija* are flavoured with wormwood. The former is milder and more refreshing than the latter, the best known being the "Gorki list" variety. *Klekovača* is juniper brandy, and *lincura* is flavoured with the root of yellow gentian. During the winter, along with mulled wine (*kuvano vino*), a very popular drink is hot brandy (*kuvana rakija*), sometimes humorously referred to as "Šumadija Tea".

Wine production in Serbia dwindled in the 1990s and, though there has been a certain recovery, it is still not very high. Top quality wines are mostly exported and local stores are left with just a few wines worth trying. Therefore when choosing from shops or wine lists go for the ones with medium to high prices (discussed in "Wine Routes" section of the Guide) as the others could be quite bad. "Plantaže" from Montenegro, with its famous Vranac wine, and "Vršački vinogradi" are ones that will neither hurt the pocket nor the palette. There are a lot of Macedonian wines on the market and most of them are fairly good. The one litre wines found in shops require you to have the glass bottle or to pay a small deposit for it.

There are 14, mostly large, breweries in Serbia-Montenegro. The beer is almost exclusively pilsner lager with the occasional dark (*tamno*) variety. It is mostly consumed from 0,5 and 0,3 bottles and cans though there are plastic bottles that seem to become ever larger (from 1,5 to 2,5 l). Draft beer (*točeno*) can be found in all bigger venues. All the beers boast an alcohol content of 4-5 %. The most famous brews are "Jelen" ("Stag") from Apatin, Nikšićko from Montenegro, "Lav" ("Lion") from Čelarevo and Weifert from Pančevo thereby covering most of the country. The quality of these beers is very good; the other less familiar sorts run a close second. International kinds of beer are widely available while "Tuborg" and "Beck's" are now brewed in Serbia-Montenegro.

Breakfast in Serbia tends to be lighter than the British breakfast but far more

A wide choice of rakijas

ample than in the Mediterranean. It usually consists of various baked goods (note the bakeries rush-hour) taken with cheese, salamis or jam. Sometimes it can be an omelet (*kajgana* is very much the same) or porridge. Lunchtime is from 2 p.m. but can nowadays be postponed to 4 or 5 p.m. This is the main meal of the day and can be quite substantial. Dinner is usually much lighter but many people treat themselves to an evening out in a restaurant from time to time, starting from 8, 9 or 10 p.m.

All Serbian towns are rife with fast food locals, mostly grills, bakeries and take-away pizza joints. There are also those specialising in sandwiches or pancakes (*palačinke*). All of them are reasonably priced and offer good value for money.

It is obvious that Serbia was not created to a vegetarians liking. Most restaurants do not have vegetarian menus but this need not be a problem with a wise selection of side dishes and salads.

Manners and Customs

This is a land of very warmhearted people, where hospitality is the dearest obligation of every host, where courtesy dictates that the guest should be offered more than he can eat or drink and where all things in the host's home will be put at the guest's disposal. It is particularly so in rural areas where the code of hospitality is treated with a great degree of seriousness. Sometimes the hospitality of overenthusiastic hosts may threaten to overwhelm, however, as it is done with the best intentions, one will have to adapt and enjoy it.

When people meet for the first time they say their first name, shake hands (try to do it sturdily with men) and say "Drago mi je" (Pleased to meet you). When meeting people you are already acquainted with, just shake hands and ask "Kako ste/si?" (How do You/you do). The usual "Hello" is "Zdravo" for younger people and "Dobro jutro"

Slatko, *served with a glass of water*

(Good morning), "Dobar dan" (literally "Good day") and "Dobro veče" (Good evening) for everyone else. Stand when meeting people, especially women and older men. When meeting after a longer time or at a celebration (birthday etc.) it is customary to kiss three times on alternating cheeks while shaking hands, or, more familiarly, embrace. The same procedure occurrs when saying goodbye – "Dovidjenja", or more informally "Zdravo" or "Ćao" (Ciao). Women, especially younger, will kiss friends lightly on the cheek just once instead of a handshake. Eye contact is valued and one can expect a fair amount of physical contact with people you meet. This just means that they consider you a good friend. On formal occasions use professional titles: "gospodin" for Mr.,

"gospodja" for Mrs. and "gospodjica" for Miss, followed by their surname.

As Serbs are, in general, open, friendly and direct, personal questions showing interest in stranger's life, politics, like and dislikes are often the basis of conversation. Do not be offended if you are openly asked about an unusual theme.

On arriving at someone's home you will be treated to a coffee (almost always a strong black one), juice and rakija (mostly home made ones in which every master of the house takes great pride). Don't miss trying the delicious preserves "slatko" (literary "sweet") of which you should take just a spoon or two followed by a sip of water. On your first entry into a household it is customary to bring a symbolic present, a bottle of alcoholic drink, an assortment of chocolates, flowers or something similar. In saying cheers – "Živeli" touch glasses and look into the eyes of the people you toast with. Note that your glass will be refilled as soon as it has been emptied, so if you donot want to continue drinking leave some in it. If offered to join a Serb for lunch, you'll have trouble talking your way out of it (and why would you?), and once there, you might easily be offered dinner and breakfast too.

The greatest honour for every guest is to be invited to a "slava", the celebration of a family's saint day. The most popular ones are St Nicolas - Sveti Nikola (December 19th), St Michaels – Sveti Arandjel (November 21st) St Georges – Djurdjevdan (May 6th) and St Johns – Sveti Jovan (January the 20th) when almost everyone goes around town visiting relatives and friends. Many privately owned institutions close earlier on these feast days. Don't forget to bring a symbolic gift. The most conventional greeting is "Srećna slava", followed by kissing three times. You will be offered "žito", a ceremonial sweet made of wheat, honey etc; you are required to make the sign of the cross (if Christian, of course), take a spoon, eat the sweet and leave it in a glass of water. All there is to do afterwards is to enjoy the hospitality and eagerly drink to all toasts.

The Serbian custom is that once one has been invited for a drink in a café

Village **slava**

A to Z

Business hours: Government and business offices usually work from 8 a.m. to 4 p.m. except Saturday and Sunday. Department stores and supermarkets are generally open from 8 a.m. to 8 or 9 p.m. on weekdays. On Saturday, most government offices are closed, albeit shops are open until 3 p.m. 24-hour shops or kiosks are quite common. Most restaurants are open until midnight.

Churches: Most of the large town churches are open throughout the day whilst those in villages are open only during the service times, usually at 7.30 a.m. (8.30 on Saturdays, 9 a.m. on Sundays) and 5 p.m. On entering a church one is required to act politely, not to laugh or raise one's voice. Enter decently dressed – no swimsuits, shorts, miniskirts or even uncovered shoulders. Take off hats. Women are expected to cover their heads although this rule is not too strictly obeyed. In orthodox churches women are not allowed into the sanctuary behind the iconostasis. Moving about during the services is not encouraged and men should keep to the right while women to the left of the church. There are no entry fees but one could bestow a small donation or buy some items, if there are any for sale (usually to the left of the entrance). Ask for permission before taking pictures, especially inside the church.

or to a restaurant, the host will pay the whole bill. Sharing payment around the table, except when there is no money around, is not considered convivial. One can ask if one may add some money but try not to be too precise; it is much better that you order a round after you enjoyed several paid by your hosts. If someone shows the clear intention of buying you a drink do not try paying for anything as it might be considered offensive.

During meals there are not too many rules to obey. Try to follow your host's pace but don't hesitate, even for a moment, in helping yourself to more. The courses (appetiser, soup, main dish, dessert) are accompanied by saying "Prijatno" (Bon Appetite) and answering "Hvala, takodje" (Thank you, the same to you).

An almost complete lack of nonsmoking zones in a country where the majority of population smokes can be a distinct inconvenience. Feel free to ask for a cigarette even if you do not know the people you are asking. It is not considered impolite.

When asking for something politely, use the phrase "molim Vas" (please).

The locals' language skills depend on their age and education: younger people even in smaller places tend to have a good knowledge of English. Amongst the middle aged and elderly people only those with a better education will know the language. Other languages that are often spoken are Italian, Russian, German and Spanish. Knowledge of any Slavic language is very useful as there are many words in common between them.

Procession through the streets of Belgrade

Cinemas in larger towns show the latest releases. All of foreign films are subtitled, never dubbed. Evening screenings are more expensive than those prior to 8 p.m.

Electric current: 220 Volts; plugs have two round pins.

Haggling is not customary and will be tolerated only in certain places (greenmarkets, for antiques etc.), provided you are willing to spend a large amount of money.

Local time is GMT + 1 hour. From the end-March to the end-October the time is GMT + 2 hrs. So, when it is noon in Belgrade, it is 11 a.m. in London and 6 a.m. in New York.

Museums rarely open every day. Most close on Monday but many do so on Sunday. Detailed opening hours are given in the text on specific museums. The last entry is usually 30 to 40 minutes before closing time. Occasionally exhibition texts are written in English and it is sometimes possible to find a booklet about the display in some of other major language. "Is there anything about the museum in English/German/French?" – *Postoji li nešto o muzeju na engleskom/ nemačkom /francuskom?*

On **photography** there are few restrictions. In many of the churches and most of the museums it is forbidden to take pictures. Photography is also forbidden near military and police objects. Most of the ruins from the NATO bombing are still considered within this category, so one should be cautious. Care should be taken before taking photos of policemen and one should always ask for permission. "May I take a picture of you?" – *Smem li da Vas slikam?*

Public holidays are: 1st-2nd January (New Year), 7th January (Orthodox Christmas), 15th February (Constitution Day), 8th-11th April (Orthodox Easter, only in 2006 as it varies), 1st-2nd May (International Labour Day).

Public toilets: There are not many around and the best places to look for them are in bus and railway stations, though these are mostly unbearably filthy. Be prepared by carrying around a small soap and some toilet paper. A far better solution is to try a restaurant or a café. "Excuse me; may I use your toilet?" – *Oprostite, smem li da se poslužim vašim Ve-ceom?* In many kafanas an elderly lady charges for the service, usually 10 dinars or so. The signs say *muški* for men's and *ženski* for women's.

Smoking is allowed in almost all places and, as many people do smoke, it can be quite annoying for the non-smokers. Some restaurants have a non-smoking area (*deo za nepušače*) but most of the bars and clubs will be full of smoke.

Tipping: Tipping is not obligatory but it is usual in taxis and in restaurants (provided you are satisfied with the service, of course) to round up the sum to the nearest whole followed by the phrase *U redu je* ("OK"). This goes for even the smallest bills.

Weights and measures: The metric system is used in Serbia, the same as in the rest of continental Europe. The unit of length is metar, of weight gram, of volume litar.

Wheelchair access is very poor and is to be found only in a few places in the larger towns.

Ravna Museum in Knjaževac

USEFUL PHRASES

In the table below are presented all 30 letters of Serb alphabet. Cyrilic letters are in black and their Latin equivalents are in gray, as both alphabets are officially in use. The pronunciation of each word and phrase is described through words in English.

A a - A a	father	Н н - N n	no	
Б б - B b	bed	Њ њ - Nj nj	onion	
В в - V v	very	О о - O o	door	
Г г - G g	good	П п - P p	pig	
Д д - D d	day	Р р - R r	room	
Ђ ђ - Đ d (Dj dj)	jag	С с - S s	son	
Е е - E e	men	Т т - T t	top	
Ж ж - Ž ž	leisure	Ћ ћ - Ć ć	chase	
З з - Z z	zoo	У у - U u	rule	
И и - I i	he	Ф ф - F f	fish	
J j - J j	you	Х х - H h	his	
К к - K k	kind	Ц ц - C c	lots	
Л л - L l	look	Ч ч - Č č	chalk	
Љ љ - Lj lj	milion	Џ џ - Dž dž	Jack	
М м - M m	me	Ш ш - Š š	she	

IN COMMUNICATION

Yes	да / da	dah
No	не / ne	ney
Please	молим вас / molim vas	moleem vas
Thank you	хвала / hvala	hvahlah
Excuse me	извините / izvinite	izeeneete
Hello	здраво / zdravo	zdravoh
Goodbye	довиђења / dovidenja	doveedyenya
Good night	лаку ноћ / laku noć	lakoo noch
morning	јутро / jutro	yootroh
afternoon	поподне / popodne	popodney
evening	вече / veče	veche
yesterday	јуче / juče	yooche
today	данас / danas	danas
tomorrow	сутра / sutra	sootrah
here	овде / ovde	ovdeh
there	тамо / tamo	tahmoh
What?	Шта? / Šta?	Shtah
When?	Када? / Kada?	Kada
Why?	Зашто? / Zašto?	Zashtoh
Where?	Где? / Gde?	Gdey
How are you?	Како си? / Kako si?	Kakoh see
Very well, thank you	Добро, хвала / Dobro, hvala	Dobroh, hvahlah
Pleased to meet you	Драго ми је / Drago mi je	Dragoh mee yey
See you soon	Видимо се / Vidimo se	Veedeemoh sey
That's fine	У реду / U redu	oo redoo
Do you speak English?	Говорите ли енглески? / Govorite li engleski?	Govoreetey lee engleskee

DURING SHOPPING

How much does it cost?	Колико ово кошта? / Koliko ovo košta?	Kolikoh ovo koshta
I would like...	Волео бих... / Voleo bih...	Voleoh bee...
Do you have...	Имате ли... / Imate li...	Eematey lee...
I'm just looking...	Само гледам... / Samo gledam...	Samoh gledam...
Do you take credit cards?	Примате ли кредитне картице? / Primate li kreditne kartice?	Preematey lee kredeetney karteetsey
What time do you close?	Када затварате? / Kada zatvarate?	Kadah zatvaratey
expensive	скупо / skupo	skoopoh
cheap	јефтино / jeftino	yefteenoh
size (clothes)	величина / veličina	veleechinah
size (shoes)	број / broj	broy
white	бело / belo	beloh
black	црно / crno	tsrnoh
red	црвено / crveno	tsrvenoh
yellow	жуто / žuto	zhootoh
green	зелено / zeleno	zelenoh
blue	плаво / plavo	plavoh

VERY USEFUL

big	велико / veliko	veleekoh
small	мало / malo	mahloh
hot	вруће / vruće	vroochey
cold	хладно / hladno	hlahdno
good	добар / dobar	dobar
bad	лош / loš	losh
open	отворено / otvoreno	otvohrenoh
close	затворено / zatvoreno	zatvohrenoh
left	лево / levo	lehvoh
right	десно / desno	desnoh
straight on	право / pravo	pravoh
near	близу / blizu	bleezoo
far	далеко / daleko	dalekoh
up	горе / gore	gorey
down	доле / dole	doley
entrance	улаз / ulaz	oolay
exit	излаз / izlaz	eeylay
toilet	ВЦ / WC	vey tsey

NUMBERING

0	нула nula	noola
1	један jedan	yedan
2	два dva	dvah
3	три tri	tree
4	четири četiri	chetiree
5	пет pet	pet
6	шест šest	shest
7	седам sedam	sedam
8	осам osam	osam
9	девет devet	devet
10	десет deset	deset
11	једанаест jedanaest	yedanaest
12	дванаест dvanaest	dvahnaest
13	тринаест trinaest	treenaest
14	четрнаест četrnaest	chetrnaest
15	петнаест petnaest	petnaest
16	шестнаест šestnaest	shestnaest
17	седамнаест sedamnaest	sedamnaest
18	осамнаест osamnaest	osamnaest
19	деветнаест devetnaest	devetnaest
20	двадесет dvadeset	dvahdeset
21	двадесет и један dvadeset i jedan	dvahdeset ee yeadan
30	тридесет trideset	treedeset
40	четрдесет četrdeset	chetrdeset
100	сто sto	stoh
101	сто и један sto i jedan	stoh ee yedan
200	двеста dvesta	dvestah
1000	хиљаду hiljadu	hilyadoo

TIME

one minute	један минут jedan minut	yedan meenoot
one hour	један сат jedan sat	yedan saht
half an hour	пола сата pola sata	polah sahta
Monday	понедељак ponedeljak	ponedelyak
Tuesday	уторак utorak	ootorak
Wednesday	среда sreda	sredah
Thursday	четвртак četvrtak	chetvrtak
Friday	петак petak	petak
Saturday	субота subota	soobota
Sunday	недеља nedelja	nedelyah

IN THE RESTAURANT

menu	јеловник jelovnik	yelovneek
wine list	винска карта vinska karta	veenskah kartah
glass	чаша čaša	chashah
bottle	флаша flaša	flashah
knife	нож nož	nozh
fork	виљушка viljuška	veeljooshkah
spoon	кашика kašika	kashikah
breakfast	доручак doručak	doroochak
lunch	ручак ručak	roochak
dinner	вечера večera	vecherah
main course	главно јело glavno jelo	glavnoh yeloh
starters	предјело predjelo	predyeloh
hamburger	пљескавица pljeskavica	plyeskavitsa
meatballs	ћевапчићи ćevapčići	chevapcheechee
soup	супа supa	soopah
vinegar	сирће sirće	seerche
oil	уље ulje	oolye
barbecued	на жару na žaru	na zharoo
baced	печено pečeno	pechenoh
fried	пржено prženo	przhenoh
cheese	сир sir	seer
rise	пиринач pirinač	peereenach
pork	свињетина svinjetina	sveenyeteenay
chicken	пилетина piletina	peeletheenah
fish	риба riba	reebah
beans	пасуљ pasulj	pasooly
bread	хлеб hleb	hleb
pie	пита pita	peetah
ice-cream	сладолед sladoled	slahdoled
cake	колач kolač	kolach
water	вода voda	vedah
caffee	кафа kafa	kafah
tea	чај čaj	chay
wine	вино vino	veenoh
beer	пиво pivo	peevoh
spirit (brandy)	ракија rakija	rakeeyah

INDEX OF PLACES

We wish you a pleasant journey!